Fulbright

ENGLISH FUNDAMENTALS

D1568450

English Fundamentals

Form B

Thirteenth Edition

Donald W. Emery
Late of The University of Washington

John M. Kierzek
Late of Oregon State University

Peter Lindblom
Miami-Dade Community College

PEARSON
Longman

New York San Francisco Boston
London Toronto Sydney Tokyo Singapore Madrid
Mexico City Munich Paris Cape Town Hong Kong Montreal

Vice President and Editor-in-Chief: Joseph Terry
Senior Acquisitions Editor: Susan Kunchandy
Development Manager: Janet Lanphier
Senior Marketing Manager: Melanie Craig
Senior Supplements Editor: Donna Campion
Media Supplements Editors: Nancy Garcia/Kim Rossi
Production Manager: Ellen MacElree
Project Coordination, Text Design, and Electronic Page Makeup: Electronic Publishing Services
    Inc., NYC
Cover Design Manager: Wendy Ann Fredericks
Cover Photos: © Stockbyte/PictureQuest
Senior Manufacturing Buyer: Dennis J. Para

Cover Printer: Phoenix Color Corps

Library of Congress Cataloging-in-Publication Data

Emery, Donald W. (Donald William), 1906–
    English fundamentals, form B / Donald W. Emery, John M. Kierzek, Peter Lindblom.—13th ed.
        p.   cm
    Includes bibliographical references and index.
    ISBN 0-321-13667-5
    1. English language—Grammar—Problems, exercises, etc.   I. Kierzek, John M., 1891–
II. Lindblom, Peter D. 1938– III. Title.

PE1112.E472   2005
428.2—dc22

                                                                                    2004044648

Please visit us at http://www.ablongman.com/emery

ISBN 0-321-13667-5

2 3 4 5 6 7 8 9 10—HT—07 06 05

Contents

Part 3

••••••••••••••••••••••••••••••••••

Sentence Building   137
Lessons, Practice Sheets, and Exercises

Part 4

••••••••••••••••••••••••••••••••••

Punctuation   179
Lessons, Practice Sheets, and Exercises

Preface

With the thirteenth edition of *English Fundamentals*, the book enters its eighth decade of service to students of the English language. Although the book is remarkably different in 2004 from its first version, produced in 1933, its fundamental qualities and its fundamental purpose remains the same. Students will still find in this new edition a straightforward and complete explanation of the language system we call English. Each basic idea is clearly explained and exemplified so that students can gain control of the operating principles of the language. Each lesson contains recognition exercises and, wherever possible, active writing exercises to reinforce the instruction in the minds of the students. A comprehensive system of tests at the end of the book allows students to check their progress and their mastery of the concepts as they work through the text.

ORGANIZATION AND APPROACH

As in previous editions, the first six lessons establish a foundation by introducing to the students the basic systems of the language by dealing with subject-verb combinations, basic sentence patterns, and systems of modification. These first lessons lay the groundwork for further study by showing the students the organizing principles of sentences. These first lessons are designed to serve as an introduction to an analysis of the language, and students should work through them first.

Once the foundation is established, the pattern of the text moves from basic structures to more complex sentence patterns. The building blocks of complex structures, clauses and phrases, offer an opportunity to learn to write more sophisticated and effective sentences. Once the more advanced principles are in place, the text provides instruction in writing correctly as well as effectively. Students learn to recognize fragments and run-on sentences, and they practice correcting these problems by revising problematic sentences. Each lesson in the advanced sections includes active production of written work through sentence combining, embedding drills, and transformation exercises. The last lessons focus the students' attention on refining their use of the language by asking them to look at punctuation, usage, spelling, and capitalization. These lessons contain short paragraphs to be revised and corrected.

The final instructional section deals with the writing process, laying out the orderly steps that allow students to develop essays and academic papers. The composition stage begins with subject selection, moves into extensive work on invention, discovering ideas, and gathering information that will naturally lead to the production of a clear, supportable thesis. From that point, students learn to select content and arrange it in an orderly presentation. The discussion of the process then shifts to revision. Revision begins with an assessment of the thesis and the content selected to support the thesis. Then the process focuses on paragraph evaluation and work on correctness. In addition to this careful explanation of the writing process, the unit contains a section on the rhetoric of the paragraph, teaching both the basic tools of paragraph development and a wide selection of paragraph patterns such as comparison/contrast, analysis, and process. The basic concepts of unity, coherence, and completeness in paragraphs are then carefully explained and exemplified. The examples and exercises in this section, as well as in the earlier sections, come from a number of disciplines, including science and business.

The text concludes with 20 progress tests and three appendices. The first appendix contains 11 sentence-combining exercises that are additional to and separate from the extensive work on combining, embedding, and transformation found in the practice sheets and exercises. The second appendix contains diagnostic tests for those who wish to identify in advance areas of language skills that need special attention. The third appendix is an answer key for the practice sheets. This key is published in the text itself to provide an opportunity for students to check their own work and thus work independently where such work is necessary and advisable.

Finally, the comprehensive index makes the text useful as a handbook after the student has worked through the lessons.

ENDURING FEATURES

- Takes a step-by-step approach so that students will progressively build on their grammar skills as they advance through the text.
- Includes examples and exercises that come from a number of disciplines, including science and business, to accommodate the interests of a wide range of students.
- Offers practice sheets, one for each lesson, that allow students to work at a beginner's level on the principles introduced in the lesson.
- Includes exercise sets in each chapter that offer intensive practice on the principles of the lesson.
- Encourages students to utilize the grammar skills they have learned within sentence and paragraph constructions.
- Offers a section on sentence combining along with accompanying sentence-combining exercises.

NEW TO THIS EDITION

Several new features appear in this thirteenth edition:

- *An emphasis on sequences.* The emphasis on sequences begins in the first lesson by showing how words, either identical or similar, change their function in sentences, as when one sentence uses *change* as a noun, the next uses *change* as a verb, and a third uses a new form of the word, *changeable.* In subsequent lessons, short units of connected text (three, four, or five sentences using the same frame of reference) accustom the students to viewing text as communication. Finally, the units on punctuation, usage, spelling, and capitalization contain exercises that are blocks of text made up of a paragraph of narrative or discussion.
- *Review pages called Check Sheets.* Review pages have been included at the end of units 1–5. The basic concepts dealt with in the lessons in the unit appear in a simplified, somewhat less technical presentation in these Check Sheets. It is nearly impossible to study the working principles of a language without using technical terms, in the same way that no one studies biology or chemistry without learning

the terminology of the discipline. At the same time, however, every textbook needs to accommodate a variety of learning styles. These new Check Sheets, because they present material in a simplified way and are graphically more open in style, assist students whose learning style works better with such a format.

- *Updated Practice Sheets and Exercises.* As in previous editions, the Practice Sheets and Exercises work in concert to lead the students from a simple presentation for basic understanding of principles to examples of more sophisticated applications of the same principles. It is perhaps easiest to think of the Practice Sheets as short examples that focus attention directly on the principle and the Exercises as a longer, more sophisticated presentation of that same principle as it works together with others to form more effective sentences. This new edition contains more than 45 pages requiring active production of sentences.

- A *Companion Website* offers students even more opportunities for grammar and writing practice.

TEXT-SPECIFIC SUPPLEMENTS

A complete *Answer Key* is available to accompany *English Fundamentals*. Please see your Longman book representative for details. ISBN: 0-321-14247-0

A *Test bank* offering additional testing options is also available. An answer key is provided with the tests so that, in addition to use in evaluation, they can be used as higher-level practice tests. ISBN: 0-321-16211-0

New to this edition! A *Companion Website* offers students even more opportunities for grammar and writing practice. Visit *English Fundamentals* online at **http://www.ablongman.com/emery.**

THE LONGMAN BASIC SKILLS PACKAGE

In addition to the book-specific supplements discussed above, many other skills-based supplements are available for both instructors and students. All of these supplements are available either free or at greatly reduced prices.

For Additional Reading and Reference

The Dictionary Deal. Two dictionaries can be shrinkwrapped with this text at a nominal fee. *The New American Webster Handy College Dictionary* is a paperback reference text with more than 1,000 entries. *Merriam Webster's Collegiate Dictionary*, 10th edition, is a hardback reference with a citation file of more than 14.5 million examples of English words drawn from actual use. For more information on how to shrinkwrap a dictionary with your text, please contact your Longman sales representative.

Penguin Quality Paperback Titles. A series of Penguin paperbacks is available at a significant discount when shrinkwrapped with this text. Some titles available are Toni Morrison's *Beloved*, Julia Alvarez's *How the Garcia Girls Lost Their Accents*, Mark Twain's *Huckleberry Finn*, *Narrative of the Life of Frederick Douglass*, Harriet Beecher Stowe's *Uncle Tom's Cabin*, Dr. Martin Luther King Jr.'s *Why We Can't Wait*, and plays by Shakespeare, Miller, and Albee. For a complete list of titles or more information, please contact your Longman sales consultant.

Penguin Academics: Twenty-Five Great Essays, Fifty Great Essays, and One Hundred Great Essays, edited by Robert DiYanni. These alphabetically organized essay collections are published as part of the Penguin Academics series of low-cost, high-quality offerings intended for use in introductory college courses. All essays were selected for their teachability, both as models for writing and for their usefulness as springboards for student writing. For more information on how to shrinkwrap one of these anthologies with your text, please contact your Longman sales consultant.

100 Things to Write About. This 100-page book contains 100 individual assignments for writing on a variety of topics and in a wide range of formats, from expressive to analytical. Ask your Longman sales representative for a sample copy. 0-673-98239-4

***Newsweek* Alliance.** Instructors may choose to shrinkwrap a 12-week subscription to *Newsweek* with any Longman text. The price of the subscription is 59 cents per issue (a total of $7.08 for the subscription). Available with the subscription is a free "Interactive Guide to *Newsweek*," a workbook for students who are using the text. In addition, *Newsweek* provides a wide variety of instructor supplements free to teachers, including maps, Skills Builders, and weekly quizzes. For more information on the *Newsweek* program, please contact your Longman sales representative.

For Instructors

Electronic Test Bank for Writing. This electronic test bank features more than 5,000 questions in all areas of writing, from grammar to paragraphing, through essay writing, research, and documentation. With this easy-to-use CD-ROM, instructors simply choose questions from the electronic test bank, then print out the completed test for distribution. CD-ROM: 0-321-08117-X. Print version: 0-321-08486-1.

Competency Profile Test Bank, Second Edition. This series of 60 objective tests covers ten general areas of English competency, including fragments; comma splices and run-ons; pronouns; commas; and capitalization. Each test is available in remedial, standard, and advanced versions. Available as reproducible sheets or in computerized versions. Free to instructors. Paper version: 0-321-02224-6. Computerized PC: 0-321-02633-0. Computerized Mac: 0-321-02632-2.

Diagnostic and Editing Tests and Exercises, Sixth Edition. This collection of diagnostic tests helps instructors assess students' competence in Standard Written English for purpose of placement or to gauge progress. Available as reproducible sheets or in computerized versions, and free to instructors. Paper: 0-321-19647-3. CD-ROM: 0-321-19645-7.

ESL Worksheets, Third Edition. These reproducible worksheets provide ESL students with extra practice in areas they find the most troublesome. A diagnostic test and post-test are provided, along with answer keys and suggested topics for writing. Free to adopters. 0-321-07765-2

Longman Editing Exercises.   Fifty-four pages of paragraph editing exercises give students extra practice using grammar skills in the context of longer passages. Free when packaged with any Longman title. 0-205-31792-8. Answer key: 0-205-31797-9.

80 Practices.   A collection of reproducible, ten-item exercises that provide additional practices for specific grammatical usage problems, such as comma splices, capitalization, and pronouns. Includes an answer key, and is free to adopters. 0-673-53422-7

CLAST Test Package, Fourth Edition.   These two 40-item objective tests evaluate students' readiness for the CLAST exams. Strategies for teaching CLAST preparedness are included. Free with any Longman English title. Reproducible sheets: 0-321-01950-4. Computerized PC version: 0-321-01982-2. Computerized Mac version: 0-321-01983-0.

TASP Test Package, Third Edition.   These 12 practice pre-tests and post-tests assess the same reading and writing skills covered in the TASP examination. Free with any Longman English title. Reproducible sheets: 0-321-01959-8

Teaching Online: Internet Research, Conversation, and Composition, Second Edition.   Ideal for instructors who have never surfed the Net, this easy-to-follow guide offers basic definitions, numerous examples, and step-by-step information about finding and using Internet sources. Free to adopters. 0-321-01957-1

Using Portfolios.   This supplement offers teachers a brief introduction to teaching with portfolios in composition courses. This essential guide addresses the pedagogical and evaluative use of portfolios, and offers practical suggestions for implementing a portfolio evaluation system in a writing class. 0-321-08412-8

The Longman Instructor's Planner.   This all-in-one resource for instructors includes monthly and weekly planning sheets, to-do lists, student contact forms, attendance rosters, a gradebook, an address/phone book, and a mini almanac. Ask your Longman sales representative for a free copy. 0-321-09247-3

For Students

My Skills Lab (www.ablongman/myskillslab) (Student Pin Card/0-321-26323-5 or Instructor/0-321-26322-07.   This website houses all media tools for developmental English (reading, writing, and study skills) in one place: Avoiding Plagiarism, Exercise Zone, Research Navigator, Longman Writer's Warehouse, Reading Roadtrip, Longman Vocabulary Website, and Longman Study Skills Website. The Longman Writer's Warehouse is the first developmental writing program that allows students to actually write on the Web—to save their work in various stages and see a piece of writing through the complete writing process. In addition to full coverage of the writing process, The Longman Writer's Warehouse offers full coverage of grammar (including diagnostic tests, whose results help students target areas of weakness), an online writer's journal, a handbook with thousands of interactive grammar exercises, research coverage, a collaborative network, Web-based activities, and multimedia (audio, video, and image-based) writing activities. Instructors receive class reporting through classroom management capabilities. MySkillslab is free when packaged with a Longman textbook.

New! *Research Navigator Guide for English,* **by H. Eric Branscomb and Linda R. Barr.** (Student 0-321-20277-5). Designed to teach students how to conduct high-quality online research and to document it properly. Research Navigator guides provide discipline-specific academic resources; in addition to helpful tips on the writing process, online research, and finding and citing valid sources. Free when packaged with any Longman text. Research Navigator guides include an access code to Research Navigator™, providing access to thousands of academic journals and periodicals, the *New York Times* Search by Subject Archive, Link Library, Library Guides, and more. FREE when packaged with a Longman textbook/VALUEPACK ONLY.

Learning Together: An Introduction to Collaborative Theory.   This brief guide to the fundamentals of collaborative learning teaches students how to work effectively in groups, how to revise with peer response, and how to co-author a paper or report. Shrinkwrapped free with this text. 0-673-46848-8

A Guide for Peer Response, Second Edition.   This guide offers students forms for peer critiques, including general guidelines and specific forms for different stages in the writing process. Also appropriate for freshman-level course. Free to adopters. 0-321-01948-2

Ten Practices of Highly Successful Students.   This popular supplement helps students learn crucial study skills by offering concise tips for a successful career in college. Topics include time management, test-taking, critical reading, stress, and motivation. 0-205-30769-8

The Longman Student Planner.   This daily planner for students includes daily, weekly, and monthly calendars, as well as class schedules and a mini-almanac of useful information. It is the perfect accompaniment to a Longman reading or study skills textbook, and is available free to students when shrinkwrapped with this text. 0-321-04573-4

The Longman Writer's Journal.   This journal for writers, free with any Longman English text, offers students a place to think, write, and react. For an examination copy, contact your Longman sales consultant. 0-321-08639-2

The Longman Researcher's Journal.   This journal for writers and researchers, free with this text, helps students plan, schedule, write, and revise their research project. An all-in-one resource for first-time researchers, the journal guides students gently through the research process. 0-321-09530-8

The Longman Writer's Portfolio.   This unique supplement provides students with a space to plan, think about, and present their work. The portfolio includes an assessing/organizing area (including a grammar diagnostic test, a spelling quiz, and project planning worksheets), a before-and-during-writing area (including peer review sheets, editing checklists, writing self-evaluations, and a personal editing profile), and an after-writing area (including a progress chart, a final table of contents, and a final assessment). Ask your Longman sales representative for ISBN 0-321-10765-9.

STATE-SPECIFIC SUPPLEMENTS

[FOR FLORIDA ADOPTIONS] Thinking Through the Test, by D. J. Henry. This special workbook, prepared specially for students in Florida, offers ample skill and practice exercises to help students prep for the Florida State Exit Exam. To shrinkwrap this workbook free with your textbook, please contact your Longman sales representative. Available in two versions: with answers and without answers. Also available: Two laminated grids (one for reading, one for writing) that can serve as handy references for students preparing for the Florida State Exit Exam.

[FOR NEW YORK ADOPTIONS] Preparing for the CUNY-ACT Reading and Writing Test, edited by Patricia Licklider. This booklet, prepared by reading and writing faculty from across the CUNY system, is designed to help students prepare for the CUNY-ACT exit test. It includes test-taking tips, reading passages, typical exam questions, and sample writing prompts to help students become familiar with each portion of the test.

[FOR TEXAS ADOPTIONS] The Longman THEA Study Guide, by Jeanette Harris. Created specifically for students in Texas, this study guide includes straightforward explanations and numerous practice exercises to help students prepare for reading and writing sections of the Texas Higher Education Assessment Program Test. To shrinkwrap this workbook free with your textbook, please contact your Longman sales representative.

ACKNOWLEDGMENTS

Our thanks go to all those who offered advice and suggestions for improving this and previous editions: Edwin J. Blesch, Jr., Nassau Community College; Ladson W. Bright, Cape Fear Community College; James Vanden Bosch, Calvin College; Bernadine Brown, Nassau Community College; Alma G. Bryant, University of South Florida; Kitty Chen Dean, Nassau Community College; Patricia Derby, Chabot College; Neil G. Dodd, East Los Angeles College; Loris D. Galford, McNeese State University; Harold J. Herman, University of Maryland; William T. Hope, Jefferson Technical College; Sue D. Hopke, Broward Community College; Clifford J. Houston, East Los Angeles College; George L. Ives, North Idaho College; Edward F. James, University of Maryland; Thomas Mast, Montgomery College; Walter Mullen, Mississippi Gulf Coast Community College; Mary E. Owens, Montgomery College; Jill Peacock, Santa Monica College; Deborah Pounders, Ouachita Baptist University; Crystal Reynolds, Indiana State University; Bill Sartoris, Camden College; Albert Schoenberg, East Los Angeles Community College; Ines Shaw, North Dakota State Unviersity; Barbara Stout, Montgomery College; Robert S. Sweazy, Vincennes University Junior College; Barbara Van Voorden, University of Missouri, St. Louis; and Larry Weirather, Clark College.

Donald W. Emery
John M. Kierzek
Peter Lindblom

Basic Sentence Patterns
Lessons, Practice Sheets, and Exercises

Lesson 1   *The Simple Sentence; Subjects and Verbs*

While you might find it difficult to produce a satisfying definition, you probably know that the sentence is a basic unit of written or oral expression. Thus, if you were asked, you might define a sentence as "an orderly arrangement of words that makes sense." If you wished to be more specific and more formal, you might say a sentence is "a self-contained grammatical unit, usually containing a subject and a verb, that conveys a meaningful statement, question, command, or exclamation."

You need to understand the basic construction of the sentence in order to write and speak effectively and correctly. In the first few lessons of this book, you'll examine the parts that make up a sentence and the distinctive characteristics of a few types of sentences that serve as the basic structures of more complicated units.

To begin, be sure you can recognize the two indispensable parts of a sentence:

1. The **subject:** the unit about which something is said.

2. The **predicate:** the unit that says something about the subject.

Although the predicate usually includes other modifying words and phrases, the indispensable part of a predicate is the verb, the word (or words) that says what the subject does or is. Here are a few things to remember about the subject–verb relationship:

1. In a sentence that reports a specific action, the verb is easily recognized. For instance, to find the subject and verb in *The rusty bumper on the front of my truck rattles noisily*, ask the question, "What happens?" The answer, *rattles*, gives the verb. Then, by asking the question "Who or what rattles?", you will find the subject, *bumper*. Notice that neither "front rattles" nor "truck rattles" makes the basic statement of the sentence.

2. Some sentences do not report an action. Instead, the sentence says something about the *condition* of the subject. It points out a descriptive quality of the subject or says that something else resembles or is the same thing as the subject. In this kind of sentence, you must look for verbs like *is, are, was, were, seem,* and *become.* Such types of verbs are often called *describing (linking) verbs.* They are words that are almost impossible to define because they lack the concrete exactness and action of verbs like *rattle, throw, smash,* and *explode.*

In a sentence using a describing verb, the subject usually reveals itself easily. For example, in the sentence "The long first chapter seemed particularly difficult," the verb is

1

seemed. The question "Who or what seemed?" provides the subject, *chapter.* The other possible choices—*long, first, particularly,* and *difficult*—do not make sense as answers to the question "Who or what seemed?"

3. Very often the subject of a sentence has material between it and its verb:

> The *price* of potatoes *is* high. [The subject is *price,* not *potatoes.*]
> *Each* of my sisters *is* tall. [The subject is *each,* not *sisters.*]
> Only *one* of these watches *works.* [The subject is *one,* not *watches.*]

4. Most modern English sentences place the subject before the verb, but in some sentences, the verb precedes the subject:

> Behind the house *stood* [verb] an old *mill* [subject].
> Under the table *sat* [verb] a large *cat* [subject].

A very common type of sentence with the verb–subject arrangement uses *here* or *there* preceding the verb:

> There *are* [verb] three willow *trees* [subject] in our yard.
> Here *is* [verb] the *list* [subject] of candidates.

5. Casual, informal language often combines short verbs and subjects with apostrophes representing the omitted letters:

> I'm (I am)   It's (It is)   You've (You have)   They're (They are)

For your first practice work, you'll be using only a single subject for each sentence. Within this limitation, the subject is always a noun or a pronoun. Before the first practice, it would be wise to review a few facts about nouns, pronouns, and verbs so that you can recognize them easily.

NOUNS

A **noun** is a word that names something, such as a person, place, thing, quality, or idea. If the noun names just any member of a group or class, it is called a *common noun* and is not capitalized:

man, city, school, relative

A noun is a *proper noun* and is capitalized if it refers to a particular individual in a group or class:

Albert Lawson, Toledo, Horace Mann Junior High School, Aunt Louise

Most nouns have two forms; they show whether the noun is naming one thing (singular number) or more than one thing (plural number, which adds *s* or *es* to the singular): one *coat,* two *coats*; a *lunch,* several *lunches.* Proper nouns are rarely pluralized, and some common nouns have no plural form—for example, *honesty, courage, ease,* and *hardness.* (Lesson 28 examines in detail the special spelling problems of plural nouns.)

Nouns often follow *the, a,* or *an*, words that are called **articles.** A descriptive word (an adjective) may come between the article and the noun, but the word that answers the question "What?" after an article is a noun:

Article	$\begin{pmatrix} optional \\ adjective \end{pmatrix}$	noun
A (or The)	happy	girl.

Another way to identify nouns is to recognize certain suffixes. A **suffix** is a unit added to the end of a word or to the base of a word (see Supplement 1).* Here are some of the common suffixes found in hundreds of nouns:

age [break*age*]; ance, ence [resist*ance*, insist*ence*]; dom [king*dom*]; hood [child*hood*]; ion [prevent*ion*]; ism [national*ism*]; ment [move*ment*]; ness [firm*ness*]; or, er [invest*or*, los*er*]; ure [expos*ure*]

PRONOUNS

A **pronoun** is a word that substitutes for a noun. There are several classes of pronouns. (See Supplement 2.) The following classes can function as subjects in the basic sentences that you will examine in these early lessons:

Personal pronouns substitute for definite persons or things: *I, you, he, she, it, we, they.*

Demonstrative pronouns substitute for things being pointed out: *this, that, these, those.*

Indefinite pronouns substitute for unknown or unspecified things: *each, either, neither, one, anyone, somebody, everything, all, few, many,* and so on.

Possessive pronouns substitute for things that are possessed: *mine, yours, his, hers, its, ours, theirs.*

VERBS

A **verb** is a word that expresses action, existence, or occurrence by combining with a subject to make a statement, to ask a question, or to give a command. One easy way to identify a word as a verb is to use the following test:

Let's _____
    (action word)

Any word that will complete the command is a verb: "Let's *leave.*" "Let's *buy* some popcorn." "Let's *be* quiet." This test works only with the basic present form of the verb, not with forms that have endings added to them or that show action taking place in the past: "Let's *paint* the car" (not "Let's *painted* the car").

---

*In some lessons of this book, you will find notations referring you to a supplement that appears at the end of the lesson. Read the supplement *after* you have thoroughly studied the lesson. The lesson contains the essential information that is vital to your understanding of subsequent lessons and exercises. The supplement presents material that has relevance to some points of the lesson. The supplements at the end of this lesson are found on page 4.

SUPPLEMENT 1

Hundreds of nouns have distinctive suffix endings. The definitions of some of these suffixes are rather difficult to formulate, but you can quite readily figure out the meanings of most of them: *ness*, for instance, means "quality or state of" (thus *firmness* means "the state or quality of being firm"); *or* and *er* show the agent or doer of something (an *investor* is "one who invests").

A unit added to the beginning of a word is called a **prefix.** Thus, to the adjective *kind*, we add a prefix to derive another adjective, *unkind*, and a suffix to derive the nouns *kindness* and *unkindness*. An awareness of how prefixes and suffixes are used will do far more than aid you in your ability to recognize parts of speech: Your spelling will improve and your vocabulary will expand.

SUPPLEMENT 2

Two classes of pronouns, the **interrogative** and the **relative,** are not listed here. Because they are used in questions and subordinate clauses but not in simple basic sentences, they will not be discussed until later lessons.

Another type of pronoun that you use regularly (but not as a true subject) is the **intensive** or **reflexive** pronoun, the "self" words used to add emphasis:

You *yourself* made the decision.

or to name the receiver of an action when the doer is the same as the receiver:

The boy fell and hurt *himself.*

The first example is the intensive use; the second is the reflexive. Pronouns used this way are *myself, yourself, himself* (not *hisself*), *herself, itself, ourselves, yourselves,* and *themselves* (not *themself, theirself,* or *theirselves*).

The "self" pronouns are properly used for these two purposes only. They should not be substituted for regular personal pronouns:

Mary and I [not *myself*] were invited to the dance.
Tom visited Eric and me [not *myself*] at our ranch.

A fourth type of pronoun is the **reciprocal pronoun,** which denotes a mutual relationship—for example, *one another, each other:*

We try to help *each other* with our homework.

NAME _____ SCORE _____

Directions: In the space at the left, copy the word that is the verb of the italicized subject.

_____ 1. *Everyone* in our office drives to work every day.

_____ 2. The *drive* to the office follows the shore of a beautiful lake.

_____ 3. The office *building* stands in the middle of a beautiful park.

_____ 4. The *company* built the office in 1993.

_____ 5. The *employees* park in a huge underground garage.

_____ 6. The *company* now employs 150 people.

_____ 7. Five years ago there were only fifty *employees.*

_____ 8. *One hundred* of the workers in the company came here last year.

_____ 9. *Sales* of the company's products increased significantly two years ago.

_____ 10. The *company* sells a line of custom-made golf clubs.

_____ 11. *Trees* line the shore of the lake behind the office.

_____ 12. The *lake* provides us with a beautiful view from our offices.

_____ 13. Yesterday the *company* held a picnic beside the lake.

_____ 14. The *picnic* occurred late in the afternoon.

_____ 15. Such *parties* are regular occurrences in our company.

_____ 16. The *company* offers many generous benefits to its employees.

_____ 17. The company's *generosity* attracts good people.

_____ 18. The attractive *grounds* around the buildings are a delight to most of the workers.

_____ 19. The pleasant working *atmosphere* led me to the company.

_____ 20. The *company* decorated the shops and the office spaces attractively.

Directions: In the space at the left, copy the word that is the subject of the italicized verb.

_____ 1. Some of the people at last night's dinner *made* large political contributions.

_____ 2. Some men from our office *went* home early today.

_____ 3. They *came* to work quite early yesterday morning.

_____ 4. Last spring Jim *gave* his sister a computer for her graduation present.

_____ 5. For her, that gift *is* very useful at college.

_____ 6. The salesperson *computed* the cost of my purchases at the register.

_____ 7. I *purchased* a new set of tires for my car last week.

_____ 8. Jamie *registered* for three classes for next semester.

_____ 9. Tom soon *grew* tired of the constant noise from the football field.

_____ 10. The shortstop *fielded* the hard grounder quite easily.

_____ 11. The batter *grounded* out to the shortstop.

_____ 12. Out of the hollow tree *crawled* a beautiful black snake.

_____ 13. The line of students *snaked* its way all around the building.

_____ 14. The craftsman *lined* the small chest with blue velvet cloth.

_____ 15. The crawl on the bottom of the TV screen *announced* an impending tornado.

_____ 16. The announcement *caused* the cancellation of this afternoon's game.

_____ 17. The coaches *canceled* the game because of the danger from the tornado.

_____ 18. My sister *coaches* softball at a nearby high school.

_____ 19. The cause of the problem with the electrical system *remains* a mystery.

_____ 20. The last play of the game *electrified* the crowd in the grandstand.

Exercise 1

Subjects and Verbs

NAME _____ SCORE _____

Directions: In the first space at the left, copy the subject of the sentence. In the second space, copy the verb.

_____ 1. My expenditures for last month exceeded my income.

_____

_____ 2. The purple haze of twilight filled the canyon.

_____

_____ 3. Underneath the rotting planks I found three scarlet king snakes.

_____

_____ 4. After last Friday the new pay scale was in effect.

_____

_____ 5. That was probably the last concert of the season.

_____

_____ 6. New supplies of insecticide arrived yesterday.

_____

_____ 7. One of our men inspected the job.

_____

_____ 8. The work of these scientists contributed significantly to our

_____ program.

_____ 9. There go your two would-be helpers with their broken tools.

_____

_____ 10. The loss of the quarterback and two linebackers led to a disastrous

_____ season.

_____ 11. The governor, assisted by two aides, used her influence to sway

_____ the delegation.

_____ 12. There stands a huge monument to man's disregard for nature.

_____

_____ 13. Marge certainly regretted that decision.

_____

_____ 14. Two of the ships survived the storm.

_____

_____ 15. Right next to my foot lay the dead snake.

_____

_____ 16. We soon found out the reason for Jim's absence.

_____

_____ 17. We studied the map more carefully.

_____

_____ 18. The last of my patience evaporated.

_____

_____ 19. A representative from the national headquarters arrived yesterday.

_____

_____ 20. In the trunk of the car lay two fishing rods.

_____

_____ 21. Neither of these answers is correct.

_____

_____ 22. My opinion, along with those of others, was enough to change

_____ her mind.

_____ 23. The players looked exhausted before the end of the first half.

_____

_____ 24. In front of us in the middle of the road was a giant black bear.

_____

_____ 25. The sight of those three men with guns upset the townspeople.

_____

_____ 26. One cannot be too careful with stocks, bonds, and insurance

_____ papers.

_____ 27. They soon made a decision about their course of action.

_____

_____ 28. Neither of my two brothers lives here.

_____

_____ 29. You arrived here a few minutes earlier than usual.

_____

_____ 30. I'm no longer sure about that candidate's qualifications.

_____

_____ 31. Among those tall trees stands our summer cabin.

_____

_____ 32. For everyone in attendance there was a small but tasteful gift.

_____

_____ 33. There's only one thing to do under these circumstances.

_____

_____ 34. Never before was there such an opportunity for profit in a small

_____ business.

_____ 35. My decision, together with the rationale behind it, stands at the

_____ end of my report.

_____ 36. Last month I paid my tuition for this semester.

_____

_____ 37. The instigator of all those troubles was a five-year-old girl.

_____

_____ 38. You determined the shortest route to the picnic grounds with your

_____ GPS.

_____ 39. From the looks of it, that car suffered a terrible accident.

_____

_____ 40. One of the versions of that story appeared last year in a national

_____ magazine.

In Lesson 1 you learned how to recognize a verb. Every verb has a **base** or **infinitive**. This form of the verb "names" the verb. But verbs change their form according to various conditions, three of which are person, number, and tense. You should learn these forms because they occur in nearly every sentence that you speak or write.

Person specifies the person(s) speaking (first person: *I, we*); the person(s) spoken *to* (second person: *you*); and the person(s) or thing(s) spoken *about* (third person: *he, she, it, they*).

Number shows whether the reference is to *one* thing (*singular* number) or to more than one thing (*plural* number).

Tense refers to the time represented in the sentence, whether it applies to the present moment (I *believe* him) or to some other time (I *believed* him, I will *believe* him).

To demonstrate these changes in form, you can use a chart or arrangement called a *conjugation*. In the partial conjugation that follows, three verbs are used: *earn, grow,* and *be*. The personal pronoun subjects are included to show how the person and number of the subject affect the form of the verb.

Indicative Mood
Active Voice*

Present Tense

	Singular	*Plural*
1st person	I earn, grow, am	We earn, grow, are
2nd person	You earn, grow, are	You earn, grow, are
3rd person	He earns, grows, is†	They earn, grow, are

Past Tense

1st person	I earned, grew, was	We earned, grew, were
2nd person	You earned, grew, were	You earned, grew, were
3rd person	He earned, grew, was	They earned, grew, were

continued on next page

---

*Indicative mood indicates that the verb expresses a fact as opposed to a wish, command, or possibility. *Active voice* indicates that the subject of the verb is the *doer,* rather than the receiver, of the action of the verb.

†The pronoun *he* is arbitrarily used here to represent the third-person singular subject, which may be any singular pronoun (*she, it, who, nobody*); singular noun (*girl, neighbor, elephant, misunderstanding, Alice, Christopher Robert Klein III*); or word groups constituting certain types of phrases or clauses that will be studied in later lessons.

9

Future Tense

1st person	I will earn, grow, be*	We will earn, grow, be
2nd person	You will earn, grow, be	You will earn, grow, be
3rd person	He will earn, grow, be	They will earn, grow, be

Present Perfect Tense

1st person	I have earned, grown, been	We have earned, grown, been
2nd person	You have earned, grown, been	You have earned, grown, been
3rd person	He has earned, grown, been	They have earned, grown, been

Past Perfect Tense

1st person	I had earned, grown, been	We had earned, grown, been
2nd person	You had earned, grown, been	You had earned, grown, been
3rd person	He had earned, grown, been	They had earned, grown, been

Future Perfect Tense

1st person	I will have earned, grown, been	We will have earned, grown, been
2nd person	You will have earned, grown, been	You will have earned, grown, been
3rd person	He will have earned, grown, been	They will have earned, grown, been

---

Notice that in the past tense, *earn* adds an *ed* ending, but *grow* changes to *grew*. This difference illustrates **regular** and **irregular verbs,** the two groups into which all English verbs are classified. *Earn* is a regular verb; *grow* is an irregular verb. (Lesson 21 discusses irregular verbs in more detail.)

Notice also that some verb forms consist of more than one word (*will earn, have grown, had earned, will have been*). In such uses, *will, had,* and *have* are called **auxiliary verbs.** More auxiliary verbs are examined in Lesson 5.

With the "naming" words (nouns and pronouns) and the "action" words (verbs), you can construct true sentences:

Janice arrived.

He laughed.

Power corrupts.

But to make sentences more varied and complete, you need modifiers or "describing" words (adjectives and adverbs) and prepositional phrases.

ADJECTIVES

An **adjective** is a word that describes or limits—that is, gives qualities to—a noun. Adjectives are found in three positions in a sentence:

---

*Earlier, some writers made distinctions in the use of *shall* and *will* in the future and future perfect tenses. *Shall* was always used with the first person singular and *will* was used in the second and third person plural. In addition, there was an emphatic mood created by reversing *shall* and *will*. So in the emphatic mood, people employed *I will* and *you* or *he shall*. In recent years, those distinctions have been lost, and we now employ *will* for all three persons in both tenses.

1. Preceding a noun that is in any of the noun positions within the sentence

> The *small* child left. He is a *small* child. I saw the *small* child. I gave it to the *small* child.

2. Following a describing (linking) verb and modifying the subject

> The child is *small*. Mary looked *unhappy*. We became *upset*.

3. Directly following the noun (less common than the two positions described above)

> He provided the money *necessary* for the trip. The hostess, *calm and serene,* entered the hall.

Certain characteristics of form and function help you recognize adjectives. There are several suffixes that, when added to other words or roots of other words, form adjectives. Here again, an understanding of the meaning of a suffix can save trips to the dictionary. For instance, in the hundreds of adjectives ending in *able* (*ible*), the suffix means "capable of" or "tending to"; thus, *usable* means "capable of being used" and *changeable* means "tending to change."

> able, ible [read*able,* irresist*ible*]; al [internation*al*]; ant, ent [resist*ant,* diverg*ent*]; ar [lun*ar*]; ary [budget*ary*]; ful [meaning*ful*]; ic, ical [cosm*ic,* hyster*ical*]; ish [fool*ish*]; ive [invent*ive*]; less [blame*less*]; ous [glamor*ous*]; y [greas*y*]

One note of warning: Many other words in English end with these letters, but you can easily see that they are not employing a suffix. T*able*, fer*ment*, ar*rive*, d*ish*, and pon*y*, for instance, are not adjectives. (See Supplement 1 for more information on adjectives.)

ADJECTIVES USED IN COMPARISONS

Nearly all adjectives, when they are used in comparisons, can be strengthened or can show degree by changing form or by using *more* and *most:*

> *great* trust, *greater* trust, *greatest* trust
> *sensible* answer, *more sensible* answer, *most sensible* answer

The base form (*great* trust, *sensible* answer) is the **positive degree**. The second form (*greater* trust, *more sensible* answer) is the **comparative degree**: it compares two things. The third form (*greatest* trust, *most sensible* answer) is the **superlative degree** and distinguishes among three or more things. (See Supplement 2.)

ADVERBS

Another modifier is the **adverb,** a word that modifies anything except a noun or a pronoun. Most adverbs modify verbs (She walked *quickly*). Other adverbs modify adjectives and other adverbs (The *very* old man walked *quite slowly*). Some adverbs modify whole sentences (*Consequently*, we refused the offer).

Adverbs tell certain things about the verb, the most common being:

1. **Manner:** John performed *well*. We worked *hard*. The child laughed *happily*. I would *gladly* change places with you.

2. **Time:** I must leave *now.* I'll see you *later. Soon* we shall meet *again.*

3. **Frequency:** We *often* go on picnics, *sometimes* at the lake but *usually* in the city park.

4. **Place:** *There* he sat, alone and silent. *Somewhere* we shall find peace and quiet.

5. **Direction:** The police officer turned *away.* I moved *forward* in the bus.

6. **Degree:** I could *barely* hear the speaker. I *absolutely* refuse to believe that story.

The most frequently used adverbs answer such questions as "How?" (manner or degree), "When?" (time or frequency), and "Where?" (place or direction).

Adverbs of a subclass called **intensifiers** modify adjectives or adverbs but not verbs—for example, a *very* good meal, his *quite* surprising reply, *too* often, *somewhat* reluctantly.

Many adverbs change form the way adjectives do, to show degree:

to drive *fast,* to drive *faster,* to drive *fastest*

to perform *satisfactorily,* to perform *more satisfactorily,* to perform *most satisfactorily*

See Supplement 2 for details on some common irregular intensifiers.

PREPOSITIONS

A **preposition** is a word that introduces a phrase and shows the relationship between the object of the phrase and some other word in the sentence. Notice that many prepositions show a relationship of space or time. Here are some common prepositions; those in the last column are called *group prepositions:*

about	beside	inside	through	according to
above	besides	into	throughout	because of
across	between	like	till	by way of
after	beyond	near	to	in addition to
against	by	of	toward	in front of
around	down	off	under	in place of
at	during	on	until	in regard to
before	except	out	up	in spite of
behind	for	outside	upon	instead of
below	from	over	with	on account of
beneath	in	since	without	out of

A preposition always has an object; with its object and any modifiers, the preposition makes a **prepositional phrase.** You can easily illustrate the function of prepositions by constructing sentences like the following:

After breakfast I walked *to* town *without* my friend. [Objects: *breakfast, town, friend.*]

On account of the rain, I canceled my plans *for* a game *of* tennis *at* the park *with* John. [Objects: *rain, game, tennis, park, John.*]

The trees *outside* the window *of* the kitchen are full *of* blossoms *during* the spring. [Objects: *window, kitchen, blossoms, spring.*]

SUPPLEMENT 1

Besides what could be called true adjectives are other classes of words that modify nouns. If you concentrate on the *functions* of the various kinds of words, however, you can safely classify as adjectives all words that precede nouns and limit their meaning. Such adjectives include articles, numerals, and possessives (*an* apple, *the* weather, *my three* roommates); modifiers that can be used also as pronouns (*these* people, *some* friends, *all* workers); and nouns that modify other nouns (*basketball* players, *summer* days, *crop* failures).

Many words can be used as adjectives or as pronouns; the position of a word within the sentence determines which part of speech it is:

Several [*adj.*] classmates of mine [*pron.*] read this [*adj.*] report.

Several [*pron.*] of my [*adj.*] classmates read this [*pron.*].

SUPPLEMENT 2

A few commonly used modifiers form their comparative and superlative degrees irregularly:

good (*adj.*)	better	best
well (*adv.*)	better	best
bad (*adj.*)	worse	worst

NAME _____ SCORE _____

Directions: In each space at the left, write one of the following numbers to identify the part of speech of the italicized words:

1. noun   3. verb   5. adverb
2. pronoun   4. adjective   6. preposition

_____ 1. *On* the back seat of the car lay several of my friend's *textbooks*.

_____ 2. He *left* the books there *several* days ago.

_____ 3. *He* missed *several* assignments because of his carelessness.

_____ 4. *Several* of our *friends* commented on Jim's carelessness.

_____ 5. The books on the *seat cost* about $250 at the bookstore.

_____ 6. The new *students seated* themselves at the back of the room.

_____ 7. The professor asked *all of* them to move to the front of the room.

_____ 8. *They* walked *slowly* to the front of the classroom.

_____ 9. *First*, they stopped *beside* the seats in the front row.

_____ 10. Then *each* of them selected a seat *at* the front of the room.

_____ 11. "Please *sit* in the same seat *every* day," said the professor.

_____ 12. *From* that day on, the *new* students sat in the same seats in the front row.

_____ 13. *Some* of the seats at the top of the lower deck of the *stadium* are blocked by columns.

_____ 14. Therefore, we always select our seats in the stadium *very carefully.*

_____ 15. We take *great care* in the selection of our seats.

_____ 16. An *early* arrival at the stadium on game day is very *important*.

_____ 17. The *importance* of an early arrival at the stadium *governs* our plans on game day.

_____ 18. At the last game, the *governor* of the state sat on the *fifty-yard* line.

_____ 19. The *last* of his group arrived at the *end* of the first quarter of play.

_____ 20. One of the defensive *ends* is the lieutenant governor's *son*.

_____ 21. The *defense* played *very* well during that game.

_____ 22. On one *play* the *offense* lost the ball on an interception.

_____ 23. "We *went* to the *well* once too often and lost the ball," said the coach.

_____ 24. *Except* for that one *play,* the offensive team played very well.

_____ 25. *Unfortunately*, the defense *weakened* in the fourth quarter.

_____ 26. Our weak *pass* defense allowed *two* touchdowns.

_____ 27. Our offense *touched* the ball *only* five times in the last quarter.

_____ 28. In the *middle* of the fourth period, a *quarter* of the fans walked out.

_____ 29. The *middle* section of the bleachers was *completely* empty.

_____ 30. My friends and *I* stayed for the *entire* game.

_____ 31. Of course, *nobody* in the stands was *completely* happy with the outcome.

_____ 32. The *afternoon, however,* was not a total disaster.

_____ 33. The *beautiful* weather and the good *company* made up for the loss.

_____ 34. Two people from the row *behind us* accompanied us to a barbecue restaurant.

_____ 35. "Please go *with* us for supper after the game," my friend said to *them.*

_____ 36. The night *before* my departure for college this term, my sister *barbecued*
_____   chicken for all of us.
_____ 37. The *barbecue* sauce tasted *delicious.*

_____ 38. My sister cooked a *most delicious* meal for us.

_____ 39. The *cook* at the restaurant should use my sister's *recipe* for barbecued chicken.

_____ 40. Then his *barbecued* chicken would taste *delicious.*

Parts of Speech

NAME _____ SCORE _____

Directions: In each space at the left, write one of the following numbers to identify the part of speech of the italicized words:

1. noun 3. verb 5. adverb
2. pronoun 4. adjective 6. preposition

_____ 1. Beth's *enthusiasm* for her new job is *commendable*.

_____ 2. We *often commend* her for her enthusiastic attitude.

_____ 3. The *harshness* of the sergeant's *voice* startled us.

_____ 4. The supervisor *voiced* her displeasure *harshly*.

_____ 5. *This* is the only *usable* plan.

_____ 6. Many other laboratories *use this* plan.

_____ 7. *After* the lecture from his dad, Jerry worked *harder*.

_____ 8. The coating gives the table a *much harder* surface.

_____ 9. *Some* of the stranded passengers seemed quite *helpless*.

_____ 10. The mechanic's *helper* gave us *some* assistance.

_____ 11. *Later,* Jones became moderately *famous* for his poetry.

_____ 12. In fact, his *fame* spread *far* and wide.

_____ 13. Another plane took off *from* the *far* runway.

_____ 14. I *objected* to *many* of his recommendations.

_____ 15. I found *many* remarks of his *quite* objectionable.

_____ 16. We placed the new piano *against* an *inside* wall of the house.

_____ 17. Our *father advised* us on this delicate matter.

_____

_____ 18. We always benefit from his *fatherly advice.*

_____ 19. *All* of these suggestions *proved* beneficial.

_____ 20. *All* seniors will receive their final grades *soon.*

_____ 21. TV *reception* in our neighborhood *finally* improved.

_____ 22. You *noticed* the *improvement* also.

_____ 23. Your recent *loss* of weight is *noticeable.*

_____ 24. I sometimes *question* my landlord's *sanity.*

_____ 25. Sane people would *unquestionably* agree with *me.*

_____ 26. The hostess's *sincerity warmed* the hearts of the travelers.

_____ 27. The *warmth* of the welcome *heartened* the weary travelers.

_____ 28. *Undoubtedly* the election will be a close *one.*

_____ 29. *Without* a *doubt* the club will elect the right person.

_____ 30. *Payment* of the entire debt before next month is *doubtful.*

_____ 31. Your account is *payable before* the end of the month.

_____ 32. We all *admit* that she is a *likeable* person.

_____ 33. *Several* of the lawyers think that the testimony is not *admissible.*

_____ 34. I'm impressed *by* these *testimonials.*

_____ 35. Your nephew made an *extremely* favorable *impression* on us.

_____ 36. *Yours* is *probably* a cheaper model.

_____ 37. *These* can be bought more *cheaply* in the city.

_____ 38. *Everyone* admired your *lovely* children.

_____ 39. There was much applause *after* the governor's *admirable* speech.

_____ 40. The children performed *admirably,* and we *applauded* them.

Directions: Each of these words is labeled as a noun, verb, adjective, or adverb. In the space following each word, write related words of the part of speech indicated. (Do not use adjectives ending in *ing* or *ed*.)

Example:

worry (n.) _____worry_____ (v.) _____worried_____ (adv.)

1. argument (n.) _____(v.) _____ (adv.)

2. brave (v.) _____(adv.) _____ (adj.)

3. bashfully (adv.) _____(n.) _____ (adj.)

4. cancel (v.) _____(n.) _____ (adj.)

5. dirty (v.) _____(adj.) _____ (n.)

6. charitable (adj.) _____(adv.) _____ (n.)

7. denial (n.) _____(v.) _____ (adj.)

8. embarrass (v.) _____(adv.) _____ (n.)

9. empathy (n.) _____(v.) _____ (adv.)

10. fall (v.) _____(n.) _____ (adj.)

11. free (adj.) _____(adv.) _____ (n.)

12. gladness (n.) _____(adj.) _____ (adv.)

13. injure (v.) _____(n.) _____ (adj.)

14. luxurious (adj.) _____(v.) _____ (adv.)

15. mystery (n.) _____(adj.) _____ (adv.)

16. offend (v.) _____(n.) _____ (adj.)

17. recognizable (adj.) _____(v.) _____ (n.)

18. ridiculous (adj.) _____(adv.) _____ (v.)

19. roughly (adv.) _____(v.) _____ (adj.)

20. tame (adj.) _____(adv.) _____ (v.)

NAME _____   SCORE _____

Directions: In the first space at the left, copy the word that is the subject of the sentence. In the second space, copy the verb. Many of the verbs consist of more than one word.

_____   1. Yesterday three of my friends flew to Spain.
_____

_____   2. With the opening of the new highway, we heard a great deal of
_____   traffic noise in our house.

_____   3. A few of the visitors had recently come from Vancouver.

_____   4. A shortage of skilled workers in the shop has caused serious
_____   delays in production.

_____   5. The recent graduates from boot camp will soon be departing for
_____   advanced training at other bases.

_____   6. The real surprise in that game was Willard, the designated hitter.

_____   7. The next arrival of a flight from Toronto will be tomorrow at noon.

_____   8. Beside the books on that table were my car keys.

_____   9. By this time next week there will be no books on that subject left
_____   in the library.

_____   10. Behind the farmhouse stands a large grove of walnut trees.

_____   11. Monday is the first day of exams for this term.

_____   12. I've never heard a better performance from our local orchestra.

_____   13. My hardest course last term was calculus.

_____   14. In the attic behind the doorway into the storage room, you'll find
_____   that trunk full of old papers.

_____   15. Everybody in that building knows about the faulty air conditioner.

_____   16. Without that information, we will need an entirely new method
_____   for determining our prices.

_____   17. Neither of the people at the interview yesterday seemed familiar
_____   to me.

_____   18. On the floor behind her running shoes, Marge located her lost belt.
_____

_____ 19. Jan's the only member of our staff with a private office.

_____ 20. Even with all the work in preparation for the exam, Jack still
_____   didn't make a good grade.

_____ 21. The company president, along with his new assistant, rode to the
_____   banquet in a limousine.

_____ 22. After two unsuccessful efforts, we finally reached an academic
_____   advisor.

_____ 23. My father, with two of his colleagues, is leaving for the convention
_____   this morning.

_____ 24. One of Mary's friends had arrived on campus during that first class.

_____ 25. A brief stop for lunch became a tiresome experience because of a
_____   dead battery.

_____ 26. A response to my letter of complaint came by return mail.

_____ 27. Barb's interested in a major in art history.

_____ 28. The team's quarterback, with a shy smile and a wave to the
_____   crowd, left the stage after his speech.

_____ 29. After the end of the winter semester, many of the rooms in the
_____   dormitories are empty.

_____ 30. People from all over the valley come to that beautiful spring for
_____   their drinking water.

_____ 31. Good advice about course selection, along with ideas from former
_____   students, appears in that short pamphlet.

_____ 32. Under the couch in the den the puppy has hidden one of my shoes.

_____ 33. That small stretch of sand is the most beautiful beach on the entire
_____   coastline.

_____ 34. Alongside the President walk his two Secret Service agents.

_____ 35. Five staff members have worked for two weeks on the reports.

_____ 36. The arrival of Mickey Mouse at the theaters inspired an excited
_____   cheer from all the children in the audience.

_____ 37. My father has owned that boat for ten years.

_____ 38. Jane's excited about the prospects of the tennis team in the new
_____   season.

_____ 39. The new football coaches, along with their wives, will move to
_____   town next month.

_____ 40. There's little opportunity for practice on that particular course.

_____

Lesson 3

Basic Sentence Patterns with Intransitive Verbs

As you know from Lesson 1, the sentence, which is a subject and predicate arranged to make a statement, is the basic unit of written and oral communication. There are just five sentence types or patterns, and learning to recognize those five patterns can help you become a more effective communicator. In this lesson and the following lesson, we look at the five patterns so that you can learn to use them in your writing.

The nature of the verb is the key to recognizing sentence patterns. There are two types of verbs, transitive and intransitive. The prefix *trans* means "across," and the letters *it* come from the Latin word meaning "to go," so *transit* means "to go across." The additional prefix *in* means "not," so *intransit* means "not to go across." (Don't confuse the Latin word with the colloquial *in transit*, which means in the act of going somewhere.)

When an **intransitive verb** is used, the verb does not transfer its action to an object. In the sentence "John spoke softly," the action is *spoke* and the actor is *John*. The action does not "go across" to a noun that receives that action. The verb is intransitive. Some intransitive verbs do not express an action; they simply connect or link the subject to a noun that renames the subject or to an adjective that modifies the subject. These types of intransitive verbs are called **linking verbs.** In the following sentences there is no action:

> John *is* a genius.
> John *is* brilliant.

The subject *John* is simply linked by the verb to a word that identifies or modifies it.

Sentence Patterns 1 and 2 use intransitive verbs. Sentence Patterns 3, 4, and 5 use transitive verbs and are addressed in Lesson 4.

SENTENCE PATTERN 1

Sentence Pattern 1 contains an intransitive verb and is the only sentence pattern that does not require a word to complete the sense of the action. Some activity takes place in each of these sentences, but no completer is needed because the action of the verb is not transferred to anything.

> The child *runs*.
> The tree *fell*.
> The customer *complained* loudly.
> The professor *walked* into the room unexpectedly.

The action of the verb is complete within itself. Pattern 1 sentences nearly always contain modifiers that tell how, when, and where the action occurred:

> Yesterday the neighborhood children played noisily in the vacant lot.

23

Notice that the material associated with the verb is all adverbial: "When?" *Yesterday.* "How?" *Noisily.* "Where?" *In the vacant lot.* The important characteristic of a Pattern 1 sentence is that there is no noun answering the question "What?" after the verb. The best way to recognize an intransitive verb is to spot the lack of a noun answering the question "What?" after the verb.

In some Pattern 1 sentences, the purpose of the statement is simply to say that the subject exists. Usually some adverbial material is added to show the place or the time of the existence:

> The glasses *are* in the cabinet.
> Flash floods often *occur* in the spring.
> There *were* several birds around the feeder.

Now we need to define a term that identifies an important part of the sentences in the four remaining patterns. As you know, the two parts of any sentence are the subject and the predicate. The core of the predicate is the verb, but the predicate also often includes words that complete the thought of the sentence. Words that follow the verb and complete the thought of the sentence are called **complements.** Complements can be nouns, pronouns, or adjectives, but all serve the same purpose in the sentence: They complete the idea or sense of the sentence.

SENTENCE PATTERN 2

Pattern 2 includes two closely related kinds of sentences. The purpose of the first type of Pattern 2 sentence is to rename the subject, to say that the subject is the same as something else. In the sentence "John is a genius," the noun *genius* is called a **subjective complement** because it completes the verb and renames the subject. (See Supplement.) The intransitive linking verb used in Pattern 2 sentences is often a form of *be.*

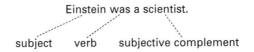

Note that both words, *Einstein* and *scientist,* refer to the same thing. There is no action; rather, a connection is established between the subject and the verb.

In the second type of Pattern 2 sentence, the subjective complement is an adjective, a word that describes rather than renames the subject. For example, in the sentence "The child is clever," the subject is joined by the verb to an adjective, again called a subjective complement. Comparatively few verbs serve the linking function. For convenience, you can think of them in three closely related groups:

1. *Be,* the most commonly used linking verb, and a few others meaning essentially the same thing: *seem, appear, prove, remain, continue,* and so forth:

   > John *is* a talented musician.
   > The performer *seemed* nervous.
   > He *remained* calm.
   > His words *proved* meaningless.

2. *Become*, and a few others like it: *turn, grow, work, get, wear,* and so forth:

> Later she *became* an accountant.
> Soon he *grew* tired of the game.
> Billy *turned* red from embarrassment.

3. A few verbs referring to the senses (*look, smell, taste, feel, sound*), which can be followed by adjective subjective complements that describe the condition of the subject:

> The roses *look* beautiful in that vase.
> This milk *tastes* sour.

The ability to recognize Pattern 2 sentences will help you understand a few troublesome usage problems that are examined in a later lesson—to understand why, for instance, careful writers use "feel bad" rather than "feel badly": "I *feel* bad about the election results."

SUPPLEMENT

A note about grammatical terminology is needed here. A noun following a linking verb and renaming the subject is sometimes called a *predicate noun* or a *predicate nominative;* an adjective following a linking verb and describing the subject is sometimes called a *predicate adjective.*

> subjective complement (n.) = predicate noun
>   predicate nominative
> subjective complement (adj.) = predicate adjective

NAME _____ SCORE _____

Directions: Each of the following sentences is a Pattern 2 sentence with a noun (or a pro-noun) subjective complement. ~~In the space at the left, copy the subjective complement.~~

_____ 1. My little brother is an outstanding soccer player.

_____ 2. My sister recently became a soccer fan.

_____ 3. Soccer is a good sport for young kids.

_____ 4. Soccer has become an important source of entertainment for all of us.

_____ 5. In some countries, soccer is an important part of daily life.

_____ 6. Yesterday, our neighbor became president of the local bank.

_____ 7. She has been a faithful employee of the bank for years.

_____ 8. She is also a graduate of a famous business school.

_____ 9. My mother is a director of the bank.

_____ 10. She has always been a mentor to that woman.

_____ 11. This year Tom became a history major.

_____ 12. History has become a fascinating study for him.

_____ 13. The history of the American Revolution is his specialty.

_____ 14. His special interest is the writers of the U.S. Constitution.

_____ 15. Those men were valuable contributors to our welfare and safety.

_____ 16. The teacher of my biology class is a famous scholar.

_____ 17. He is also a very successful inventor.

_____ 18. One of his inventions is a popular exercise machine.

_____ 19. The machine has been a valuable asset for many athletic teams.

_____ 20. The teacher has become an immensely wealthy man because of the success of the machine.

Directions: Each of the following sentences is a Pattern 2 sentence containing an adjective subjective complement. In the space at the left, copy the subjective complement.

_____ 1. The team became extremely exhausted by the end of the practice.

_____ 2. We grew more confident with every successful presentation of our proposal.

_____ 3. With little effort, we were able to finish the yard before noon.

_____ 4. My sister's chocolate chip cookies are the best in the entire world, according to my friends.

_____ 5. My family has been enthusiastic about those cookies for generations.

_____ 6. The cookies taste especially good with a cold glass of milk.

_____ 7. As a cook, my sister is especially brilliant.

_____ 8. Her recipe for peanut butter sandwiches is renowned all over our neighborhood.

_____ 9. For our football fans, only a conference championship will be acceptable.

_____ 10. The expectations of the fans are extraordinarily high this season.

_____ 11. Our quarterback is highly skilled.

_____ 12. He has become famous throughout the conference for his passing accuracy.

_____ 13. Last season he became more successful with every game.

_____ 14. Prior to his arrival, the fans had grown weary of losing all the time.

_____ 15. Their opinion of the coach had turned quite sour.

_____ 16. With the new quarterback's success, the fans became happier with every game.

_____ 17. In the eyes of the fans, the coach became more talented.

_____ 18. Victory has become customary for our team.

_____ 19. Thus, the team has become comfortable with success.

_____ 20. All in all, the season has been extremely successful.

Exercise 3   *Subjects and Verbs*

Directions: In the first space at the left, copy the subject of the sentence. In the second space, copy the verb. Many of the verbs consist of more than one word. ~~If the sentence is a Pattern 2 sentence, circle the subjective complement~~.

_____   1. Last week two of my friends left for Colorado.

_____   2. With decreasing quality, the newspaper experienced a sharp drop
_____   in circulation.

_____   3. A few of the laborers had originally come from Portugal.

_____   4. An enormous decrease in the number of engineering graduates has
_____   reduced our technological productivity.

_____   5. A new manager for the accounting department will soon be arriving
_____   from the division headquarters.

_____   6. The unsung hero of yesterday's game was Watkins, the shortstop.

_____   7. The earliest day for an appointment with the dentist will be next
_____   Monday.

_____   8. In the room next to this one is the new server.

_____   9. By the day after tomorrow, there will be a new coat of paint on
_____   this building.

_____   10. Out in the pasture grazed a beautiful Tennessee walking horse.

_____   11. Tomorrow is the first day of the new term.

_____   12. She'd never seen a more beautiful dress in any local store.

_____   13. Your earliest opportunity for that course is Winter Term.

_____   14. On the dashboard under the corner of the windshield, you'll find
_____   the vehicle identification number.

_____   15. Everyone in the company knows about your monumental efforts
_____   on that project.

_____   16. Along with that questionnaire, we have developed a new method
_____   for tabulating the results of our opinion polls.

_____   17. Neither of the last two questions on my history test rang any bells
_____   with me at all.

_____   18. Under the bed in his room in the dorm, Sam found the library book.

_____

_____ 19. Mark's the only one of my friends with a cell phone in both of his
_____ cars.

_____ 20. With all of that work on my new diet, I didn't lose a single pound.

_____ 21. The homecoming queen, along with her escort, sat in a special
_____ seat on the fifty-yard line.

_____ 22. With the Vice President rode a pair of Secret Service agents.

_____ 23. The arrival of Hank Aaron at the Old Timers' Game caused a
_____ tremendous roar of applause.

_____ 24. A few of the little kids from the camp took the front seats in the
_____ auditorium.

_____ 25. A large majority of the people at the town meeting had not studied
_____ the proposed bond issue.

_____ 26. Several volunteers have worked long hours on the new picnic area
_____ at the elementary school.

_____ 27. My family has owned this property since 1935.

_____ 28. The soap opera star, with a bright smile and a silly giggle, accepted
_____ the roses from the mayor.

_____ 29. At this time of year, the campgrounds around the lake are almost
_____ all full.

_____ 30. Many people from nearby towns maintain their interest in our
_____ football team despite its dismal record this year.

_____ 31. My response to your ideas, along with comments by other members,
_____ will appear in the minutes of this meeting.

_____ 32. High up on that top shelf, I have hidden my textbooks from last
_____ semester.

_____ 33. That computerized index is the most useful research tool in the
_____ library.

_____ 34. Mack's always looking for some new adventure.

_____ 35. There is no chance for a retake on that test.

_____ 36. A repetition of my dismal failure on the previous algebra test
_____ seemed impossible.

_____ 37. The pleasant supper by the lake became a grim exercise in
_____ endurance because of the sudden thunderstorm.

_____ 38. One of Harry's friends had brought his little brother along on the
_____ canoe trip.

_____ 39. My brother, with two buddies from his fraternity, is coming home
_____ for the weekend.

_____ 40. After a very rocky first inning, Shaughnessy pitched almost
_____ flawlessly for five innings.

Lesson 4   Basic Sentence Patterns with Transitive Verbs

In Sentence Pattern 2 the intransitive verb links the subject to a noun or adjective that completes the idea of the sentence: "Maria is our pitcher"; "Maria is brilliant." When a **transitive verb** is used, the action expressed by the verb "goes across" to some noun that receives the action. That noun is called the **direct object** and is the receiver of the action expressed in the verb. In the sentence "John watched a movie," the action (the verb) is *watched*, and the actor (the subject) is *John;* the receiver of the action (the direct object) is *movie*. The direct object can be found by asking the question "What?" after the subject and verb have been found. "John watched what? John watched a movie."

SENTENCE PATTERN 3

In Pattern 3 sentences the verb is a transitive verb. It does not link or connect; instead, it identifies an action and transfers that action to a receiver or object of the action (the direct object). The subject-verb combination of the sentence does not complete a thought unless there is an object to receive the action named in the verb. For example, in the sentence "The child hits the ball," the subject-verb combination (*child hits*) does not make a complete statement. A complete statement requires that the child hit *something*.

The direct object is always a noun or a noun equivalent, such as a pronoun:

I broke my glasses. What names the activity? *Broke* is the verb. Who broke? *I* is the subject. I broke what? *Glasses.* Thus, *glasses* is the direct object.

Someone saw us. What names the activity? *Saw.* Who saw? *Someone* saw. Someone saw what? *Us* is the direct object.

We need to draw a contrast between a Pattern 2 sentence and a Pattern 3 sentence. Although both patterns require a complement, in a Pattern 2 sentence such as "The child is a genius," the subject is either renamed or modified by the subjective complement. In the sentence "Someone saw us," it is clear that *someone* and *us* are not the same. *Us* is the receiver of the action *saw* and simply cannot be taken to be the same as the *someone* who saw. In both Pattern 2 and Pattern 3 sentences, the thought of the sentence is not complete without a complement, but in Pattern 3 the subject acts upon the complement, the direct object.

SENTENCE PATTERN 4

Pattern 4 sentences also contain a direct object. But because Pattern 4 sentences use verbs such as *give* or *show*, the sentences need a **second** complement to complete their thought. After a transitive verb such as *shows, gives,* or *tells*, the direct object (the receiver of the action) answers the question "What?" and an **indirect object** answers the question "To whom?" or "For whom?" Thus, "She sang a lullaby" is a Pattern 3 sentence, but "She gave the children a gift" is a Pattern 4 sentence.

In the sentence "The parents give the child a present," you can easily see that two complements are used. The sentence mentions the thing that is given (*present*, the direct object) and the person to whom the direct object is given (*child*, the indirect object). Although the indirect object usually names a person, it can name a nonhuman thing, as in "We gave your *application* a careful reading."

Other verbs that are commonly used this way and therefore produce a Pattern 4 structure are *allow, assign, ask, tell, write, send, pay, grant,* and so on. Nearly all sentences using such verbs can make essentially the same statement by using a prepositional phrase, usually beginning with the preposition *to* or *for.* When the prepositional phrase is present in the sentence, it is a Pattern 3 sentence.

> The postman brought me a letter. [Pattern 4; *me* is an indirect object.]
> The postman brought a letter to me. [Pattern 3; *me* is the object of a preposition.]
> Mother bought us some candy. [Pattern 4]
> Mother bought some candy for us. [Pattern 3]

SENTENCE PATTERN 5

Pattern 5 sentences regularly use verbs such as *consider, call, think, find, make, elect, appoint,* and *name.* There are two closely related types of Pattern 5 sentences. Each type begins like a Pattern 3 sentence:

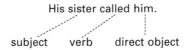

> His sister called him.
>
> subject   verb   direct object

But the nature of the verb *called* allows the use of a second complement answering the question "What?" after *called him.* His sister called him what?

> His sister called him a genius.

The reference of the two nouns following the verb is a key to the difference between this type of sentence and a Pattern 4 sentence. In a Pattern 4 sentence the two noun complements refer to different things, but in a Pattern 5 sentence they refer to the same thing.

> Mother made us some fudge. [Pattern 4: *us* and *fudge* refer to different things.]
> This experience made John an activist. [Pattern 5: *John* and *activist* are the same thing.]

Thus, there are two complements in Pattern 5 sentences. The one closer to the verb is the direct object. The second complement is called the **objective complement.** In the first type of Pattern 5 sentence, the objective complement is a noun that *renames* the direct object. In the second type of Pattern 5 sentence, the objective complement is an adjective that *describes* the direct object.

> His sister called him a genius.
> His sister called him brilliant.

Because the objective complement renames or describes the direct object, we can use a handy test to help us recognize Pattern 5: The insertion of *to be* between the complements will give us an acceptable English wording.

> We appointed Jones [to be] our representative.
> I thought this action [to be] unnecessary.

Sometimes the word *as* is used between the direct object and the objective complement in Pattern 5 sentences:

> We appointed Jones as our representative.

Some adjective objective complements are very important to the meaning of the verb. Thus, it is sometimes effective to place these objective complements immediately after the verb and before the direct object:

> *Usual order:* He set the caged animals [D.O.] free [O.C.].
> *Variation:* He set free [O.C.] the caged animals [D.O.].

SUPPLEMENT

One special kind of verb makes it difficult to distinguish between a direct object and the object of a preposition. Here are two examples:

> Harry jumped off the box.
> Harry took off his raincoat.

The first sentence is Pattern 1. *Off* is a preposition, *box* is the object of the preposition, and the prepositional phrase is used as an adverbial modifier because it tells *where* Harry jumped. The second sentence is Pattern 3. The verb, with its adverbial modifier *off*, is the equivalent of the transitive verb *remove*. *Raincoat* is the direct object.

There is another way to distinguish between the adverbial use and the prepositional use of such a word as *off* in the preceding examples. When the word is a vital adverbial modifier of the verb, it can be used in either of two positions: following the verb or following the direct object.

> Harry took off his raincoat.
> Harry took his raincoat off.

When the word is a preposition, the alternate position is not possible: "Harry jumped the box off" is not an English sentence. Here are some other examples of verbs with adverbial modifiers. Notice that in each case you can easily find a transitive verb synonym for the combination:

> Give up [*relinquish*] her rights.
> Leave out [*omit*] the second chapter.
> Put out [*extinguish*] the fire.
> Make over [*alter*] an old dress.
> Make up [*invent*] an excuse.

SUMMARY OF VERBS USED IN DIFFERENT SENTENCE PATTERNS

1. **Verbs that serve a linking function and commonly form Pattern 2 sentences:**
   be, seem, appear, prove, remain, continue, become, turn, grow, work, get, wear, look, smell, taste, feel, sound

2. **Verbs that commonly produce Pattern 4 sentences:**
   allow, assign, ask, tell, write, send, pay, grant

3. **Verbs that commonly produce Pattern 5 sentences:**
   consider, call, think, find, make, elect, appoint, name

NAME _____　SCORE _____

Directions: Each of these sentences is a Pattern 3 sentence. Circle the subject and underline the verb. In the space at the left, copy the direct object.

_____ 1. All of us want a holiday from class soon.

_____ 2. Last week we took three tests within two days.

_____ 3. The professor's assistant announced a term paper assignment this
morning.

_____ 4. The term paper will provide an in-depth treatment of a subject
related to the professor's lectures.

_____ 5. Many people in the class have chosen topics for the paper already.

_____ 6. Last night the reporters on television issued a frightening warning
about this week's weather.

_____ 7. A cold front will cover the northern part of the state.

_____ 8. The bad weather threatens our baseball game this Saturday.

_____ 9. The game will probably decide the conference championship.

_____ 10. The college might postpone the game until the following Monday.

_____ 11. One of my friends hiked a long mountain trail over the weekend.

_____ 12. She carried a pack with a tent and some food in it.

_____ 13. On the trail she saw a huge black bear.

_____ 14. The bear was stealing honey from a huge hollow tree.

_____ 15. The bear frightened my friend very badly.

_____ 16. On a shelf in the back of the library I found a copy of a rare book.

_____ 17. Some of the people in my office held a meeting yesterday afternoon.

_____ 18. A few people in the office left the meeting early.

_____ 19. Every person in my office needs a raise before next year.

_____ 20. None of the people in my office make very much money.

Directions: The following are Pattern 3, 4, or 5 sentences. Identify the italicized complement by writing one of the following in the space at the left:

      D.O. (direct object)   I.O. (indirect object)   O.C. (objective complement)

_____ 1. Grandma gave *me* her recipe for drop biscuits.

_____ 2. I saw your *dog* out behind my house today.

_____ 3. That new project made Harry very *happy* yesterday.

_____ 4. My father desperately wants a new *car.*

_____ 5. In the hallway on the bookshelf, I saw a *copy* of an old magazine.

_____ 6. Jim showed *Cheryl* pictures of his new car.

_____ 7. That new house down the street has a dark green *door.*

_____ 8. Someone painted that new house a bright *orange.*

_____ 9. The football team has won the last *three* of its games.

_____ 10. The coach called the last victory the most *important* of his career.

_____ 11. Several players earned special *awards* for their play in that game.

_____ 12. The quarterback told *me* a funny story about the coach.

_____ 13. The coach gave some *players* special awards.

_____ 14. The coach gave special *awards* to some players.

_____ 15. The coach's speech made those awards quite *special.*

_____ 16. The president of the college appointed Jim as a student *representative* to the Board of Trustees.

_____ 17. Once in a while, I enjoy a hot fudge *sundae.*

_____ 18. The taste of the hot fudge makes the sundae a wonderful *treat.*

_____ 19. Please show *us* the pictures from your last sailboat race.

_____ 20. The high winds during the race made it both *difficult* and *dangerous.*

Exercise 4   *Complements*

NAME _____ SCORE _____

Directions: Circle the subject and underline the verb in each of the following sentences. Identify the italicized complement by writing one of the following in the space at the left.

S.C. (subjective complement)   D.O. (direct object)
I.O. (indirect object)   O.C. (objective complement)

_____ 1. The president made Ms. Sharpe his *chief of staff*.

_____ 2. The inventor suggested a new *product* for the company.

_____ 3. The book reviewer paid the *author* a very high compliment.

_____ 4. Hal offered *me* $150 for that pair of skis.

_____ 5. The television sportscaster called our team the *underdog* in the tournament.

_____ 6. The exhausted elderly man called a *taxi*.

_____ 7. The team gave *Freeman* a huge bonus for signing the contract.

_____ 8. To the people from Alaska, the humidity in Louisiana seemed extremely *high*.

_____ 9. June's nephew colored the wallpaper *blue*.

_____ 10. In response to my story, the teacher granted me an *extension* on the paper.

_____ 11. The stylist left Mary's hair very *curly*.

_____ 12. Uncle Sal told the *officer* a very lame story.

_____ 13. He's *one* of the best teachers in the entire college.

_____ 14. The boss called Mike's *departure* a great loss to our department.

_____ 15. Bob sang the school fight *song* backward.

_____ 16. The cinnamon buns in the oven smell *spicy*.

_____ 17. All afternoon Helen has been searching the *house* for her lost car keys.

_____ 18. Mrs. Cooper promised the kindergarten *children* a special dessert for tomorrow's lunch.

_____ 19. The brief shower was a welcome *relief* from the heat.

_____ 20. Every child recited the *poem* perfectly.

Directions: Using appropriate forms of the verbs indicated, write twenty original sentences illustrating the following Patterns:

Sentences 1–5: Pattern 2

Sentences 6–10: Pattern 3

Sentences 11–15: Pattern 4

Sentences 16–10: Pattern 5

Circle every subject complement and every direct object; underline with one line every indirect object; underline with two lines every objective complement.

1. be _____

2. seem _____

3. remain _____

4. appear _____

5. grow _____

6. grow _____

7. ask _____

8. build _____

9. throw _____

10. tell _____

11. tell _____

12. give _____

13. bring _____

14. show _____

15. make _____

16. make _____

17. elect _____

18. paint _____

19. find _____

20. select _____

In this lesson you will examine a few more forms and uses of verbs, including some additional auxiliary verbs. With these forms and those that you have already examined, you will be acquainted with nearly all of the verb forms that the average speaker and writer will ever use.

In Lesson 2 you examined the partial conjugation of three verbs: *earn, grow,* and *be.* You may want to refer to that conjugation (pages 9–10) as we discuss a few more points about changes in verb form.

Third-person singular verbs in the present tense end in *s* (or *es*): *earns, teaches, is, has.* Notice that on nouns the *s* (*es*) ending shows a plural form; whereas on verbs it shows a singular form:

dogs, noses	(plural nouns)
wags, sniffs	(singular verbs)

If you review the conjugation of the verb *be* in Lesson 2, you will notice the verb is completely irregular. Unlike any other verb in the language, it has three forms (*am, is,* and *are*) in the present tense and two forms (*was* and *were*) in the past tense.

In general, the tenses are used as follows:

Present:	Action occurring at the present moment. He *earns* a good salary.
Past:	Action occurring at a definite time before the present moment. Last year he *earned* a good salary.
Future:	Action occurring at some time beyond the present moment. Next year he *will earn* a good salary.
Present perfect:	Action continuing up to the present moment. So far this year he *has earned* ten thousand dollars.
Past perfect:	Action continuing to a fixed moment in the past. Before leaving for college, he *had earned* $10,000.
Future perfect:	Action continuing to a fixed moment in the future. By next Christmas he *will have earned* $10,000.

In Lesson 21 you will be reminded of a few usage problems involving tenses.

PRINCIPAL PARTS

We noted in Lesson 2 that *earn* is a regular verb and *grow* is an irregular verb. We customarily make use of three distinctive forms, called the **principal parts** of the verb, to show the difference between regular and irregular verbs. The following are the principal parts:

- *Base* or *infinitive*, the "name" of the verb, used in the present tense with *s* (*es*) added in the third-person singular

- *Past,* the form used in the simple past tense
- *Past participle,* the form used in the three perfect tenses

   In all regular verbs, the past and the past participle are alike, formed simply by the addition of *ed* to the base form (or only *d* if the base word ends in *e*). Thus, *earn* becomes *earned.* Irregular verbs are more complicated because, for nearly all of them, the past tense and the past participle are not spelled alike. Thus, the past tense of *grow* is *grew,* and the past participle of *grow* is *grown.* Following are the three forms of some irregular verbs illustrating spelling changes and endings:

Base	Past	Past Participle
be	was, were	been
become	became	become
bite	bit	bitten
break	broke	broken
catch	caught	caught
do	did	done
eat	ate	eaten
put	put	put
ring	rang	rung
run	ran	run
see	saw	seen

(You will study more principal parts of verbs and the usage problems associated with them in Lesson 21.) Both regular and irregular verbs add *ing* to their base form to produce the **present participle.** The present participle is often used with auxiliary verbs.

AUXILIARY VERBS

In the sample conjugation in Lesson 2, you observed the use of *will* and *have* as auxiliary verbs in the future tense and the perfect tenses. Another important auxiliary is *be,* used with the present participle (the *ing* form of the main verb) to produce what is called the **progressive form.** As an example of its use, suppose someone asks you what you are doing in your English class. You probably would not reply, "Right now, we *review* parts of speech." Instead, you probably would say, "Right now, we *are reviewing* parts of speech," to show that the action is not fixed in an exact moment of time but is a continuing activity. This very useful type of verb occurs in all six tenses:

   We are reviewing.
   We were reviewing.
   We will be reviewing.
   We have been reviewing.
   We had been reviewing.
   We will have been reviewing.

Another type of auxiliary verb includes *may, might, must, can, could, would,* and *should. May, can,* and *might* are used to suggest possibility. *Can* sometimes also suggests capability.

I may go to town tomorrow.   (If certain conditions exist.)
I might go to town tomorrow.   (If certain conditions exist.)
I can go to town tomorrow.   (I am able to go.)

Must indicates an obligation:

I must go to town.

Could is used to indicate ability, possibility, or permission in the past tense:

I could have gone to town.   (If I had wanted to go.)

These words are called **modal auxiliaries,** and they are used the way *will* is used:

I *should study* this weekend.
I *should have studied* last weekend.

Occasionally, *do* acts as a modal auxiliary and combines with the base form of a main verb to make an "emphatic" form: "But I *did* pay that bill last month." In Lesson 6 you will examine the much more common use of the *do* auxiliary in questions and negatives.

Other variations of some modals and time auxiliaries make use of *to* in the verb phrase:

Mr. Nelson *has to retire* [must retire] early.
You *ought to eat* [should eat] more vegetables.
I *used to be* a secretary.
Jim *was supposed to be* here at 10 o'clock.
I *am to depart* for Miami early in the morning.
I *am going to depart* for Miami early in the morning.
We *meant to leave* much earlier today.

Here are a few other points to remember about auxiliary verbs:

1. *Have, be,* and *do* are not used exclusively as auxiliaries; they are three of the most commonly used main verbs:

    I *have* a brown pen. [Main verb]
    I *have* lost my brown pen. [Auxiliary]
    He *is* a good speaker. [Main verb]
    He *is* becoming a good speaker. [Auxiliary]
    He *did* a good job for us. [Main verb]
    Yes, I *did* embellish the story somewhat. [Auxiliary]

2. When the verb unit contains auxiliaries, short adverbial modifiers may separate parts of the whole verb phrase:

    We *have* occasionally *been* sailing.
    He *has*, of course, *been telling* the truth.

3. In a few set expressions following introductory adverbs (usually adverbs of time), the subject is placed within the verb phrase between an auxiliary and the main verb:

Only lately *have* I *learned* to drive.
Rarely *do* we *turn on* the television set.

NAME _____ SCORE _____

Directions: Each of these sentences contains at least one auxiliary verb. (Some have two; some have three.) Copy the auxiliary verb(s) in the first space at the left. In the second space, write 1, 2, 3, 4, or 5 to identify the sentence pattern.

_____ _____ 1. Without his generous contribution, the club could not have finished that playground for the neighborhood kids.

_____ _____ 2. We would have been about $1,000 short of our goal without his contribution.

_____ _____ 3. By tomorrow, the company will have been working on that proposal for two weeks.

_____ _____ 4. We have, of course, been working night and day to get the proposal completed.

_____ _____ 5. Will the men have finished that wall by late afternoon today?

_____ _____ 6. Can we bring in more people as additional staff on that project?

_____ _____ 7. The family down the street could not find its cat last night.

_____ _____ 8. My sister is supposed to leave for college next week.

_____ _____ 9. I should have been studying during last night's televised football game.

_____ _____ 10. Only rarely do we leave the house before 7:30 A.M.

_____ _____ 11. That dog has been my mother's faithful companion for years.

_____ _____ 12. My brother's fraternity has elected him its president.

_____ _____ 13. Can you tell me the price of that pair of roller blades?

_____ _____ 14. Doesn't that seem quite expensive to you?

_____ _____ 15. We ought to check that cash register again before closing time.

_____ _____ 16. Seats for tonight's game should still be available.

_____ _____ 17. I might have run that program ten times yesterday.

_____ _____ 18. Will you make a run to the grocery store for me?

_____ 19. After forty-five minutes, I could not have run any farther.

_____ 20. Those men should have finished the race by this time.

_____ 21. Those men did not give us their best effort.

_____ 22. The coach has called those men the slowest runners in the world.

_____ 23. Those men need to work harder on their speed.

_____ 24. I have been training very hard now for several weeks.

_____ 25. I have probably run fifty miles or more in the last several weeks.

_____ 26. My father has called this winter the worst in many years.

_____ 27. Our team should have appointed James Crane as its representative to the Athletic Council.

_____ 28. Arthur did not take his computer with him on the flight to Houston.

_____ 29. We will need to ship the computer to him immediately.

_____ 30. I have been looking for a good used truck for several weeks.

_____ 31. A good used truck might be a rare thing in this part of the country.

_____ 32. Perhaps I should look for a truck in the classified ads in the new paper.

_____ 33. My cousin Barbara has located a fine used truck on the Internet.

_____ 34. I might find a truck suitable for me in a big city newspaper.

_____ 35. Please, will you give me directions to that nice Italian restaurant?

_____ 36. Yes, Joan did pay me the money for that textbook.

_____ 37. Alex used to be a professional soccer player back in Spain.

_____ 38. With good weather, I might sail to the island tomorrow for lunch.

_____ 39. By the end of the year, Maria will have been working here for twenty years.

_____ 40. Really, you should have told me that story about two weeks ago.

Complements

Copyright © 2005 by Pearson Education, Inc.

NAME _____   SCORE _____

Directions: In the space at the left, write one of the following to identify the italicized word:

      S.C. (subjective complement)   I.O. (indirect object)

      D.O. (direct object)   O.C. (objective complement)

If the italicized word is not a complement, leave the space blank. Circle every auxiliary verb.

_____ 1. The two accountants should find that *error* without much difficulty.

_____ 2. Competent people will not find that work *difficult*.

_____ 3. I, however, have always had great *difficulty* with problem solving.

_____ 4. Can you solve a simple quadratic *equation*?

_____ 5. Complex weather patterns can make a forecast of the hurricane's track almost *impossible*.

_____ 6. These storms respond to *forces* in the upper atmosphere.

_____ 7. They often move away from *areas* of high pressure.

_____ 8. Slow movement across the open sea often produces an *increase* in wind velocity.

_____ 9. More rapid movement, interestingly enough, often causes a decrease in wind *velocity*.

_____ 10. A large, powerful hurricane can push a storm *surge* of fifty to sixty feet in front of it.

_____ 11. Often, rising water is the most dangerous *effect* of a hurricane.

_____ 12. The Hurricane Service calls September 10 the *peak* of the hurricane season in the Atlantic Ocean.

_____ 13. We can follow the *track* of a hurricane by using satellite technology.

_____ 14. Hurricane forecasters often call perfectly formed hurricanes a beautiful *sight*.

_____ 15. The rest of us consider such *pictures* frightening.

_____ 16. The town's mayor gave *one* of the candidates for city council a ringing endorsement.

45

_____ 17. The mayor gave a long *speech* at a civic club meeting yesterday.

_____ 18. She praised the *candidate* for his long service in the municipal government.

_____ 19. The candidate provided *us* with her resume and a short biography.

_____ 20. The audience found her resume very *interesting*.

_____ 21. She seems highly *qualified* for the job of town council member.

_____ 22. She also appears very *confident* in her abilities.

_____ 23. Many members of that audience will probably vote for the *candidate*.

_____ 24. Perhaps the voters should consider other *candidates* before the election.

_____ 25. The town needs to elect only the best-qualified *candidate*.

_____ 26. Many consider Norton the best-qualified *candidate*.

_____ 27. Out in the marsh Jason saw a very rare *hawk*.

_____ 28. Will you, along with the rest of the staff, go down to the second floor *office* for the rest of the day?

_____ 29. On the platform at the front of the *auditorium* stood the college president and his assistant.

_____ 30. Many people consider the new president perfectly *qualified* for the job.

_____ 31. They give *her* credit for great success in her last job.

_____ 32. The Board of Trustees considered her record *impeccable*.

_____ 33. Apparently, she accomplished great *things* in that earlier position.

_____ 34. For one thing, she doubled the *size* of the college's endowment fund.

_____ 35. For many people, that one accomplishment made *her* a good candidate for the job.

_____ 36. The breeze from that pine forest smelled *wonderful*.

_____ 37. Did the professor allow *us* an extra week for that project?

_____ 38. The two women walked slowly down the *concourse* to the restaurant.

_____ 39. Isn't that scene on the postcard incredibly *beautiful*?

_____ 40. I left out the second *chapter* of the textbook from my test preparation.

Any long piece of writing made up exclusively of basic sentences would be too monotonous to read. You should think of the basic sentences not as models for your writing but as elementary units, important because they are the structures from which more effective sentences develop. In this lesson, we look at two alterations of basic sentence patterns:

1. Sentences that use passive verbs
2. Sentences in the form of a question

Lessons 7 through 11 then show how basic sentences can be combined and certain elements can be reduced to subordinate clauses and phrases to produce varied, well-developed sentences.

PASSIVE VOICE

In Lesson 2 you examined a partial conjugation of the verb *earn*. The forms listed there are in the active voice, which means that the subject is the doer of the action. A more complete conjugation would include the passive voice. In the passive voice, the subject is not the doer of the action; it is the receiver of the action. Thus the verb is always transitive. Passive verb forms make use of the auxiliary verb *be* combined with the past participle of the verb, as shown in the following illustration of the third-person singular in the six tenses:

> This amount is earned.
> This amount was earned.
> This amount will be earned.
> This amount has been earned.
> This amount had been earned.
> This amount will have been earned.

The present and past tenses of progressive verbs can also be shifted to the passive voice, giving us forms in which *be* is used in two auxiliary capacities in the same verb form:

> These cars *are being sold* at a loss.
> These cars *were being sold* at a loss.

Because only transitive verbs have passive forms, only sentence patterns 3, 4, and 5 can be altered to the passive voice. When the idea of a Pattern 3 sentence in the active voice is expressed with a passive verb, there is no direct object (complement) in the sentence:

Active voice:	Children play games.
Passive voice:	Games are played [by children].

If the doer of the verb's action is expressed in a sentence using a passive verb, the doer must occur as the object of the preposition *by*. When a Pattern 4 sentence is altered to form a passive construction, the indirect object that follows the active verb sometimes becomes the subject of the passive verb:

Active voice: John gave Allen a model plane.

Passive voice: Allen was given a model plane [by John].

Here the passive verb is followed by a complement, *plane*, which we continue to call a direct object in spite of the fact that it follows a passive verb. It is also possible, in a Pattern 4 sentence, to make the direct object the subject of a passive verb, making the sentence read thus:

The model plane was given to Allen (by John).

Notice also how a Pattern 5 sentence can be given a different kind of expression by means of a passive verb:

Active voice: The parents consider the child a genius.
The parents consider the child clever.

Passive voice: The child is considered a genius [by the parents].
The child is considered clever [by the parents].

In these sentences the direct object becomes the subject, but the passive verb requires a complement (*genius, clever*). Because the complement renames or describes the subject, it is called a subjective complement.

The passive voice serves a real purpose in effective communication: It should be used when the *doer* of the action is unknown or is of secondary interest in the statement. In such a situation, the writer, wishing to focus attention on the *receiver* of the action, places that unit in the emphatic subject position. The passive verb form makes this arrangement possible. Thus, instead of some vague expression such as "Somebody should wash these windows," we can say, "These windows *should be washed*."

Sometimes the passive voice is described as "weak." Admittedly, some writers do get into the habit of using the passive form when there is little justification for it. In most narrative writing, the doer of the action is logically the subject of the verb. "The fullback crossed the goal line" would certainly be preferred to "The goal line was crossed by the fullback," a version that gives the same information but tends to stop any action suggested by the sentence. The passive voice also lends itself to a kind of muddied, heavy-footed writing that produces prose like this:

It *is* now *rumored* that the secretary of defense *has been informed* that contingent plans *have been made* to....

The writer of such a sentence, however, probably finds the passive voice effectively hides the identity of the person who is spreading the rumor, who has informed the secretary of defense, or who has made the plans. This use of the passive voice creates an impersonal, bureaucratic language popular in many institutions.

You should practice with passive constructions so you can use this important device when it is called for. Equally important, if a criticism of your writing mentions doubtful uses of the passive voice, you need to be able to recognize passive verbs in order to change them when necessary.

QUESTIONS

In the sentence types you examined in earlier lessons, you noted the normal positioning of the main sentence parts: the subject first, followed by the verb, followed by the complement, if any. In questions, however, other arrangements are possible. As we study these new structures, we must first recognize the fact that there are two kinds of questions:

1. Questions answered by *yes* or *no*
2. Questions answered by information

QUESTIONS ANSWERED BY *YES* OR *NO*

In the following paired sentences, the first sentence is a statement and the second sentence a related question. These sentences demonstrate how the structure of a yes/no question differs from that of a statement.

1. Beth is happy. Is Beth happy?

2. You were there. Were you there?

3. You see Ms. Locke often. Do you see Ms. Locke often?

4. You heard the announcement. Did you hear the announcement?

Notice from these examples that if the verb is *be* in the present or past tense, the subject and the *be* form (*am, are, is, was,* or *were*) reverse positions. With other one-word verbs in the present or past tense, the proper form of the auxiliary *do* is used, followed by the subject and the base form of the main verb.

If the verb already has an auxiliary, the subject follows the auxiliary verb. If there are two or more auxiliaries, the subject follows the first one.

5. You have seen the movie. Have you seen the movie?

6. They will arrive later. Will they arrive later?

7. The house is being painted. Is the house being painted?

8. He should have been told. Should he have been told?

When the verb is *have* in the present tense, two versions of the question are possible: the subject-verb reversal and the *do* auxiliary. (See Supplement 1.)

9. You have enough money. Have you enough money?

10. You have enough money. Do you have enough money?

QUESTIONS ANSWERED BY INFORMATION

Some questions ask for information rather than for a *yes* or *no* response. These questions make use of words called **interrogatives,** words that stand for unknown persons, things, or descriptive qualities. The most commonly used interrogatives are these:

pronouns:	*who (whom), which, what*
adjectives:	*whose, which, what*
adverbs:	*when, where, why, how*

The interrogative pronoun *who*, which stands for an unknown person or persons, has three forms:

1. *Who*, when it is used as a subject or a subjective complement
2. *Whose*, when it is used as a possessive modifier of a noun
3. *Whom*, when it is used as an object

(In a later lesson you will learn that these three forms of *who* have another important use in subordinate clauses; the choice between *who* and *whom* as a problem of usage is discussed more extensively in Lesson 24.)

In questions using these interrogatives, the normal arrangement of the main sentence parts is retained only when the interrogative is the subject or a modifier of the subject. Here again we use paired statements and related questions to demonstrate these structures:

1. *My brother* [S.] paid the bill. *Who* [S.] paid the bill?

2. *Five cars* [S.] were damaged. *How* many cars [S.] were damaged?

In all other situations the subject-verb position is altered as it is with yes/no questions. The interrogative word, or the unit containing the interrogative word, stands at the beginning of the sentence to signal that a question, not a statement, is forthcoming:

I studied *geometry* [D.O.] last night.
What [D.O.] did you study last night?

You saw *Jim* [D.O.] at the party.
Whom [D.O.] did you see at the party?

She is Mother's *cousin* [S.C.].
Who [S.C.] is she?

We can use Bill's *car* [D.O.].
Whose car [D.O.] can we use?

You spent 15 *dollars* [D.O.].
How much money [D.O.] did you spend?

You [S.] called *Bob* [D.O.] a *thief* [O.C.].
Who [S.] called Bob a thief?

Whom [D.O.] did you call a thief?
What [O.C.] did you call Bob?

When the interrogative unit is the object of a preposition, two arrangements of the question are often possible:

1. The entire prepositional phrase may stand at the beginning.

2. The interrogative may stand at the beginning with the preposition in its usual position.

The speaker was referring *to the mayor.*
To whom was the speaker referring?
Whom was the speaker referring to?

(See Supplement 2.)

SUPPLEMENT 1

The type of verb also determines the structuring of sentences that are negative rather than positive. The positioning of the negator *not* (or its contraction, *n't*) depends on the presence or absence of an auxiliary verb. Sentences using *be* or *have* must be considered special cases.

1. If the verb is *be* in the present tense or in the past tense, used either as the main verb or as an auxiliary verb, the *not* follows the *be* form:

   I *am not* pleased with the report.
   He *was not* [wasn't] available.
   They *were not* [weren't] invited.

2. With other one-word verbs in the present or past tense, the proper form of the auxiliary *do* is used followed by the negator and the base form of the main verb:

   I *do not* [don't] expect a reward.
   He *does not* [doesn't] attend regularly.
   We *did not* [didn't] respond.

3. If the verb already has an auxiliary, the negator follows the auxiliary. When there are two or more auxiliaries, the *not* follows the first one:

   We *could not* [couldn't] see very well.
   I *may not* have understood him.
   They *will not* [won't] refund my money.
   This cake *ought not* to have been baked so long.

4. When *have* in the present tense is the main verb, two negative forms are possible:

   I *have not* [haven't] enough time to play.
   I *do not* [don't] have enough time to play.

SUPPLEMENT 2

At the informal language level, another version—"*Who* was the speaker referring to?"—is often found, despite the traditional demand for the objective case for the object of a preposition. The formal level of both spoken and written English calls for "*To whom* was the speaker referring?"

NAME _____ SCORE _____

Directions: These sentences are Pattern 3, 4, or 5 sentences. In the first space at the left, write the pattern number. In the second space, write the verb form used when the italicized word in the sentence is made the subject.

_____4_____   Later I will send you a *copy* of the bulletin.
will be sent

_____   1. Jan included my *idea* in her presentation.

_____   2. The county elected *Mrs. Johnson* mayor.

_____   3. Johnny found that old *sword* in an old barn down the road.

_____   4. The crowd in the gym gave *Marcia* a huge ovation.

_____   5. The sales manager keeps those *statistics* a secret from his staff.

_____   6. You should have reported your *change of address* to the Post Office.

_____   7. You should have told *Marta* about your change of address.

_____   8. The committee could not have discovered those *facts* about the candidate.

_____   9. None of the people on that boat recognized the *dangers* from the storm.

_____   10. Few people can recall a sight more amazing than that plane's short flight.

Directions: The purpose of this exercise is to contrast the structure of a question with that of a statement. In the space at the left, copy the word from the question that serves the function indicated.

S. (subject)	O.C. (objective complement)
D.O. (direct object)	O.P. (object of preposition)
S.C. (subjective complement)	

The statement following the question has the same basic structure as that of the question.

_____ 1. How many cookies did she bake?
(D.O.)   She baked 100 cookies (D.O.).

_____ 2. How many copies are ready for the meeting?
(S.)   Ten copies (S.) are ready for the meeting.

_____ 3. What are you concerned about in this situation?
(O.P.)   I am concerned about tomorrow's weather (O.P.).

_____ 4. Whose proposal did you select?
(D.O.)   I selected Tom's proposal (D.O.).

_____ 5. Whose car did you drive?
(D.O.)   I drove Martin's car (D.O.).

_____ 6. Whose car is that?
(S.C.)   That is Martin's car (S.C.).

_____ 7. How many errors did you find on that page?
(D.O.)   I found three errors (D.O.) on that page.

_____ 8. Whom should the president choose as her assistant?
(D.O.)   The president should choose Robert (D.O.) as her assistant.

_____ 9. Who will be president's assistant?
(S.)   Robert (S.) will be the president's assistant.

_____ 10. Who will the president's assistant be?
(S.C.)   The president's assistant will be Robert (S.C.).

_____ 11. To whom was that message sent?
(O.P.)   That message was sent to Mr. Worth (O.P.).

_____ 12. What color did she paint her room?
(O.C.)   She painted her room a soft pink (O.C.).

_____ 13. Who sang Charley that corny love song?
(S.)   Anne (S.) sang Charley that corny love song.

_____ 14. What did Anne sing to Charley?
(D.O.)   Anne sang a corny love song (D.O) to Charley.

_____ 15. To whom did Anne sing that corny love song?
(O.P.)   Anne sang that corny love song to Charley (O.P.).

NAME _____ SCORE _____

Directions: Each of the following sentences uses a passive verb. Underline the verb. Rewrite each sentence using an active form of the verb. (You will have to supply a logical subject if the passive verb does not.) If your rewrites are done correctly, your first four sentences will be Pattern 3, your next three will be Pattern 4, and the final three will be Pattern 5.

1. By noon all the tickets to the concert had been bought by people in the lines at the stadium.

   _____

2. That paper must be proofread and corrected very carefully.

   _____

3. That building was designed by two young architects from Southern California.

   _____

4. That book has been read by almost two million people in the past five years.

   _____

5. The students should have been told the format for that paper by the professor.

   _____

6. One change of schedule is allowed each student at the beginning of each semester by the college.

   _____

7. Every employee was given a letter of explanation for the changes in medical insurance.

   _____

8. That man should have been held liable for his careless mistakes in the design of that building.

   _____

9. That campsite is considered impossibly primitive by all but a few hardy campers.

   _____

10. Manny was always considered the class comedian by most of his fellow students.

    _____

Directions: The italicized word in each of the following questions is a complement or the object of a preposition. In the space at the left, write one of the following abbreviations to identify the function of the italicized word:

      D.O. (direct object)   O.C. (objective complement)

      S.C. [subjective complement   O.P. (object of preposition)

_____ 1. To which companies did you send that *proposal*?

_____ 2. Which *companies* did you send that proposal to?

_____ 3. What award shall we give to *Mark*?

_____ 4. *What* was the cost of last night's dinner?

_____ 5. What present did you give *Jaime*?

_____ 6. How *elated* was Tom by the team's victory?

_____ 7. Whom has the organization selected as its *representative* to the convention?

_____ 8. Has the organization selected *Barbara Jones* as its representative to the convention?

_____ 9. Will Barbara Jones be our *representative* to the convention?

_____ 10. How many people attended yesterday's *game*?

_____ 11. How *short* has our supply of printing supplies grown?

_____ 12. Why didn't you tell me about that *problem* sooner?

_____ 13. *Whom* did you send that e-mail to?

_____ 14. Where in the building did you send that new *computer*?

_____ 15. To what *department* did you send that new computer?

_____ 16. How much did you tell *Mari* about that problem in accounting?

_____ 17. How much *money* did the company lose in that last deal?

_____ 18. *What* is Michelle's batting average this season?

_____ 19. How many people did you send that *message* to?

_____ 20. How long a *drive* is the trip from here to Sable Beach?

Check Sheet

You can use Check Sheets in three ways. You can use them as a quick review at the end of each unit; you can use them as another, shorter presentation of the materials in the unit; or you can use them as a quick reference guide to refresh your understanding of a principle as you write papers for English or other classes.

PARTS OF SPEECH

☐ **Nouns**

☐ Common nouns are the names of persons, places, things, qualities, or ideas.

☐ Proper nouns are the names of specific individuals in a class.

Common	Proper
girl	Maria
city	Minneapolis
bat	Omaha Classic
honesty	(no proper form)
economic theory	Marxism

☐ Common nouns are not capitalized, but proper nouns are.

☐ Nouns are singular if they indicate one of the class, plural if they indicate two or more.

☐ **Pronouns**

☐ Pronouns take the place of nouns when reusing the noun would be repetitive.
- *Personal pronouns:* I, you, he, she, it, we, they
- *Demonstrative pronouns:* this, that, these, those
- *Indefinite pronouns:* each, either, neither, one, anyone and others
- *Possessive pronouns:* mine, yours, his, hers, its, ours, theirs

☐ Nouns and pronouns answer the question Who? or What?

☐ **Verbs**

☐ Verbs express action, existence, or condition, and they combine with nouns or pronouns used as subjects to make a statement.
> Maria is tired.
> Tom runs.
> Tyrone sees the dog.

☐ Verbs answer the question What happens? or What is?

☐ Verbs change form to indicate
- *Person:* first I, we; second you; third she, they
- *Number:* singular indicates one thing, plural indicates two or more

- *Tense:* time of the action or existence
  Present: I run
  Past: I ran
  Future: I will run
  Present perfect: I have run
  Past perfect: I had run
  Future perfect: I shall have run

☐ Verb forms for the various tenses are developed from the principal parts of the verb: base, past, and past participle.

☐ The sense of verbs may be changed by adding forms of *to be* and an *-ing* ending to the verb to create progressive tenses.

☐ The sense of verbs can be changed to indicate condition and possibility by adding modal auxiliaries such as *may, might, would, could,* and *should.*

☐ Transitive verbs change voice from active (*The boy saw the dog.*) to passive (*The dog was seen by the boy.*).

☐ Adjectives

☐ Adjectives modify nouns—that is, adjectives change our sense of the noun by adding a limit, description, or quality to the noun. Adjectives occur in three positions:

Preceding the noun	The tall girl ran.
Following a linking verb	The tall girl is happy.
Directly after the noun	The girl, happy....

☐ Adjectives can show degree or strength by changing their form:
  The girl is happy.
  She is happier than I am.
  She is the happiest girl in our class.

☐ Adjectives answer questions such as How big? What shape? What color?

☐ Adverbs

☐ Adverbs change our sense of—modify—verbs, adjectives, other adverbs, or whole sentences:
  The girl walked quickly.
  She walked quite slowly.
  The very young girl walked out of the room.
  Certainly, we'll be there on time.

☐ Adverbs most frequently answer the question How? When? or Where?

☐ Prepositions

☐ Prepositions establish relationships between a noun (the object of the preposition) and another word in a sentence.
  The plane flew into the cloud, under the cloud, behind the cloud.

☐ Sentence Patterns

☐ The parts of speech are combined into sentences that follow five specific patterns. The first two patterns employ intransitive verbs—that is, verbs that transfer no action to an object.

- Pattern 1 (intransitive verb with no complement needed to complete action)
  The bird flies.
- Pattern 2 (intransitive linking verb with subjective complement, either a noun or adjective)
  The man is a scientist.
  The man is brilliant.

The next three patterns employ transitive verbs—that is, verbs that transfer action from the subject to object.

- Pattern 3 (transitive verb with a direct object receiving the action)
  The pilot flies the plane.

Note that some verbs—for example the verb *to fly*—can be intransitive or transitive.

- Pattern 4 (transitive verbs such as *give* and *show,* with a direct object and an indirect object)
  The woman showed us two coats.

- Pattern 5 (transitive verb such as *call, think, find,* and *elect,* with a direct object and an objective complement, either a noun or an adjective)
  The teacher called her a genius.
  The teacher called her brilliant.

☐ All of these sentence patterns can be enriched with the use of adjective and adverb modifiers and prepositions.

☐ Questions

- Questions answered by *yes* or *no* employ a change in order to indicate the question:
  Maria is happy.
  Is Maria happy?
- Questions employ interrogatives to request information:
  Pronouns: who, whom, which, that
  Adjectives: whose, which, what
  Adverbs: when, where, why, how

Clauses and Phrases

Lessons, Practice Sheets, and Exercises

Lesson 7 — *Coordination: Compound Sentences*

To begin to study sentences that build on the simple patterns discussed in the previous lessons, let's examine a student writer's description of a snowstorm. Each sentence is numbered for later reference.

(1) The first really serious snowfall began at dusk and had already spread a treacherous powdering over the roads by the time the homeward-bound crowds reached their peak. (2) As the evening deepened, porch and street lights glowed in tight circles through semi-solid air. (3) The snow did not fall in a mass of fat, jovial flakes; it squatted in a writhing mist of tiny particles and seemed less snow than a dense, animated fog. (4) Through the night the wind rose, worrying the trees as a puppy shakes a slipper. (5) It rushed round the corners of buildings and tumbled over roofs, from which it snatched armfuls of snow to scatter in the streets. (6) Save for the occasional grumble of a sanitation truck sullenly pushing its plow, all sound stopped. (7) Even the wind was more felt than heard. (8) Day did not dawn. (9) The world changed from charcoal gray to lead between six and seven, but the change was one from night to lesser night. (10) The snow still whirled. (11) Drifts had altered the neat symmetry of peaked roofs into irregular mountain ranges ending in sheer cliffs four or five feet above the leeward eaves. (12) The downwind side of every solid object cast a snow shadow that tapered away from a sharp hump until it merged into the surrounding flat pallor. (13) Along the street, windshield wipers, odd bits of chrome, startling blanks of black glass, and isolated headlights decorated large white mounds. (14) Men and women shut off their alarm clocks, stretched, yawned, looked out of their windows, paused in a moment of guilt, and went back to bed. (15) Snow had taken the day for its own, and there was no point in arguing with it.

The 15 sentences of this paragraph are all made up of groups of related words called clauses. A **clause** is a group of words that always contains a subject and a verb in combination. Recalling the scenes, actions, and responses associated with the event, the author has created a series of clauses (subject-verb combinations): the snowfall began, the snowfall had spread a powdering, the homeward-bound crowds reached their peak, the evening deepened, lights glowed, and so on.

Although it may not be apparent when you first read the paragraph, the entire passage is based on short, simple sentences of the patterns studied in the preceding lessons. The writer's problem was to combine or alter these short statements in order to put them into their most pleasing and effective form. Presenting all of them as basic sentences would communicate the author's ideas but in a form that, in addition to being monotonous, would not give proper

61

emphasis to the most important ideas. Only two sentences (8 and 10) are retained as one-subject, one-verb basic sentences. Some of the sentences (3, 9, and 15) combine two basic sentences, giving each clause equal force. Two sentences (1 and 5) join more than one verb to the same subject. Sentence 13 joins four subjects to the same verb, and Sentence 14 has two subjects joined to six verbs.

In the next several lessons, we examine the word groups—independent clauses, subordinate clauses, and phrases—that are the language tools allowing a writer to apply various strategies to produce effective sentences.

COMPOUNDING SENTENCES

A sentence, as you learned in Lesson 1, is a word group containing a subject and a verb. From this definition, and from the one already given for a clause, it would seem that a sentence and a clause are identical. And this is true for one kind of clause, the **independent clause** (also called the *main clause* or *principal clause*). The independent clause can stand by itself as a sentence. Every example sentence and every exercise sentence that you have worked with thus far in this book has been made up of one independent clause. We call a sentence consisting of one independent clause a **simple sentence.**

One means of combining or altering short, simple sentences is called *compounding,* joining grammatically equal parts so they function together. We can join two or more subjects, verbs, complements, or modifiers by using a **coordinating conjunction. (Conjunctions** are words that join words, phrases, or clauses; conjunctions that join grammatically equal units are called *coordinating.*) The three common coordinating conjunctions are *and, but,* and *or;* other coordinators are *nor, for, yet,* and *so.* With the use of a coordinating conjunction, we can join two very short sentences and create a longer, more readable sentence.

Dad read the notice. I read the notice.
Dad *and* I read the notice. [Compound subjects]

Margo enjoys golf. Margo enjoys tennis.
She enjoys golf *and* tennis. [Compound direct objects]

I studied very hard. I failed the test.
I studied very hard *but* failed the test. [Compound verbs]

I found the lecture interesting. I found the lecture instructive.
I found the lecture interesting *and* instructive. [Compound objective complements]

I can see you during your lunch hour. I can see you after 5 o'clock.
I can see you during your lunch hour *or* after 5 o'clock. [Compound prepositional phrases]

Compounding is often used with two (sometimes more than two) independent clauses; the result is a common type of sentence called the **compound sentence.** We can create compound sentences in two ways.

CLAUSES JOINED BY A COORDINATING CONJUNCTION

Any of the coordinating conjunctions already mentioned can be used to join two independent clauses. The normal punctuation is a comma before the conjunction:

I had reviewed the material, and I did well on the test.

It is important to distinguish this sentence from a nearly identical version using a compound verb:

> I had reviewed the material and did well on the test.

In this version, the sentence is not a compound sentence because there is no separate subject for the second verb. It is a simple sentence with a compound verb and should be written without a comma.

CLAUSES JOINED BY A SEMICOLON

Sometimes the two independent clauses stand side by side with no word tying them together:

> No one was in sight; I was alone in the huge auditorium.

Often, the second of the two clauses joined by a semicolon begins with an adverbial unit that serves as a kind of tie between the clauses. This adverbial unit may be:

1. A simple adverb

> *Currently,* we are renting an apartment; *later,* we hope to buy a house.
> These were last year's highlights; *now* we must look at plans for next year.

2. A short phrase

> I cannot comment on the whole concert; *in fact,* I slept through the last part of it.

3. A conjunctive adverb

> Your arguments were well presented; *however,* we feel that the plan is too expensive.

The most common conjunctive adverbs are *therefore, however, nevertheless, consequently, moreover, otherwise, besides, furthermore,* and *accordingly.* These words, often followed by a comma, should be used cautiously; they usually contribute to a heavy, formal tone. To lessen this effect, writers often place them, set off by commas, within the second clause:

> Your arguments were well presented; we feel, *however,* that the plan is too expensive.

Because adverbial units like *later* and *therefore* are *not* coordinating conjunctions, the use of a comma to join the two clauses is inappropriate. This error is often called a *comma splice* or a *comma fault.* The important thing to remember is that when independent clauses are joined by a coordinating conjunction, the use of a comma is the custom. When there is no coordinating conjunction, the comma will not suffice; the customary mark is the semicolon. We study these punctuation rules thoroughly in Lesson 17.

Coordination: Compound Sentences

NAME _____ SCORE _____

Directions: The following twenty-five sentences illustrate three types of sentences:

Type 1. The sentence is a simple sentence with a subject and a compound verb—that is, two verbs joined by a coordinating conjunction (*and, but, or, nor, for, yet, so*). Normal punctuation: none.

> *We worked all day in the yard but finished only half the job.*

Type 2. The sentence is a compound sentence—that is, two independent clauses joined by a coordinating conjunction. Normal punctuation: comma before the conjunction.

> *We worked all day in the yard, but we finished only half the job.*

Type 3. The sentence is a compound sentence joined with no coordinating conjunction joining the two clauses. (The second clause often begins with an adverbial unit such as *now, thus,* or *therefore.)* Normal punctuation: semicolon.

> *We worked very hard in the yard; thus we finished all the work in one day.*

In each of the following sentences, a *caret* ^ marks a point of coordination. If the sentence is Type 1, write **0** in the space at the left. If the sentence is Type 2, write **C** (for comma) in the space. If the sentence is Type 3, write **S** (for semicolon) in the space.

_____ 1. The woman on that motorcycle is Jim's sister ^ for one so young, she rides very well.

_____ 2. We must have been misinformed about the due date ^ for everyone else turned the paper in today.

_____ 3. The two men put their boat in the river ^ but forgot to install the drain plugs in the stern of the boat.

_____ 4. The water rose slowly in the bottom of the boat ^ and it sank gracefully to the bottom of the river.

_____ 5. I am happy about your victory ^ but I wish that I had won my match also.

_____ 6. You won your first match ^ therefore you are ahead of me in the tournament.

_____ 7. I did not win my second match ^ and was eliminated from the tournament.

_____ 8. The books in the library are not arranged correctly on the shelves ^ thus I was not able to find a copy of that book.

_____ 9. I found the books arranged incorrectly on the shelves ^ and was unable to locate a copy of one of the sources for my paper.

_____ 10. I found the books arranged incorrectly on the shelves ^ but located a new source for my paper despite it all.

_____ 11. Once Joanie knew everyone on our hall ^ but last week a new couple moved into the apartment next door.

_____ 12. She went next door to meet the new couple ^ the people, however, had gone out of town for the weekend.

_____ 13. One of the men in our office recently caught a record largemouth bass ^ so he now has a huge picture of the fish in his office.

_____ 14. "I rarely fish in that spot ^ but went there that day because of a bad storm on the other side of the lake," he said.

_____ 15. He is an avid angler ^ so fishes almost every weekend.

_____ 16. Usually, he drives great distances for his fishing trips ^ but he stays closer to home during bad weather.

_____ 17. The other people in our office admire the fish very much ^ and they often stop in his office for a quick look at the picture.

_____ 18. Marge and Angela are leaving Monday for a trip to New Mexico ^ they will talk to companies about our new software product.

_____ 19. The women have little sales experience ^ nor have they ever been to New Mexico.

_____ 20. Either their experience with the software will help them in their efforts ^ or they'll come back empty-handed from a long, expensive trip.

_____ 21. They came back with two big orders ^ for people so young, they did a wonderful job.

_____ 22. They came back with an order from a large company ^ for they were very convincing in their sales presentations.

_____ 23. The two women had little sales experience ^ yet accomplished a great deal on their trip.

_____ 24. They experienced great success on this trip ^ so the boss will probably send them out again soon.

_____ 25. They experienced great success on this trip ^ so will probably be sent out again soon.

Exercise 7   *Coordination: Compound Sentences*

NAME _____   SCORE _____

Directions: The twenty-five sentences here illustrate three types of sentences:

Type 1. The sentence is a simple sentence with the subject having two verbs joined by a coordinating conjunction. Normal punctuation within the sentence: none.

> *We worked all day on the car but could not find the trouble.*

Type 2. The sentence is a compound sentence with the two independent clauses joined by a coordinating conjunction: *and, but, or, nor, for, yet,* or *so.* Normal punctuation: a comma before the conjunction.

> *We worked all day on the car, and now it runs well.*

Type 3. The sentence is a compound sentence without one of the coordinating conjunctions joining the independent clauses. (The second clause often begins with an adverbial unit such as *now, thus,* or *therefore.*) Normal punctuation: a semicolon.

> *We worked all day on the car; now it runs well.*

In each of the following sentences, a caret ^ marks a point of coordination. If the sentence is Type 1, write **O** in the space at the left. If the sentence is Type 2, write **C** (for comma) in the space. If the sentence is Type 3, write **S** (for semicolon) in the space.

_____   1. Yesterday, the men finished the project ^ therefore they stayed home today.

_____   2. The shortstop dove for the ball ^ but was not able to field it cleanly.

_____   3. That politician made promises to every group in the county ^ thus she has assured herself of major conflicts in the future.

_____   4. Usually Jim takes his vacation in August ^ he's never been to the mountains in October before.

_____   5. The service in this restaurant has always been excellent ^ last night, however, our waiter was very slow.

_____   6. I enrolled yesterday in History 211 ^ several of my friends enjoyed the course very much last semester.

_____   7. The secretary is searching everywhere for that lost file ^ for we need it desperately for this afternoon's meeting.

_____   8. The people in the stands whistled and stamped their feet ^ for them only a victory would be satisfactory.

_____   9. "We need to get to the station early today," said Tom ^ "that train always leaves exactly on time."

_____ 10. I looked for that book for an hour ^ it is definitely not on the shelves in our library.

_____ 11. Maria will either take that job in Los Angeles ^ or take a tour of Europe immediately after graduation.

_____ 12. Maria will either take that job in Los Angeles ^ or she will take a tour of Europe immediately after graduation.

_____ 13. Mark studied hard for that test ^ yet everyone else in the class made a better grade.

_____ 14. I wanted to go to last night's game ^ but I hadn't finished my report for today's meeting.

_____ 15. Laura came late to class today ^ she turned off her alarm clock by mistake this morning.

_____ 16. Anna made an appointment with an advisor today ^ for she wants to change her major to computer science.

_____ 17. Anna wants to change her major to computer science ^ for some reason she no longer enjoys music courses.

_____ 18. You can print out seven copies of that report ^ or take the original to the Copy Center for the extra copies.

_____ 19. Several people left the movie early ^ the talkative audience made them very angry.

_____ 20. "Please help me look for my contact lens," begged Robert ^ "I've already lost one this week."

_____ 21. Radar was first used in World War II for tracking enemy planes ^ now it has many uses in civilian life.

_____ 22. We need to pay close attention to that map ^ several people have gotten lost on that road in the last few days.

_____ 23. We need to pay close attention to that map ^ for several people have gotten lost on that road in the last few days.

_____ 24. Check your work on that problem very carefully ^ for that problem the answer in the key is incorrect.

_____ 25. The two girls had looked everywhere for that jacket ^ thus they were surprised to find it in the trunk of the car.

Directions: Combine the short sentences in each numbered item into one longer sentence.

1. Alice loves to listen to jazz.
   She occasionally enjoys a little country and western music.

   _____

2. We were all forced to work late on Thursday night.
   Therefore I had little time to study for Friday morning's test.

   _____

3. The traffic into the stadium was backed up for several blocks.
   We still made it to our seats in time for the kickoff.

   _____

4. We are thinking of going to the library tonight.
   We might do our research over the Internet instead.

   _____

5. Jackie did not find a new phone number for that customer.
   She did not find a new address.

   _____

6. Walt and his two friends finished baseball practice.
   Then they went to a nearby restaurant for supper.

   _____

7. Maria got up quite early this morning.
   She needed to study for another hour for her history test.

   _____

8. Lightning struck very close to the parking garage.
   Several car alarms went off noisily.

   _____

9. John needs to leave an hour early for the airport.
   Otherwise he might get caught in that rush hour traffic on I-50.

   _____

10. I could not find any No. 2 pencils for tomorrow's test.
    I will need to stop at the store on my way to school.

    _____

Lesson 8   *Subordination: Adverb Clauses*

To this point you have had practice with the simple sentence (one independent clause) and the compound sentence (two or more independent clauses). Basic as these sentences are to your thinking and writing, you need to move beyond these structures in order to make your writing flexible and effective. Often you can improve the precision of your statements if you use slightly more complex structures.

"Rain began to fall, and we stopped our ball game" is a perfectly correct sentence. But notice these slightly altered versions of that sentence:

When rain began to fall, we stopped our ball game.

After rain began to fall, we stopped our ball game.

Because rain began to fall, we stopped our ball game.

These three, in addition to lessening the singsong tone of the compound sentence, are more informative. The first two tell the time at which the game was stopped—and notice that *when* and *after* point out slightly different time frames. The third version gives a different relation between the two statements; it tells not the time of, but the reason for, stopping the game.

If, instead of writing the compound sentence "Rain was falling, and we continued our ball game," you write "Although rain was falling, we continued our ball game," you have refined your thinking and your expression. Your readers now interpret the sentence exactly as you want them to; they now know that the ball game was continued in spite of the fact that rain was falling.

The process by which a statement is reduced to a secondary form to show its relation to the main idea is called subordination. The grammatical unit that expresses a secondary idea as it affects a main idea is the subordinate, or dependent, clause, which we define as a subject-verb combination that cannot stand alone as a sentence. A subordinate clause works in a sentence in the same way that a single part of speech—an adverb, an adjective, or a noun—works. Instead of a single word—*quickly, quick, quickness*—used as an adverb, an adjective, or a noun, a group of words is used. A sentence made up of one independent clause and at least one dependent clause is a **complex sentence**.

ADVERB CLAUSE

The **adverb clause** works in exactly the same way a one-word adverb works: It provides information by modifying a verb, an adjective, or another adverb. The most common types of adverb clauses modify verbs. In fact, they answer direct questions about the action: When? (time); Where? (place); Why? (cause); and How? (manner). The role of the adverb clause is shown by the conjunction that introduces the adverb clause. The conjunction—the structural signal of subordination—is not an isolated word standing between the two clauses; it is part of the subordinate clause. In such a sentence as "We left the house after the rain stopped," the unit "the rain stopped" could stand alone as an independent clause. But the clause is made dependent by the inclusion of the conjunction *after.* The dependent clause "after the rain stopped" establishes the time when "we left the house." Thus, the clause works as an adverb of time in the same way that the one-word adverbs work in the following sentences:

We left the house *early.*
We left the house *late.*
We left the house *yesterday.*

Various types of adverb clauses and their most common conjunctions are listed here with examples.

Time (*when, whenever, before, after, since, while, until, as, as soon as*):

The baby cried *when the telephone rang.*
The cat ran out *before Lou could shut the door.*
After the bell rings, no one can enter.
I've known Palmer *since he was in high school.*
You should not whisper *while Dr. Fuller is lecturing.*
You may leave *as soon as your replacement arrives.*

Place (*where, wherever*):

We parted *where the paths separated.*
I shall meet you *wherever you want me to.*

Cause (or Reason) (*because, since, as*):

I walk to work every day *because I need the exercise.*
Since she could not pay the fine, she could not drive the car.
As you are the senior member, you should lead the procession.

Purpose (*so that, in order that*):

We left early *so that we could catch the last bus.*
They died *that their nation might live.*
They came to America *in order that they might find freedom.*

Manner (*as, as if, as though*):

Raphael acted *as if the party bored him.*
Please do the work *as you have been instructed.*

Result (*so...that, such...that*):

Derek arrived *so late that he missed the concert.*
The workmen made *such a racket that I got a headache.*

Condition (*if, unless, provided that, on condition that*). This kind of adverb clause gives a condition under which the main clause is true:

Sit down and chat *if you are not in a hurry.*
He will not give his talk *unless we pay his expenses.*
She will sign the contract *provided that we pay her a bonus.*
If I were you, I would accept the offer.
If you had told me earlier, I could have helped.

There is an alternate arrangement for certain kinds of conditional clauses. In this arrangement, *if* is not used; instead, a subject-verb inversion signals the subordination. Sentences like the last two preceding examples sometimes take this form:

Were I you, I would accept the offer.
Had you told me earlier, I could have helped.

Concession (*although, though, even if, even though, since*). This clause states a fact in spite of which the main idea is true:

Although she is only nine years old, she plays chess.
Our car is dependable *even though it is old.*

Comparison (*than, as*). Two distinctive characteristics of the adverb clause of comparison should be noted. First, part or all of the verb, although it is needed grammatically, is usually not expressed. Second, when an action verb is not expressed in the subordinate clause, the appropriate form of the auxiliary *do* is often used even though the *do* does not occur in the main clause:

Gold is heavier *than iron* [is].
Your computer is not as new *as mine* [is].
Her theme was better *than any other student's in the class* [was].
Ellen earned more bonus points *than her brother* [did].

Adverb clauses may also modify verbs, adjectives and adverbs. In this type of clause, the conjunction *that* is sometimes unexpressed.

Jim slept *as late as possible.* [Modifies the verb *slept*]
We are sorry *that you must leave early.* [Modifies the adjective *sorry*]
I am sure *(that) he meant no harm.* [Modifies the adjective *sure*]
The car is running better *than it did last week.* [Modifies the adverb *better*]

ELLIPTICAL CLAUSE

Ellipsis means *omission,* to *leave something out.* A clause that leaves some parts understood or unexpressed is called an **elliptical clause**. There are many types of elliptical clauses. You should be aware of them because they can lend variety to your writing. In the following examples, brackets enclose the parts of the clauses that may be unexpressed. (See Supplement.) Note that all the types of adverb phrases (time, place, cause, purpose, manner, result, condition, concession, and comparison) may be elliptical.

While [I was] *walking home,* I met Mr. Rodriguez.

When [he is] *in Cleveland,* he stays with us.

Call your office *as soon as* [it is] *possible.*

Adjustments will be made *whenever* [they are] *necessary.*

Mary, *although* [she is] *a talented girl,* is quite lazy.

If [you are] *delayed,* call my secretary.

Your ticket, *unless* [it is] *stamped,* is invalid.

A NOTE ON SENTENCE VARIETY

Although some adverb clauses—those of comparison, for instance—have a fixed position within the sentence, many adverb clauses may be placed before, inside, or following the main clause:

When they deal with the unknown, Greek myths are usually somber.

Greek myths, *when they deal with the unknown,* are usually somber.

Greek myths are usually somber *when they deal with the unknown.*

Notice that no comma is used in the third example above. Usually a comma is not needed when the adverbial clause is the final element of the sentence, as the third example below also illustrates:

Although he did not have authority from Congress, President Theodore Roosevelt ordered construction of the Panama Canal.

President Theodore Roosevelt, *although he did not have authority from Congress,* ordered construction of the Panama Canal.

President Theodore Roosevelt ordered construction of the Panama Canal *although he did not have authority from Congress.*

You should practice various arrangements to relieve the monotony that comes from reliance on too many main-subject-plus-main-verb sentences.

SUPPLEMENT

Occasionally, an elliptical adverb clause of comparison must be recast because the exact meaning is unclear when parts of the clause are unexpressed. Here are two sentences that are ambiguous in the shortened forms of the clauses:

Mr. Alton will pay you more *than Stan.*

Probable meaning:	Mr. Alton will pay you more than [he will pay] Stan.
Possible meaning:	Mr. Alton will pay you more than Stan [will pay you].

Parents dislike homework as much *as their offspring.*

Probable meaning:	Parents dislike homework as much as their offspring [dislike homework].
Possible meaning:	Parents dislike homework as much as [they dislike] their offspring.

SUMMARY OF ADVERB CLAUSES

1. *Function:* to modify a verb, an adjective, or an adverb

2. *Position:* fixed for some types (She sold more tickets *than I did*); others may be at the beginning, in the interior, or at the end of main clause

3. *Subordinators:* conjunctions, most of which show adverbial relationships such as time (*when, since, while*), cause (*because, as*), and so on

4. *Special structures:*
   a. An adverb clause modifying an adjective subjective complement and subordinated by *that* sometimes has the subordinator *that* unexpressed:

   I'm sure *(that) you are wrong.*

   b. Elliptical clauses:
   Mary is older *than I (am).*
   If (you are) unable to attend, call me.
   While (she was) preparing lunch, Mary cut her finger.

NAME _____ SCORE _____

Directions: Identify each of the following adverb clauses by writing one of the following in the space at the left:

1. Time   4. Purpose   7. Condition   10. Modification of an
2. Place   5. Manner   8. Concession   adverb or adjective
3. Cause   6. Result   9. Comparison

_____ 1. Yesterday I stayed at work as long *as I possibly could.*

_____ 2. Her test grade was higher *than any other student's test score.*

_____ 3. The dog ran out of the yard *before Tim could shut the gate.*

_____ 4. *Even though we gave it our best effort,* we were unable to finish that job on time.

_____ 5. We left that road and went off-road *where the blacktop ended.*

_____ 6. *If we don't return before nightfall,* please call the Coast Guard.

_____ 7. We went to work early *so that we could avoid that traffic jam on the express-way.*

_____ 8. The air conditioner is working better *than it ran before the repair.*

_____ 9. The temperature is lower today *than it was yesterday.*

_____ 10. *Since you can't go skiing with me,* I've invited Al in your place.

_____ 11. *Since we drove onto this road,* the traffic has been moving very slowly.

_____ 12. *As I was closing the door of my apartment this morning,* the phone rang.

_____ 13. I canceled my tennis match for today *as I could not run on my sprained ankle.*

_____ 14. We'll meet you *wherever you want us to.*

_____ 15. Sherry was so late *that the group had to leave without her.*

_____ 16. We were quite sorry *that we had to leave her behind.*

_____ 17. *Unless we study very late tonight,* I probably won't make a very good grade on that test.

_____ 18. *After the men left for the basketball game,* the three women went to a restaurant for dinner.

77

_____ 19. We found Jim *where that tall tree shades the sidewalk.*

_____ 20. The two men continued their hike *even though they were in a heavy rain.*

_____ 21. My father will advance us the money for the trip *on the condition that we pay him back this summer.*

_____ 22. Is the work in that class any easier *than it was in the first week?*

_____ 23. Mark is much taller *than Manny.*

_____ 24. *As soon as Jim returns to the office,* we'll ask for his help on that project.

_____ 25. We sat quietly under the tree *as though we hadn't a care in the world.*

_____ 26. "*When you find that letter,* please fax me a copy of it," said Ms. Smythe.

_____ 27. Last night we stayed home and watched an old movie *because the weather was very cold outside.*

_____ 28. We were certain *that you would be here on time.*

_____ 29. "I followed the instructions exactly *as they were written,*" complained Mario, "but I still couldn't put that bookcase together."

_____ 30. The people outside the store came early today *so that they could be among the first to buy tickets for that concert.*

_____ 31. Mr. Harrison is such a smart investor *that he doubled his money on that stock in only two years.*

_____ 32. *When we get the car repaired,* I would like to visit my sister in the state capital.

_____ 33. Liz found the puppy wandering *where the creek turns back through the pasture.*

_____ 34. No one has ever scored more goals in one of our games *than Angela.*

_____ 35. The Marshalls were very sorry *that we could not join them for dinner.*

_____ 36. Joanne did better work on that project *than I ever could have done.*

_____ 37. *Although we were a little hesitant to enter the race,* we finished quite well and had a great time.

_____ 38. The men crossed the creek *where the two boulders stand near the bank.*

_____ 39. *Because the storm was approaching rather rapidly,* we canceled our fishing trip.

_____ 40. *Since that man moved in next door,* the appearance of the house has improved greatly.

Exercise 8   *Adverb Clauses*

NAME _____ SCORE _____

Directions: Each sentence contains an adverb clause. Underline each adverb clause. In the space at the left, write one of the following numbers to identify the type of clause:

1. Time	4. Purpose	7. Condition	10. Modification of an
2. Place	5. Manner	8. Concession	adjective or an adverb
3. Cause	6. Result	9. Comparison	

_____ 1. Whenever Tim arrives, please call my secretary.

_____ 2. Although we had not heard any noise, the books had fallen off the shelf in the library.

_____ 3. Jamie's GPA is slightly higher than mine.

_____ 4. That fishing license, if it contains a trout stamp, will allow you to catch three trout a day during the season.

_____ 5. My mother was convinced that we should leave early in the morning.

_____ 6. The three little kids ran as if their lives were in danger.

_____ 7. Because the test covers so much material, I started studying early yesterday morning.

_____ 8. How can we plan if there is no established goal for our work?

_____ 9. Please fax your answer to us so that we can begin work immediately.

_____ 10. Please make a check mark wherever you find an error in computation.

_____ 11. If I were you, I would take the introductory course first.

_____ 12. The boys walked so fast that they left the rest of us far behind.

_____ 13. Jim is confident that he can get an interesting summer job.

_____ 14. The contractor says that this old house is built better than most newer houses.

_____ 15. That blue shirt, although old, is still very comfortable.

_____ 16. The boss hired eight new workers in order that we might finish the work on time.

_____ 17. The children acted as if they did not want to leave the zoo.

_____ 18. Since we added a voice mail system, communication in the office has been much improved.

_____ 19. Since she lost her driver's license, Mary has been taking the bus to work.

_____ 20. Please leave the office as early as possible today.

_____ 21. I'm not sure that I understand that first problem in the textbook.

_____ 22. That bill won't leave the committee unless Senator Jackson votes for it.

_____ 23. Even though Julia presented a convincing argument, the class voted against her proposal.

_____ 24. The cross country team is certainly glad that the heat wave has broken.

_____ 25. Please do not line up until your group has been called.

_____ 26. You must provide a cover sheet for your paper exactly as you were instructed.

_____ 27. Bob has taken a course in Spanish so that he can talk to people on his vacation in Costa Rica.

_____ 28. The people in the back of the room chanted so loudly that we could not hear the speaker.

_____ 29. If I had known about that mixed doubles tournament, Jennifer and I would have entered.

_____ 30. My little brother is now taller than I am.

_____ 31. As he was walking toward our table, the waiter dropped our entire order.

_____ 32. We found a place to pick blueberries where the bushes are high and the ground is not steep.

_____ 33. Jim usually watches television while doing his homework.

_____ 34. I'll play ball with you after I finish my dessert.

_____ 35. Although dark clouds have moved in from the west, it has not yet begun to rain.

_____ 36. If you want to see the birds, you have to get up early in the morning.

_____ 37. Little Billy hits the baseball farther than his older friends do.

_____ 38. Jessica is pleased that she won a full scholarship to the university.

_____ 39. Her mouth puckered as if she had eaten something very sour.

_____ 40. Because the blizzard had felled so many trees, we were unable to drive up our driveway.

Directions: In the first space at the left, write the subordinating conjunction that fits logically in the blank in the sentence. In the second space, write one of the following numbers to identify the type of clause:

1. Time	4. Purpose	7. Condition	10. Modification of an adverb
2. Place	5. Manner	8. Concession	or adjective
3. Cause	6. Result	9. Comparison	

_____
_____   1. _____ conditions improve rather quickly, we should probably postpone the picnic.

_____
_____   2. We will need to stay late at the track tonight _____ we can get the car ready for tomorrow's race.

_____
_____   3. The staff can't work on that estimate _____ the plans have not arrived from the architect's office.

_____
_____   4. _____ the people next door moved out, the neighborhood has been much more peaceful.

_____
_____   5. I turned my paper in on time _____ my printer ran out of ink and I had to go to the store late last night.

_____
_____   6. I'll put that report _____ you can find it easily.

_____
_____   7. Their proposal is considerably longer _____ mine.

_____
_____   8. Were you surprised _____ Al and Margie agreed to come to the reunion?

_____
_____   9. _____ I saw Al and Margie at the reunion, we had a very pleasant conversation.

_____
_____   10. _____ you don't get organized in the next few minutes, you will be late for the presentation of your report.

_____
_____   11. The players worked on that particular play _____ they could do it perfectly every time.

_____
_____   12. The venues for the concerts are so far from here _____ I won't be able to see my favorite group play.

_____
_____   13. I copied the quotation exactly _____ I found it in the article, but the whole thing didn't seem to make sense in my paper.

_____
_____   14. _____ Alex was very tired at the end of the day, he was very proud of the finished project.

_____
_____   15. _____ the two young boys finally reached the top of the mountain, they found the trail down the other side quite easy.

Directions: Rewrite the sentence or sentences in each item as a complete sentence using an adverbial clause; use the subordinating conjunction that properly establishes the relationship between the two sentences or clauses.

1. On Monday we left the office early in order to avoid the usual Friday traffic jam on I-17. (purpose)

   _____

2. We came to the on-ramp for the interstate and found it totally jammed with cars. (time)

   _____

3. The interstate was totally backed up. As a result, we had to take a detour on a surface street. (result)

   _____

4. We turned off onto Jones Street near that new restaurant. We decided to stop for a sandwich and a cup of coffee. (cause)

   _____

5. Because we were very hungry, we were happy that something happened. We decided to stop for a late lunch. (modification of adjective)

   _____

6. We entered the restaurant and saw Mario and his wife, Jean. (time)

   _____

7. We had not seen Mario and Jean for quite some time, but they were very glad to see us. (concession)

   _____

8. We picked up our conversation as though nothing had happened. We had seen them just last week. (manner)

   _____

9. We had such an enjoyable time with them that we agreed to do something. We agreed to go to a movie with them next weekend. (result)

   _____

10. We spent a very pleasant hour at lunch, and then we drove back onto the interstate and went to the farm. (time)

   _____

Just as a single-word adjective modifies a noun or pronoun, clauses that begin with *who, whom, whose, which,* or *that* can modify nouns or pronouns. A clause that modifies a noun or pronoun is called an **adjective** or **relative clause.** An adjective clause gives information about the noun in the same way that the one-word adjectives do. Both one-word adjectives and adjective clauses can be seen as basic sentences that have been worked into a main clause.

I looked into the sky. The sky was blue.
I looked into the blue sky.

I looked into the sky. The sky was filled with towering cumulus clouds.
I looked into the sky, which was filled with towering cumulus clouds.

In Item 1 the sentence "The sky was blue" becomes the one-word adjective *blue* and modifies the noun *sky.* In Item 2 the sentence "The sky was filled with towering cumulus clouds" cannot become a one-word adjective; therefore, the sentence becomes an adjective or relative clause opened by the word *which.* The clause modifies the word *sky* in the sense that it provides us with information about the sky.

ADJECTIVE CLAUSES

Nearly all of the adjective clauses you read, write, or speak use *who, whose, whom, which,* or *that* to tie the adjective clause to the noun it modifies. These words, in spite of the fact that they join one clause to a word in another clause, are not conjunctions. They are pronouns that have a connective or *relating* function; thus they are called **relative pronouns.** (See Supplement.) Relatives can function *within* the adjective clause as subjects, direct objects, or objects of prepositions.

It is helpful to think of an adjective clause as a simple sentence that is incorporated within another sentence. The relative pronoun, by substituting for a noun, refers ("relates") the clause directly to the word being modified. Because the relative pronoun is the word signaling the subordination, the pronoun, sometimes preceded by a preposition, always begins the adjective clause.

Examine the following paired units. Every A unit has two simple sentences; the second repeats a noun from the first sentence. The B sentence shows how the second idea has been reduced to an adjective clause and has become part of the first sentence. Notice that the normal position of an adjective clause is immediately following the noun or the pronoun it modifies.

A. This is a well-built truck. *The truck* will save you money.
B. This is a well-built truck *that* will save you money.
   [The clause modifies *truck. That* is the subject in the adjective clause.]

A. Alice has a new boyfriend. *The new boyfriend* [or *He*] sings in a rock group.
B. Alice has a new boyfriend *who* sings in a rock group.
   [*Who* is the subject in the clause that modifies *boyfriend*.]

A. Here is the book. I borrowed *the book* [or *it*] yesterday.
B. Here is the book *that* I borrowed yesterday.
   [*That* is the direct object in the adjective clause.]

A. The firm hired Chet Brown. The boss had known *Chet Brown* [or *him*] in Omaha.
B. The firm hired Chet Brown, *whom* the boss had known in Omaha.
   [*Whom* is the direct object in the adjective clause.]

A. May I introduce Dick Hart? I went to college *with Dick Hart* [or *him*].
B. May I introduce Dick Hart, with *whom* I went to college?
   [The clause modifies *Dick Hart.* Notice that the preposition *with* stands at the beginning of the clause with its object *whom.* At the informal level of language usage, the preposition in this structure is sometimes found at the end of the clause. See Supplement 2 of Lesson 6 on page 52.]

A. She is a young artist. I admire the young *artist's* [or *her*] work.
B. She is a young artist *whose* work I admire.
   [*Work* is in this position because, although it is the direct object of *admire,* it cannot be separated from its modifier, the relative adjective *whose,* which must be placed at the beginning of the adjective clause.]

We also use the adverbs *when* and *where* as relatives. *When* and *where* introduce adjective clauses in combinations meaning "time when" and "place where." The following examples show that the subordinator is really the equivalent of an adverbial prepositional phrase. (The B sentences are complex sentences combining the material of the two A sentences.)

A. Beth and I recalled the time. We considered ourselves rebels *at that time*.
B. Beth and I recalled the time *when* we considered ourselves rebels.

A. This is the spot. The explorers came ashore at this spot.
B. This is the spot *where* the explorers came ashore.

These clauses are logically considered adjective clauses because they immediately follow nouns that require identification, and the clauses give the identifying material. If you remember "time-when" and "place-where," you will not confuse this type of adjective clause with other subordinate clauses that may use the same subordinators.

Note: In certain adjective clauses, the relative word is unexpressed; the meaning is instantly clear without it: the food *(that) we eat,* the house *(that) he lived in,* the man *(whom) you saw,* the time *(when) you fell down,* and so on.

RESTRICTIVE AND NONRESTRICTIVE ADJECTIVE CLAUSES

Depending on their role in a sentence, adjective clauses are restrictive or nonrestrictive. A **restrictive clause** provides identification of the noun it modifies. A **nonrestrictive clause** provides information that is not essential for identification. Thus, in the sentence "The man who owns that car just walked up," the man is identified by the clause *who owns that car.* But in the sentence "John Williams, who owns that car, just walked up," the clause *who owns that car* does not identify John Williams (he is identified by his name). The clause tells us something additional; it adds information about John Williams.

Restrictive Clauses

The restrictive adjective clause is not set off by commas because it is essential to the identification of the word being modified.

> The grade *that I received on my report* pleased me.
> Anyone *who saw the accident* should call the police.

Without the modifying clauses (*that I received on my test; who saw the accident*), the nouns are not identified. What grade and what anyone are we talking about? But when we add the modifiers, we identify the *particular* grade and the *particular* anyone. In other words, this kind of clause restricts the meaning of a general noun to one specific member of its class.

Nonrestrictive Adjective Clauses

The nonrestrictive adjective clause does require commas. Although the clause supplies additional or incidental information about the word that it modifies, the information is not needed for identifying the noun. (Don't, however, get into the habit of thinking that a nonrestrictive clause is unimportant; unless it has some importance to the meaning of the sentence, it has no right to be in the sentence.) Nonrestrictive modifiers are usually found following proper nouns (*Mount Everest, Philadelphia, Mr. Frank Smith*); nouns already identified (the oldest *boy* in her class, her only *grandchild*); and one-of-a-kind nouns (Alice's *mother,* the *provost* of the college, the *writer* of the editorial).

The following examples contrast restrictive and nonrestrictive adjective clauses. (See Supplement.)

> I visited an old friend *who is retiring soon.* [Restrictive]
> I visited my oldest and closest friend, *who is retiring soon.* [Nonrestrictive]
>
> The man *whose car had been wrecked* asked us for a ride. [Restrictive]
> Mr. Ash, *whose car had been wrecked,* asked us for a ride. [Nonrestrictive]
>
> A small stream *that flows through the property* supplies an occasional trout. [Restrictive]
> Caldwell Creek, *which flows through the property,* supplies an occasional trout. [Nonrestrictive]
>
> She wants to retire to a place *where freezing weather is unknown.* [Restrictive]
> She wants to retire to Panama City, *where freezing weather is unknown.* [Nonrestrictive]

SUPPLEMENT

A few distinctions in the use of *who, which,* and *that* in adjective clauses are generally observed. *Which* refers only to things; *who* refers to people; and *that* refers to things or people. *That* is used only in restrictive clauses; in other words, a "that" adjective clause is not set off by commas. Because *which* is the relative pronoun that must be used in a nonrestrictive clause modifying a thing, there is a convention that *which* should not introduce a restrictive adjective clause. This convention is generally, but by no means always, observed. People tend to use *which* in their writing when *that* would be better.

SUMMARY OF ADJECTIVE CLAUSES

1. *Function:* to modify a noun or a pronoun

2. *Position:* follows the noun or pronoun that it modifies

3. *Subordinators:*
   a. relative pronouns (*who, whom, which, that*), which function within the adjective clause as subjects, direct objects, or objects of prepositions
   b. relative adjectives (*whose, which*)
   c. relative adverbs (*when, where*)

4. *Special problem:* Adjective clauses vital to the identification of the nouns being modified are restrictive and do not require commas. Clauses not necessary for identification are nonrestrictive and are set off by commas.

NAME _____ SCORE _____

Directions: Each italicized unit is an adjective clause. In the space at the left, copy the word that is the antecedent of the relative pronoun in the clause. Note that some of the adjective clauses occur inside an adverbial clause and others have adverbial clauses within them.

_____ 1. My grandfather was in North Carolina in 1903, *when the Wright brothers made their historic flight.*

_____ 2. Before that flight, many people had experimented with gliders, *in which they were able to make very short flights.*

_____ 3. The wings of the gliders, *which were slightly curved,* simulated the shape of birds' wings.

_____ 4. The first flight *that had a person aboard* was in France in a hot-air balloon.

_____ 5. Because hot-air balloons, *which had no controls,* could not be steered, inventors continued to study possibilities for powered flight.

_____ 6. The first glider *that could be controlled by a pilot* was flown by Otto Lilienthal in Germany.

_____ 7. The gliders, *which depended on air currents for their flight,* were not practical for transportation.

_____ 8. In the 1800s inventors developed gasoline engines, *which were then available to power airplanes.*

_____ 9. Thus, Nikolaus Otto, *whom most people identify as the inventor of the four-cycle gasoline engine,* became a major contributor to our ability to fly airplanes.

_____ 10. Wilbur and Orville Wright ran a bicycle shop in Dayton, *where they developed the first airplane.*

_____ 11. They worked for several years to develop gliders *that could be controlled by a pilot.*

_____ 12. They actually built a small wind tunnel *in which they studied the effects of air pressure on the wings of the gliders.*

_____ 13. They flew the gliders from a sandy strip *where updrafts carried the gliders into the air.*

_____ 14. The updrafts, *which are called thermals,* occurred when the sun heats the air above the sand.

_____ 15. Following the design *that Otto and others had perfected,* the brothers installed an engine in a glider.

Directions: Each sentence contains one adjective clause. Underline the adjective clause and copy the word it modifies in the space at the left.

_____ 1. The material I failed to study was in the first section of the test.

_____ 2. The material in Chapter 1, which I failed to study, was in the first ten questions on that test.

_____ 3. The instructors who wrote that test played a trick on us poor students.

_____ 4. Mr. Smith and Mrs. Babson, who wrote that test, played a trick on us poor students.

_____ 5. All students that are enrolled in an American history course need to read these two articles.

_____ 6. All classes that meet at 8:00 A.M. were canceled last week because of heavy construction on the roads near the campus.

_____ 7. My biology class, which meets at 8:00 A.M., was canceled yesterday.

_____ 8. Yesterday I got a letter from my friend Joe, who attends a college in the northern part of the state.

_____ 9. All students who attend that school must own a laptop computer.

_____ 10. Joe, who doesn't have a lot of money, is borrowing his older brother's laptop.

_____ 11. Joe is trying to buy a laptop that is older and less expensive than a new one.

_____ 12. A laptop that is older, however, will run at a slow speed and won't have much RAM.

_____ 13. Joe's other option, which doesn't seem very wise, is to borrow enough money to buy a new computer.

_____ 14. He does have an aunt who has quite a bit of money.

_____ 15. Perhaps he can borrow the money he needs from her.

Directions: Each of these sentences contains an adjective clause, but appropriate commas are omitted. Underline each adjective clause. In the first space at the left, write the antecedent of the adjective clause. In the second space write R if the clause is restricted and N if it is nonrestrictive. Remember that nonrestrictive clauses are set off by commas.

_____ _____   1. That bulletin should tell you everything you need to know about next week's trip.

_____ _____   2. Roberta is buying a four-cylinder Ford which will give her good gas mileage.

_____ _____   3. Roberta is trying to find a car that will give her good gas mileage.

_____ _____   4. To join the new bowling league, you should call Jack Franklin who is one of the league's organizers.

_____ _____   5. Jack Franklin is one of the people who are organizing the new bowling league.

_____ _____   6. My uncle gave me a truck that is nearly as old as I am.

_____ _____   7. Most of the people I knew in high school have gone on to college.

_____ _____   8. Are you sure that the textbook was the only thing you studied for today's test?

_____ _____   9. At the ball game last night I saw Marge Thompson who is in my British history class.

_____ _____   10. I wish I could find the person who sold me this coat last month.

_____ _____   11. If you take the new bypass which circles the entire city you will save a great deal of time.

_____ _____   12. My brother often goes to the mountains during the months when the snow is quite deep.

_____ _____   13. I usually go to the mountains in June when there is never any snow visible.

_____ _____   14. This spring the snow which usually melts in March was still quite deep in April.

_____ _____   15. Few people who are environmentalists are in favor of the construction of that highway through the gorge.

_____ _____   16. According to the letter I received yesterday, Kim will be back in town at the end of the month.

_____ _____   17. According to Kim's last letter which came yesterday she will be back in town at the end of the month.

_____ 18. According to the weather report, there is a huge cold front over
_____   Boise which is the capital of Idaho.
_____ 19. John Grisham whose first novel was *A Time To Kill* was at one
_____   time a lawyer.
_____ 20. The last day of registration is September 2 which is also the day
_____   before the Labor Day weekend.
_____ 21. Mark is excited because he made a sale that put him in the lead in
_____   the sales contest.
_____ 22. The last piece of evidence which the prosecutor introduced was a
_____   gun recovered from the scene of the crime.
_____ 23. That book belongs to a girl with whom I worked when I was out
_____   of school last term.
_____ 24. When I registered this term, someone had already taken the last
_____   seat in a class I needed for graduation.
_____ 25. I plan to spend the summer with an uncle who lives in Wyoming.
_____
_____ 26. I plan to spend the summer with Uncle Will who lives in Wyoming.
_____
_____ 27. The student with whom we rode to Snellville when semester
_____   break began is not returning to school next term.
_____ 28. Marge bought that truck in 1992 when turquoise was a very
_____   popular color for trucks.
_____ 29. The police force has offices in a building that has often been
_____   condemned but never destroyed.
_____ 30. Three books that I needed for my research paper were not on the
_____   shelves in the library.

Directions: The two sentences in each item can be combined into one by changing the second into an adjective clause. Write the combined sentence in the blank.

1. Mary Allen has been promoted to district manager. She once managed our local office.

   _____

2. Mary Allen has been promoted to district manager. The president trusts her judgment without any reservation.

   _____

3. Mary Allen has been promoted to district manager. Landis Corporation had offered a similar job to her last year.

   _____

4. Mary Allen has been promoted to district manager. I have always admired her.

   _____

5. Mary Allen has been promoted to district manager. My friends and I have always enjoyed working with her.

   _____

6. My family and I want to move to a small town. The town has an old-fashioned drugstore.

   _____

7. Any town would suit my family and me. The town has an old-fashioned drugstore.

   _____

8. My grandfather grew up in a small town. The town had an old-fashioned drugstore.

   _____

9. Old-fashioned drugstores had counters. The clerk stood behind the counter and sold ice cream cones.

   _____

10. The counter at the drugstore had a menu. The menu offered two kinds of sandwiches and three flavors of ice cream.

   _____

An adverbial clause such as *after the rain stopped* can work to set the time of the main verb just as the single-word adverb *yesterday* does. The adjective clause *whom I knew well* can modify our understanding of a noun in the same way the single-word adjective *tall* does. A noun clause works in a similar way: It does the work of a regular noun.

NOUN CLAUSES

A **noun clause** is a group of words containing a subject-verb combination and a subordinating word. The subordinating words that serve to introduce noun clauses are conjunctions (*that, if, whether*); pronouns (*who, whom, what, which, whoever, whatever, whichever*); adjectives (*whose, which, what*); and adverbs (*when, where, why, how*). Remember that the subordinating word is part of the clause and always stands at or near the beginning of the clause.

Jill now wonders *if her answer was the correct one.*
[Noun clause subordinated by the conjunction *if* and used as a direct object.]

All of us hope *that you'll return soon.*
[Noun clause subordinated by the conjunction *that* and used as a direct object.]

I do not know *who he is.*
[Noun clause subordinated by the pronoun *who* used as the subjective complement within the clause.]

I know *what I would do with the extra money.*
[Noun clause subordinated by the pronoun *what* used as the direct object within the clause.]

Tell me *whom Mary is feuding with now.*
[Noun clause subordinated by the pronoun *whom* used as the object of the preposition *with.*]

You must decide *which car you will use today.*
[Noun clause subordinated by the adjective *which* modifying the direct object *car.*]

Why Morton left school still puzzles his friends.
[Noun clause subordinated by the adverb *why.*]

As you can see from these examples, a noun clause, like a noun, can be a subject, direct object, subjective complement, object of a preposition, or appositive (see page 95). You can understand the uses of the noun clause if you think of it as a clause equivalent to a "something" or a "someone" in one of these noun slots.

Subject (S)

The girl opened the window. [Single-word noun as S.]
Whoever came in first opened the window. [Noun clause as S.]
His *story* is very convincing. [Noun as S.]
What he told us is very convincing. [Noun clause as S.]

93

Subjective Complement (S.C.)

This is his *story*. [Single-word as S.C.]

This is *what he told us*. [Noun clause as S.C.]

Direct Object (D.O.)

Mr. Allen announced *his resignation*. [Single-word as D.O.]

Mr. Allen announced *that he would resign*. [Noun clause as D.O]

Can you tell me your *time* of arrival? [Single-word as D.O.]

Can you tell me *when you will arrive?* [Noun clause as D.O.]

Object of a Preposition (O.P.)

Give the package to the *man*. [Single-word as O.P.]

Give the package to *whoever opens the door*. [Noun clause as O.P.]

Note that the choice between *who/whoever* and *whom/whomever* depends on its use in the clause. This rule creates apparently awkward and sometimes tricky choices:

Give the book to whomever you see first. [*whomever* is the object of the verb *see*]

Give the book to whoever answers the door. [*whoever* is the subject of the verb *answers*]

(See Supplement 1.)

In noun clauses used as direct objects, the conjunction *that* is often unexpressed because the meaning is usually clear without it.

I know *that you will be happy here.*

[Noun clause subordinated by the conjunction *that*.]

I know *you will be happy here.*

[Noun clause with subordinating word omitted.]

This omission of the subordinating word creates an ellipsis, a construction similar to an elliptical adverbial clause. In adverbial clauses, the subject and part of the verb (the auxiliaries) are omitted. In this construction, only the subordinating word is omitted.

Most of the noun clauses that you read and write will be used as subjects, direct objects (the most common use), subjective complements, or objects of prepositions. However, two rather special uses should be noted, the *delayed* noun clause and the *appositive* noun clause.

DELAYED NOUN CLAUSE

One common use of a noun clause is as a delayed subject. The signal for this construction is the word *it* standing in the subject position, with the meaningful subject being a noun clause following the verb.

It is unfortunate *that you were delayed.*

Although the sentence begins with *It* and the clause follows the verb, the clause is the real subject. The meaning of the sentence is "That you were delayed is unfortunate."

A related noun clause use puts the word *it* in the direct object slot with a noun clause following an objective complement. This use, which is encountered less frequently than the delayed subject, gives us a clause that we can call a delayed direct object.

We think it unlikely *that Jones will be reelected.*

APPOSITIVE NOUN CLAUSE

To understand the other special noun clause, you must know what an appositive is. An **appositive** is a noun unit inserted into a sentence to rename another noun that usually immediately precedes the appositive. A simple example occurs in the following sentence:

Senator Jackson, a dedicated environmentalist, objected.

Because any noun unit can be used as an appositive, noun clauses sometimes function in this position. Some noun clause appositives are separated from the noun they are renaming by at least a comma, sometimes by a heavier mark.

There still remains one mystery: *how the thief knew your name.* [The noun clause renames the preceding noun, *mystery.*]

A rather special type of appositive noun clause, subordinated by *that* and following such nouns as *fact, belief, hope, statement, news,* and *argument,* is usually not set off by any mark of punctuation.

You cannot deny the fact *that you lied under oath.*

Your statement *that the boss is stupid* was undiplomatic.

(See Supplement 2.)

SUPPLEMENT 1

You have probably already noticed that the pronouns, adjectives, and adverbs that subordinate noun clauses are essentially the same words that are used in questions (Lesson 6). The two uses are alike in the important fact that they always stand at the beginning of the clause. The two uses differ in that, as interrogatives, the words bring about the subject-verb inversion, whereas in noun clauses the subject-verb position is the normal one.

Whom will the mayor appoint?

[This sentence is a direct question; it calls for an answer. *Whom* is the D.O. of the main verb.]

I wonder *whom the mayor will appoint.*

[This sentence is a statement, not a direct question. Notice that a question mark is not required. *Whom* is the D.O. within the noun clause.]

SUPPLEMENT 2

Because an appositive is a renamer, it represents a reduced form of a Pattern 2 sentence in which the subject and a noun subjective complement are joined by a form of *be.* The writer of the sentence "Senator Jackson, a dedicated environmentalist, objected" could have written two simple sentences, the second one repeating a noun used in the first:

Senator Jackson objected.
Senator Jackson [or He] is a dedicated environmentalist.

The adjective clause offers the writer one device for compressing this information into one sentence.

Senator Jackson, who is a dedicated environmentalist, objected.

The appositive represents a further compression.

Senator Jackson, a dedicated environmentalist, objected.

If you think of the appositive as a renamer of the preceding noun (the two nouns could be joined by a form of *be*), you have a handy test to help you recognize any noun clause appositive use.

There still remains one mystery: *how the thief knew your name.*
[Test: The mystery *is* how the thief knew your name.]

You can't deny the fact *that she has real talent.*
[Test: The fact *is* that she has real talent.]

Your contention *that the witness lied* has some merit.
[Test: The contention *is* that the witness lied.]

If you remember a few points about the form, function, and positioning of adjective and noun clauses, you should have little difficulty in distinguishing between them. Although certain kinds of noun clauses in apposition may, at first glance, look like adjective clauses, a few simple tests clearly show the difference.

The news *that you brought us* is welcome. [Adjective clause]
The news *that Bob has recovered* is welcome. [Noun clause]

If you remember that an adjective clause is a describer and that an appositive noun clause is a renamer, you can see that in the first sentence the clause describes—in fact, identifies—the noun *news,* but it does not tell us what the news is. In the second sentence the clause does more: It tells us what the news is. Remember the *be* test. "The news is *that you brought us* ..." does not make sense, but "The news is *that Bob has recovered* ..." does; therefore, the second clause is a noun clause in apposition.

Another test that can be applied to these two types of sentences is based on the fact that in adjective clauses, but not in noun clauses, *which* can be substituted for *that.* "The news *which* you brought us ..." is acceptable English; the clause, in this case, is an adjective clause. But because we can't say "The news *which* Bob has recovered ..." the clause is a noun clause; it cannot be an adjective clause.

SUMMARY OF NOUN CLAUSES

1. *Function:* to work as a noun within the main clause

2. *Positions:* subject (or delayed subject), renaming subjective complement, direct object (or delayed direct object), object of preposition, or appositive

3. *Subordinators:*
   a. conjunctions: *that, if, whether*
   b. pronouns: *who, whom, which, what,* and ... *ever* forms, standing for unknown persons or things
   c. adjectives: *whose, which, what*
   d. adverbs: *when, where, why, how*

4. *Special problem:* Some noun appositive clauses closely resemble adjective clauses. They differ in that, in addition to describing the noun, the appositive clause renames the noun:

   The remark *that Jim made* (adjective clause) was unwise.

   The remark *that Mr. Smith cannot be trusted* (appositive noun clause) was unwise.

Practice Sheet 10

Noun Clauses

NAME _____ SCORE _____

Directions: Identify the function of each italicized noun clause by writing one of the following abbreviations in the space at the left:

S. (subject or delayed subject)	S.C. (subjective complement)
D.O. (direct object or delayed direct object)	O.P. (object of preposition)
	Ap. (appositive)

_____ 1. Your statement *that she is very intelligent* certainly pleased Marisol.

_____ 2. No one knows *who is running for campus president.*

_____ 3. *Whoever leaves the room last* should turn out the lights.

_____ 4. I decided *which of those two coats I intend to order.*

_____ 5. Give that note to *whomever you see at the front desk.*

_____ 6. Give that note to *whoever is sitting at the front desk.*

_____ 7. Jim had forgotten the fact *that the paper is due next Tuesday.*

_____ 8. Jim had forgotten *that the paper is due next Tuesday.*

_____ 9. The fact *that the paper is due next Tuesday* had slipped Jim's mind.

_____ 10. *How he can finish the paper by Tuesday* is a mystery to me.

_____ 11. The big question is *whether Jim can finish that paper by Tuesday.*

_____ 12. Do you know *whose car is parked behind mine in the driveway?*

_____ 13. His casual comment *that my shirt looks funny* hurt my feelings.

_____ 14. *Whether my shirt looks funny or not* is none of his business.

_____ 15. Did Alicia tell you *when her plane will land?*

_____ 16. *When her plane will land* has never been made clear to any of us.

_____ 17. It is not clear *when her plane will land.*

_____ 18. We think it likely *that the plane will land early tomorrow morning.*

_____ 19. I know *you will become good friends with the people in this office.*

_____ 20. Well, that is *what he hopes to accomplish over the next two weeks.*

99

Directions: Each of the following sentences contains a noun clause. Put parentheses around each noun clause and identify its function by writing one of the following abbreviations in the space at the left:

S. (subject or delayed subject) S.C. (subjective complement)
D.O. (direct object or O.P. (object of preposition)
    delayed direct object) Ap. (appositive)

_____ 1. Sam does not know where he put his history textbook.

_____ 2. How he manages to lose so much of his stuff amazes all his friends.

_____ 3. Apparently, the fact that he loses his books constantly doesn't bother him very much.

_____ 4. Whatever table is handy when he walks in the door is the place he drops his books.

_____ 5. The place where he eats lunch is often where he leaves his books.

_____ 6. It seems very inconvenient that he is so absentminded.

_____ 7. Some people believe that absentmindedness is caused by stress.

_____ 8. But everyone agrees that Sam is always very relaxed.

_____ 9. Some people find it offensive that Sam does not seem to care about his possessions.

_____ 10. Sam, however, just hopes that his friends will be understanding about his attitude.

_____ 11. We all wonder who will take care of Sam next year in graduate school.

_____ 12. We intend to hand his care over to whoever is willing to do the job.

_____ 13. Whoever takes on that job will certainly be busy.

_____ 14. Whomever he finds for that job will certainly be busy.

_____ 15. Last year, Sam suddenly remembered that he had left his brother in a restaurant.

_____ 16. Unfortunately, the thought that he had left his brother behind occurred to him after about an hour's drive down the road.

_____ 17. For a few minutes, Sam could not remember where he had left his brother.

_____ 18. Finally, it dawned on him that they had been having lunch together.

_____ 19. The fact that he had eaten a pastrami sandwich for lunch reminded Sam of the name of the restaurant.

_____ 20. His friends can only hold on to the hope that, in the future, his memory will improve.

NAME _____ SCORE _____

Directions: Each of the following sentences contains a noun clause. Put parentheses around each noun clause and identify its function by writing one of the following in the space at the left.

S. (subject or delayed subject)   S.C. (subjective complement)
D.O. (direct object or   O.P. (object of preposition)
      delayed direct object)   Ap. (appositive)

_____ 1. Leah's teacher does not realize how sensitive the child is.

_____ 2. I am slightly uneasy about what Ellen will do next.

_____ 3. How my roommate ever survived prep school is a mystery to me.

_____ 4. The lawyer assured us that we had a foolproof case.

_____ 5. It can now be revealed that Simpson had once been an agent of the CIA.

_____ 6. Can you tell me when the next bus from Newark will arrive?

_____ 7. I know only one thing: Jack is now trying to move to Mobile.

_____ 8. You'll have to work with whatever tools are available.

_____ 9. The reason for Mike's resignation is that he hates to be away from home.

_____ 10. Where the treasure was buried has never been learned.

_____ 11. It is unfortunate that you arrived too late for the main speech.

_____ 12. The two girls promised us they would clean up the kitchen.

_____ 13. The reporters' version was quite different from what I really said.

_____ 14. One of Bernardo's real skills is that he programs computers well.

_____ 15. That he programs computers well is one of Bernardo's real skills.

_____ 16. Sherwood's main objection was that the interest rate was high.

_____ 17. We should pack nothing except what we will use on the trip.

_____ 18. What I will need for the trip fills three suitcases.

_____ 19. Melinda never understood why her parents like Ross so much.

_____ 20. But that is not what I said.

_____ 21. The fact that the commissioner's brother owns that land had no effect on her vote on the zoning change.

_____ 22. I don't know if I'm right, but I will take the next left turn.

_____ 23. The fact is that there is no need for a new shopping center in that part of town.

_____ 24. Her prediction that the renovations would far exceed the original budget was accurate.

_____ 25. Were you told that you could pass the course only if you took several trips to the local museums?

_____ 26. Whoever takes the most trips to the museums gets the best grade.

_____ 27. Norman is a man who never seems to think about what he will do in the future.

_____ 28. Will the campus police think it unusual that you left your car on campus when you went home for the weekend?

_____ 29. The girl in the seat next to you was interested in how you were solving that last equation.

_____ 30. That is exactly what I have been advising her for months now.

_____ 31. No one seems to know why a new shirt has so many pins in it.

_____ 32. Truman heard that a new company had taken control of the bankrupt shopping center.

_____ 33. Why the new owners reduced the size of the sales force remains a mystery to many people.

_____ 34. The fact that the man can operate several of our computerized milling machines makes him extremely valuable to the company.

_____ 35. The old hands chuckled when the new man asked where the left-handed monkey wrenches are kept.

_____ 36. The Financial Aid Office gave Norma one last option: that she should try to obtain a government loan.

_____ 37. The company president gave the consultant whatever advice and assistance she could.

_____ 38. My mother becomes frustrated because she cannot remember where she has put her car keys.

_____ 39. When it was announced that Coach Hartshorn was leaving, several new people signed up for the team.

_____ 40. The dilemma that faces us is that no one yet knows the extent of the damage.

Directions: Combine the following pairs of word groups into a single sentence by joining the second to the first as a noun clause.

1. The only question is (something). Why you decided to move into that apartment in the first place.

   _____

2. Your friends will have only one question. Why you decided to move into that apartment in the first place.

   _____

3. Please give this message to (someone). Whoever comes to the door when you knock.

   _____

4. (Something) was not clear from that phone call. Whether you still want to meet for lunch.

   _____

5. (Someone) should be a little embarrassed. Whoever did the proofreading on that first page in the paper.

   _____

6. That announcement did not surprise anyone. (The announcement was) that Jim is leaving next week for a new job.

   _____

7. Did you know (something)? We were having lunch downtown at the time.

   _____

8. Some staff members think (something) is possible. This policy will be changed soon.

   _____

9. The teacher told Marcia (something). She needs to study harder for the next test.

   _____

10. (Something) was very fortunate. The people in that car were wearing seat belts.

   _____

NAME _____ SCORE _____

Directions: The italicized material in each of these sentences is a subordinate clause. In the first space at the left write one of the following to identify the clause:

> Adv. (Adverb clause)
>
> Adj. (Adjective clause)
>
> N. (Noun clause)

Then in the second space, write one of the following abbreviations to identify the use within the noun clause of the word printed in heavy type.

> S. (subject)   I.O. (indirect object)   O.C. (objective complement)
>
> D.O. (direct objective)   S.C. (subjective complement)

_____ 1. **Whoever** *told you that story* was guilty of gross exaggeration.

_____

_____ 2. The boss never explained to us *why he had made Mr. Farley his chief **assistant**.*

_____

_____ 3. You will be held responsible for *whatever **mistakes** your trainees make.*

_____

_____ 4. A current rumor is *that the company will make the **union** another wage offer.*

_____

_____ 5. The secretary of the union tells me *there is no **truth** in the rumor.*

_____

_____ 6. It is quite possible *that someone had turned off the burglar **alarm**.*

_____

_____ 7. Mrs. Smiley is firm in her belief *that this is the **best** of all possible worlds.*

_____

_____ 8. *Whatever contribution you can send **us*** will be greatly appreciated.

_____

_____ 9. In those days none of us thought it likely *that Eric would ever become a successful **architect**.*

_____

_____ 10. Every housewife is concerned about *how **expensive** basic foods are becoming.*

_____

_____ 11. I hope you will remember *why I offered **you** that other position.*

_____

_____ 12. *How this new rule will change the **practice** of law* is not clear at this time.

_____

_____ 13. The person *who wrote **me** that letter* is a very skilled writer.

_____

_____ 14. The important concepts in today's lecture became less clear *as I became more **fatigued**.*

_____ 15. *Because the voters found those two amendments* **confusing,** they
_____   refused to pass either of them.

_____ 16. We all laughed at Allan because he said *that the last history test*
_____   *was not very* **difficult.**

_____ 17. James was amused when the children were surprised by **what** *they*
_____   *saw at the end of the movie.*

_____ 18. Larry was able to use the book *I sent* **him** as a source for his
_____   research paper.

_____ 19. A student who *considered the prerequisites for the chemistry*
_____   *course too* **demanding** took her case to the dean.

_____ 20. No one in the administration knows **whom** *the President will*
_____   *nominate for that cabinet position.*

_____ 21. No one in the administration knows **who** *the President's cabinet*
_____   *nominee will be.*

_____ 22. *That movie, because it is quite* **suspenseful,** became very popular.
_____

_____ 23. I'm afraid *that the last two miles of that race will leave Becky*
_____   **exhausted**.

_____ 24. Martha is new to politics; she believes *everything the candidates*
_____   *tell* **her**.

_____ 25. Martha is new to politics; she believes **whatever** *the candidates*
_____   *tell her.*

_____ 26. When our class toured the city's new aquarium, we learned *that*
_____   *strange* **creatures** *live in the sea.*

_____ 27. *If you can keep your feet* **dry**, you may be able to avoid blisters
_____   during the long hike.

_____ 28. Jack refused to show any of us **what** *he paid for his new car.*
_____

_____ 29. The only advice *the coach could give* **us** was that we need to try
_____   harder next time.

_____ 30. The only advice **that** *the coach could give us* was that we need to
_____   try harder next time.

Directions: In each pair of word groups, use the first group as a main clause and add the second to the first by making it an adjective clause, an adverb clause, or a noun clause. Rewrite enough of the two word groups to make the new sentence clear. Identify the subordinate clause you have created by writing one of the following in the space at the left:

Adv. (adverb clause)   Adj. (adjective clause)   N. (noun clause)

_____   1. Jensen was delighted.
He landed a big contract.

_____

_____   2. Not everyone in the class knew (something).
The due date for the paper had been changed.

_____

_____   3. Andrew always remembers with great fondness that spot.
(The spot is) where he proposed to his wife.

_____

_____   4. By noon it was certain.
The game would be rained out.

_____

_____   5. The weight was so heavy (that something happened).
I dropped it with a crash in the middle of the floor.

_____

_____   6. You need to follow the steps in the instructions (in a certain way).
Exactly as I have written them.

_____

_____   7. Please give this message to (anyone).
Who comes to the meeting from my office.

_____

_____   8. Please give this message to (someone).
Whoever comes to the meeting from my office.

_____

_____   9. The person is sitting at the first desk on your right.
The person can help you with your problem.

_____

_____   10. We might need to cut down that tree.
Lightning struck it last night.

_____

Directions: In place of the *someone* or *something* in the first sentence, put a noun clause formed from the idea of the second sentence or phrase. The suggested subordinating word is provided in parentheses.

Example:
Someone should turn on the heat. (whoever)
The person who gets to the cabin first

<u>Whoever gets to the cabin first should turn on the heat.</u>

1. I know *something*. (what)
   The thing that needs to be done to solve that problem.

   _____

2. They all hope *something*. (that)
   We can finish this project by Friday.

   _____

3. Jim understands *something*. (how)
   How that program works.

   _____

4. Have you decided *something*? (where)
   The place you want to spend your vacation.

   _____

5. We need to tell Dad *something*. (when)
   The time he should pick us up at the airport.

   _____

6. You should have *something* by tomorrow morning. (whatever)
   The things you need to finish the new cabinets.

   _____

7. *Someone* should move that car. (whoever)
   The person who left it in my driveway.

   _____

8. They think *something* is unlikely. (that)
   Jim will arrive in time for the meeting.

   _____

9. *Someone* should return my textbook and lecture notes. (whoever)
   The person who picked them up by mistake.

   _____

10. I just figured *something* out. (how)
    The way I can print my article in three columns per page.

    _____

A **phrase** is a group of related words that does *not* contain a subject and a verb in combination. Like the subordinate clause, the phrase is used in a sentence as a single part of speech. Many of the sentences that you have studied so far have contained a prepositional phrase, which consists of a preposition, a noun or a pronoun used as its object, and any modifiers of the object. Most prepositional phrases are used as adjectives or adverbs:

> Most *of my friends* live *in the East.*
> [The first phrase is used as an adjective to modify the pronoun *most;* the second is used as an adverb to modify the verb *live.*]

Much less commonly, a prepositional phrase is used as a noun:

> *Before lunch* is the best time for the meeting.
> [The phrase is the subject of the verb *is.*]

> She waved to us from *inside the phone booth.*
> [The phrase is the object of the preposition *from.*]

Another important kind of phrase makes use of a verbal. A **verbal** is a word formed from a verb but used as a different part of speech. There are three kinds of verbals: the gerund, the infinitive, and the participle.

GERUNDS

A **gerund** is a noun formed by adding -*ing* either to the base of the verb *(studying)* or to an auxiliary *(having studied, being studied, having been studied).* You might think of the gerund phrase as the equivalent of a noun. It can appear in any place in a sentence where a noun might appear: subject, direct object, renaming subjective complement, object of preposition, or (rarely) appositive.

> *Studying* demands most of my time. [Subject]
> I usually enjoy *studying.* [Direct object]
> My main activity is *studying.* [Renaming subjective complement]
> You won't pass the course without *studying.* [Object of preposition]
> Might I suggest to you another activity: *studying*? [Appositive]

These single-word gerund uses are uncomplicated. "He enjoys *studying*" and "He enjoys football" are alike in their structure; the only difference is that in one the direct object is a word formed from a verb and in the other it is a regular noun. Because they are formed from verbs and are thus "verbal nouns," gerunds can have a direct object or a subjective complement. The following examples will help clarify this important point.

> He enjoys *walking in the snow.*
> [The gerund has no complement. Compare "He walks in the snow."]

109

She enjoys building model airplanes.

[*Airplanes* is the direct object of the gerund *building*. Compare "She builds model airplanes."]

He enjoys *being helpful*. He enjoyed *being elected treasurer*.

[*Helpful* is the subjective complement of the gerund *being; treasurer* is the subjective complement of the passive gerund *being elected*. Compare "He is helpful" and "He was elected treasurer."]

She enjoyed *telling us the good news.*

[*Us* is the indirect object and *news* is the direct object of the gerund *telling*. Compare "She told us the good news."]

He enjoyed *making our vacation pleasant.*

[*Vacation* is the direct object of the gerund *making,* and *pleasant* is the objective complement of *vacation*. Compare "He made our vacation pleasant."]

INFINITIVES

An **infinitive** is a verbal consisting of the base of the verb, usually preceded by *to* (*to* is called the sign of the infinitive). The infinitive uses auxiliaries to show tense and voice: *to study, to have studied, to be studying, to have been studying, to be studied, to have been studied.* An **infinitive phrase** consists of an infinitive plus its modifiers and/or complements. Infinitive units are used as nouns, as adjectives, and as adverbs:

To attend the party without an invitation would be tactless.

[The infinitive phrase is used as the subject of the sentence. Within the phrase, *party* is the direct object.]

It would be tactless *to attend the party without an invitation.*

[In this pattern, the infinitive phrase is called a delayed subject; hence it serves a noun use. The signal word is *it;* although *it* stands in subject position, the infinitive phrase is the meaningful subject. Sometimes the *it* is in the direct object slot with the delayed infinitive phrase following an objective complement: I would consider it tactless *to attend the party without an invitation.* Compare a similar noun clause use in Lesson 10.]

I wanted *to give Charles another chance.*

[The infinitive phrase is the direct object of *wanted*. Within the phrase, *Charles* is the indirect object and *chance* the direct object of the infinitive. Compare "I gave Charles another chance."]

My plan is *to become an active precinct worker.*

[The infinitive phrase is used as a noun; it is a subjective complement that renames the subject *plan*. Within the phrase, *worker* is the subjective complement of the infinitive. Compare "I became an active precinct worker."]

The test *to be taken next Friday* is an important one.

[The infinitive phrase is used as an adjective modifying *test.*]

I am happy *to meet you.*

[The infinitive phrase is used as an adverb modifying the adjective *happy.*]

To be sure of a good seat, you should arrive early.

[The infinitive phrase is used as an adverb modifying *should arrive.*]

Infinitive phrases sometimes include their own subjects. Notice that when a pronoun is used as the subject of an infinitive, the pronoun is in the objective case (see Lesson 24).

We wanted *her to resign.*

We know *him to be a good referee.*

In a rather common sentence type, the subject of an infinitive is preceded by *for,* which in this case is considered part of the phrase.

For us to leave now would be impolite.

It's silly *for you to feel neglected.*

The infinitive without *to* may form a phrase that is used as the direct object of such verbs as *let, help, make, see, hear,* and *watch:*

The teacher let *us leave early.*

Martha watched *her son score the winning touchdown.*

The infinitive without *to* is also sometimes used as the object of a preposition, such as *except, but,* and *besides:*

He could do nothing except *resign gracefully.*

He did everything but *write the paper for me.*

SUPPLEMENT 1

In Lesson 6, you learned that an interrogative unit in a direct question stands at the beginning of the sentence. Notice how this positioning can affect the internal makeup of a gerund phrase or an infinitive phrase:

How many natives did the missionaries succeed in *converting*?

[*Converting* is the gerund form of a transitive verb and therefore requires a direct object—in this case, *natives.*]

Which car did you finally decide *to buy*?

[*Car* is the direct object of the infinitive *to buy.*]

SUPPLEMENT 2

When the gerund is preceded by a pronoun, the pronoun should be in the possessive case.

The audience *enjoyed Maria's dancing in the first act.*

[Compare "The audience enjoyed Maria's dance in the first act."]

We appreciated *your helping the class with that project.*

[Compare "We appreciated your help with that project."]

SUMMARY OF GERUND AND INFINITIVE PHRASES

Gerund Phrases

1. Forms: *studying, having studied, being studied, having been studied*

2. Function: as a noun within the larger unit

3. Positions: subject, renaming subjective complement, direct object, object of preposition, and (rarely) appositive

Infinitive Phrases

1. Forms: *to study, to have studied, to be studying, to have been studying, to be studied, to have been studied.* Some infinitive phrases have subjects (We wanted her to run for office) in the objective case.

2. Function: as adjective (Here are the letters *to be mailed today*), as adverb (I am happy *to meet you*), or as noun (*To leave* now would be unwise)

3. Positions: subject (or delayed subject), direct object (or delayed direct object), renaming subjective complement, and (rarely) object of preposition.

4. Special structures:
   a. *For* sometimes introduces an infinitive phrase that has a subject.

   For you to criticize his work would be presumptuous.

   b. A phrase with a subject but without the marker *to* is often used as a direct object following one of these verbs: *let, help, make, see, hear, watch:*

   Mother let *us mix the cookie dough.*
   Ms. Jones heard *the man threaten the cashier.*

   c. The infinitive without *to* is used as object of prepositions *except, but, besides.*

   He could do nothing but *leave quietly.*

NAME _____ SCORE _____

Directions: In the space at left, copy the abbreviation that identifies the use of the italicized gerund phrase.

    S. (subject)   S.C. (subjective complement)

    D.O. (direct object)   O.P. (object of preposition)

_____ 1. For about two weeks, Alex considered *moving to a new apartment.*

_____ 2. We should start *counting those tickets before 5 o'clock.*

_____ 3. Wasn't your brother amused by *your trying to play football?*

_____ 4. *Polishing the silverware* was the hardest job for all of us on the wait staff.

_____ 5. *"Leaving that work for tomorrow* is probably a good idea," said the boss.

_____ 6. My summer internship will include *going to Brazil to study the rain forest.*

_____ 7. Thomas can't think of math courses without *getting nervous.*

_____ 8. When did Sharon begin *running marathons?*

_____ 9. Does *being the youngest person on the staff* affect your work very much?

_____ 10. The toughest job for any business leader is *communicating ideas to the staff.*

_____ 11. I finished my work on that paper by *saving it to my floppy disk.*

_____ 12. Everyone in the class wishes that she would stop *asking all those silly questions.*

_____ 13. Before this semester, Jan never believed that *learning to type* was important.

_____ 14. You can extend the life of your car's engine by *changing the oil regularly.*

_____ 15. One of life's simple pleasures is *drinking a hot cup of coffee on a cold morning.*

_____ 16. We finished work on the report by *printing copies of it this morning.*

_____ 17. For a good laugh, you should try *listening to my brother talk about his puppy.*

_____ 18. Jim's job last summer was *pouring concrete in a housing development.*

_____ 19. Mom is very proud of Alexis for *making all A's last semester.*

_____ 20. After we finished *doing all those exercises,* we were totally exhausted.

Directions: Each sentence contains one infinitive phrase (some with subjects). Underline each infinitive phrase. In the space at the left, write the abbreviation that identifies the use of the phrase in the sentence.

N. (noun)　　　　Adj. (adjective)　　　　Adv. (adverb)

_____ 1. We need to know more about your experience in your last job before we can offer you a position with our company.

_____ 2. Everyone should know the way to change a tire on a car.

_____ 3. To find that program in your computer, click the left button on the mouse on the proper icon.

_____ 4. Jim left so early this morning that we did not have an opportunity to talk to him.

_____ 5. One of the advisors can help you select your courses for next term.

_____ 6. When the car broke down, we couldn't do anything but walk home.

_____ 7. They should be able to find those books somewhere in the college library.

_____ 8. For a skilled thief, it was a fairly simple matter to pick the lock and enter the hotel room.

_____ 9. For a skilled thief, it was fairly simple to pick the lock and enter the hotel room.

_____ 10. The list of chapters to be studied for the next test is on the bulletin board.

_____ 11. It's hard to know which trail to the top of the mountain is easier.

_____ 12. I think I will stay home this weekend to study for the big test in history.

_____ 13. Since we had worked hard all day on that project, we were too tired to play tennis.

_____ 14. "I've never liked to exercise early in the morning," said Barb.

_____ 15. Before you leave this afternoon, you have a chance to drive that car on the test track.

_____ 16. My little brother is always only too eager to make fun of my unsuccessful woodworking projects.

_____ 17. The men have decided to let Al choose the menu for the staff banquet.

_____ 18. To be sure you get the courses you need, you should register as early as possible.

_____ 19. Maria wants to spend the day looking for a new dress for that dance.

_____ 20. The list of books to be read for that class is almost two pages long.

Exercise 11   *Gerund and Infinitive Phrases*

NAME _____ SCORE _____

Directions: Each sentence contains one gerund phrase. Underline the gerund phrase. In the space at the left, write the abbreviation that identifies the use of the gerund phrase.

S. (subject)   S.C. (subjective complement)

D.O. (direct object)   O.P. (object of preposition)

_____ 1. Balancing my checkbook is much easier now that I use my computer.

_____ 2. Jerry's young cousin learned much about geography by collecting stamps from across the world.

_____ 3. Although she enjoys math, Cary has never considered becoming an accountant.

_____ 4. Alan's toughest job each month is balancing his checkbook.

_____ 5. Before adjourning the meeting, we need to set a date for the next meeting.

_____ 6. Senator Bell does not oppose increasing the sales tax to build new schools.

_____ 7. Without a computer, registering all these students would be very difficult.

_____ 8. The idea of running for class president had never crossed Adam's mind.

_____ 9. Running for class president was not something that Adam had ever considered.

_____ 10. Most people would never consider running for class president.

_____ 11. Finding that last source of information allowed me to finish my paper early.

_____ 12. Perhaps we could improve voter turnout by declaring election day a national holiday.

_____ 13. The last thing we considered in the meeting was appointing a new treasurer.

_____ 14. "If I can do it without upsetting everyone, I'd like to postpone that test by one week," said the instructor.

_____ 15. Living in the small cabin for an entire year must have been a great challenge for that pioneer family.

_____ 16. Painting those chipped, scarred walls would greatly improve the appearance of the classroom.

_____ 17. Our first priority should be painting those chipped, scarred walls.

_____ 18. Have you considered moving your desk to a spot under that window?

_____ 19. I certainly enjoyed watching that game from the box seats.

_____ 20. Watching that game from the box seats was great fun.

Directions: In the space at the left, write the abbreviation that identifies the use of the italicized infinitive phrase within the sentence.

N/s (subject, delayed subject) Adj. (adjective)

N/sc (subjective complement) Adv. (adverb)

N/d (direct object)

N/op (object of preposition)

_____ 1. *To be sure of the best deal*, check prices in at least three stores.

_____ 2. In all the thunder and lightning, we couldn't do anything except *run for cover.*

_____ 3. It is always difficult *to find materials on popular subjects.*

_____ 4. McDaniel does, in fact, want *us to work on his political campaign.*

_____ 5. His great desire *to finish his first marathon* made Max a dedicated runner.

_____ 6. Mark told us *to take the pie out of the oven at 2 o'clock.*

_____ 7. Alma was delighted *to receive a call from her cousin Barbara last night.*

_____ 8. After all that work, I'm looking forward to a chance *to rest up over the weekend.*

_____ 9. The extra day's work will let *us finish that project without any problems.*

_____ 10. Are you interested enough in that author *to buy two of her novels?*

_____ 11. Arthur and Jose have been chosen *to serve on the party's nominating committee.*

_____ 12. "Can anyone here show me *how to open this computer program?*" asked Anna.

_____ 13. Sol was on the Internet for three hours today trying *to find new sources for his paper.*

_____ 14. It was almost impossible *for us to find our way from your directions.*

_____ 15. "*To speak to a personal representative*, please punch 2 on your touch-tone phone," said the recorded voice.

_____ 16. They hope we will try our very best *to finish that project by the end of the week.*

_____ 17. That error in the outfield gave them a chance *to tie the score.*

_____ 18. Robert recently moved to a new apartment *to be within walking distance of work.*

_____ 19. Jill's plan is *to get up very early and finish writing that paper.*

_____ 20. Any one of us would jump at the chance *to go sailing for two weeks in the Caribbean.*

Directions: Combine the two sentences in each item into a single sentence by resolving one sentence into a gerund phrase or an infinitive phrase to replace the italicized word(s) in the other sentence.

1. Alice washes her new car twice a week.
   She enjoys *doing that job.*

   _____

2. Mark wants to become a computer programmer.
   At this time *this* is his goal.

   _____

3. When Shirley first came to town, she needed to find a job.
   Finding one was her first important task.

   _____

4. When she was young, Caroline studied karate.
   Doing this gave her great powers of concentration.

   _____

5. Tammy did not say goodbye to her friends.
   Without *doing something*, Tammy left the restaurant.

   _____

6. If you ask your advisor, perhaps she will be able *to do something.*
   She will be able to help you select a course.

   _____

7. Your best option at this point is *something.*
   You should study the material and take the test again.

   _____

8. You can register for next term by telephone.
   It is a fairly simple thing *to do something.*

   _____

9. Painting the walls and the trim in that room is our job for today.
   Our job for the day is *to do something.*

   _____

10. Studying for the test was easy.
    It was easy *to do something* once I outlined the chapters in the text.

    _____

A participle is an adjective formed from a verb by adding *-ing* or *-ed* to the base form of the verb (*studying, studied*) or to an auxiliary (*having studied, being studied, having been studied*). (Note that many verbs have irregular past participles. See pages 224–226 for lists of such verbs.) By itself, a participle works exactly as any one-word adjective works:

> The *injured* bird clung to the *swaying* branch.
>
> [The past participle *injured* modifies the noun *bird;* the present participle *swaying* modifies the noun *branch.*]

Often, however, the participle is combined with other words to form a **participial phrase** that modifies a noun.

> The taxi driver, *being a war veteran,* signed the petition.
>
> [The participial phrase modifies the noun *taxi driver.* Within the phrase, *veteran* is a subjective complement.]
>
> *Calling the man a hero,* the mayor gave him an award.
>
> [The participial phrase modifies the noun *mayor.* Within the phrase, *man* is a direct object and *hero* is an objective complement.]

PARTICIPIAL PHRASES

The similarity between an adjective clause and a participial phrase is obvious:

1. A man grabbed the microphone. The man [*or* He] was wearing a painted mask.
   [Two independent clauses.]

   a. A clown *who was wearing a painted mask* grabbed the microphone.
   [Adjective clause. *Mask* is a direct object of the verb.]
   b. A clown *wearing a painted mask* grabbed the microphone.
   [Participial phrase. *Mask* is a direct object of the participle.]

2. Jo's parents left the concert early. They found the music uncomfortably loud.
   [Two independent clauses.]

   a. Jo's parents, *who found the music uncomfortably loud,* left the concert early.
   [Adjective clause. *Music* is a direct object and *loud* an objective complement.]
   b. Jo's parents, *finding the music uncomfortably loud,* left the concert early.
   [Participial phrase. *Music* is a direct object and *loud* an objective complement.]

These two examples point out another similarity: Like the adjective clause, the participial phrase can be either restrictive or nonrestrictive. The phrase in the first example identifies the clown; it is restrictive and is not set off by commas. The phrase in the second example is not needed to identify parents; it requires commas because it is nonrestrictive.

Like adjective clauses, participial phrases must be very close to the noun they modify. An adjective clause must follow the noun it modifies. A restrictive (identifying) participial phrase normally follows the noun it modifies, as in the example, "A man wearing a black mask. . . ." Unlike a nonrestrictive adjective clause, however, a nonrestrictive participial phrase can move into another position in the sentence. Observe the positions of the participial phrase in the following sentences:

Steve, having passed the test with flying colors, decided to celebrate.

Having passed the test with flying colors, Steve decided to celebrate.

Occasionally, the participial phrase can be moved to the end of the clause:

Steve decided to celebrate, having passed the test with flying colors.

Because a participle is an adjective formed from a verb and thus suggests an action, the participial phrase can be used to relieve the monotony of a series of short, independent clauses:

Pam wanted desperately to hear the rock concert, but she was temporarily short of funds, and she knew that her cousin Alice had an extra ticket, and so she decided to call her. [Four independent clauses]

Wanting desperately to hear the rock concert but being temporarily short of funds, Pam decided to call her cousin Alice, knowing that she had an extra ticket. [One independent clause and three participial phrases]

Jensen stood at home plate. He waggled his bat. He eyed the pitcher coldly. He took a mighty swing at the first pitch. He hit the ball out of the park. [Five independent clauses]

Standing at home plate, waggling his bat, and eyeing the pitcher coldly, Jensen took a mighty swing at the first pitch, hitting the ball out of the park. [One independent clause and four participial phrases]

ABSOLUTE PHRASES

The **absolute phrase** is a special kind of phrase, different from the standard participial phrase in both form and function. Within the absolute phrase, the participle follows a noun or a pronoun that is part of the phrase. The phrase adds to the meaning of the whole sentence, but it does not directly modify any noun or pronoun in the sentence. The absolute phrase is a versatile structure capable of many variations and widely used in modern writing to point out subtle relationships underlying the ideas within a sentence:

All things being equal, Mary should easily win the race.

The storm having passed, the ball game resumed.

The police recovered eight of the paintings, *three of them badly damaged.*

The mob reached the palace gates, *the leader (being) a burly, red-haired sailor.*

[Occasionally an absolute phrase having a noun and a complement appears with the participle unexpressed.]

A special kind of phrase using *with* to introduce the absolute phrase can add subtle modifying and narrative coloring to a sentence:

With the band playing and the crowd applauding furiously, Jim Kinman was obviously uncomfortable as he stood on the stage.

They held the funeral on the second day, *with the town coming to look at Miss Emily beneath a mass of bought flowers, with the crayon face of her father musing profoundly above the bier....* (William Faulkner)

But we can't possibly have a garden party *with a dead man just outside the front gate.* (Katherine Mansfield)

The face was a curious mixture of sensibility, *with some elements very hard and others very pretty*—perhaps it was in the mouth. (Katherine Anne Porter)

Notice that the *with* in this construction is quite unlike *with* in its common prepositional use:

The acquitted woman left the courtroom *with her* lawyer.
[*with* used as a preposition]

The acquitted woman left the courtroom *with her head held high.*
[*with* used to introduce the absolute phrase]

SUMMARY OF PARTICIPIAL AND ABSOLUTE PHRASES

Participial Phrases

1. Forms: *studying, studied, having studied, being studied, having been studied, having been studying*

2. Function: to modify a noun or pronoun. Those that identify the noun or pronoun are restrictive and require no punctuation; others are nonrestrictive and are set off by commas.

3. Position: if restrictive, always following the word it modifies. Nonrestrictive phrases may stand after the noun, at the beginning of the sentence, and occasionally at the end of the sentence.

Absolute Phrases

1. Form: a noun or pronoun followed by a participle
   The crops having failed, Grandfather sold the farm.

2. Function: adds to the meaning of the entire sentence but does not modify a word or fill a noun slot

3. Position: at the beginning, in the interior, or at the end of the larger unit; usually set off by commas

4. Special structures:
   a. The participle *being* is sometimes unexpressed.

   Its chairman [being] a retired military person, the committee is well disciplined.

   b. The phrase sometimes begins with the word *with.*

   With its supply of ammunition exhausted, the garrison surrendered.

NAME _____   SCORE _____

Directions: The italicized unit in each sentence is either a participial phrase or an absolute phrase. If the unit is a participial phrase, copy in the space at the left the noun or pronoun that the phrase modifies. If the unit is an absolute phrase, leave the space blank. **Note:** Study also the other verbal phrases. Of the following sentences, six contain gerund phrases and seven contain infinitive phrases.

_____ 1. The candidate's advertising campaign relied heavily on television commercials *attacking the incumbent.*

_____ 2. Only those *wearing red or white jackets* will be admitted to the special cheering section.

_____ 3. *The noise of the sirens having shattered the quiet,* the campers all raced to safety up the side of the hill.

_____ 4. My sister has a serious case of lateral epichondylitis, *commonly known as tennis elbow.*

_____ 5. Forrest definitely needs a tutor, *the instructor having criticized him for making several errors in math.*

_____ 6. *Sensing that there was only one chance for escape,* John left the classroom before his name was called.

_____ 7. *The only other strong runner having dropped out of the race,* Juanita moved easily into the lead.

_____ 8. Without turning another page, she closed the book and walked away, *leaving the book on the table where it lay.*

_____ 9. My previous boss had carefully retained every memo and note *written to him by anyone in the company.*

_____ 10. *Having left his heavy coat back in the dorm,* Harry shivered as he walked to his first class.

_____ 11. *The evening news being exceptionally bleak,* we turned off the television and listened to music during dinner.

_____ 12. My brother, *being an avid baseball card collector,* pushed his way to the front of every autograph line.

_____ 13. Tell me why you, *knowing that such food is bad for your health,* continue to eat donuts and candy.

_____ 14. *My keys being locked inside my car,* I'm afraid I won't be on time for class this morning.

_____ 15. Anyone *having seen that precious little brown dog* is asked to call me as soon as possible.

_____ 16. A number of those books will be discarded, *most of them having simply worn out through constant use.*

_____ 17. Martha James, *once thought of as an up-and-coming defense attorney,* has taken a job as a prosecutor.

_____ 18. While running, Marie listens to a personal stereo, *with the strains of Beethoven wafting gently around her.*

_____ 19. *Looking enormously happy,* the monkey ate the banana he had stolen from his neighbor.

_____ 20. Anita, *no longer struggling with quantitative analysis,* seems very much at peace with the world.

_____ 21. Three police officers, *the tallest one scarcely able to fit through the door,* were standing in the hotel lobby.

_____ 22. By noon, *with the smoke still rising slowly from the ashes,* the investigators were hard at work.

_____ 23. A woman *covered with tattoos* began calling people into the carnival tent.

_____ 24. *Observed from a distance,* the prison looks like a college campus.

_____ 25. *Observing the prison from a distance,* one notices that it looks very much like a college campus.

_____ 26. The cleanup crew found several old pizza boxes, *two of them dating from last semester.*

_____ 27. The view down the valley is a little foggy, *the waterfall in the distance showering the area with mist.*

_____ 28. *Talking with the engineer for the first time,* I was impressed by his ability to simplify technical matters.

_____ 29. After searching for several hours, the soldiers found a second road *leading into the valley.*

_____ 30. Martha selected a second topic, *the teacher having told everyone to select one with ample source material.*

Exercise 12 — Participial and Absolute Phrases

Copyright © 2005 by Pearson Education, Inc.

NAME _____   SCORE _____

Directions: Each of the following sentences contains one participial phrase or one absolute phrase. Underline these phrases. If the phrase is a participial phrase, copy in the space at the left the noun or pronoun that phrase modifies. If the phrase is an absolute phrase, leave the space blank.

_____ 1. Having passed the bar exam, Marie began searching for a job with a small law firm.

_____ 2. With only one day remaining before vacation, I gave my important cases to a colleague.

_____ 3. All the people standing in line now must be registered before we start closing for the night.

_____ 4. The report containing all the important figures for this year will be available soon.

_____ 5. Several of us intend to go to the mountains next week, exams being over for this term.

_____ 6. The last of the glasses having been packed for shipment, we took all the boxes to the post office.

_____ 7. Everyone holding a ticket for tonight's game needs to read the policy on rain-outs.

_____ 8. My friend Lisa, her degree finally finished, is going to Europe this summer.

_____ 9. The arrival of the new computers stopped our work for today, giving us a much-needed break.

_____ 10. My replacement having just arrived, I think I will go home now.

_____ 11. Having found two good sources for her short paper, Tammy copied the articles and went out for a pizza.

_____ 12. The audience left the auditorium, laughing together at the speaker's closing story.

_____ 13. For Mike the term ended on a high note, two Bs and an A being the best grades he had ever made.

_____ 14. "Those of you needing rooms for the convention should sign up with Marcia now," said Alex.

_____ 15. Those books are old and tattered, their titles covered with green mold.

_____ 16. Running ahead of schedule on their project, the team members took a long lunch hour today.

_____ 17. The team having scored three touchdowns early, the coach put in the second-string players in the second half.

_____ 18. Encouraged by her success in calculus class, Tina considered registering for another math course.

_____ 19. At 6:00 P.M. the registrar closed the doors, all the classes for next term being filled.

_____ 20. Those boots ought to work well out on the trail, having a stout lug sole to prevent slipping.

_____ 21. Having already run four miles earlier, Melissa declined our invitation to run down to the river and back.

_____ 22. Interest rates being reasonably low now, prospects for buying a house are excellent.

_____ 23. Taking everything into account, I think that a pontoon boat is a great idea.

_____ 24. Totally captivated by the young children's singing and dancing, Jo spent a wonderful afternoon in the theater.

_____ 25. Mr. Johnson having been transferred to Cleveland, Ms. Amato is now handling all those accounts.

_____ 26. The school board, having convened at 1:00 P.M., finally adjourned at 8:30 P.M. last night.

_____ 27. Jenny's paper, with a large B written on the top of the first page, was returned yesterday afternoon.

_____ 28. Having overslept almost an hour, Max rushed into work late and missed an important meeting.

_____ 29. The chicken, having been in the smoker for several hours, looked and tasted delicious.

_____ 30. The last student having finished the exam, the teacher picked up the papers and left the room.

_____ 31. Finally finishing her exam, the last student handed in her paper and left the room.

_____ 32. With the jury deadlocked after six votes, the judge reluctantly declared a mistrial.

_____ 33. The sidewalk downtown being torn up, pedestrians were forced to walk in the busy street.

_____ 34. The President having signed the treaty, it was sent to the Senate for ratification.

_____ 35. The young boy walked aimlessly down the street, softly whistling a tune from the movie.

_____ 36. These interviews will be of interest to anyone thinking of a career in engineering.

_____ 37. Having picked up my tickets for the concert, I drove back to the dorm.

_____ 38. The youngest of the five children invested her money wisely, always living rather frugally.

_____ 39. The engineer, his shirt pockets stuffed with pencils and scraps of paper, worked feverishly on the calculations.

_____ 40. Never paying much attention to details, Beverly forgot to record three checks in her checkbook.

NAME _____ SCORE _____

Directions: In the first space at the left, write one of the following letters to identify the italicized verbal phrase:

G (gerund phrase)   I (infinitive phrase)

P (participial phrase)   A (absolute phrase)

In the second space, write one of the following abbreviations to identify the complement printed in heavy type within the phrase.

S.C. (subjective complement)   I.O. (indirect object)

D.O. (direct object)   O.C. (objective complement)

_____ 1. Aunt Lois and the interior designer discussed *painting the hallway*
_____   *a soft* **blue**.

_____ 2. *Having been appointed* **CEO** *only recently,* Ms. Wharton has not
_____   been able to make many changes yet.

_____ 3. The electrician, by failing *to find the frayed* **insulation**, might
_____   have caused a serious problem.

_____ 4. *Having several* **options** *for summer jobs,* Bill and Tom have still
_____   not decided what they will do.

_____ 5. *To get some* **information** *on the local job market,* the college
_____   conducted an extensive telephone survey.

_____ 6. No one who knows Marian would ever accuse her of *being* **unkind** *to*
_____   *another student.*

_____ 7. I'm indebted to you for *helping* **me** *when I fell behind in math class.*
_____

_____ 8. The carpenters began to pack up their tools, *the sky having become quite*
_____   **dark** *very suddenly.*

_____ 9. *After handing* **Barbara** *the small present,* her father stood beside her while
_____   she opened it.

_____ 10. You can probably get concert tickets by *calling the ticket* **office** *early in*
_____   *the morning.*

_____ 11. Sri Lanka, *formerly called* **Ceylon**, is located in the Indian Ocean.
_____

_____ 12. I always seem *to feel mentally* **exhausted** at the end of a hard tennis match.
_____

_____ 13. We had to send for a key, *Mark having locked the* **door** *accidentally as he left.*

_____

_____ 14. *Being the most experienced* **cashier,** William is often called on to help others
_____ correct their mistakes.

_____ 15. *My white shirt being extremely* **wrinkled,** I was forced to iron it before I wore
_____ it to work.

_____ 16. We were asked *to keep our valuables* **secure** by putting them in the hotel safe.

_____

_____ 17. Tom Ansley expects *to be elected* **Parks Commissioner** *in next*
_____ *month's election.*

_____ 18. How did we manage *to spend so much* **money** in such a short period of time?

_____

_____ 19. I made a small mistake at work yesterday—*turning off my* **computer** *before I*
_____ *saved the data.*

_____ 20. Despite her long explanation, Mary Ellen succeeded only in *making us*
_____ *more* **confused** *about the first problem on the test.*

_____ 21. We did not see *Mother give* **James** *that message.*

_____

_____ 22. *Having written two new* **songs,** the young musician is trying to sell them to
_____ a recording company.

_____ 23. The traffic jam cleared up a few minutes after five, *the wreckers having towed*
_____ *away the two* **cars.**

_____ 24. *The chess match having been declared a* **draw,** the two players agreed to
_____ play another match the following day.

_____ 25. *Giving* **me** *one more day to complete my paper* was a kind thing for
_____ Professor Larson to do.

_____ 26. "We are trying *to find another* **solution** *to that problem,*" said Mr. Lopez.

_____

_____ 27. *Finding the traffic jam almost* **impassible,** we turned off onto a side road.

_____

_____ 28. *With traffic proving to be an almost impossible* **mess,** we turned off onto
_____ a side road.

_____ 29. When we could find no way *to work our* **way** *through traffic,* we turned off
_____ onto a side road.

_____ 30. When *working our* **way** *through traffic* became quite difficult, we turned off
_____ on a side road.

Directions: Combine the two sentences in each item into a single sentence by converting the second sentence into a participial phrase or an absolute phrase.

1. We all sat down to dinner.
   The last guest had arrived.

   _____

2. The newly registered freshmen assembled in the auditorium.
   All were carrying their bright red registration packets.

   _____

3. Jenny sat down and opened the letter.
   A brief frown crossed her face.

   _____

4. The two men ran up the ramp into the stadium.
   They were trying desperately to make the kickoff.

   _____

5. The woman watched as her daughter left for college.
   She wiped away a few tears with her handkerchief.

   _____

6. I looked for days in the reference books.
   I was trying to find facts about my grandmother's family.

   _____

7. Thomas searched eagerly through the classified ads for a good used car.
   His present car had blown an engine.

   _____

8. Christina identified those actors immediately.
   She had watched the movie for the third time just last night.

   _____

9. All the phone lines at the ticket center were busy.
   Tickets for the popular concert had gone on sale at 9:00 A.M.

   _____

10. All the fans stood during the seventh-inning stretch.
    The announcer led them in "Take Me Out to the Ball Game."

    _____

Check Sheet

☐ Sentences, also known as *independent clauses,* can be joined to make writing more effective.

☐ Compound Sentences

☐ Two independent clauses joined by a comma and a coordinating conjunction (*and, but, or, nor, for, yet, so*) or by a semicolon create a compound sentence.

> The two men left work at noon, and the three women left at 12:30 P.M.
> The two men left work at noon; then the three women left at 12:30 P.M.

Punctuation note: Omitting the comma before the coordinating conjunction creates an error called a *run-on sentence;* omitting the coordinating conjunction creates an error called a *comma splice.*

☐ Each coordinating conjunction establishes a different relationship (time, cause, etc.) between the two clauses. Considerable care must be exercised to select the proper coordinating conjunction. The relationships between clauses joined with a semicolon are often established by using conjunctive adverbs such as *therefore* and *however.* Note that compound verbs—that is, a subject with two verbs—require no punctuation.

> John picked up the book and left the room.

☐ Complex Sentences

☐ Sentences formed by subordinating one clause and including it with a second sentence to form a complex sentence.

☐ Adverbial Clauses

☐ Adverbial clauses are word groups opened with subordinating conjunctions such as *when, since, after, although, if, unless, because,* and others. The clauses perform the same functions as one-word adverbs that modify verbs.

> The men left town early.
> After the rain stopped, the men left town.
> The men, after the rain stopped, left town.
> The men left town after the rain stopped.

The clause stands as an opening element, an interrupting element between subject and verb, or as the final element of a sentence.

Punctuation note: When an adverbial clause stands as the opening element of a sentence, it is joined to the main clause with a comma. That same clause, when

131

it stands between the subject and verb, it is set off with commas. The adverbial clause requires no punctuation when it stands as the final element of the sentence.

☐ Adjective or Relative Clauses

☐ Just as adjectives modify (change the reader's conception of) nouns,

> the red rose
> the changeable weather

clauses that begin with *who, whose, whom, which,* and *that* can also modify nouns. The words opening these clauses are called relative pronouns. Most adjective clauses stand immediately after the noun they modify; occasionally, a preposition or even a prepositional phrase intervenes between the noun and the modifying clause, but the position of the clause must clearly establish the relationship between the clause and the noun (called the *antecedent*) it modifies.

> The man *who won the award* will be here soon.
> The man *whose brilliant discovery* won the prize will soon be here.
> The man to *whom we will give the prize* will appear soon.
> The man *whom I pointed out* is the winner of the prize.
> The man of the hour, about *whom you have heard so much,* just walked into
> the room.

☐ Some adjective clauses identify the noun modified by the clause. All of the clauses in the examples above identify the noun. Such clauses, called *restrictive relative* or *adjective clauses,* are not set off with commas. Adjective clauses that modify but do not identify are called *nonrestrictive relatives* and *are* set off by commas.

> The person *who owns that car* should move it from my driveway.
> June Williams, who owns that car, should move it from my driveway.

☐ Remember certain distinctions in using *who, which,* and *that. Who* refers only to people; *which* refers only to things. *That* is used only in restrictive clauses, and there is a convention (though not a hard-and-fast rule) that *which* is never used to open a restrictive clause.

☐ The adverbs *when* and *where* are sometimes used as though they are relative pronouns. In sentences such as

> I carefully searched the place in which I had dropped my wallet.

we sometimes say

> I carefully searched the place where I had dropped my wallet.

In the same way, *when* can be used as a replacement for *in which.*

> Jan recalled the very minute when she met Tom.

☐ Noun Clauses

☐ In the same way that adjective clauses can replace one-word adjectives, word groups containing a subject-verb combination and a subordinating word can do the work of a noun. These structures, called *noun clauses,* can do whatever simple nouns can do in a sentence: They can be the subject, subjective complement, direct object, object of a preposition, and an appositive.

Whoever answered the phone (S.) asked *what we wanted from the store.* (D.O.)
The next question was *how we intended to pay for it.* (S.C.)
The person then gave the phone to *whoever was standing next to her.* (O.P.)
He objected to the fact *that we were taking so much time.* (Ap.)

The subordinating words can be conjunctions, adjectives, or adverbs.

Jill wonders *if* Mom and Dad are coming. (conjunction)
Jill wonders *when* they will arrive. (adverb)
Jill wonders *which* car they be driving. (adjective)
Jill wonders *what* they will do tomorrow. (pronoun)

☐ Gerunds, Infinitives, and Verbal Phrases

☐ Word groups that employ a form of a verb and associated words can be used as noun replacements and perform most of the functions that ordinary nouns perform in a sentence.

☐ Gerunds Phrases

☐ Gerunds are formed by adding *-ing* to a verb's base form or to an auxiliary.

flying, having flown, having been flown

☐ Gerunds can stand alone in sentences: *Running* is good exercise. Barb enjoys *running.*

☐ Gerunds can also be joined with other words to create gerund phrases.

Running three miles can be exhausting.
Maria enjoys *operating that video camera.*

These phrases can serve any purpose in a sentence that a simple noun serves: subject, subjective complement, direct object, object of preposition.

☐ Infinitive Phrases

☐ An infinitive is a verbal formed from the base of the verb and the word *to.* Infinitives change tense and voice by adding auxiliaries. Modifiers and complements are added to infinitives to create infinitive phrases. Infinitives and infinitive phrases serve as nouns, adjectives, and adverbs.

To find that source was a difficult task. (subject)
It was a difficult task *to find that source.* (delayed subject)
My next step is *to find that source.* (subjective complement)
Jill wanted desperately *to find that source.* (direct object)
My plan *to find that source* did not work. (adjective)
To find that source, you should check on the Internet. (adverb)

☐ Infinitive phrases sometimes contain their own subjects.

> The instructor asked *Mary to find that source.*

☐ Infinitive phrases can open with *for* and the subject of the infinitive.

> *For us to find that source* was an almost impossible task.

☐ Infinitive phrases without the word *to* can serve as the direct object of verbs such as *let, help, make, see, hear,* and *watch.*

> Anne let *Mary find that source first.*

☐ Infinitive phrases without *to* can serve as the object of a preposition such as *except, but,* and *besides.*

> There is nothing left for me to do *but find that source.*

☐ Participial Phrases

☐ A participle is a verbal adjective formed by adding *-ing* or *-ed* to the base of a verb or to an auxiliary. Participles can be used as simple adjectives.

> The *exhausted* man faced another *exhausting* climb.

☐ Participles can be joined by other words to form a participial phrase that modifies a noun.

> *Exhausted from the first long climb,* the girl stopped to rest on a ledge.
> *Exhausting every ounce of energy,* the girl finally reached the summit.

☐ Participial phrases, like adjective clauses, can be either restrictive or nonrestrictive. Usually, restrictive phrases follow the noun being modified.

> The girl just reaching the summit is my sister.

The nonrestrictive phrase can appear in three positions in the sentence, but it must always be clearly related to the noun it modifies.

> *Having reached the summit at last,* the girl raised her hands in triumph.
> The girl, *having reached the summit at last,* raised her hands in triumph.
> The girl raised her hands in triumph, *having reached the summit at last.*

Note that, in the third version, no confusion is created by moving the phrase to the end of the sentence because the closest noun cannot sensibly be modified by the phrase. In another sentence,

> The girl shook hands with Jim, having reached the summit at last.

it is possible to make the phrase modify the word *Jim,* so the phrase must not be moved to the end of the sentence if the phrase modifies the word *girl.*

☐ Absolute Phrases

☐ Phrases composed of a noun plus a participle sometimes modify the sentence as a whole without being closely related to any noun in the rest of the sentence. In fact, the phrase should not include a noun that appears in the rest of the sentence. The absolute phrase, although it is not a sentence, is in that one sense independent of the rest of the sentence.

> *The job having been completed,* the workers left for the day.
> The workers left for the day, *the job having been completed.*

☐ An absolute phrase can be opened by the word *with.*

> *With the hard part of the work already finished,* the workers began to relax.

3 Sentence Building

Lessons, Practice Sheets, and Exercises

Lesson 13 | *Completeness: Dealing with Sentence Fragments*

To be complete, a sentence must

1. Contain a subject and a verb.
2. Be able to stand alone as an independent unit.

A group of words without both a subject and a verb cannot be a complete sentence. A group of words containing both a subject and a verb but opening with a subordinating conjunction cannot be a complete sentence. The subordinating conjunction makes the clause dependent instead of independent.

SENTENCE FRAGMENTS

A group of words that does not have a subject and a verb and cannot stand alone is called an incomplete sentence, or **sentence fragment.** Sometimes a sentence fragment is punctuated as if it were a sentence. This mistake of punctuation is called a **period fault.** Sentence fragments almost always fit one of the following patterns:

1. A subordinate clause standing as a sentence. (But remember that *and, but, or, nor, for, yet,* and *so* do not subordinate. A clause introduced by one of these words may stand as a sentence.)

    Fragments: The clerk finally let us see the contract. *Although she clearly hated to reveal its contents.*

    Bob tried to start the old lawn mower. *Which never seemed to work properly for him.*

2. A verbal phrase punctuated as a sentence:

    Fragments: The delegates agreed on a compromise wage scale. *Realizing that the strike could not go on indefinitely.*

    Nell had ordered her tickets a month ago. *To be sure of getting good seats.*

3. A noun followed by a phrase or a subordinate clause but lacking a main verb:

Fragments: The committee should include Ms. Jones. *A tireless worker with many constructive ideas.*

The mayor asked Bentley to take the job. *Bentley being the only available person with field experience.*

The coach thinks our prospects are good. *A chance, perhaps, to wln back the conference championship.*

Junior will require a special kind of tutor. *Someone who will realize how sensitive the child really is.*

You should learn to avoid using fragments in your writing. Usually a close reading of anything you have written will reveal sentence fragments so that you can correct them. You can improve your skill at identifying fragments by using the following strategy: When you check what you have written, read the sentences in a paragraph in reverse order. Start with your last sentence and work back to your first. This process, which breaks the tie between a fragment and the sentence that it depends on, makes any grammatically incomplete sentence stand out.

CORRECTING SENTENCE FRAGMENTS

When you have discovered a fragment in your writing, any one of several possible corrections is easy to make.

- You can attach the fragment to the preceding sentence by doing away with the fragment's capital letter and supplying the right punctuation.
- You can change the fragment to a subordinate clause and attach it to the appropriate main clause by means of the right connective.
- You can change the fragment to an independent clause by supplying a subject or a verb or both.
- You can change the fragment to an appositive or some other appropriate phrase.

Consider the following corrected sentences:

The clerk finally let us see the contract, *although she clearly hated to reveal its contents.*
Bob tried to start the old lawn mower, *which never seemed to work properly for him.*
The delegates agreed on a compromise wage scale *because they realized that the strike could not go on indefinitely.*
To be sure of getting good seats, Nell had ordered her tickets a month ago.
The committee should include Ms. Jones, *a tireless worker with many constructive ideas.*
The mayor asked Bentley to take the job, *Bentley being the only available person with field experience.*
The coach thinks our prospects are good; *we have a chance, perhaps, to win back the league championship.*
Junior will require a special kind of tutor. *He or she must be someone who will realize how sensitive the child really is.*

There are a few types of word groups that are not considered fragments. Although they lack a complete subject-verb combination, these types of word groups are accepted as legitimate language patterns. They are

1. **Commands:** in which the subject *you* is understood:

    > Please be seated. Put your name on a slip of paper. Pass the papers to the left aisle.
    > [See Lesson 21, Supplement.]

2. **Exclamations:**

    > What excitement! Only two minutes to go! Good Heavens, not a fumble? How terrible!

3. **Bits of dialogue:**

    > "New car?" she asked. "Had it long?"
    > "Picked it up last week," he replied.

4. **Occasional transitions between units of thought:**

    > On with the story.
    > And now to conclude.

You have very likely observed in your reading that experienced writers sometimes use sentence fragments, especially in narrative and descriptive writing. But these writers are skilled workers who know how to use fragments to achieve particular stylistic effects. You should first master the fundamental forms of the sentence. Once you have learned to write clear, correct sentences without faltering, there will be plenty of time for experimenting.

NAME _____ SCORE _____

Directions: Study the following word groups for completeness. In the space at the left, write **S** if the word group is a grammatically complete sentence, **F** if the word group is a fragment.

_____ 1. Joe's garage always cluttered and smelling like spilled oil.

_____ 2. Flying low over the small town and frightening all the animals in the nearby countryside.

_____ 3. Flying low over the small town and frightening all the animals in the nearby countryside was one of Marcie's chief delights as a pilot.

_____ 4. Ever since Janie began to work on her novel and keep herself isolated from the rest of us.

_____ 5. Ever since, Janie began to work on her novel and keep herself isolated from the rest of us.

_____ 6. Please don't leave the lights on when you leave the building.

_____ 7. Don't leave the lights on when you leave the building.

_____ 8. Leaving the lights on when you leave the building increases our electric bill unnecessarily.

_____ 9. Leaving the lights on when you leave the building and increasing our electric bill unnecessarily.

_____ 10. Excited by the prospect of attending the playoff game, we closed up shop and left early for the ballpark.

_____ 11. The exciting prospect of closing up shop early and attending the playoff game.

_____ 12. His next car, he promised himself, would be fast, exciting, and fun to drive.

_____ 13. His next car, he promised himself, fast, exciting, and fun to drive.

_____ 14. His next car, which would, he promised himself, be fast, exciting, and fun to drive.

_____ 15. Buy yourself a new car, one that is fast, exciting, and fun to drive.

_____ 16. "A new car? How do you like it?" asked his friend.

_____ 17. "Great! Fast as lightning! Want to drive it?" he exclaimed.

_____ 18. The quarterback, usually very skilled, but who today played very poorly.

_____ 19. The quarterback is usually very skilled, but today he played very poorly.

_____ 20. We need someone who is very skilled and plays very consistently.

_____ 21. That is a man who never seems to lose his focus on the goals of the organization.

_____ 22. A man who never seems to lose his focus on the goals of the organization.

_____ 23. The goals of the organization never seem to be far from that man's mind.

_____ 24. That man, however, has never been known to take a vacation.

_____ 25. He has burning ambition, which seems to drive him at all times.

_____ 26. A man of burning ambition, which seems to drive him at all times.

_____ 27. A man whose burning ambition seems to drive him at all times.

_____ 28. It is important, on occasion, to control one's ambition.

_____ 29. A balanced life, one which allows a focus on work and other areas of life.

_____ 30. We should strive for a balanced life, one that allows a focus on work and other areas of life.

NAME _____   SCORE _____

Directions: Each numbered unit consists of a sentence followed by a fragment. Be prepared to discuss in class the structuring of the fragments. In the space provided, rewrite enough of the material to show how you would correct the error, by either attaching the fragment to the sentence or recasting the fragment so that it becomes a complete sentence.

1. Many people do not enjoy camping because of its many inconveniences. Especially because of cold and rain they might encounter on hikes.

_____

2. These days, many people are trying to improve their physical fitness. Running, jogging, or exercising in some way to reduce weight.

_____

3. My sister loves animals and tries to bring home every stray dog she sees. Although she lives with two other girls in a small apartment.

_____

4. We did not try to locate you in the airport. Since we thought your plane had already left.

_____

5. Mr. Jones is a dedicated collector of old jazz recordings. Especially those of Benny Goodman, who is, he says, the greatest clarinetist who ever lived.

_____

6. He was a very lonely young man, making few friends at the college. Always trying to avoid meeting new people.

_____

7. My brother tripped over a root and broke his ankle. Running through the woods chasing his hound, which seemed to move farther away all the time.

_____

8. Ms. Detweiler is taking my qualitative analysis class. A fine young woman, brilliant in mathematics and science.

_____

9. We all need to find ways of reducing tension. Fishing, napping, or developing an interest in some hobby that will take our minds off the day's troubles.

_____

10. My friends advise me against entering the field of law. A profession greatly overcrowded, filled with people who make only a scant living in their practices.

   _____

11. All the men stopped their work early today. Discouraged by the problems they had encountered.

   _____

12. Mr. Jones is one of the leading citizens of Mill City. A man who possesses great business skill and financial acumen.

   _____

13. Not very many people like Mary. Because she has a bad temper and a vicious tongue.

   _____

14. Many people are eating less beef these days to avoid cholesterol. Even though they don't really enjoy chicken and tuna fish.

   _____

15. We do not know when John will return from school this year. Probably not till the end of the second term.

   _____

16. Under the circumstances we had only two options. Neither of them very good.

   _____

17. We looked down from the cliff into a valley with two long rivers. One of them running into a broad, shallow lake.

   _____

18. The Smiths moved into the house across the street from us. That house being the only one on the block big enough to hold six kids and three big dogs.

   _____

19. John is hoping to make straight A's the rest of the term so that he can improve his D– average. Which doesn't seem like a very good possibility.

   _____

20. Hard work and long hours offer many rewards for the college student. The biggest one being a heavy case of fatigue.

   _____

Exercise 13A   *Correcting Sentence Fragments*

NAME _____   SCORE _____

Directions: Each numbered unit consists of a sentence plus a fragment. In the space provided, rewrite enough of the material to show how you would correct the error either by attaching the fragment, properly punctuated, to the sentence, or recasting the fragment so that it becomes a complete sentence.

1. Morgan began a new program for improving his grades. Including regular study sessions, library work, and some tutoring in one difficult class.

   _____

2. Maria spends every night reading romance novels. Although her friends want her to go out with them.

   _____

3. The men definitely worked hard in that last hour. Thinking the whole time that it was necessary to finish the job before they left.

   _____

4. Even the most dedicated students need some recreation. Perhaps taking up the guitar or listening to music.

   _____

5. Mr. Nash's son is learning to program computers. A bright, inquisitive boy of ten who is quite skilled for his age.

   _____

6. Martha had soon made several new friends. Spending all her time outside of class in the Student Union or the Recreation Center.

   _____

7. My sister Ella has a large collection of recordings by great blues singers. Including all the records of the great Muddy Waters.

   _____

8. Jason read the fine print on the contract for almost two hours. Giving him a pounding headache.

   _____

9. Martha is trying to raise her GPA to 3.1. A possibility if she makes all A's this term.

   _____

145

10. We have a full tank of gas and $20 each. Which is enough for us to get safely home for the weekend.

11. Paul has postponed graduation for one more term. Hoping to be here for one more football season.

12. We have ordered several additional pieces of equipment. A new lathe, for example, and a fine new milling machine.

13. The company continues the search for a new marketing director. A search that has been going on for five months.

14. The football team has signed a blue-chip prospect at quarterback. Thought by some to be a future Heisman Trophy winner.

15. The dean offered Barbara two possible strategies. Improving her grades or finding a job after this semester.

16. The college makes great efforts to help students with academic difficulties. Providing tutors and offering review classes before exams.

17. The coach has scheduled cross-country practice at 5:00 A.M. Temperatures in midafternoon often reaching 100 degrees at this time of year.

18. That novel has been read by most people on campus. A suspense thriller that frightens almost everyone who reads it.

19. We need to paint the house in the near future. But not until after the winter storms.

20. My advisor suggested that I take an introductory computer course. A useful class and one that might lead me to study computer science.

Proper arrangement of the parts of your sentence will help make your meaning clear. Ordinarily the main parts—the subjects, the verbs, the complements—cause no problems. Modifying words and phrases and subordinate clauses can be problematic if they are not located carefully. Here we consider five possible trouble spots in the placing of modifiers.

1. Although we sometimes use a rather loose placement for some common adverbs, such as *only, nearly, almost,* and *hardly,* we can write precise sentences only when such adverbs are placed close to the words they modify:

Loose:	This will *only* take five minutes.
	Jill *nearly* saw 90 movies last year.
Better:	This will take *only* five minutes.
	Jill saw *nearly* 90 movies last year.

2. Words and phrases that attach themselves to the wrong word can confuse the reader:

Loose:	I wish every person in this class could know the man I'm going to talk about *personally.*
Better:	I wish every person in this class could know *personally* the man I'm going to talk about.
Loose:	It was reported that the Italian premier had died *on the 8 o'clock newscast.*
Better:	*On the 8 o'clock newscast,* it was reported that the Italian premier had died.
Loose:	The police department will be notified of all reported obscene phone calls *by the telephone company.*
Better:	The police department will be notified *by the telephone company* of all reported obscene phone calls.

3. The **squinting modifier** is one that is placed between two units, either of which it could modify:

Loose:	Students who can already type *normally* are put into an advanced class.
Better:	Students who can already type are *normally* put into an advanced class.
Loose:	He said *after the dinner* some color slides would be shown.
Better:	He said some color slides would be shown *after the dinner.*

4. The **split infinitive** results from the placing of an adverbial modifier between the *to* and the verb stem of an infinitive. Although greatly overemphasized by some as an error, the split infinitive, particularly with a modifier consisting of more than one word, is usually avoided by careful writers:

Loose:	Dad likes to *once in a while* plan and cook a dinner.
Better:	*Once in a while,* Dad likes to plan and cook a dinner.

147

5. The conjunctions *both . . . and, not only . . . but also, either . . . or,* and *neither . . . nor* are used in pairs and are called **correlatives.** Because they point out the equal relationship between units, they should be placed immediately before the parallel units that they connect:

Loose:	We sent invitations *both* to Webster *and* Jenkins.
Better:	We sent invitations to *both* Webster *and* Jenkins.
	[The parallel words are *Webster* and *Jenkins.*]
Loose:	This woman *not only* can get along with young people *but also* with their parents.
Better:	This woman can get along *not only* with young people *but also* with their parents.
Loose:	You must *either* promise me that you will come *or* send a substitute.
Better:	You must promise me that you will *either* come *or* send a substitute.

DANGLING MODIFIERS

The relationship between a word being modified and the modifying phrase should be clear. Any modifying phrase that does not attach itself clearly to the word it is supposed to modify is called a **dangling modifier.** A dangling modifier can create a confusing sentence. Participial phrases are especially apt to float free in a sentence.

> *Stepping into the boat,* my camera fell into the water.

This sentence contains a participial phrase and a main clause, but the phrase does not actually modify any word in the main clause. The sentence is made up of two thoughts that can be expressed as

> I stepped into the boat.
> My camera fell into the water.

We can make the two sentences into a compound sentence:

> I stepped into the boat, and my camera fell into the water.

Or we can make the first clause an introductory adverbial element:

> As I stepped into the boat, my camera fell into the water.

But we cannot convert the first sentence into a participial phrase because the only noun the phrase could modify is *camera,* and the camera did not step into the boat. The sentence, if read literally, becomes nonsense. We could rework the sentence by changing the subject of the second clause in a way that allows the participial phrase to modify the new subject:

> Stepping into the boat, I dropped my camera into the water.

Because the person who dropped the camera and the person who is stepping into the boat are the same, *I,* the sentence is now correct.

Gerund Phrases and Infinitive Phrases

Gerund phrases and infinitive phrases can also cause problems when they are randomly inserted into sentences:

> *After studying all morning,* a nap was Mary's only goal for the afternoon.

The intended meaning of the sentence is clear, but the literal meaning is that the nap studied all morning; the phrase attaches itself to the first available noun—in this case, a noun that produces a nonsense statement.

> *To qualify for that job,* good typing skills are a necessity.

Again, the intended meaning is clear, but the literal meaning is nonsense. Good typing skills are not qualifying for that job; a person with good typing skills is qualifying for that job. Remember the phrase that contains the verbal must have a word to refer to, and that word must be close enough to the phrase so that the reader does not associate the phrase with the wrong word.

CORRECTING DANGLERS

The easiest way to correct a dangler is to supply the word that the phrase should modify and to place the phrase next to that word. Another way is to change the dangling phrase to a subordinate clause with a subject and verb expressed.

1. Participial phrase at the beginning of a sentence

Dangler:	*Burned to a cinder,* I could not eat the toast. [The sentence sounds as if I were burned to a cinder. The word that the dangler should modify is *toast,* but this word is too far from the phrase immediately associated with it.]
Better:	Burned to a cinder, the toast could not be eaten. I could not eat the toast because it was burned to a cinder.

2. Gerund following a preposition

Dangler:	Before *making a final decision,* other cars should be driven. [Are the other cars making a final decision? That is not what is meant, and yet that is what the sentence states.]
	On graduating from high school, my father let me work in his office. [The sentence says that your father let you work in his office when he, not you, graduated from high school.]
	Since *breaking my leg,* my neighbors have helped with my farm chores. [A logical sentence only if the neighbors broke your leg.]
Better:	Before making a final decision, drive other cars. Before you make a final decision, you should drive other cars.
	On graduating from high school, I went to work in my father's office. After I had graduated from high school, my father let me work in his office.

Since breaking my leg, I have been helped with my farm chores by my neighbors.

My neighbors have helped with my farm chores since I broke my leg.

3. Elliptical "time" clause (see Lesson 8), usually introduced by *when* or *while*

Dangler: *When ten years old,* my father sold the farm and moved to Dallas.

While weeding my vegetable garden, a garter snake startled me.

[The understood subject of the adverb clause is different from the subject of the main clause, but the reader assumes that both clauses have the same subject. The result is a ridiculous meaning that the writer never intended.]

Better: When ten years old, I moved to Dallas after my father sold the farm.

When I was ten years old, my father sold the farm and we moved to Dallas.

While weeding my vegetable garden, I was startled by a garter snake.

While I was weeding my vegetable garden, a garter snake startled me.

4. Introductory infinitive phrase naming a specific action

Dangler: *To enter the contest,* a box top must be sent with your slogan.

[A *box top* is not entering the contest. To avoid this problem, be sure that the word that the phrase attaches to names the logical doer of that action.]

Better: To enter the contest, you must send a box top with your slogan.

If you want to enter the contest, a box top must be sent with your slogan.

When you enter the contest, send a box top with your slogan.

NAME _____ SCORE _____

Directions: From each of the following pairs of sentences select the one that is clearer and write its letter in the space at the left. Be prepared to justify your choice.

_____ 1. a. We have only a few minutes left before the plane leaves.
　　　　　　 b. We only have a few minutes left before the plane leaves.

_____ 2. a. She must either promise us that she will send the book soon or that she will buy us another copy.
　　　　　　 b. She must promise us that she will send the book soon or that she will buy us another copy.

_____ 3. a. Last month I nearly spent $250 repairing my car.
　　　　　　 b. Last month I spent nearly $250 repairing my car.

_____ 4. a. When Marge caught sight of him, Jim turned quickly and ran down the street.
　　　　　　 b. Jim turned quickly when Marge caught sight of him and ran down the street.

_____ 5. a. The music at the concert not only was loud but also monotonous.
　　　　　　 b. The music at the concert was not only loud but also monotonous.

_____ 6. a. Either you must arrive on time for the test or you will not be allowed to take it.
　　　　　　 b. You must either arrive on time for the test or you will not be allowed to take it.

_____ 7. a. For six months Jill has been doing aerobics every day to lose weight.
　　　　　　 b. Jill has been doing aerobics every day to lose weight for six months.

_____ 8. a. It seems that my teammates were not all prepared to face a pitcher with a great curve ball.
　　　　　　 b. It seems that not all my teammates were prepared to face a pitcher with a great curve ball.

_____ 9. a. I had only been asleep for a few minutes when my boss called to tell me to come to work.
　　　　　　 b. I had been asleep for only a few minutes when my boss called to tell me to come to work.

_____ 10. a. Growing your own tomatoes often is more expensive than buying them at the store.
　　　　　　 b. Growing your own tomatoes is often more expensive than buying them at the store.

Directions: In the space at the left, write either **A** or **B** to indicate the logical placement of the modifier in the parentheses.

_____ 1. *(either)* To get into Professor Windham's class, **A** you must **B** enroll very early or get a special permit to enroll.

_____ 2. *(once a week)* As part of her internship, Beth had to **A** work at the day care center **B**.

_____ 3. *(for a long time)* The woman who missed that last bus **A** stood in the rain **B**.

_____ 4. *(only)* The sale on men's suits will **A** last **B** a few days longer.

_____ 5. *(with high hopes)* The climbing team set out **A** for the top of the mountain **B**.

_____ 6. *(not only)* "I'm **A** happy to report that we have **B** reached our sales quota for the month but also set a new record for the quarter," said Mr. Conway.

_____ 7. *(ordinarily)* People who have been playing tennis **A** are **B** assigned to the intermediate class.

_____ 8. *(on her day off)* Fran was accustomed to **A** go the beach **B**.

_____ 9. *(just)* Dr. Fonseca has **A** been practicing in Colorado for **B** three months.

_____ 10. *(while the boss was out of the office)* **A** We amused ourselves **B** playing computer games.

_____ 11. *(almost)* In the last five pages of her paper Marge **A** discovered **B** ten typographical errors.

_____ 12. *(often)* Making wisecracks in class **A** is **B** a way of hiding insecurities.

_____ 13. *(from the local police)* I heard **A** that several cars had been stolen **B** last week.

_____ 14. *(not all)* The reporter said that **A** the delegates were **B** convinced that Watson would make the best candidate.

_____ 15. *(when the students became drowsy)* **A** The teacher would tell about how he had been a fighter pilot **B** in the War in the Gulf.

Exercise 14   *Misplaced Modifiers*

NAME _____   SCORE _____

Directions: In each of the following sentences is a poorly positioned word or phrase. Rewrite each sentence.

1. Either you need to deposit your check or cash it before September 30.

   _____

   _____

2. We neither enjoyed the book or the movie.

   _____

   _____

3. Her program of study only contains one laboratory science course.

   _____

   _____

4. Everyone attending that meeting was urged to complain to the city council on our campus.

   _____

   _____

5. My grandmother seems to, no matter the circumstances, remain cheerful.

   _____

   _____

6. Those club members not only were interested but also helpful.

   _____

   _____

7. The movie star was discovered while eating a hamburger in a Burger King by a talent scout.

   _____

   _____

8. My parents only made a few dollars profit on the sale of their house.

   _____

   _____

9. Jim should not watch television, for watching television often gives him a headache.

   _____

   _____

10. Mr. Grammas liked to secretly and generously support his alma mater's football team.

   _____

   _____

Directions: In the space at the left, write **A** or **B** to indicate the logical placing of the italicized modifier with the parentheses.

_____ 1. *(with a smile on her face)* **A** The delighted child told her mother about the new doll **B**.

_____ 2. *(not)* We know that **A** all our members will **B** get involved in the fund drive.

_____ 3. *(from the crowd)* Smith's arrival at home plate brought forth **A** loud boos **B**.

_____ 4. *(diligently)* Janet's intention is to **A** work **B** on her law degree for the next three years.

_____ 5. *(not only)* Learning to play bridge will **A** give you **B** an interesting hobby but also allow you to make new friends.

_____ 6. *(not only)* Learning to play bridge **A** will give you **B** a new hobby but also new friends.

_____ 7. *(every morning)* Jill tries to check **A** the Dow Jones Average and the prices of her stocks **B**.

_____ 8. *(as an assignment for history class)* **A** I studied two historical novels written in the eighteenth century **B**.

_____ 9. *(nearly)* Yesterday my little brother **A** fell **B** ten feet from the roof of our garage.

_____ 10. *(after several telephone calls)* **A** The store agreed to **B** credit my account for the shirts mistakenly charged last month.

_____ 11. *(not only)* On the first day of class Jim **A** had to buy **B** several expensive text-books but also a new dictionary.

_____ 12. *(not only)* On the first day of class Jim **A** had **B** to buy several expensive text-books but also to locate his new dictionary.

_____ 13. *(after taking a short nap)* **A** Jim was rested enough to mow the lawn **B**.

_____ 14. *(eagerly)* The woman who had won the prize **A** walked **B** to the front of the auditorium to receive it.

_____ 15. *(only)* We should have known that a chance to go to Australia probably **A** comes **B** once in a lifetime.

NAME _____ SCORE _____

Directions: One sentence of each pair contains a dangling modifier. Underline the dangling modifier. In the space at the left write the letter that identifies the correct sentence.

_____ 1. a. Being the end of the race, my legs were cramped and tired.
             b. This being the end of the race, my legs were cramped and tired.

_____ 2. a. While walking down the street, a red car ran across the curb and hit a fire plug.
             b. While we were walking down the street, a red car crossed the curb and hit a fire plug.

_____ 3. a. Trimmed with a beautiful white lace, Nancy's gown was admired by all the guests.
             b. Trimmed with a beautiful white lace, all the guests admired Nancy's gown.

_____ 4. a. When he was only six, my Aunt Barbara taught my little brother the multiplication tables.
             b. When only six, my Aunt Barbara taught my little brother the multiplication tables.

_____ 5. a. Walking down through that beautiful valley, tall, stately white pine trees were seen on both sides of the trail.
             b. Walking down through that beautiful valley, we saw tall, stately white pine trees on both sides of the trail.

_____ 6. a. Since spraining my ankle, my sister has been grooming the horses every morning.
             b. Since I sprained my ankle, my sister has been grooming the horses every morning.

_____ 7. a. Before anyone can be made a partner in that firm, approval of all the partners is needed.
             b. To be made a partner in that firm, approval of all the partners is needed.

_____ 8. a. In making a choice of careers, it would be a good idea to check on the expected number of job opening for the next ten years.
             b. In making a choice of careers, you should check on the number of expected job openings for the next ten years.

_____ 9. a. To be sure of a good finish on that tabletop, work in a clean, dry place.
             b. To be sure of a good finish on that tabletop, the work should be done in a clean, dry place.

_____ 10. a. While flying back from Japan, Justin lost his camera and three lenses.
             b. While flying back from Japan, Justin's camera and three lenses were lost.

_____ 11. a. When I called Martha yesterday, we decided to go to the movies Friday night.
          b. Calling Martha yesterday, we decided to go to the movies Friday night.

_____ 12. a. Observing that, after covering the pan, the eggs cook much more quickly.
          b. Observe that, after you cover the pan, the eggs cook much more quickly.

_____ 13. a. While living in Alaska, Richard often received photographs of sandy beaches from his friends.
          b. While living in Alaska, Richard's friends often sent him photographs of sandy beaches.

_____ 14. a. To order those fabulous knives you must send twenty dollars in check or money order to the distributor.
          b. To order those fabulous knives, twenty dollars in check or money order must be sent to the distributor.

_____ 15. a. While riding in the front seat beside me, my dog's leash got caught in the power window.
          b. While she was riding in the front seat beside me, my dog's leash got caught in the power window.

_____ 16. a. After waiting in line for twenty minutes, my luggage was checked very quickly by the customs inspector.
          b. After I waited in line for twenty minutes, my luggage was checked very quickly by the customs inspector.

_____ 17. a. Encouraged by the early polls in her district, a full-scale campaign was launched by the novice politician.
          b. Encouraged by the early polls in her district, the novice politician launched a full-scale campaign.

_____ 18. a. Having finished painting the kitchen, Kay's mother asked us to continue into the hallway.
          b. After we finished painting the kitchen, Kay's mother asked us to continue into the hallway.

_____ 19. a. Mark's foot slipped when pulling the board out of the pile of lumber.
          b. Mark's foot slipped when he pulled the board out of the pile of lumber.

_____ 20. a. Working every day for two weeks, Will's research paper came along very nicely.
          b. Because he worked every day for two weeks, Will's research paper came along very nicely.

Exercise 14A   *Dangling Modifiers*

NAME _____   SCORE _____

Directions: Rewrite each of the following sentences twice:
    a. Change the dangling modifier to a complete clause with subject and verb.
    b. Retain the phrase but begin the clause with a word that it can logically modify.

1. Having worked the first equation incorrectly, the rest of Jim's work on that problem was also incorrect.
    a. _____
       _____
    b. _____
       _____

2. After working in the fields on a hot day, a swim in the cold creek is very refreshing.
    a. _____
       _____
    b. _____
       _____

3. To find your way down that trail at night, a good flashlight is necessary.
    a. _____
       _____
    b. _____
       _____

4. When almost finished with the survey, the computer lost all our data.
    a. _____
       _____
    b. _____
       _____

5. Having practiced that formation every day for a month, it seemed easy to the members of the band.
    a. _____
       _____
    b. _____
       _____

6. Continuing down the road, tall, beautiful redwood trees rose on both sides of us.

   a. _____

   _____

   b. _____

   _____

7. Upon reading the letter, Karen's eyes filled with tears.

   a. _____

   _____

   b. _____

   _____

8. Exhausted by the long climb, the hot meal and the rest at the summit were appreciated by the hikers.

   a. _____

   _____

   b. _____

   _____

9. While carrying an armload of firewood, a small garter snake frightened my sister.

   a. _____

   _____

   b. _____

   _____

10. To receive the rebate, that coupon must be mailed to the factory.

    a. _____

    _____

    b. _____

    _____

Beginning writers sometimes string together too many short sentences, or they tie clauses together with conjunctions—*and, but, or*—that fail to establish precise relations between the clauses.

Poor:	Sally usually attends each concert. She missed this one. She went to the airport to meet her cousin Ellen. Ellen was arriving from Atlanta.
	I rode around town for three days, but I couldn't find a place to stay, and then I located this apartment, and so I am comfortable.

If you use the methods of creating and combining sentences that we have studied, you will make your writing more precise, more economical, and more meaningful:

Improved:	Although Sally usually attends each concert, she missed this one because she went to the airport to meet her cousin Ellen, who was arriving from Atlanta.
	After riding around town for three days without finding a place to stay, I finally located this apartment, where I am comfortable.

Get into the habit of trying different methods of subordinating material. Notice in the following sentences how an idea can be expressed in a variety of ways:

Two Sentences:	The small car was inexpensive to drive. It had only four cylinders.
Compound Verb:	The small car had only four cylinders and was inexpensive to drive.
Compound Sentence:	The small car was inexpensive to drive, for it had only four cylinders.
Adverbial Clause:	Because the small car had only four cylinders, it was inexpensive to drive.
Adjective Clause:	The small car, which had only four cylinders, was inexpensive to drive.
Participial Phrase:	The small car, having only four cylinders, was inexpensive to drive.
	Having only four cylinders, the small car was inexpensive to drive.
	The small car was inexpensive to drive, having only four cylinders.
Absolute Phrase:	The small car having only four cylinders, it was inexpensive to drive.
Prepositional Phrase:	The small car with only four cylinders was inexpensive to drive.
Appositive:	The small car, a four-cylinder model, was inexpensive to drive.
Adjective Modifier:	The small four-cylinder car was inexpensive to drive.

The use of subordination produces more than a pleasing sound in writing. It makes a crucial contribution to meaning by eliminating uncertainty about what is most important in a message. Consider the following string of simple sentences:

The management and union representatives announced an agreement. A strike had been threatened but was averted. The employees of Grantex Company reported for work today. They were relieved.

There is no way of knowing from these sentences which fact is most significant: The agreement? The avoidance of a strike? The workers' reporting for work? Their relief? Rewritten with proper subordination, the news reveals what the writer believes is most significant:

> The relieved employees of Grantex Company reported for work today after the management and union representatives announced an agreement that averted a threatened strike.

The only independent clause in the sentence concerns the workers' return to work. That is the important message. A writer more interested in strikes and their effect on the general economy might report the event thus:

> The threatened strike was averted at Grantex Company when the management and union representatives announced an agreement, after which the relieved employees reported for work today.

A NOTE ON SENTENCE VARIETY

Preceding lessons have demonstrated how subordinate clauses and phrases, by compressing material, help the writer avoid tiresome strings of independent clauses. You have also seen that certain subordinate units—adverbial clauses and participial phrases in particular—can be put in several places within the sentence, thus helping prevent monotony in your sentences.

Another unit useful for achieving compression and variety is the appositive. (See Lesson 10.) As noun renamers, appositives closely resemble—they might be called the final reduction of—Pattern 2 clause and phrase modifiers of nouns:

> Ted could explain the trick to us. Ted [or He] is an amateur magician. [two independent clauses]
>
> Ted, *who is an amateur magician,* could explain the trick to us. [adjective clause]
>
> Ted, *being an amateur magician,* could explain the trick to us. [participial phrase]
>
> Ted, *an amateur magician,* could explain the trick to us. [appositive]

Although the usual position of an appositive is immediately following the noun it renames, many appositives, like many nonrestrictive participial phrases, can precede the main noun (in which case they are called *pre-positional appositives*); sometimes they are effectively placed at the end of the clause:

> Lawyer Somers, *a master of wit and guile,* cajoles and browbeats in the courtroom.
>
> *A master of wit and guile,* Lawyer Somers cajoles and browbeats in the courtroom.
>
> Lawyer Somers cajoles and browbeats in the courtroom, *a master of wit and guile.*

As a final example of language tools for renaming and modifying nouns, study this tightly constructed sentence:

> One of the five largest towns in Roman England, home of King Arthur's legendary Round Table, seat of Alfred the Great, whose statue looks down its main street, early capital of England, and victim of Cromwell's destructive forces, Winchester is an enchanting cathedral city in which layer after layer of history is visibly present.
>
> Elisabeth Lambert Ortiz, "Exploring Winchester," *Gourmet,*
> March 1978, p. 21

This sentence is made up of one independent clause, which includes an adjective clause, and five pre-positional appositives, the third of which contains an adjective clause. The statements underlying this sentence might be charted as follows:

[Winchester was] one of the five largest towns in Roman England.

[Winchester was] the home of King Arthur's legendary Round Table.

[Winchester was] the seat of Alfred the Great.

[Alfred the Great's] statue looks down its main street.

[Winchester was] the early capital of England.

[Winchester was] the victim of Cromwell's destructive forces.

Winchester is an enchanting cathedral city.

[In this city] layer after layer of history is visibly present.

We see here that eight statements—enough to make up a paragraph of clear but unrelieved simple sentences—have been shortened into one complex sentence. The layering of appositives and adjective clauses produces compression, sentence variety, and proper emphasis.

NAME _____ SCORE _____

Directions: Each of the following numbered units consists of two independent clauses in the form of a compound sentence or two short sentences. One of the independent clauses is italicized. The second sentence is rewritten to include the italicized clause as a subordinate clause or phrase. In the space at the left of each item, write one of the following numbers to identify the italicized subordinate unit in the rewritten sentence:

1. Adverb clause   4. Gerund phrase   7. Infinitive phrase
2. Adjective clause   5. Absolute phrase
3. Participial phrase   6. Appositive

_____ 1. *The old car had been sitting in the garage for years*, but it seems to be in near-perfect condition. *Although the old car had been sitting in the garage for years,* it seems to be in near-perfect condition.

_____ 2. *The old car had been sitting in the garage for years.* But it seems to be in near-perfect condition. The old car, *which had been sitting in the garage for years,* seems to be in near-perfect condition.

_____ 3. *The old car had been sitting in the garage for years,* but its condition seems to be nearly perfect. *The old car having sat in the garage for years,* its condition still seems nearly perfect.

_____ 4. Mark came to work quite late today. *He is usually very punctual.* Mark, *who is usually very punctual,* came to work quite late today.

_____ 5. Mark came to work quite late today. *He is usually very punctual.* Mark, *usually quite punctual,* came to work quite late today.

_____ 6. Paraphrase the important points in your textbook, *for it will help you to remember the ideas. To help you remember the ideas,* paraphrase the important points in your textbook.

_____ 7. Paraphrase the important points in your textbook, *for it will help you to remember the ideas.* Paraphrase the important points in your textbook *because it will help you to remember the ideas.*

_____ 8. *Paraphrase the important points in your textbook,* for it will help you to remember the ideas. *Paraphrasing the important points in your textbook* will help you to remember the ideas.

_____ 9. *Julie saw the dog run from the yard*; she immediately began to chase it down the street. *Seeing the dog run from the yard,* Julie immediately began to chase it down the street.

_____ 10. *Julie saw the dog run from the yard*; she immediately began to chase it down the street. *When Julie saw the dog run from the yard,* she immediately began to chase it down the street.

_____ 11. *The gates to the stadium opened at 11:00 A.M.* The people rushed immediately to their seats. *When the gates to the stadium opened at 11:00 A.M.,* the people rushed immediately to their seats.

163

_____ 12. *The gates to the stadium opened at 11:00 A.M.* The people rushed immediately to their seats. *The gates to the stadium having opened at 11:00 A.M., the people rushed immediately to their seats.*

_____ 13. *The gates to the stadium opened at 11:00 A.M.* The people rushed immediately to their seats. *With the gates to the stadium opening at 11:00 A.M.,* the people rushed immediately to their seats.

_____ 14. *Adjust the brightness level on your computer screen,* and you will decrease eye strain. *Adjusting the brightness level on your computer screen* will decrease eye strain.

_____ 15. *Adjust the brightness level on your computer screen,* and you will decrease eye strain. *If you adjust the brightness level on your computer screen,* you will decrease eye strain.

_____ 16. Adjust the brightness level on your computer screen, *and you will decrease eye strain. To decrease eye strain,* adjust the brightness level on your computer screen.

_____ 17. *Manuel is not at work today,* so I will need to answer his phone. *Because Manuel is not at work today,* I will need to answer his phone.

_____ 18. *Manuel is not at work today,* so I will need to answer his phone. *With Manuel not at work today,* I will need to answer his phone.

_____ 19. *Manuel is not at work today,* so I will need to answer his phone. Today I will need to answer the phone for Manuel, *who is not at work.*

_____ 20. Martina will help you to learn that program. *She attended a workshop on its operation last week.* Martina, *who attended a workshop on the operation of that program last week,* will help you to learn it.

_____ 21. Martina will help you to learn that program. *She attended a workshop on its operation last week.* Martina will help you to learn that program *because she attended a workshop on its operation last week.*

_____ 22. Martina will help you to learn that program. *She attended a workshop on its operation last week.* Martina, *having attended a workshop on the operation of that program last week,* will help you to learn it.

_____ 23. *You must fill out that form very carefully,* or you will not get a rebate on that purchase. *If you do not fill out that form very carefully* you will not get a rebate on that purchase.

_____ 24. You must fill out that form very carefully, and *you will get a rebate on that purchase. To get a rebate on that purchase,* you must fill out the form very carefully.

_____ 25. *Max Carlson is our new purchasing agent.* He will start work next Monday. Max Carlson, *who is our new purchasing agent,* will start work next Monday.

NAME _____   SCORE _____

Directions: Preceding lessons have demonstrated various types of noun modification. When two sentences employ the same noun or pronoun, one sentence can be incorporated into the other by being reduced to an adjective clause, a participial phrase, or an appositive. In the following pairs of sentences, the word printed in heavy type in the first sentence is the noun or pronoun to be modified. Combine the sentences by reducing the second sentence to the kind of unit indicated by the following letters:

   a. Adjective clause
   b. Participial phrase following the noun
   c. Participial phrase preceding the noun
   d. Appositive

You need not write the entire sentence; write only enough to show how the combining is done.

1. To get to the head of the trail, we had to make a steep **climb.** It goes up the west side of the mountain.

   a. _____

   b. _____

2. A short, squat **man** stood beside the trail. He was carrying a backpack.

   a. _____

   b. _____

3. **James Ortiz** met us at the head of the trail. He is a professional guide.

   a. _____

   d. _____

4. **Ortiz** pulled out a map of the trail. He spoke very softly.

   a. _____

   c. _____

5. He spread out the map and pointed to a **spot** on the map. The spot lay very near a river.

a. _____

b. _____

6. He said, "Right here is a beautiful **spot**. The spot overlooks the big rapids.

a. _____

c. _____

7. The **campsite** provides a beautiful view of the rapids. It has a flat area for pitching tents.

a. _____

b. _____

8. The **campsite** also has a plentiful supply of potable water. It is a state park.

a. _____

c. _____

d. _____

9. We hiked the **trail**. It was a six-mile climb.

a. _____

d. _____

10. At dusk, the last of us **hikers** straggled into the campsite. We were all footsore and exhausted.

a. _____

c. _____

d. _____

Lesson 16 *Parallel Structure; Comparisons*

There are two other situations in which the underlying logic of the sentence requires the writer to select carefully the structure and position of the sentence units.

PARALLEL STRUCTURE

When two or more parts of a sentence are similar in function, they should be expressed in the same grammatical construction; in other words, they should be **parallel.** The principle of parallelism implies that, in a series, nouns should be balanced with nouns, adjectives with adjectives, prepositional phrases with prepositional phrases, clauses with clauses, and so forth. The following sentence owes much of its clarity and effectiveness to its careful parallel arrangement: Two adjective clauses are joined with *and*, two adverbs with *but*, and three noun direct objects with *and*.

> Anyone who studies world affairs *and* who remembers our last three wars will realize, sadly *but* inevitably, that another conflict will endanger the economic strength of our nation, the complacency of our political institutions, *and* the moral fiber of our people.

Anyone	who studies world affairs *and*	
	who remembers our last three wars will realize,	sadly *but*
		inevitably,
that another conflict will endanger	the economic strength of our nation,	
	the complacency of our political institutions,	
	and the moral fiber of our people.	

Two types of errors, the *false series* and the *and who* construction, work to destroy parallelism by using coordinate conjunctions to join grammatical units that are not alike.

1. The false or shifted series

> **Weak:** Most people play golf for exercise, pleasure, and so they can meet others. [The *and* ties an adverb clause to two nouns.]
>
> **Better:** Most people play golf for exercise, for pleasure, and for social contacts.
>
> **Weak:** Our new teacher was young, tall, slender, and with red hair. [The *and* suggests that it will be followed by a fourth adjective, not a prepositional phrase.]
>
> **Better:** Our new teacher was young, tall, slender, and red-haired.
>
> **Weak:** Mr. Little's speech was tiresome, inaccurate, and should have been omitted.
>
> **Better:** Mr. Little's speech was tiresome, inaccurate, and unnecessary.

2. The *and who* or *and which* construction

Weak:	Their son is an athlete with great talent *and who* will soon be well known.
Better:	Their son is an athlete who has great talent and who will soon be well known.
	Their son is a greatly talented athlete who will soon be well known.
	[Here the unbalanced modification is avoided.]
Weak:	I am taking Physics 388, a difficult course *and which* demands much time.
Better:	I am taking Physics 388, which is a difficult course and demands much time.
	I am taking Physics 388, which is difficult and demands much time.

COMPARISONS

When you write sentences that make comparisons or contrasts, you must observe certain forms if your writing is to be clear and precise.

1. Be sure that you compare only those things that are capable of being compared:

Faulty:	The storage capacity of this computer is much greater than our old one. [*One* refers to computer; thus, two unlike things, storage capacity and the computer, are being compared.]
Improved:	The storage capacity of this computer is much greater than *the storage capacity of* our old one.
	The storage capacity of this computer is much greater than *that of* our old one.
Faulty:	The influence of the political leader is more ephemeral than the artist. [Here, *influence,* an abstract quality, is being compared to a person, the artist.]
Improved:	The influence of the political leader is more ephemeral than *the influence of* the artist.
	The influence of the political leader is more ephemeral than *that of* the artist.
	The political leader's influence is more ephemeral than *the artist's.*

2. When you use the comparative form of an adjective in a comparison, use *any other* when it is necessary to exclude the subject of the comparison from the group:

Faulty:	Wilson, the first-string center, is heavier than any man on the team. [In this version the writer is comparing Wilson to the members of a group that includes Wilson.]
Improved:	Wilson, the first-string center, is heavier than *any other* man on the team.

3. When your sentence contains a double comparison, be sure to include all the words necessary to make the idiom complete:

Faulty:	He is now as tall as his mother, if not taller.
Improved:	He is now as tall *as,* if not taller *than,* his mother.
Faulty:	She is one of the best runners in the club, if not the best.
Improved:	She is one of the best *runners,* if not the best *runner,* in the club.

Double comparisons may create sentences that sound awkward even though they form the comparison correctly and completely. You may want to recast the sentence to make it read more smoothly.

1. Try forming two sentences:

> He is now as tall as his mother. He may, indeed, be taller than she.
> She is one of the best runners in the club. She may even be the best runner in the club.

2. Try writing two independent clauses:

> He is now as tall as his mother, and he may be even taller than she is.
> She is one of the best runners in the club, and she may be the best runner in the club.

(See Supplement for more details on sentences used to compare and contrast.)

SUPPLEMENT

In addition to requiring the structural units already mentioned, comparison-contrast sentences place a few constraints on the form of the adjective or adverb.

1. When your comparison is limited to two things, use the comparative degree:

> Both Jane and Laura sing well, but Jane has the *better* voice.
> Which takes *more* time, your studies or your job?

2. Use the superlative for more than two things:

> January is the *worst* month of the year.

You learned in Lesson 2 that there are two ways of forming the comparative and superlative degrees. In general, *er* and *est* are used with short words, and *more* and *most* with longer words.

> When I was *younger,* I was *more apprehensive* about thunder and lightning.
> This encyclopedia is the *newest* and the *most comprehensive.*
> Maria works *faster* than I and also *more accurately.*

Remember that in present-day standard English, *er* or *est* is not combined with *more* or *most* in the same word. We don't say, for example, *more pleasanter, most loveliest,* or *more faster.*

NAME _____ SCORE _____

Directions: In the space at the left of each pair of sentences, copy the letter identifying the sentence that is logically structured.

_____ 1. a. Jose is a man who is highly skilled in that field and with considerable ability to improvise.
b. Jose is a man who is highly skilled in that field and has considerable ability to improvise.

_____ 2. a. On the other side of the field, a man stumbled as he crossed the brook and falling into the water.
b. On the other side of the field, a man stumbled as he crossed the brook and fell into the water.

_____ 3. a. My friend plays tennis because it's fun, it improves his fitness, and it develops friendships.
b. My friend plays tennis for fun, fitness, and because he likes the friendships he develops.

_____ 4. a. That story in the lecture distracted us from the point and was completely unnecessary.
b. That story in the lecture distracted us from the point and which was completely unnecessary.

_____ 5. a. That road is rocky, twisting, and has a great number of potholes.
b. That road is rocky, twisting, and full of potholes.

_____ 6. a. Our efforts to repair the damage were very focused and we completed them much sooner than we expected.
b. Our efforts to repair the damage were very focused and completed much sooner than we expected.

_____ 7. a. The people in that office are intelligent, dedicated, and hard-working.
b. The people in that office are intelligent, dedicated, and work hard.

_____ 8. a. You will be in charge of raising funds in your precinct, and transportation to the polling places must be arranged.
b. You will be in charge of raising funds in your precinct, and you must arrange transportation to the polling places.

_____ 9. a. The voters want to elect someone who is intelligent and helpful to people in difficult circumstances.
b. The voters want to elect someone who is intelligent and helping people in difficult circumstances.

_____ 10. a. Julia wishes to move away from the farm and find a job in the city.
b. Julia wishes to move away from the farm and that she could find a job in the city.

Directions: From each of the following pairs of sentences, select the one that makes a correct comparison and copy its letter in the blank at the left.

_____ 1. a. As our new baseball coach we have hired Jaime Ruiz, one of the best coaches in our area, if not the best coach.
   b. As our new baseball coach we have hired Jaime Ruiz, one of the best, if not the best, coaches in our area.

_____ 2. a. Every man in town wants to own a car that is faster than his neighbors.
   b. Every man in town wants to own a car that is faster than his neighbors'.

_____ 3. a. Working out with weights will make you a more stronger hitter after a few months.
   b. Working out with weights will make you a stronger hitter after a few months.

_____ 4. a. My cousin Janie operates that drill press better than any person I know.
   b. My cousin Janie operates that drill press better than any other person I know.

_____ 5. a. Johnson and Smith both field very well, but Smith has the stronger throwing arm.
   b. Johnson and Smith both field very well, but Smith has the strongest throwing arm.

_____ 6. a. People once believed that the cost of living in small towns was lower than big cities.
   b. People once believed that the cost of living in small towns was lower than it was in big cities.

_____ 7. a. Of the three pitchers on the softball team, Jessica has the best curve ball.
   b. Of the three pitchers on the softball team, Jessica has the better curve ball.

_____ 8. a. The new bank building downtown is taller than any building there.
   b. The new bank building downtown is taller than any other building there.

_____ 9. a. That truck is one of the most powerful, if not the most powerful, sold in this country.
   b. That truck is one of the most powerful trucks, if not the most powerful truck, sold in this country.

_____ 10. a. The company's financial condition is better than last year.
   b. The company's financial condition is better than last year's.

NAME _____   SCORE _____

Directions: Rewrite each sentence to correct the faulty parallelism.

1. Fred's old car was rusty, dented, and had bald tires.

   _____

2. My Uncle Roy avidly pursues three hobbies: fly fishing, collects stamps, and reading mystery stories.

   _____

3. Professor Yelling is strict, demanding, and who gives fairly low grades.

   _____

4. I enjoy tennis for the exercise, the competition, and because it takes my mind off school work.

   _____

5. A notebook computer will be lightweight, compact, and have a fast operating speed.

   _____

6. The workshop on spreadsheets taught me several useful techniques and which was quite entertaining.

   _____

7. It is a fine school, with an excellent library, new laboratories, and has a fairly small student body.

   _____

8. The instructional manual for the computer was somewhat useful, but one in which most of the information was far too technical for me.

   _____

9. That particular drill improved my play at the net, and my stamina increased also.

   _____

10. The three men took up skydiving for the excitement and so they could brag to their friends about their courage.

   _____

Directions: Rewrite each sentence so that the comparison in it is logical.

1. Jim's time in the 10K race was as good, if not better than, the times of the other runners from our club.

   _____

2. Although the weather here is a bit colder and wetter, I like it better than Atlanta.

   _____

3. Now that I've taken both the history and the literature courses, I think I like the history courses the most.

   _____

4. Marcia, the executive secretary, often says her work is more important than the company presidents.

   _____

5. Our textbook says that the operation of American universities is much more structured than European universities.

   _____

6. Alex is changing jobs, and he hopes he can be more happier and productive in his new position.

   _____

7. Walt's attitudes toward work are far different from other workers.

   _____

8. Little Mary's reaction to that vaccination was as bad, if not worse than, any I've ever seen.

   _____

9. I've noticed that Grandma likes horror movies more than her daughters.

   _____

10. Sailing conditions in the nearby bay are far better than any location on the East Coast.

    _____

SENTENCE BUILDING

☐ **Completeness**

☐ To be a sentence, a complete sentence, a word group must

1. Contain a subject and a verb.

2. Be independent rather than subordinate.

☐ Sentences tend to be incomplete for three reasons:

1. They are actually subordinate clauses.

   Although we never tried to drive that car again

   This clause must be attached to a main clause because the word *although* is a subordinating conjunction.

2. They are verbal phrases.

   Running down the street with a large kite suspended overhead

   To be sure of an early arrival

   Participles and infinitives cannot stand alone; they must function in or be attached to a main clause.

3. They are an incomplete construction made up of a noun and a phrase or subordinate clause.

   A man of good reputation who needs no introduction to this group because he has

   performed so many vital services to the city where he has lived for so many years...

   No matter how long the word group continues, no matter how many phrases and subordinate clauses it contains, it can't be a sentence unless it has a subject and a verb.

☐ Correcting fragments is relatively easy once they are detected:
   • Attach the fragment to the previous sentence or to the following sentence as the sense of the sentence allows.
   • Change the fragment to a subordinate clause with an appropriate subordinating word and attach it to a main clause.
   • Change the fragment to an independent clause by supplying either a subject or verb or both as the sense of the sentence demands.

☐ Some expressions that lack a subject-verb combination are not considered fragments:
   • Commands (The subject *you* is not voiced in such expressions.)
      Step right up. Take a ticket. Go to your seat.
   • Exclamations
      Wow! Triplets? What a surprise!
   • Bits of dialog (Note that much of our day-to-day, informal conversation is couched in sentence fragments.)
      "Running late?" she asked. "Better hurry. Only a few seats left."
   • Short transitional expressions
      Now for the last step. On to the next stop.

175

☐ Traps

☐ *Misplaced Modifiers*

We often place modifiers rather loosely in sentences in our conversation and informal writing, but in more formal writing and when precise expression is important, modifying words, phrases, and clauses must be located carefully.

1. Putting adverbs such as *only, nearly, almost,* and *hardly* in the wrong place can change the meaning of the sentence. Put modifying words, phrases, and clauses as close as possible to the word they modify.

   James nearly found $100 on the beach yesterday.

   technically means that James almost found, but did not find, money on the beach. Someone found the money ahead of James, or James walked past it without seeing it.

   James found nearly $100 on the beach.

   means that he found money on the beach, probably between $90 and $99. Changing the position of the adverb changes the meaning of the sentence.

2. Putting modifying words and phrases where they can attach themselves to the wrong word can confuse the reader.

   We heard that a forest fire burned thousands of acres of land on the evening news.

   literally means that the acreage burned on the news—that is, while the reporters watched—or perhaps the burning occurred in the newsroom. In either case, the reader can be confused. The intended meaning is that we heard the report on the news.

3. Putting modifiers where they can apply equally to two words can confuse the reader. In the sentence

   Students who can solve this problem easily can succeed in my logic course.

   the meaning might be

   Students who can easily solve this problem can succeed...

   or it might mean

   Students who can solve this problem can easily succeed...

   Position the modifier so that it can apply to only one word.

4. Place modifying words and phrases outside an infinitive, not between *to* and the verb stem.

   My brother likes to once in a while visit the zoo.

   is a clear but awkward statement.

   Once in a while, my brother likes to visit the zoo.

   is a much smoother expression.

5. Place the correlatives such as *both...and* and *not only...but also* immediately before the parallel units they connect

	We sent tickets to both Janice and Joan.
not	We sent tickets both to Janice and Joan.
and certainly not	We both sent tickets to Janice and Joan.

☐ Dangling Modifiers

Any phrase that does not attach itself clearly to the word it modifies is called a *dangling modifier*. Connect participial, gerund, and infinitive phrases as closely as possible to the words they modify. In the sentence

> Coming into town, the stately trees shaded both sides of the road.

the literal meaning of the structure has the trees coming into town and shading both sides of the road. The participial phrase modifies the noun following it closely in the sentence. Unless the trees are coming into town—perhaps on a truck—make the sentence read

> As we came into town, the stately trees shaded both sides of the road.
>
> or Coming into town, we saw the stately trees shading both sides of the road.

Be sure that gerund and infinitive phrases, especially those that serve as opening elements of the sentence, can attach themselves logically to the next noun in the sentence.

> To work as a truck driver, a commercial driver's license is required.

Logically, the commercial driver's license is not going to work as a truck driver; while the meaning is probably clear, it is better to say

> To work as a truck driver, you need a commercial driver's license.

or, more formally,

> To work as a truck driver, one needs a commercial driver's license.

☐ Sentence Building

☐ *Subordination*

Use compound verbs and sentences and subordinate clauses and phrases to create varied sentences.

- Two simple sentences: The gun fired. The runners broke from the starting blocks.

Compound verb: (not a possible construction because the two sentences have different subjects)

Compound Sentence: The gun fired, and the runners broke from the starting blocks.

Adverbial clause: When the gun fired, the runners broke from the starting blocks.

Participial phrase: (not a possible construction)

Absolute phrase: With the gun having fired, the runners broke from the starting blocks.

Other constructions are possible when the subjects of the sentences are the same:

> I raised the flag. I unlocked the gate.

Compound verb: I raised the flag and unlocked the gate.

Compound sentence: I raised the flag; then I unlocked the gate.

Participial phrase: Having raised the flag, I unlocked the gate.

☐ Parallel Structures

Two or more parts of sentences that are similar in function should be similar in grammatical construction—that is, parallel. Nouns should be balanced with nouns, verbs with verbs, and so on.

- Avoid the false or shifted series.

    He took that job for its challenges, its high pay, and *because it allowed him to travel.*

- Avoid the *and who, and which* construction.

    That is a job that offers challenges, high pay, *and which allows Hank to travel extensively.*

☐ Comparisons

☐ Be sure that comparisons and contrasts are made at the same level.

Her car's engine is more powerful *than my car.*

Engines cannot logically be compared to cars.

In using the comparative form of an adjective in a comparison, use *any other* to exclude the subject of the comparison from the group.

Our state university is bigger than any university in the state.

If "our state university" is in the state, it must be compared to *any **other** university* in the state.

In making double comparisons, include all the words necessary to make the expression complete.

Alicia is easily as smart as Robert, if not smarter.

Alicia is easily as smart as, if not smarter *than,* Robert.

☐ Use the comparative degree of the adjective or adverb when two items are compared.

Alicia is *smarter* than Robert.

☐ Use the superlative degree when three or more items are involved.

Alicia is the *smartest* person in the entire class.

Punctuation

Lessons, Practice Sheets, and Exercises

Lesson 17 — *Commas to Separate*

As your writing grows more precise and more economical, you will need to use commas to separate certain parts of sentences so that your work cannot be misunderstood. Five rules cover the occasions when commas are used to separate parts of a sentence.

THE FIVE RULES FOR COMMAS TO SEPARATE

1. Use commas before *and, but, or, nor, yet, for,* and *so* when they join the clauses of a compound sentence:

> I placed the typed sheet on his desk, and he read it slowly.
>
> His face turned red, but he did not say a word.
>
> I knew he was angry, for he rose and stomped out of the room. [Note that no comma is used before the conjunction in a compound predicate.]

At this point, you might reread Lesson 7. Remember that a semicolon rather than a comma is usually required in a compound sentence when no coordinating conjunction is present.

2. Use a comma between the items of a series.

> The land looked brown, parched, lifeless, and ominous. [four adjectives]
>
> Volunteers may be students, office workers, housewives, or retirees. [four nouns]
>
> The dog charged through the door, down the steps, and into the garage. [three phrases]
>
> He understands what he must do, when he must do it, and why it must be done. [three subordinate clauses]
>
> Larry brought the wood, Mark built the fire, and I got the steaks ready. [three independent clauses]

A series is composed of three or more words, phrases, or clauses of equal grammatical rank. A series usually takes the form of *a, b, **and** c;* sometimes it may be *a, b, **or** c.* Although commas may be used to separate a series of short clauses, the punctuation must change if the clauses have commas within them.

> Larry, who has a pickup truck, brought the wood, Mark, who was once a Boy Scout, built the fire, and I got the steaks ready.

Obviously commas do not effectively separate the independent clauses in this sentence, so we need to use a mark with greater strength—in this case, the semicolon.

> Larry, who has a pickup truck, brought the wood; Mark, who was once a Boy Scout, made the fire; and I got the steaks ready.

In journalism, writers often omit the comma before the final conjunction. It is easier to remember the rule if you develop a consistent pattern of using the comma before the final conjunction.

3. Use a comma between coordinate adjectives preceding a noun.

> the harsh, cold wind

When applied to adjectives, the word **coordinate** indicates that two adjectives modify a single noun with equal force. We usually separate coordinate adjectives with a comma. Sometimes it is difficult to know whether or not two adjectives are equal. Consider the following:

> the harsh cold wind
> the difficult final exam

Two tests will help you to decide if the adjectives are equal.

First, if you can use the word *and* instead of a comma between the two words and still produce a correct statement, the adjectives are equal, and a comma should be used to separate them. *The harsh and cold wind* makes perfect sense in English, demonstrating that the adjectives are equal in force and need a comma. But you would never say *the difficult and final exam;* thus, the adjectives are not coordinate, and the comma is not needed.

Second, if the adjectives sound natural in reversed position, they are equal and can be separated by a comma if the word *and* is not used. The phrase *the cold, harsh wind* is just as readable as *the harsh, cold wind*, again demonstrating that the adjectives are equal.

When you use more than two adjectives before a noun, you should use the *and* test, checking the adjectives by pairs—the first with the second, the second with the third, and so on—to determine the need for commas. It may help you to know that we usually do not use commas before adjectives denoting size or age. And remember that you never use a comma between the last adjective and the noun.

Observe how use of these tests determines punctuation like the following:

> a neat, courteous little boy
> a hot, steamy summer day

Because we don't say "a neat and courteous and little boy," we would place a comma between neat and courteous, but not between courteous and little. We could say *a hot, steamy summer day* or *a steamy, hot summer day*, but not *a hot and steamy and summer day*.

4. Use a comma after most introductory modifiers. The following specific applications of this rule will help you use it correctly.

    a. Put commas after introductory adverbial clauses:

> *Unless the floodwater recedes soon,* we're in trouble.
> *If we can prove that the signature was forged,* we will win the case.
> *Before sophomores will be admitted to courses numbered 300 or above,* they must have official permission.
> *Before I answer you,* I want to ask another question.
> *When he arrived,* he seemed distraught.

    b. Put commas after introductory verbal-phrase modifiers:

> *Having climbed the steep trail up Cougar Mountain,* Bob decided to take some pictures.
> *To get the best view of the valley,* he walked to the edge of the cliff.
> *After opening his backpack,* he searched for his new telephoto lens.

    c. Put a comma after an introductory absolute element, such as a phrase, an adverb modifying the whole sentence, a mild exclamation, and *yes* and *no*.

> *In fact,* there was no way to keep the front door closed.
> *Certainly,* I'll be glad to help you.
> *Well,* what are we to do now?
> *No,* we are not in danger.

    d. Ordinarily, do not put a comma after a single prepositional phrase at the beginning of a sentence. If the opening element contains two or more phrases, use a comma to separate the phrases from the main clause. A long introductory prepositional phrase is not followed by a comma when the subject and verb are reversed.

> *After a heavy dinner* we usually went for a short walk.
> *In early summer* many birds nested there.
> *In spite of the very heavy wind and the pelting hailstones,* the third race was completed.
> *In the name of justice,* please help these people.
> *After school, or during the evening,* teachers were expected to find time for grading papers and preparing lessons.
> *Between the dusty night table and the unmade bed* were all the magazines that I wanted to read.

5. Use a comma between any two words that might be mistakenly read together:

> *Before,* he had been industrious and sober. [not *before he had been*]
> *Once inside,* the dog scampered all over the furniture. [not *inside the dog*]
> *While we were eating,* the table collapsed. [not *eating the table*]
> *After we had washed,* Mother prepared breakfast. [not *washed Mother*]
> *Ever since,* he has been afraid of deep water. [not *ever since he has been*]
> *Shortly after ten,* thirty new recruits appeared. [not *shortly after ten thirty*]

NAME _____ SCORE _____

Directions: Each of the following sentences is missing two commas. Add the commas where they are necessary. Then, in the space at the left, write the number of the rule that applies to each comma you have added:

1. Before a coordinating conjunction in a compound sentence
2. In a series
3. Between coordinate adjectives
4. After an introductory modifier
5. To prevent misreading

_____ 1. Soon after the men left for work and the coffee shop closed for the day.

_____
_____ 2. Soon after the men left for work the coffee shop owner closed the shop after a long hard day's work.

_____ 3. Looking at the engine the boss said, "That thing is so heavy that it would take two men, a boy and an engine hoist to lift it into the truck."
_____

_____ 4. My sister stood up, walked through the door and slammed it loudly as the women in the room gave her a short loud cheer.
_____

_____ 5. After a short break in the action the players came back on the court and the game resumed after the television commercial.
_____

_____ 6. A few minutes after we finished eating the dog climbed up on the table and he devoured the rest of the turkey.
_____

_____ 7. The short steep climb to the top of the hill left all of wishing for a cold drink, a nap and a ride back down to the bottom of the hill.
_____

_____ 8. Having located the last important pieces of information for our report Jim and I finished the work and he left the library to go back to his dorm.
_____

_____ 9. The three women pitched the tents cooked a tasteless uninviting meal, and then fell into a deep and dreamless sleep.
_____

_____ 10. Shortly after five thirty cars drove into the parking lot the drivers got out of the cars, and they began to set up the food for the tailgate party.
_____

_____ 11. Shortly after five men had left for town the rest of the men on the shift went back to work and they finished the digging before the others returned.
_____

_____   12. The difficult final exam left us all exhausted for we had studied very hard for
_____   the past three days and most of us were tired when the exam started.

_____   13. The crew neither ate nor slept during the storm yet they did not seem fatigued
_____   at the end of the long difficult trip.

_____   14. As long and difficult as the trip might have been the crew told the story
_____   excitedly to relatives, friends and acquaintances.

_____   15. All along we had expected to find John and Marge at the restaurant but they
_____   had not arrived by the time we finished eating dinner.

_____   16. After the men finished mending the tear in the sail we hoisted it, the wind filled
_____   the sail and we set off on the windward leg of the voyage.

_____   17. Once before I had visited my brother in Canada and we had spent the time
_____   camping on an isolated lake.

_____   18. Although the girls had never been to the northern part of the city they set out
_____   without a map and tried to find the location of that old quirky thrift shop.

_____   19. Looking back over my high school career I sense that I should have spent more
_____   time on such basics as reading, writing and math.

_____   20. Although no one ever seems to find the perfect vacation spot we all spend a
_____   great deal of time energy, and money looking for it.

_____   21. Alicia's short intense burst of speed carried her up and over the last difficult
_____   hill in the cross- country race and let her pass Jennie, Barb and three girls from
                another school.

_____   22. In spite of our best efforts to figure out Andrew's scribbled note we did not
_____   understand that we had to buy the hamburgers, buns and charcoal for the picnic.

_____   23. In spite of our best efforts to decipher Andrew's scribbled note proved to be an
_____   almost impossible task so we did not understand what we had to buy for the
                picnic.

_____   24. Once before we had run into that difficulty with Andrew's handwriting so
_____   Wendy suggested that we always communicate with him by telephone.

_____   25. The coaches the team managers, and the trainers had left earlier in the day
_____   for they wanted to get to the field earlier than the rest of us.

NAME _____ SCORE _____

Directions: Each of the following sentences has two commas missing. Add the commas where they are necessary. Then, in the blanks at the left, write the number of the rules that apply to the commas you have added:

1. Before a coordinating conjunction in   3. Between coordinate adjectives
   a compound sentence   4. After an introductory modifier
2. In a series   5. to prevent misreading

_____   1. June has taken the required courses in history psychology, and math but she
_____   must also take a course in biology.

_____   2. Because Jim found two new sources for that long difficult report his work is
_____   going more quickly now.

_____   3. The handsome well-dressed television anchor looked once more at his script,
_____   cleared his throat and began to read.

_____   4. Working to catch up with the rest of the runners Marta ran hard up the long
_____   winding hill.

_____   5. Raquel ordered the artwork, the titles and the slides but she still needs to
_____   write the script for her new sales presentation.

_____   6. The children in that class can play on the swings this afternoon or they can play
_____   a noisy colorful video game.

_____   7. After the dog wandered away the boys looked in the barn, the pasture and
_____   the corn fields.

_____   8. After waking up the girls wandered over to the restaurant for a leisurely
_____   delicious breakfast.

_____   9. Kate had once ridden with a police officer on patrol; after that training to
_____   become an officer became an immediate compelling goal.

_____   10. Arriving early for the meeting Audrey sat down in the back for a short
_____   refreshing nap.

_____   11. Carla tried valiantly to start the car but she had to call her sleepy reluctant
_____   brother for help.

_____   12. Because the women want to study computer graphics they must also take math,
_____   computer programming and an art course.

_____   13. I've tried for three years to grow big juicy tomatoes but the bugs have killed
_____   the plants every year.

_____   14. Overwhelmed by the number of choices Arthur decided to buy only the
_____   simplest least expensive MP3 player he could find.

_____   15. The girls already have the tables, chairs and umbrellas but they will have to set
_____   them up on the patio.

Directions: Under each rule, write two sentences of your own composition to illustrate the punctuation designated. The purpose of the exercise is to practice correct comma usage.

1. Comma used before a coordinating conjunction in a compound sentence

    a. _____

    _____

    b. _____

    _____

2. Commas used in a series (one series of single words and one series of phrases)

    a. _____

    _____

    b. _____

    _____

3. Comma used after an introductory modifier (one adverb clause and one verbal phrase)

    a. _____

    _____

    b. _____

    _____

4. Comma used between coordinate adjectives

    a. _____

    _____

    b. _____

    _____

5. Commas used to prevent misreading

    a. _____

    _____

    b. _____

    _____

NAME _____   SCORE _____

Directions: One sentence in each of the following pairs is correctly punctuated. Copy the identifying letter of the correct sentence in the space at the left. Be prepared to explain in class why the punctuation of the other sentence is faulty.

_____ 1. a. As the days passed my sister resisted calling the tall handsome boy in her class but she finally dialed his number.
    b. As the days passed, my sister resisted calling the tall, handsome boy in her class, but she finally dialed his number.

_____ 2. a. Thinking back to my childhood days, I remember starting a collection of snuffboxes; my first one was made of buffalo horn.
    b. Thinking back to my childhood days I remember starting a collection of snuffboxes; my first one was made of buffalo horn.

_____ 3. a. "I predict a long, bitterly fought campaign; the political writers are in the back rooms sharpening their pencils," said the reporter.
    b. "I predict a long bitterly fought campaign, the political writers are in the back room, sharpening their pencils," said the reporter.

_____ 4. a. The behavior of some delegates was rude and disruptive, for some of us the convention was a disappointment.
    b. The behavior of some delegates was rude and disruptive; for some of us the convention was a disappointment.

_____ 5. a. She has invested a small fortune in her car; a powerful stereo, special seats and a sophisticated alarm system were just a modest beginning of her effort.
    b. She has invested a small fortune in her car; a powerful stereo, special seats, and a sophisticated alarm system were just a modest beginning of her effort.

_____ 6. a. The dog eyed the meat hungrily but the small quick fox snatched it up, and ran into the thicket.
    b. The dog eyed the meat hungrily, but the small, quick fox snatched it up and ran into the thicket.

_____ 7. a. Noting a slight swirl in the water, Sue cast the lure into the center of it, and a huge trout struck just as the lure hit the water.
    b. Noting a slight swirl in the water Sue cast the lure into the center of it and a huge trout struck, just as the lure hit the water.

_____ 8. a. While she had been running the clock had stopped, it failed to record her best time ever in this long difficult race.
    b. While she had been running, the clock had stopped; it failed to record her best time ever in this long, difficult race.

_____ 9. a. Seeing the grouse rise out of the sage, the woman raised her gun, shot skillfully, and dropped the bird cleanly.
    b. Seeing the grouse rise out of the sage the woman raised her gun, shot skillfully and dropped the bird cleanly.

_____ 10. a. "When you walk, walk very carefully, but try not to look at the water two hundred feet below," advised the guide.
b. "When you walk walk very carefully but try not to look at the water, two hundred feet below," advised the guide.

_____ 11. a. Our teacher was a mild-mannered kindly old gentleman, he often went to obvious extremes to avoid embarrassing any of us.
b. Our teacher was a mild-mannered, kindly old gentleman; he often went to obvious extremes to avoid embarrassing any of us.

_____ 12. a. There is only one gas station in our village, and the owner always goes home for lunch, sometimes not returning till the middle of the afternoon.
b. There is only one gas station in our village and the owner always goes home for lunch; sometimes not returning till the middle of the afternoon.

_____ 13. a. The calm, friendly garage attendant assured us that the bridge had been repaired and was now safe to cross.
b. The calm, friendly, garage attendant assured us that the bridge had been repaired, and was now safe to cross.

_____ 14. a. Several kinds of exotic flowers grow in this warm humid climate, everywhere one sees hibiscus, oleander and orchids.
b. Several kinds of exotic flowers grow in this warm, humid climate; everywhere one sees hibiscus, oleander, and orchids.

_____ 15. a. Yesterday we awoke to find the ground covered with wet heavy snow, today's newspaper reports that not since 1937, have we had snow this late.
b. Yesterday we awoke to find the ground covered with wet, heavy snow; today's newspaper reports that not since 1937 have we had snow this late.

_____ 16. a. In the opinion of some, elementary-school teachers are more influential than parents in determining children's attitudes toward learning, and I agree with that opinion.
b. In the opinion of some elementary-school teachers are more influential than parents in determining children's attitudes toward learning and I agree with that opinion.

_____ 17. a. Many early automobiles were high, stately things, most of them were patterned after the horse-drawn carriage.
b. Many early automobiles were high stately things, most of them were patterned after the horse-drawn carriage.

_____ 18. a. Your lecture made a deep lasting impression on our class and we were still discussing it, several weeks later.
b. Your lecture made a deep, lasting impression on our class, and we were still discussing it several weeks later.

_____ 19. a. Forty years ago, I fished for bass, pike, and muskellunge in Minnesota, in those days no one worried about polluted water.
b. Forty years ago I fished for bass, pike, and muskellunge in Minnesota; in those days no one worried about polluted water.

_____ 20. a. Wanting to buy postcards, candy bars, magazines and souvenirs; I checked my luggage, and searched the airport for a newsstand.
b. Wanting to buy postcards, candy bars, magazines, and souvenirs, I checked my luggage and searched the airport for a newsstand.

Just as there are times when you need to use commas to separate items, there are times when you need to use commas to enclose items. Use commas to enclose **interrupters**—those words, phrases, or clauses that interrupt the normal word order of a sentence.

COMMON INTERRUPTERS

The most common types of interrupters are discussed below.

1. Nonrestrictive adjective clauses and phrases

> The coach's Awards Banquet speech, *which was one of her best,* should be published. [nonrestrictive adjective clause]
>
> Jan's mother, *holding a winning ticket,* went to the desk. [nonrestrictive participial phrase]
>
> Professor Angela Cheney, *at the far end of the head table,* summoned a waiter. [nonrestrictive prepositional phrase]

Clauses and phrases not essential to identify a noun are set off by commas. (See Lesson 9 to review restrictive and nonrestrictive clauses and phrases.) Note that, in some cases, the meaning of the sentence depends on whether a clause is taken as restrictive or nonrestrictive.

> My brother-in-law *who lives in Akron* is a chemist.
>
> [The writer has more than one brother-in-law. The restrictive clause is needed to distinguish this brother-in-law from other brothers-in-law.]
>
> My brother-in-law, *who lives in Akron,* is a chemist.
>
> [The writer is telling us that he or she has only one brother-in-law. Identification is not explicit.]

2. Most appositives

> One comedian, *the one with the lisp,* was booed.
>
> The major, *a veteran of three wars,* accepted the award.
>
> Mr. Tate, *our head counselor,* will speak.
>
> Our head counselor, *Mr. Tate,* will speak.

As you learned in Lesson 10, the most common type of appositive immediately follows the noun or pronoun that it renames. Appositives like these are called *loose* or *nonrestrictive appositives* and are set off. Sometimes, however, an appositive functions in the same way that a restrictive adjective clause functions: It identifies a preceding noun that, without the appositive, could refer to any member of a class. An appositive of this sort is not set off:

> my brother Jack
>
> the poet Keats

the apostle Paul
the preposition *to*

3. Absolute phrases

Today being a holiday, I plan to loaf and relax.
Her replacement having arrived early, Bea had time to shop.
He sat there in silence, *his left cheek twitching as usual.*
He stood in the doorway, *his wet cloak dripping water on the rug,* and waited for some sign of recognition.

An absolute phrase, which consists of a noun or a pronoun and a verbal (see Lesson 12), modifies the sentence as a whole, not any special part of it. Because the phrase is not restricted to any special part of the sentence, the phrase should be set off.

4. Parenthetical expressions

The text, *moreover,* had not been carefully proofread.
You will find, *for example,* that the format is not attractive.
The meal, *to tell the truth,* was quite unappetizing.
His appearance, *I must admit,* would startle anyone.

These are words, phrases, or clauses that break into the sentence to explain, to emphasize, to qualify, or to point the direction of the thought and that should be set off.

5. Words used in direct address

"Remember, *Jimmy,* that we like your work," he said.
"*Henry,*" said the teacher, "you made an A on your paper."
"I believe, *sir,* that you have been misinformed," she replied.
"And now, *dear friends and neighbors,* let's eat," said Father Jamison.

6. Expressions designating the speaker in direct quotations

"With your permission," *Tom replied,* "I'll go home for the day."
"That will have to do," *said Mrs. Garcia,* "until we think of something better."

Other punctuation marks may be used instead of the comma if the sentence justifies their use.

"How shall I tell him?" asked Mary timidly. [question mark after question]
"Silence!" he shouted. "Get to work at once!" [exclamation point]
"Two of the buildings are firetraps," replied the inspector; "moreover, the library needs a new roof." [semicolon required to avoid a comma fault between independent clauses]

7. Negative insertions used for emphasis, units out of their position, and tag questions (short interrogative clauses combined with statements)

> Our plane was an old propeller model, *not the 747 we had expected.*
> *Tired and footsore,* the hikers finally reached camp.
> The hikers finally reached camp, *tired and footsore.*
> Her answer was a good one, *don't you think?*
> You remember, *don't you,* Dr. Wade's eloquent eulogy?

8. Degrees, titles, and the like when they follow names

> Helen Lyle, *Ph.D.,* gave the opening address.
> The new ambassador is Peter Jones, *Esq.*

9. In dates and addresses

> On July 14, *1904,* in a little cottage at 316 High Street, *Mayville, Illinois,* the wedding took place.

When a year follows a month, rather than a day of the month, the year is usually not set off. No comma is needed before a ZIP code number:

> As of March 1995 his mailing address was 1675 East Union Street, Seattle, Washington 98122.

NAME _____   SCORE _____

Directions: Insert commas where they are necessary in the following sentences. Then, in the space before each sentence write one of the following numbers to indicate the rule that governs the punctuation of the sentence:

1. a nonrestrictive clause or phrase
2. an appositive
3. a noun in direct address

4. a parenthetical element
5. the speaker in dialogue
6. an absolute phrase

_____ 1. The meeting having finally ended the people walked out of the room.

_____ 2. The end of the meeting came I'm sure you understand not a minute to soon for any of us.

_____ 3. Jim Atkins the unofficial leader of our little group suggested that we walk down the street to a small restaurant for lunch.

_____ 4. "Folks," said Jim, "there is a great little Italian restaurant just around the corner."

_____ 5. "That sounds like a wonderful idea Jim," said Marianne. "Let's go."

_____ 6. So they walked down Elm Street which is lined, ironically enough, with oak trees.

_____ 7. The elm trees people say died many years ago from a strange disease.

_____ 8. The oak trees which were planted to replace the elm trees are about forty years old.

_____ 9. The oak trees having grown to about twenty feet in height the street is now pleasantly shaded all day long.

_____ 10. "The trees are certainly beautiful," said Josie. "Do you know who planted them?"

_____ 11. The city's mayor Angela Lopez led the campaign to remove the dead trees and plant new trees along the street.

_____ 12. It was the city's landscaping crew however that did the actual work of planting the trees.

_____ 13. The oak trees planted along the street are white oaks called *Quircus alba* by scientists.

_____ 14. These oaks which often live 200 to 400 years are the noblest of the oak trees.

_____ 15. There was a famous oak tree in Hartford, Connecticut, the Charter Oak.

_____ 16. During the years before American Revolution, King James II dispatched Sir Edmund Andros the governor of the Dominion of New England to seize the state's charter.

_____ 17. The legislature debated the surrender of the charter which was quite a controversial request until late into the night.

_____ 18. Suddenly, the candles all blew out and with the room dark the charter disappeared.

_____ 19. The charter which was hidden in the oak tree by Joseph Wadsworth a member of the legislature was saved from the British.

_____ 20. The Charter Oak an important part of American history was destroyed by a windstorm in 1856; a marble monument marks the spot where the oak tree grew.

Directions: Each of the following sentences contains one adjective clause or one participial phrase. Underline the clause or phrase. Insert commas where they are needed. In the space at the left of each sentence write **R** if the clause of phrase is restrictive; **N** if it is nonrestrictive.

_____ 1. Can you recommend a course that will require little outside reading?

_____ 2. I signed up for Philosophy 274 which requires much outside reading.

_____ 3. We spent the winter in El Paso where the winters are mild.

_____ 4. We want to move to some area where the winters are mild.

_____ 5. Mr. Beech having hung up his hat and coat joined our group.

_____ 6. A large man holding a small baby sat down next to me.

_____ 7. The first person who gives us the correct answer will win the prize.

_____ 8. Lily Robbins who thought she knew the answer raised her hand.

_____ 9. Our cruise ship stopped at Samoa where many of us went ashore.

_____ 10. An island I'd like to visit is Samoa.

_____ 11. Anyone knowing this man's whereabouts should notify the police.

_____ 12. My eldest son having witnessed the accident called the police.

_____ 13. Betty confided in her oldest friend whose opinion she valued highly.

_____ 14. Betty's roommate is a girl who parents live in Bermuda.

_____ 15. This is Shirley Bascom of whom you have heard me speak.

_____ 16. Can't you think of someone from whom you could borrow the money?

_____ 17. My unabridged dictionary badly scorched in the fire must be replaced.

_____ 18. Books kept in the reserve library may be checked out after five o'clock.

_____ 19. Our speaker today is a man who really needs no introduction.

_____ 20. Our speaker today is Mayor Trueblood who really needs no introduction.

Exercise 18   *Commas to Enclose*

NAME _____ SCORE _____

Directions: Recognizing typical punctuation situations in your own writing is an important skill. In the spaces provided, write two sentences to illustrate each of the rules indicated. Punctuate your sentences correctly.

1. Nonrestrictive adjective clauses

   a. _____
   _____

   b. _____
   _____

2. Nonrestrictive participial phrases

   a. _____
   _____

   b. _____
   _____

3. Appositives

   a. _____
   _____

   b. _____
   _____

4. Nouns used in direct address

   a. _____
   _____

   b. _____
   _____

5. Parenthetical elements

   a. _____
   _____

   b. _____
   _____

6. Absolute phrases

   a. _____
   _____

   b. _____
   _____

Directions: Each of the following sentences contains one adjective clause or one participial phrase. Underline the clause or phrase. Insert commas where they are needed. In the space at the left of each sentence write **R** if the clause or phrase is restrictive, **N** if it is nonrestrictive.

_____ 1. How tall is that tree standing beside the school?

_____ 2. Jimmy Thomas who played baseball here three years ago has been called up by a major league club.

_____ 3. My father needs someone who will mow his yard twice a month.

_____ 4. The maple is one of the trees that lose their leaves every fall.

_____ 5. I got a phone call yesterday from my sister Sally who calls about once a week to check up on me.

_____ 6. The little kid standing in the last row of the class is my nephew Tim.

_____ 7. Manny poking his head around the corner of the house saw the thief just as he left the yard.

_____ 8. Our new accountant is Ralph Marks who just moved to town.

_____ 9. We needed an accountant who has a good understanding of tax law.

_____ 10. A couple of men standing on the street corner helped Bertha push her car off the street.

_____ 11. This morning I met two students that had just entered school yesterday.

_____ 12. This morning I met Ron Jansen who just entered school yesterday.

_____ 13. Lois Larkin owns a shop that sells cross-country ski equipment.

_____ 14. Lois Larkin owns *The Snow Shop* which sells cross-country ski equipment.

_____ 15. A woman wearing a blue suit and a bright red tie just walked into my office.

_____ 16. Joan Williams wearing a blue suit and a bright tie just walked into my office.

_____ 17. That old truck dented and dusty will have to last through one more winter.

_____ 18. My roommate only goes to movies that are odd, old comedies.

_____ 19. The sailing club needs volunteers who know how to repair fiberglass.

_____ 20. Rich Houston who is an expert with fiberglass just joined the sailing club.

NAME _____ SCORE _____

Directions: Insert commas where they are needed. Then, in the space at the left, write the number of commas you used in each sentence.

_____ 1. Exhausted bruised but deliriously happy the players left the field at 3:15 P.M. three hours and 14 minutes after the start of the season's final game which had brought the state championship to Forest City.

_____ 2. When the session was over Millie Morse who complained most loudly during the session suggested a change in the agenda a plan that pleased nobody else in the hall it seemed to us.

_____ 3. When we had located John rounded up the two dogs and left food out for the cat we set off on our trip to the cabin a drive of about 300 miles.

_____ 4. Shortly before the sun had slipped into the sea behind the islands each tinted a fiery red by the sun's rays which also turned the waters around the islands a bright glowing orange.

_____ 5. Jumping quickly from the dock to the deck of the boat we loaded the supplies collected earlier and slipped out through the harbor making as little noise as possible.

_____ 6. After the girls checked the tennis schedule for next season they came to the conclusion that they had a very trying season ahead of them.

_____ 7. Once you have tried the new shrimp pizza down at Pezzoli Restaurant you will never want other pizzas most of which will taste bland by comparison.

_____ 8. At our last convention which was held in Taos New Mexico on April 3 1995 we decided to withdraw from the national organization and become an independent club.

_____ 9. When you have located the island on the chart plot your course measure the distance from here to the island and try to estimate your time of arrival.

_____ 10. Their tents knocked flat by a sudden gust of wind the hapless Girl Scouts who were soon soaked to the skin found a flashlight formed a haphazard line and walked dejectedly back to camp.

NAME _____ SCORE _____

Directions: The following sentences contain 40 numbered spots, some with punctuation and some without punctuation. In the corresponding numbered spaces at the left, write **C** if the punctuation is correct or **W** if the punctuation is incorrect.

1. _____ (1) Mark had some bad luck yesterday; he lost his glasses, got a parking
                        1

2. _____   ticket and missed an algebra test.
                        2

3. _____ (2) After running Harry often goes to the gym and lifts weights for an hour.
                        3   4

4. _____

5. _____ (3) We took, I'm sure a longer route; but we were able to avoid that
                        5

6. _____   monstrous traffic jam on Highway 60.
                        6

7. _____ (4) The test was long difficult, and a little tricky but Jim passed it quite easily.
                        7   8

8. _____

9. _____ (5) The new computers will arrive this Monday, everyone therefore, will need
                        9   10

10. _____   to work late on Tuesday and Wednesday.

11. _____ (6) Angie Thompson a recent graduate of the state university, has accepted
                        11

12. _____   a job as our new systems analyst.
                        12

13. _____ (7) As the storm clouds gathered the band members moved their instruments
                        13

14. _____   inside, and set up on the stage.
                        14

15. _____ (8) The trip that we planned for next weekend has been canceled, the hotels
                        15   16

16. _____   in that area are all booked up.

17. _____ (9) The only way to the waterfall is to drive to the park, walk up the hill
                        17

199

18. _____ and climb that steep rocky path to the top.

19. _____ (10) The old church once very shabby, has been completely restored by a

20. _____ company that wants to open a restaurant.

21. _____ (11) That woman is Georgie Butler the new company president, her first name

22. _____ is really Georgina.

23. _____ (12) My brothers graduated from high school on June 12, 1999, they enlisted

24. _____ in the Navy the next day.

25. _____ (13) When the hard rain started several sensitive car alarms went off in the

26. _____ parking lot.

27. _____ (14) Richard Abbott, who is well known in Texas as a horseman recently

28. _____ bought a ranch in northern Idaho.

29. _____ (15) Did it ever occur to you, that we should have studied before we were to

30. _____ take the exam?

31. _____ (16) The unhappy, frowning teacher looked straight at me and said; "Please

32. _____ answer question number two for us, Robin."

33. _____ (17) Looking quickly at the books on the shelf, Carla selected one and walked

34. _____ to the desk looking at the index as she walked.

35. _____ (18) When she returned the book lay on the table, she had not, as she thought,

36. _____ left it at work.

37. _____ (19) Although Edwin is an attorney who has little experience in actual trials

38. _____ he has a good chance to win this case.

39. _____ (20) Onto our work table the boss dropped a huge box containing the

40. _____ advertising fliers and a large number of envelopes.

This lesson covers a number of tricky punctuation marks.

APOSTROPHE

The apostrophe (') has three uses:

1. To form the possessive of nouns and indefinite pronouns
2. To mark the omitted material in contractions
3. To form certain plurals, such as those of letters and abbreviations

Forming Possessives

Any noun, whether singular or plural, that does not end in *s* shows ownership by adding an apostrophe and *s:*

> a boy*'s* hat [the hat belongs to the boy], the horse*'s* tail, Carol*'s* car, men*'s* shoes, children*'s* toys

Plural nouns that end in *s* form possessives by adding an apostrophe after the *s:*

> boy*s'* hats, horse*s'* tails, the Smith*s'* home, ladie*s'* dresses

Singular nouns ending in *s* or *z* form the possessive by adding *'s.*

> the countess*'s* castle, Frances*'s* reply, Mr. Gomez*'s* report

On rare occasions, if the pronunciation of the word with the additional *s*-sound would be awkward, it is permissible to form the possessive with an apostrophe alone.

> for goodness' sake

For the sake of uniformity, the exercises on possessives will ask that you use the *'s* after singular nouns ending in *s*.

The indefinite pronouns, but not the personal pronouns, form the possessive with the aid of the apostrophe:

> somebody*'s* sweater, anyone*'s* opinion, anybody*'s* game [But note the possessive forms of pronouns: his, hers, its, theirs, ours, yours, whose.]

Compound words and word groups form the possessive by adding an apostrophe and *s* to the last word of the group:

> My sister-in-law*'s* last visit was in December.
> Did you get anyone else*'s* opinion of your paper?

Note that establishing ownership of two or more items requires careful attention. For individual ownership, add an apostrophe and *s* at the end of both owners.

Oliver Stone's and Alfred Hitchcock's movies [indicating that each made certain movies]

For joint ownership of two or more items, add an apostrophe and *s* at the end of the second owner's name:

Rogers and Hammerstein's musicals [indicating that they wrote musicals as joint projects]

Omitted Material

The apostrophe is used to stand for the omitted material in contractions:

doesn't [does not], won't [will not], she's [she is, she has], o'clock [of the clock], rock 'n' roll [rock and roll]

You must learn to distinguish carefully between the following pairs of contractions and possessives:

Contraction	*Possessive*
it's [it is, it has]	its
there's [there is, there has]	theirs
they're [they are]	their
who's [who is, who has]	whose
you're [you are]	your

Unusual Plurals

Use an apostrophe to form the plural of letters and words that are treated as words.

the three *R's;* mostly *A's* and *B's;* too many *and's;* no *if's, and's,* or *but's* about it.

Although some authorities no longer require the formation of the plural of numbers and symbols with an apostrophe, there are times when the lack of an apostrophe creates confusion. Thus, it seems logical to retain the apostrophe for the sake of clarity.

Btu's, CPA's, 1980's, scores in the 80's and 90's

Many writers need to be reminded regularly of an important related fact: An apostrophe is never used in forming the plural of either a common or a proper noun.

There are two Kathys in the class. Two grandmas attended.

COLON

The colon (:) is a formal mark announcing an explanation, a list, or a quotation to follow.

"My fellow Americans: My speech tonight will examine...."
All hikers must bring the following: a flashlight, a small ax, and a waterproof tarp.
Mr. Rankin stood and addressed the group: "I don't intend to take much of your time today."

The colon is used in formal papers to begin a quotation of four or more lines. The text of the quotation is indented from both margins and is set off by quotation marks.

In cases where the colon sets off a quotation, the identifying tag should appear in the independent clause.

Colons are also used as a mark of separation in certain special constructions:

Hours, minutes, and seconds
> 1:14:10 P.M.

Biblical chapters and verses
> I Kings 2:1

Titles and subtitles
> *Conversations: Famous Women Speak Out*

Note that after a colon it is permissible to have an initial capital letter if the text following the colon is a complete sentence. Do not use a colon to separate a verb from its complement or a preposition from its object.

Faulty: All hikers must bring: a flashlight, a small ax, and a waterproof tarpaulin.

Faulty: The things a hiker must bring are: a flashlight, a small ax, and a waterproof tarpaulin.

Faulty: The hiker's equipment should consist of: a flashlight, a small ax, and a waterproof tarpaulin.

DASH

The dash (—) is used to show an abrupt change in thought in the sentence. It must be used sparingly and never as a substitute for other marks.

Superior students—notice that I said *superior*—will not have to take the test.

New surroundings, new friends, a challenging new job—all these helped Eugene overcome his grief.

HYPHEN

The hyphen (-) is used to divide a word at the end of a line and to join words to form various types of compounds. Divide a word between syllables only. With words having a prefix or a suffix, divide the word after the prefix and before the suffix. Avoid dividing a word so that a single letter ends or begins a line. (Consult your dictionary for problems of syllabic division.)

mathe-matics *not* mathem-atics
inter-collegiate *not* intercol-legiate
govern-ess *not* gov-erness
enough *not* e-nough
many *not* man-y

It is important to note that the use of computerized publishing programs by newspaper and magazine publishers has created a situation where words seem to be divided at random wherever the end of the line occurs. In academic writing, however, it is a good idea to continue the practice of dividing words by the rules stated here.

Use hyphens to join the parts of compound modifiers preceding nouns.

> Observe his well-kept lawn. His lawn is well kept.
> We deplore your devil-may-care attitude.

This use of a hyphen sometimes determines an exact meaning:

> a roll of 20-dollar bills; a roll of 20 dollar bills
> all-American boys; all American boys

Use hyphens with compound numbers from twenty-one to ninety-nine and with fractions:

> Twenty-two people claimed the one-third share of the reward money but received only one-eighth.

Use hyphens, particularly with prefixes and suffixes, to avoid awkward combinations of letters or to distinguish between two meanings of a word:

> anti-intellectual
> pre-Aztec
> her doll-like face
> re-cover a couch [not recover the money]

QUOTATION MARKS

Quotation marks should be used to enclose quoted material and words you may use in some special way. Use double quotation marks (" ") to enclose the exact words of a quoted speech. Quotation marks always come in pairs. The marks show the beginning and the end of a speech, whether it is part of a sentence, one sentence, or several sentences. If a speech is interrupted by material showing who said it, quotation marks set off the quoted material from the explanatory material. Use quotation marks where the directly quoted material begins and where it ends or is interrupted. Indirect quotations are *not* set off by quotation marks:

> "I admit," said Ralph, "that I was mistaken."
> [Note that the explanatory material is set off from the direct quotation.]

> Peg answered, "I didn't attend. I wasn't in town." [More than one sentence.]
> Peg answered that she hadn't attended because she hadn't been in town.
> [This is an indirect quotation. Words not directly quoted should not be enclosed in quotation marks.]

Use double quotation marks to set off the subdivisions of books, names of songs, and titles of units of less than book length, such as short stories, short poems, essays, and articles:

> The second chapter of *Moby Dick* is entitled "The Carpet-Bag."
> Eva Peron sings "Don't Cry for Me, Argentina" in the musical *Evita.*
> Our anthology includes "Threes," a poem from Sandburg's *Smoke and Steel.*

> The first article I read for my research paper was William Calvin's "The Great Climate Flip-flop" in the *Atlantic Monthly.*

Titles of books, magazines, long poems, newspapers, motion pictures, and radio and television series are not set in double quotation marks. In printed material, these items are set in italic type (*type like this*). Other special uses of italics are for foreign words and phrases and for names of ships, planes, and spacecraft. In handwritten or typewritten papers, underlining (<u>typescript like this</u>) is the equivalent of italics in printed material. Word-processors can produce effects such as bold (**bold**) and italic, which gives students a capability previously not available except through typesetting.

Double quotation marks are also used to set off slang words used in serious writing. Sometimes double quotation marks are used to set off words when they are referred to as words:

> The witness had only recently been released from the "slammer."
> Words like "seize" and "siege" are often misspelled.

Usage is divided on these uses of quotation marks. The two words in the second example would almost certainly appear in italics in printed material. Student writers of handwritten or typed material should either underline such words or set them off by quotation marks, the first method being the more common practice.

Double Quotation Marks with Other Punctuation

Follow this usage in the placing of quotation marks in relation to other marks:

1. Commas and periods always go inside quotation marks.

2. Semicolons and colons always go outside quotation marks.

3. Question marks and exclamation points go inside if they belong to the quoted part, outside if they do not.

> "Come in," said my uncle, "and take off your coats." [comma and period]
> Mr. Lowe said, "I heartily endorse this candidate"; unfortunately most of the audience thought he said *hardly* instead of *heartily.* [semicolon outside]
> "Heavens!" he exclaimed. "Is this the best you can do?" [exclamation point and question mark]
> Mother asked, "Where were you last night?" [no double punctuation]
> Did she say, "I came home early"?
> [question mark belongs to the whole sentence, not to the quoted part]
> Did Mother ask, "Where were you last night?"
> [note that there is only one question mark after a double question like this]

Single Quotation Marks

Use single quotation marks to enclose a speech within a speech:

> "I wonder what he meant," said Betty, "when he said, 'There are wheels within wheels.' "

You may not write many sentences like this one, but just the same, you should note that when you have quotes within quotes, the period comes inside both the single and double quotation marks.

NAME _____ SCORE _____

Directions: In the spaces at the left, write **C** if the punctuation is correct, **W** if it is wrong. Within the incorrect sentences, correct the faulty punctuation by adding, removing, or changing marks and adding, where needed, an additional *s* after an apostrophe.

_____ 1. Some of the coaches' drills—especially the short sprints—are very difficult and often leave the players exhausted.

_____ 2. "Morris' Movers" is the name of that amateur cross-country team; the members don't win any prizes, but they do have lot's of fun.

_____ 3. The list of prizes is impressive; five beautiful guitars, several collections of sheet music, and a biography of Carlos Santana.

_____ 4. A lawyers work must be typed perfectly, with all the *t's* crossed and all the *i's* dotted.

_____ 5. We need someone elses opinion in your case because its difficult to interpret the law in cases such as yours.

_____ 6. Wallace Brothers' Store is offering some real bargains in: women's apparel, mens' work clothes, and childrens' shoes.

_____ 7. "Tomorrow's agenda," said the speaker, "is filled with interesting and fascinating—but I see by your yawns that you've lost interest already.

_____ 8. Its not likely that anyone can replace you, with your lovely smile and great ability to allay peoples fears.

_____ 9. "Someone's coming down the walk," whispered Mary. "I don't recognize him; the footsteps are Jim's, but the whistle's Marvin's.

_____ 10. We're trying to improve our class's image; our reputation suffers because of everyones lack of motivation.

_____ 11. "Lets not panic," said the scoutmaster, "for calm action always lets us conquer trying circumstances."

_____ 12. If it's true that the dog hurt its leg, we'll surely need to find its owner before it's too late to help.

_____ 13. The new cars interior comes equipped with: leather seats, padded dashboard, and a special set of mirrors.

_____ 14. For the past few year's our teams lacked depth and experience, but this years' ought to be much more successful.

_____ 15. At 9 oclock you'll need to check the cakes progress and adjust the temperature of the oven.

Directions: Sentences 1–5 are indirect quotations. In the space provided, rewrite each sentence as a direct quotation. Sentences 6–10 are direct quotations. Rewrite each as an indirect quotation. You will have to alter some verb forms and some pronoun forms as well as the punctuation.

1. My brother said that he had lost his wallet.

2. The sales manager observed that he would need to hire two new division managers.

3. My teachers often tell me that I am too talkative in class.

4. The policeman asked if we needed directions to the next town.

5. Did she tell you that the elevator is being repaired?

6. The teller said to me, "It will take only a minute to compute your interest."

7. My father said, "I certainly appreciate all your hard work."

8. His sister answered, "I don't want to go sailing in this rainy weather."

9. The salesman asked, "Why did you select the convertible?"

10. Didn't she say, "You should take the right-hand fork after the covered bridge"?

NAME _____   SCORE _____

Directions: In the space at the left, write **C** if the punctuation is correct, **W** if it is incorrect. Within the incorrect sentences, correct the faulty punctuation by adding, removing, or changing marks.

_____   1. What's new about Jim's proposal is it's focus on the prospects open to us in the bond market, isn't it?

_____   2. You've selected the location of all the game's, haven't you?

_____   3. "Thats not right," said the captain. "I'm sure I told you to get everyones comments on that incident."

_____   4. He closed his comments with one final but very important statement: "Remember, friends, there's great hope that we can win, if we use the strength thats our's.

_____   5. Todays work list includes repairs for: the men's sauna, the womens locker room, and the childrens' play area.

_____   6. "Your assignment for Monday," said the professor, "is to read all section's on— but we don't have class on Monday, do we?"

_____   7. The equipment list for tomorrow's climb should include the following items: boots, ropes, pitons, gloves, a helmet, and a good, hearty lunch.

_____   8. "Its funny," mused Janet, "but these letters aren't addressed to me." "Perhaps they belong to the people next door."

_____   9. You'll find that todays agenda is filled with: committee meetings, general session's, subcommittee meetings, and several caucuses.

_____   10. You're probably familiar with Parkinson's Law: In any job, the work expands to fill the available time.

_____   11. "Everyone's chances in the contest are equal," said Tom. "We'll simply put all the entries into a hat and draw out the name of the winner.

_____   12. Sam's excuse for quitting football was that the X's and O's used in the coaches' diagrams were too confusing for him to understand.

_____   13. When I opened the lunch my sister had packed for me, I found: a slice of bread with it's crusts cut off, two days worth of old lunch wrappings, and a note that said, "Now we are even."

_____   14. Ms. Jones decision to stand for reelection is based on a misinterpretation of the voters' opinions of her past performances.

_____   15. Just a few day's ago—I can't remember exactly when—Joan ordered a whole years supply of pens' and pencils' for the office.

Directions: Sentences 1–5 are indirect quotations. In the space provided, rewrite each sentence as a direct quotation. Sentence 6–10 are direct quotations. Rewrite each as an indirect quotation. You will have to alter some verb forms and pronoun forms as well as the punctuation.

1. Mr. Raymond reported that he saw an unidentified flying object over his house last night.

   _____

2. Kathleen responded that the last train for the city leaves every evening at 6:30 P.M.

   _____

3. The reporter asked when the murder victim had last been seen alive.

   _____

4. Did she say that there are no rooms left in the hotel for this weekend?

   _____

5. The manager announced that all the part-time employees would receive a 10-percent raise.

   _____

6. "You must answer every question if your application is to be considered," said the receptionist to me.

   _____

7. The secretary looked up slowly from her work and said, "I wonder what the next big crisis will be."

   _____

8. The delighted child said, "This is the best party anyone ever had."

   _____

9. The announcer turned to the woman and asked, "Would you like to tell our audience exactly how you feel about winning the lottery?"

   _____

10. On the boss's wall there is a sign that asks, "Why is there always enough time to do something over and never enough time to do it right?"

   _____

Lesson 20
End Marks; Summary of Punctuation Rules

This lesson discusses end marks and summarizes all the punctuation rules presented in this book.

PERIOD

The **period** is used after a complete declarative sentence and after ordinary abbreviations. Its use as end punctuation after sentences needs no examples. Its use after abbreviations is a little more complicated.

Personal Titles

A period is used in the following abbreviations: *Mr., Mrs., Ms., Messrs., Mmes.,* and *Dr.* These abbreviations appear before the name. Periods are also used for *Jr., Sr., Esq., D.D., Ph.D.,* and so forth, which are used after names. Miss does not require a period. *Ms.,* used instead of *Miss* or *Mrs.* when marital status is not indicated, is usually considered an abbreviation and uses a period, although some modern dictionaries have entries for it either with or without a period.

Latin-Based Terms

The following initials and abbreviations, used only in documentation pages and tabulations but not in ordinary writing, require periods: *e.g. (for example), etc. (and so forth), i.e. (that is), p., pp. (page, pages),* and *vol. (volume).* A.D., B.C., B.C.E., C.E., A.M., and P.M. (usually set in small caps in printed material) are used only with figures and where necessary for clarity. Note: A.D. should precede the year (A.D. 37); B.C., however, should follow the year (31 B.C.).

Addresses

The following abbreviations require periods and are acceptable in addresses but should be spelled out in ordinary writing: *St. (Street), Ave. (Avenue), Blvd. (Boulevard), Dr. (Drive), Rd. (Road), Co. (Company),* and *Inc. (Incorporated).* Conventionally, periods are used with abbreviations of the states *(Mass., Minn., Tex., W. Va.).* However, the two-letter capitalized symbols authorized by the U.S. Postal Service *(MA, MN, TX, WV)* do not require periods.

Poor: Last Mon. P.M. I visited my two older bros., who live in N.Y. Chas. works for a mfg. co. there. Thos. attends NYU, preparing himself for a gov't. job. He's coming home for Xmas.

Right: Last Monday afternoon I visited my two older brothers, who live in New York. Charles works for a manufacturing company there. Thomas attends New York University, preparing himself for a government job. He's coming home for Christmas.

Acronyms and Measurements

In modern usage, the "alphabet" name forms, or acronyms, of various governmental or intergovernmental agencies, social or professional organizations, and units of measurement used in scientific contexts are usually not followed by periods: *ACLU, CARE, CBS, CIA, NAACP, NCAA, NATO, PTA, SEC, UNESCO, Btu* (British thermal unit), *mpg, mph, rpm*. New acronyms and abbreviated forms spring into existence nowadays with regularity. The following examples are some that have gained common acceptance fairly recently: *AIDS* (acquired immune deficiency syndrome), *CAT scan* (computerized axial tomography), *CATV* (community antenna television), *CD* (certificate of deposit), *CEO* (chief executive officer), *COLA* (cost-of-living adjustment), *CPR* (cardiopulmonary resuscitation), *DWI* (driving while intoxicated), *IRA* (individual retirement account), *MIA* (missing in action), *MRI* (magnetic resonance imaging), *OPEC* (Organization of Petroleum Exporting Countries), *PC* (personal computer), *STOL* (short takeoff and landing), *VCR* (videocassette recorder). Refer to your dictionary when in doubt about the meaning of an abbreviated form or the possibility of using periods. Be prepared to find apparent inconsistencies and divided usage.

QUESTION MARK

The **question mark** is used after a *direct question,* which is an utterance that calls for an answer. (See Lesson 6.) A question mark is not used after an *indirect question,* which is a statement giving the substance of a question but not the words that would be used in a direct question.

Direct: Who goes there? Is that you? When do we eat? How much do I owe you? "Who goes there?" he demanded. [in dialogue]

Indirect: She asked me how old I was. I wondered why she would ask such a question. [Note that these are statements, not direct questions.]

Refer to page 205 to review the use of question marks with quotation marks.

EXCLAMATION POINT

The **exclamation point** is used sparingly in modern writing and should be reserved for statements of strong feeling. Mild exclamations, such as *oh, goodness, well, yes,* and *no,* are followed by commas, not exclamation points. Be sure to place the exclamation mark after the exclamation itself.

"Help! I'm slipping!" he shouted. [Note the period after *shouted.*]

"Stop that!" she screamed. [Do not put the exclamation point after *screamed.*]

"Well, it was exciting, wasn't it?" "Oh, I had a pleasant time."

SUMMARY OF PUNCTUATION RULES

This summary covers the indispensable punctuation rules for anything you write. Colons, commas, periods, and even question marks and exclamation points do have other uses for special occasions or effects, but these occasional applications rarely cause problems for most writers.

Commas to Separate: Five Rules

1. Compound sentences
2. Items in a series
3. Coordinate adjectives
4. Introductory modifiers
5. Words that may be misread together

Colon: Two Rules

1. Use a colon to announce a list, an explanation, or a long quotation.
   a. If the text following a colon is a complete sentence, use an initial capital letter.
   b. Do not use a colon to separate a verb from its complement or a preposition from its object.
2. Use a colon to separate hours, minutes, and seconds; biblical chapters and verses; titles and subtitles.

Apostrophe: Two Rules

1. With possessives
2. With contractions

Period: Two Rules

1. After declarative sentences
2. After most abbreviations

Commas to Enclose: Eight Rules

1. Nonrestrictive clauses and phrases
2. Appositives
3. Absolute phrases
4. Parenthetical expressions
5. Words in direct address
6. The speaker in dialogue
7. Negative insertions
8. Dates, addresses, degrees, and titles

Semicolon: Two Rules

1. In compound sentences without a conjunction joining the independent clauses
2. To separate items in a series when commas occur within items

Quotation Marks: Three Rules

1. Enclose direct quotations
2. Set off titles
3. Set off words used in some special way

Question Mark: One Rule

1. After direct questions

NAME _____ SCORE _____

Directions: In the space at the left of each sentence write **C** if the punctuation is correct, **W** if it is incorrect. Within the incorrect sentences, correct the faulty punctuation.

_____ 1. "Take this message for Mr Johnson please," said the voice on the phone; "I have been unable to reach him by phone."

_____ 2. N.A.S.A. usually launched space shuttles from Cape Kennedy which is located on Cape Canaveral in Florida.

_____ 3. The FBI office in our state capital has moved its headquarters to a building that is located on the interstate highway.

_____ 4. Please mail the package to my home address 646 Seneca Avenue Madison WI 66606.

_____ 5. Do you think we should contact NOAA or OSHA about that question?

_____ 6. My dictionary tells me that NOS stands for 'not otherwise specified,' but my friend Robert says he uses 'nos' to make his car go faster in street races.

_____ 7. Should we gather all the tools—wrenches, ratchets, etc—before we begin to work on that project?

_____ 8. "Slow down!" she shouted; "None of the traffic lights on this street are working."

_____ 9. My brother's degree from law school was changed from LL.B to J.D. about five years after he graduated.

_____ 10. Some movies made in recent years, e.g., *Ocean's Eleven*, are actually remakes of movies first made many years ago.

_____ 11. I found that reference in Vol. XXXII, No. 12 of *Atlantic* magazine.

_____ 12. "Isn't my appointment with the doctor on Wednesday at 11:00 AM?

_____ 13. Can you tell me where the library, which used to be at the corner of Third and Main is now located.

_____ 14. July 4, 1776, the day the Declaration of Independence was signed, is the day officially celebrated as the birthday of the United States.

_____ 15. "When asked, the instructor said, 'The next test is on Tuesday, November fifteenth,'" Tom responded to my question about the date of the next test.

_____ 16. Uncle Dan who owns that beautiful sailboat out in the harbor once sailed as a crew member on a boat in The America's Cup Series.

_____ 17. "Can you tell me the name of the movie that tells the story of the baseball player Lou Gehrig's life?" asked Marlene.

_____ 18. "Yes, it was titled *The Pride of the Yankees*," responded Lillian, "It starred Gary Cooper as Lou Gehrig."

_____ 19. Yesterday after class had been dismissed, my instructor asked me, why I had been absent from the previous two classes?

_____ 20. With all the people assembled in the auditorium we tried to present our proposal using a computer running Power Point.

Directions: If the following sentences, correct every error in punctuation by adding or deleting punctuation marks as needed.

1. Looming over the campsite is a huge white pine that is 150 feet tall, it's branches are reflected in the lake, lying just nearby.

   _____

2. This years budget doesnt include any funds for hiring the new staff members that we need if we're going to implement that new newly proposed quality control plan.

   _____

3. Smiling broadly at the team the coach said, "I ve been coaching for almost 20 years and I don t believe I have ever had a team that plays with as much heart and courage as you displayed in todays game.

   _____

4. Al Lopez the new engineer, came to us from a construction company where he was assistant superintendent in charge of engineering for a parking garage project.

   _____

5. "My computer is older and slower than your's," laughed Nancy, "but it does what I need, and doesnt cause me any problems."

   _____

6. Its time for the 6 o'clock news, but I think, I will watch the motocross race on Channel 237 instead.

   _____

7. You need to drive back to the library where you left your books before it closes and you have to wait until tomorrow morning to get them back.

   _____

8. Laughing softly the manager looked at Gonzales and said, "I want you to play right field today even though you haven't played there since you played in Little League."

   _____

9. Stretching out below us was a beautiful valley its floor a vast green meadow and its far border a beautiful river.

   _____

10. Titan Corporation a national security company is opening a branch office in town so that it can offer its services to the new companies opening in the new industrial park outside of town.

    _____

NAME _____ SCORE _____

Directions: The following sentences contain 40 numbered spots between words or beneath words. (The number is beneath the word when the punctuation problem involves the use of an apostrophe in the word.) In the correspondingly numbered spots at the left, write **C** if the punctuation is correct or **W** if it is incorrect.

1. _____   (1) The sportscaster on the local television station has resigned, in his final
                                                                                            1

2. _____   broadcast he said he'd found a place where people are better sports than
                                    2

                    they are here.

3. _____   (2) After I had read the new women's magazine, I gave the copy to Janie Schultz,
                                                   3   4

4. _____   who is a free-lance writer of some note.

5. _____   (3) My eccentric uncle left me some unusual items in his will: an antique
                                                                                 5

6. _____   sewing machine, three advertising posters, and a small leather purse.
                                                                   6

7. _____   (4) Someone—I don't really want to know who—has left a long jagged scratch
                                                           7   8

8. _____   on the side of my new car.

9. _____   (5) Looking up from behind the book and smiling shyly Melissa said, "It must
                                                                              9

10. _____   be time for the party to start; I hear the band tuning up."
                                                    10

11. _____   (6) The weather being, as far as I was concerned far too cold for gardening;
                                                             11   12

12. _____   I picked up a book that I'd been trying to read for some time.

13. _____   (7) You need the following items to make a good omelette: eggs, milk, butter,
                                                                          13

14. _____   cheese, bacon, and a good omelette pan.
                                  14

15. _____   (8) "I checked the list before I went into the store, but I couldn't find it when
                                                                          15

16. _____   I got in the store," said Grandma, who is a trifle absent-minded.
                                  16

17. _____   (9) At last the girls have arrived, their luggage has been here for day's
                                              17   18

217

18. _____   cluttering up the front hallway.

19. _____ (10)   As there is no other way out of the valley; we cleared the logging road
                   19

20. _____   using: axes, shovels, pickaxes, and good old muscle power.
                   20

21. _____ (11)   I think I'll try to buy a new car, my old one is very dirty on the inside, and
                   21

22. _____   it's trunk has a big dent in it.
                   22

23. _____ (12)   Many industries in the country are beginning to follow the patterns of

24. _____   Japanese management; with company songs, calisthenics, and quality circles.
                   23   24

25. _____ (13)   I'm delighted to say that I'm finally going to fulfill one of my dreams,
                   25   26

26. _____   I'm going to take a trip to the Grand Canyon.

27. _____ (14)   Gathering his belongings up the stairs he walked and left the meeting;
                   27   28

28. _____   those left at the table were completely surprised.

29. _____ (15)   "Thats going to be a great boon to this small town," said Joan Shields,
                   29   30

30. _____   "not many towns have their own telephone company."

31. _____ (16)   After all our club is very small, we cannot expect to compete with a
                   31   32

32. _____   large club from a major city.

33. _____ (17)   My boss called me and said, "Jones, my boy, youre going to love your next
                   33

34. _____   assignment; and that's an order.
                   34

35. _____ (18)   "Somebody else's car would be better than mine, yours, Joan, is especially
                   35   36

36. _____   well suited to carry trash," laughed Harry.

37. _____ (19)   Mr. Wells smiled and asked, "Can I interest anyone in a free dinner at a dark,

38. _____   expensive French restaurant?"
                   37   38

39. _____ (20)   A new worker entered the room and asked "What time is lunch around
                   39

40. _____   here and how far is the cafeteria from here?"
                   40

NAME _____ SCORE _____

Directions: The following sentences contain forty numbered spaces between words or beneath words. (The number is beneath the word when the problem involves the use of an apostrophe in that word.) In the correspondingly numbered spaces at the left, write **C** if the punctuation is correct or **W** if it incorrect.

1. _____ (1) As almost everyone knows a few species of spiders are poisonous,
                                                          1   2

2. _____ but those in our gardens are almost always harmless.

3. _____ (2) Dr. Stuart, who's witticisms and puns are widely known and widely
                                        3

4. _____ deplored, laughed heartily at his own joke.
                            4

5. _____ (3) Another thing you will notice in Italy is the size of Italian paper money,
                                        5

6. _____ the bill's are larger than our's.
                            6

7. _____ (4) The bell for ten-o'clock classes having rung; I thanked Dr. Adams for
                                7   8

8. _____ her helpful suggestion and left the office.

9. _____ (5) "Our trip," said Aunt Edna, "was wonderfully exciting but I must admit
                                              9

10. _____ that theres no place like home."
                        10

11. _____ (6) The response to the remark was mild, we didn't want to encourage
                                      11

12. _____ Dr. Evans, who is easily inspired to talk endlessly.
                        12

13. _____ (7) After dinner several of us sat around the campfire discussing politics,
                                            13

14. _____ soon we were in the midst of a lively, good-natured debate.
                                  14

15. _____ (8) One of Bacon's beliefs that I do not agree with, is that parents should
                                        15

16. _____ choose their children's occupations.
                        16

17. _____ (9) I reminded the clerk that the package should be delivered to my new
                              17

18. _____ address, which is 1167 South 16th Street.
                        18

19. _____ (10) Protecting the environment is not the responsibility of governmental

20. _____   agencies alone, it must be everyones concern.
                      ₁₉   ₂₀

21. _____ (11) The opening speeches were so long, so rambling, and so dull that it's no
                                                            ₂₁   ₂₂

22. _____   wonder some of us fell asleep.

23. _____ (12) Although the child did not really understand his grandfather's little joke
                                                            ₂₃   ₂₄

24. _____   he laughed politely.

25. _____ (13) Our apartment is on Oak Street; the easiest way to reach it is by way of
                                              ₂₅

26. _____   Summit Avenue which is a one-way street.
                              ₂₆

27. _____ (14) "Recently I have noticed," the memo from the sales manager read,

28. _____   "that many of our clerk's mispronounce the word 'accessories.'"
                              ₂₇   ₂₈

29. _____ (15) Every camper should bring: hiking boots, a pup tent, and two changes of
                                        ₂₉

30. _____   heavy, winter clothing.
                      ₃₀

31. _____ (16) "Dodo" can mean either of two things: an extinct flightless bird, that once
                                        ₃₁   ₃₂

32. _____   lived on Mauritius or a stupid person.

33. _____ (17) The stranger's jacket was torn, ill fitting, and covered with mud but his
                                              ₃₃   ₃₄

34. _____   manner was quiet and gentle.

35. _____ (18) With great ceremony the roast pig was carried into the dining hall; it's
                                                                      ₃₅ ₃₆

36. _____   open mouth holding a large red apple.

37. _____ (19) "Let's not play with these tools, children," said the gardener, you might
                        ₃₇   ₃₈

38. _____   fall and cut yourselves."

39. _____ (20) Contrary to the stories, that we had heard about the new regional manager;
                              ₃₉   ₄₀

40. _____   we found him to be quite agreeable.

PUNCTUATION

There are 15 rules for the use of commas, two for semicolons, and more for using apostrophes, colons, dashes, hyphens, quotation marks, periods, and question marks, but for practical purposes you should focus on a more limited list of rules.

☐ Commas

1. Use commas to separate the independent clauses of a compound sentence when a coordinating conjunction is present. [Note that a semicolon can replace the comma and coordinating conjunction. This use is the only common use of the semicolon.]

   Maria opened her books, and she began to study.
   Maria opened her books; then she began to study.

2. Use commas to separate items in a series.

   We saw Thomas, Richard, and Harrison at the movie.

3. Use a comma between coordinate adjectives.

   We finally completed that long, difficult project.

4. Use a comma to set off introductory verbal phrases and subordinate clauses.

   Jumping into the chair, the cat curled up and went to sleep.

5. Use a comma to set off two or more prepositional phrases at the beginning of a sentence. Single phrases and, when the subject and verb are reversed, longer phrases at the beginning of a sentence are usually not set off with a comma.

6. Use a comma to prevent misreading. Misreading often occurs if an introductory element is not punctuated correctly, but some short prepositional phrases cause problems in certain contexts.

   Once inside, the dog and cat slept soundly before the fire.

   The comma is essential to maintain the sense of the sentence.

7. Most sentence interrupters, with the exception of restrictive appositives, restrictive participial phrases, and restrictive adjective clauses, are set off by commas.

   *Note that with few exceptions, participial phrases are not set off with commas when they are the final element of the sentence.

   Thus we can establish a rule of thumb: Opening elements are set off with one comma, interrupting elements are set off by two, and final elements connect to the sentence without punctuation. Some have called this generalization the rule of one, two, and zero.

8. Set off both the speaker in dialogue and any person addressed in the text.

221

☐ End Marks

☐ End marks are fairly simple: Periods end sentences. Question marks end questions.

☐ Exclamation Points

☐ Exclamation points are used sparingly, and most often in dialogue. It is better to create emphasis through the use of word choice and emphatic sentence structure than through exclamation points.

☐ Apostrophe

Use apostrophes to create possessives and to indicate contractions. Apostrophes are used for clarity's sake in creating unusual plurals. In other cases, do not use apostrophes to create plurals.

☐ Dashes, Hyphens, and Quotation Marks

☐ Dashes, hyphens, and quotation marks have special functions, and their use should be checked against the rules in this text.

5 Usage

Lessons, Practice Sheets, and Exercises

Lesson 21   *Using Verbs Correctly: Principal Parts; Tense*

In Lesson 2 you learned that some verbs are regular and others are irregular. Regular verbs add *ed* ending in the past tense (*earn, earned*), but irregular verbs change their form (*grow, grew*). Since verb forms change to indicate changes in tense and voice, it is necessary to pay close attention to the forms of all verbs. We now review certain places where incorrect forms sometimes appear because of confusion in the use of the principal parts (the base, past tense, and past participle) of verbs. (See Supplement.)

VERB FORMS

To gain assurance in your use of verbs, you must remember how the past tense and the past participle are used. The **past tense** is always a single-word verb; it is never used with an auxiliary:

I *ate* my lunch. [Not: I *have ate* my lunch.]

The **past participle**, when it is used as a verb, is *never* a single word; it is used with the auxiliary *have* (in the correct tense) to form the perfect tenses or the auxiliary *be* (in the correct tense) to form the passive voice:

I *have done* the work. [Not: I *done* the work.]
The work *was done.* [Not: I the work *was did.*]

(The past participle is, of course, used as a single word when it is a modifier of a noun: the *broken* toy, the *worried* parents, some *known* criminals.)

Four groups of verbs often cause confusion. Each group contains verbs that have similar trouble spots. The basic solution for the problem in each group is to master the principal parts of the verbs. The principal parts are listed in this lesson in the customary order: base form, past tense, and past participle (P.P.).

Past Tense Versus Past Participle

Sometimes errors occur because the past tense of a verb is confused with the past participle of the verb.

	Verb	Past Tense	P.P.
Later they *became* [not *become*] more friendly.	become	became	become
They *began* [not *begun*] to laugh at us.	begin	began	begun
He had never *broken* [not *broke*] the law.	break	broke	broken
I should have *chosen* [not *chose*] a larger car.	choose	chose	chosen
Yesterday the child *came* [not *come*] home.	come	came	come
I *did* [not *done*] what she told me to do.	do	did	done
He *drank* [not *drunk*] some water.	drink	drank	drunk
I had *driven* [not *drove*] all day.	drive	drove	driven
The lamp had *fallen* [not *fell*] over.	fall	fell	fallen
The bird has *flown* [not *flew*] away.	fly	flew	flown
Small puddles have *frozen* [not *froze*] on the sidewalks.	freeze	froze	frozen
Dad has *given* [not *gave*] me a car.	give	gave	given
Theresa has *gone* [not *went*] to school.	go	went	gone
I've never *ridden* [not *rode*] a horse.	ride	rode	ridden
We ran out when the fire alarm *rang* [not *rung*].	ring	rang	rung
Lenny has *run* [not *ran*] in two marathons.	run	ran	run
I *saw* [not *seen*] your nephew yesterday.	see	saw	seen
It must have *sunk* [not *sank*] in deep water.	sink	sank	sunk
She should have *spoken* [not *spoke*] louder.	speak	spoke	spoken
The car had been *stolen* [not *stole*].	steal	stole	stolen
The witness was *sworn* [not *swore*] in.	swear	swore	sworn
John has *swum* [not *swam*] across the lake.	swim	swam	swum
Someone had *torn* [not *tore*] the dollar bill.	tear	tore	torn
You should have *worn* [not *wore*] a hat.	wear	wore	worn
I have already *written* [not *wrote*] my essay.	write	wrote	written

Regular Versus Irregular

Sometimes errors occur because an irregular verb is thought to be regular.

	Verb	Past Tense	P.P.
The wind *blew* [not *blowed*] steadily all day.	blow	blew	blown
John *brought* [not *bringed*] Mary some flowers.	bring	brought	brought
This house was *built* [not *builded*] in 1795.	build	built	built
Barbara *caught* [not *catched*] two trout.	catch	caught	caught
Slowly they *crept* [not *creeped*] up the stairs.	creep	crept	crept
He *dealt* [not *dealed*] me a good hand.	deal	dealt	dealt
The men quickly *dug* [not *digged*] a pit.	dig	dug	dug
She *drew* [not *drawed*] a caricature of me.	draw	drew	drawn
All the men *grew* [not *growed*] long beards.	grow	grew	grown
Ben *hung* [not *hanged*] his cap on the hook.	hang	hung	hung
I *knew* [not *knowed*] him at college.	know	knew	known
I have never *lent* [not *lended*] him money.	lend	lent	lent
We *sought* [not *seeked*] shelter from the rain.	seek	sought	sought
The sun *shone* [not *shined*] all day yesterday.	shine	shone	shone
The prince *slew* [not *slayed*] the fierce dragon.	slay	slew	slain
I soon *spent* [not *spended*] the money.	spend	spent	spent
Ms. Andrews *taught* [not *teached*] us algebra.	teach	taught	taught

Lou *threw* [not *throwed*] the receipt away.	throw	threw	thrown
The old man *wept* [not *weeped*] piteously.	weep	wept	wept

Obsolete or Dialectal Forms

A third type of error results from the use of an obsolete or dialectal form of the verb, a form not considered standard now:

	Verb	*Past Tense*	*P.P.*
I *am* [not *be*] working regularly.	be*	was, were	been*
I *have been* [not *been*] working regularly.			
The child *burst* [not *bursted*] out crying.	burst	burst	burst
I've *bought* [not *boughten*] a car.	buy	bought	bought
I *climbed* [not *clumb*] a tree for a better view.	climb	climbed	climbed
The women *clung* [not *clang*] to the raft.	cling	clung	clung
The dog *dragged* [not *drug*] the old shoe home.	drag	dragged	dragged
The boy was nearly *drowned* [not *drownded*].	drown	drowned	drowned
At the picnic I *ate* [not *et*] too many hot dogs.	eat	ate	eaten
Betty *flung* [not *flang*] the stick away.	fling	flung	flung
You *paid* [not *payed*] too much for it.	pay	paid	paid
It had been *shaken* [not *shooken*] to pieces.	shake	shook	shaken
He had never *skinned* [not *skun*] an animal.	skin	skinned	skinned
A bee *stung* [not *stang*] me as I stood there.	sting	stung	stung
The girl *swung* [not *swang*] at the ball.	swing	swung	swung
I wonder who could have *taken* [not *tooken*] it.	take	took	taken

Confusing Verb Forms

A fourth type of verb error results from a confusion of forms of certain verbs that look or sound almost alike but are actually quite different in meaning, such as *lie, lay; sit, set;* and *rise, raise.* Note that three of these troublesome verbs—*lay, set,* and *raise*—in their ordinary uses take an object. The other three—*lie, sit, rise*—do not take an object.

	Verb	*Past Tense*	*P.P.*
Please *lay* your books [D.O.] on the table.	lay	laid	laid
Mary *laid* several logs [D.O.] on the fire.			
The men have *laid* some boards [D.O.] over the puddle.			
Our cat often *lies* [not *lays*] on the couch.	lie	lay	lain
Yesterday our cat *lay* [not *laid*] on the couch.			
Our cat has *lain* [not *laid*] on the couch all morning.			
She *sets* the plate [D.O.] in front of me.	set	set	set
An hour ago Tom *set* out some food [D.O.] for the birds.			
I had *set* the camera [D.O.] at a full second.			

*As you learned in Lesson 2, the irregular verb *be* has three forms (*am, are, is*) in the present tense and two forms (*was, were*) in the past tense.

I usually *sit* in that chair. Yesterday he *sat* in my chair. I have *sat* at my desk all morning.	sit	sat	sat
At her command they *raise* the flag [D.O.]. The boy quickly *raised* his hand [D.O.]. He had *raised* the price [D.O.] of his old car.	raise	raised	raised
He *rises* when we enter the room. Everyone *rose* as the speaker entered the room. The water has *risen* a foot since midnight.	rise	rose	risen

Exceptions

The rules and illustrations given here are an adequate guide in most situations. They show the importance of knowing the principal parts of these verbs. Note, however, that there are a few exceptions, such as the intransitive uses of *set:*

A *setting* [not *sitting*] hen *sets.* [Of course, a hen, like a rooster, may be said to *sit* when that is what is meant.]

The sun *sets* in the west.

Cement or dye *sets.*

A jacket *sets (fits)* well.

With a few verbs, special meanings demand different principal parts. For example, the past tense and the past participle of *shine,* when the verb is used as a transitive verb, are *shined:*

This morning I *shined* [not *shone*] my shoes.

The verb *hang* with the meaning "to execute by suspending by the neck until dead" uses *hanged,* not *hung,* for the past tense and the past participle. When in doubt, always refer to your dictionary.

SEQUENCE OF TENSES

In Lesson 2 you studied a partial conjugation showing the forms of three sample verbs as they occur in six tenses. In Lesson 5 you were told the basic uses of the six tenses. Although most student writers usually have little difficulty in establishing and maintaining logical time relationships in their sentences, a few situations sometimes cause confusion.

Subordinate Clauses

The tense in a subordinate clause is normally the same as that in the main clause unless a different time for the subordinate statement is clearly indicated.

We think that Mary studies hard all the time.

We think that Mary studied hard for the last test.

We think that Mary will study hard for the next test.

We think that Mary has studied hard for all her tests.

We think that Mary had studied hard before last week's test.

We thought that Mary studied hard all the time.
We thought that Mary studied hard in the past.
We thought that Mary would study hard for the next test.
We thought that Mary has studied hard all year.
We thought that Mary had studied hard last semester.

Universally True Statements

The present tense is used for a statement that is universally true.

The dietitian reminded us that whipped cream *is* (not *was*) fattening.
I wonder who first discovered that oysters *are* (not *were*) edible.

Shifting Tenses

In narrative writing a shift from past tense to present tense or from present to past should be avoided.

The library *was* silent except for an occasional whisper, when suddenly a side door *opened* [not *opens*] and a disheveled young man *dashed* [not *dashes*] in and *started* [not *starts*] yelling, "Man the lifeboats!" After the librarians *had managed* to restore order...

Present Perfect Tense

The perfect form of an infinitive should not be used when the controlling verb is in the present perfect tense.

Correct: I would have liked to see that performance.
Incorrect: I would have liked to have seen that performance.

In the indicative mood, there is rarely any confusion over the correct form of the infinitive.

Correct: I have wanted to run that marathon for years.

SUPPLEMENT

When a sentence makes a statement or asks a question, the verb is said to be in the **indicative mood** or **mode** (see Lesson 2). Two other moods indicate a different purpose in the sentence.

Imperative Mood

When a sentence gives a direction or command, the verb is in the **imperative mood.** The imperative of all regular verbs simply uses the base form of the verb without a subject.

Please *give* me the ball.
Take out your pen and paper.

Even the verb *to be*, irregular in most formations, uses the base to form the imperative.

Be careful; the steps are slippery.
Please *be* on time; the bus will depart promptly.

Subjunctive Mood

The present subjunctive uses the base form of the verb, regardless of the subject.

> The catalog recommends that she *study* accounting in the first semester.

The past subjunctive takes the same form as the past tense of the verb. (The auxiliary *be* is always *were* regardless of the number or person of the subject.)

> I wish I *were* at home today.

The past perfect subjunctive has the same form as the past perfect.

> I wish I *had gone* home earlier.

We also use the subjunctive in these special ways:

1. In clauses beginning with *that* when they follow words such as *ask, suggest, require, recommend,* and *demand.*

> The policy requires that we *submit* our requests in writing.
> The manager insisted that we *be* present for the ceremony.

2. In clauses beginning with *if* when the clause makes a statement that is clearly and unmistakably contrary to fact.

> If I *were* able to sing, I would try out for the Met.
> If he were young again, he would live life differently.

NAME _____ SCORE _____

Directions: In the space at the left, write the correct form of the verb shown in parentheses. Do not use any *–ing* forms.

_____   1. After the truck driver had (drink) his coffee, he (climb) back into
_____   the cab and started off again.

_____   2. Some of my prize tulips have had their stems (break) because last
_____   night a neighbor's dog (dig) a hole in my garden.

_____   3. One man nearly (drown) when the volunteers tried to salvage the
_____   boat that had (sink) in the bay.

_____   4. Betsy came in crying and reported that Bobby had (tear) her
_____   jacket and that a bee had (sting) her.

_____   5. By ten o'clock the crew had (drag) away the tree limbs that the
_____   storm had (blow) across the road.

_____   6. Although she had never (ride) a horse before, Letty bravely
_____   (swing) herself into the saddle.

_____   7. Mr. Jensen had (bring) to the party some of his homemade pickled
_____   eels, but we (eat) very little of this delicacy.

_____   8. Willy (run) into the cabin to get his camera, but by the time he
_____   returned, the beautiful hummingbird had (fly) away.

_____   9. "Why have you (choose) this run-down hamburger joint when we
_____   could have (go) to my favorite restaurant?" asked Annie.

_____   10. A cold rain had (begin) to fall, and my hands and feet felt nearly
_____   (freeze).

_____   11. As soon as he had (eat) his pie, Lawton (lay) aside the newspaper
_____   and left the restaurant.

_____   12. You (do) a very unwise thing when you (lend) your brother-in-law
_____   enough money for his new car.

_____   13. Last month we (spend) two weeks in Aruba, and the sun (shine)
_____   every day that we were there.

_____   14. You should not have (buy) that old car; it's been (drive) nearly
_____   120,000 miles.

_____   15. Three years ago the firm's bookkeeper (steal) some funds, and the
_____   police have not yet (catch) him.

229

_____ 16. After being (swear) in, the witness said that he had (know) the

_____   defendant for twenty years.

_____ 17. "If you are looking for your sweater," said Mother, "it has (lie) all

_____   day exactly where you (lay) it last night."

_____ 18. Yesterday Jerry (hang) on the walls of his den all of the pictures

_____   that he had (take) on his vacation.

_____ 19. After the dam (burst), the flood waters in the valley (rise)

_____   alarmingly.

_____ 20. "Every afternoon this week after class, I've (go) to the municipal

_____   pool and (swim) a half-mile," boasted Loretta.

_____ 21. "It has been (bring) to my attention," said the secretary, "that a

_____   few members of our club have not yet (pay) their dues."

_____ 22. By the end of the first week, I (become) convinced that the boys

_____   had (take) advantage of the new coach's trusting nature.

_____ 23. I'm pleased to report that your son has (do) careful work on every

_____   theme he has (write) in class this semester.

_____ 24. After Bert had (swim) across the lake and back, he (lie) down for

_____   a short rest before lunch.

_____ 25. After being sentenced, the thief (swear) that he did not know

_____   where his accomplices hid the money they had (steal).

_____ 26. We could have (come) into town for the game, but we (choose) to

_____   stay on the farm and watch it on TV.

_____ 27. I had (lie) on the ground so long that I felt stiff when I (begin) to

_____   hoe the garden again.

_____ 28. A friendly farmer stopped his antique truck for us; we (throw) our

_____   packs on the top of some potato sacks and (climb) aboard.

_____ 29. Over last weekend as I (lie) in the hospital, I regretted having

_____   (eat) the wild mushrooms we had found.

_____ 30. Little Anne had never (fly) in a plane before, and, as she walked

_____   up the steps, she (cling) desperately to her father's arm.

Directions: Each sentence has two italicized verb units. If the principal part or tense of the verb is the form proper in serious writing, write **C** in the corresponding space at the left. If the verb is incorrect, write the correct form in the space.

_____ 1. "I really feel that I've *grown* up since I *come* to college," said Brett.

_____

_____ 2. "I *been* living here for thirty years, and I never *seen* a sunset like

_____ that one," said the old-timer.

_____ 3. I wish you would *lay* aside your garden tools and *lie* down for a

_____ short rest.

_____ 4. "If I had *known* that you were to be out of town, I would have

_____ *chose* another time for my party," said Elizabeth.

_____ 5. It would have been wiser for you *to have admitted* that you had

_____ *taken* the car without the owner's permission.

_____ 6. Two of the young campers decided to sleep outside, but eventually

_____ they *become* cold and *crept* back into the main tent.

_____ 7. "Twice I have *written* to the landlord notifying him that the

_____ dishwasher is *broke*," she complained.

_____ 8. The astronaut *begun* his lecture by reminding the audience that

_____ the moon *was* approximately 250,000 miles from the earth.

_____ 9. A fresh breeze had *blowed* away the morning fog, and the sun had

_____ *climbed* up over the hills to our east.

_____ 10. As I was *laying* in the hammock for a short rest, a stray cat *come*

_____ up to and demanded to be petted.

_____ 11. The golf ball *rose* in the air almost vertically, it seemed, and then

_____ *sank* into a clump of poison ivy.

_____ 12. Benny stomped into the kitchen, *lay* his brief case on the table,

_____ and *announces*, "I'm tired, I'm hungry, and I want a cup of coffee."

_____ 13. "You've *took* the wrong seat," Janine said to the new boy. "I *been*

_____ *setting* in this seat all semester."

_____ 14. " I could have *swore* that the man I just *seen* leaving the bank is a

_____ college friend of mine," said Paul.

_____ 15. Outside the restaurant a panhandler stopped Elmer and *says*,

_____ "Now that you've *eaten*, how about buying me a cup of coffee?"

_____ 16. "This fancy ski outfit is nearly *wore* out," said Eunice, "and it

_____   isn't completely *payed* for yet."

_____ 17. If the old skinflint doesn't *raise* our salaries soon, some of us are

_____   going to *rise* up in rebellion.

_____ 18. "I admit that I *been* arrested a few times for misdemeanors," he

_____   admitted, "but I have never *stoled* anything."

_____ 19. Mrs. Little *set* aside her needlepoint and asked her visitor to *sit*

_____   beside her.

_____ 20. "That old tire you *threw* away last week is still *lying* in the alley, "

_____   complained Stew's neighbor.

NAME _____   SCORE _____

Directions: In the space at the left, write the correct form of the verb shown in parentheses. Do not use any *–ing* forms.

_____
_____ 1. Yesterday afternoon two suspicious-looking men had been (see) loitering near the shop that was (break) into last night.

_____
_____ 2. At the homecoming dance, Annabelle (wear) a dress that I would not have (choose) for such an occasion.

_____
_____ 3. Our visiting lecturer (lay) great stress on the fact that responsibility for government (lie) ultimately with the voters.

_____
_____ 4. Shortly after the prime minister had (go) to bed, someone (throw) a brick through her bedroom window.

_____
_____ 5. The young people eagerly (drink) the hot coffee because, after their descent from the mountain, they were nearly (freeze).

_____
_____ 6. The sun has (shine) every day this week; winter has nearly (run) its course.

_____
_____ 7. By the time she was twenty-five, Lenore had (climb) Denali and had (fly) over the South Pole.

_____
_____ 8. You certainly (do) a wise thing when you demanded that the new contract should be (write) by your lawyer.

_____
_____ 9. Henry (grow) suspicious when he learned that his partner had (become) involved in shady stock speculations.

_____
_____ 10. The old man took off his glasses, (lay) his magazine on the table, and (lie) down on the couch.

_____
_____ 11. I have (eat) at this restaurant many times, but never before have I (pay) such exorbitant prices.

_____
_____ 12. At the Grange meeting, one farmer (rise) from his chair and complained that the price of cattle feed had (rise) again.

_____
_____ 13. Not a word was (speak) as the children picked up the shattered vase that had (fall) to the floor.

_____
_____ 14. After winning the third set, the champion (lay) his tennis racket aside and (blow) on his hands to warm them.

_____
_____ 15. Later this year Dennis, having (spend) most of his inheritance, (begin) to think about getting a job.

Directions: Each sentence has two italicized verb units. If the principal part or tense of the verb is the form proper in serious writing, write **C** in the corresponding space at the left. If the unit is incorrect, write the correct form in the space.

_____ 1. The sun has *shone* every day for a week, but Cranston Creek is
_____ still *froze* solid.

_____ 2. The spy got out of the car, silently *crept* under the fence, and *lay*
_____ the package on the driveway.

_____ 3. Hearing the strange noise, Dad *run* to the front window to see
_____ who had *driven* onto our parking strip.

_____ 4. "You'll stay in your highchair until you've *ate* your cereal and
_____ *drank* your hot chocolate, " Mother told her grandchild.

_____ 5. "It would have been fun to *have gone* to the movie with you
_____ guys," said Bobby Jo, "but I *seen* the show last week in Atlanta.

_____ 6. To this day Jason has never *flown* in an airplane; on every trip he
_____ has *ridden* in either a bus or a train.

_____ 7. "Many ships have *sank* off this cape," said Captain Adams, "and
_____ many good sailors have *drownded.*"

_____ 8. Larry *set* outside on the porch and waited while Ben *shined* his
_____ boots.

_____ 9. "I never did like that blouse," said Trina, "and so I *threw* it away
_____ after I'd *wore* it only twice."

_____ 10. Later the janitor found the receipt *laying* on the floor, where it had
_____ apparently *fallen* from the secretary's desk.

_____ 11. Ellen's father *done* a good job or repairing the three *broken*
_____ appliances.

_____ 12. "You *been* a bad dog, Bowser," said Jan to her pet. "You've
_____ chewed on your blanket until it's nearly *tore* in two."

_____ 13. By the time we had *went* ten miles we realized that the filling
_____ station attendant had *given* us inaccurate directions.

_____ 14. "I admit," said Harwood, "that these reports were hastily *wrote*
_____ and that I should have *spent* more time on them."

_____ 15. Ben had found a smooth section of the beach and had just *set*
_____ down on his blanket when a nearby child looked at him and *says*,
"Hi there, Gramps."

_____ 16. The children *burst* out laughing when they looked at the pictures
_____ that the babysitter had *drew* on the paper napkins.

_____ 17. "The church bells for early service have already *rang* and you are
_____ still *lying* in bed," said Mrs. Stewart.

_____ 18. "Truer words were never *spoke*," said the editor to himself as he
_____ *begun* to write another editorial.

_____ 19. You surely should have *knew* that Rhode Island *was* the smallest
_____ of all the states.

_____ 20. As the lifeguard rowed toward him, the exhausted man *swam* to
_____ the raft and desperately *clung* to it.

Examine the following conjugation. Note that in the present tense, the third-person singular *(he, she, it)* verb form differs from the third-person plural *(they)* verb form.

I earn	We earn
You earn	You earn
He, She, It *earns*	They *earn*

We refer to this change as a change in number. As noted in Lesson 2, **singular number** refers to only one thing; **plural number** refers to more than one thing. Notice how verbs and nouns differ in this respect: The *s* ending on nouns is a plural marker, but on verbs it designates the singular form.

The following examples show how the number of the subject (one or more than one) affects the form of the verb. (See Supplement.) The verbs *have, do,* and *be* are important because they have auxiliary uses as well as main-verb uses. *Be* is an exceptional verb; it changes form in the past tense as well as in the present tense.

Singular	*Plural*
She *walks* slowly.	They *walk* slowly.
Mother *seems* pleased.	My parents *seem* pleased.
Mary *has* a new dress.	All of the girls *have* new dresses.
He *has traveled* widely.	They *have traveled* widely.
She *does* her work easily.	They *do* their work easily.
Does he *have* enough time?	*Do* they *have* enough time?
He *is* a friend of mine.	They *are* friends of mine.
My brother *is coming* home.	My brothers *are coming* home.
His camera *was taken* from him.	Their cameras *were taken* from them.

VERB AGREES IN NUMBER

The relation of verb form to subject follows an important principle of usage: The verb always agrees in number with its subject. Although the principle is simple, some of the situations in which it applies are not. You will avoid some common writing errors if you keep in mind the following seven extensions of the principle. The first is probably the most important.

1. The number of the verb is not affected by material that comes between the verb and the subject.

> Immediate *settlement* of these problems *is* [not *are*] vital. [The subject is *settlement*. Problems, being here the object of the preposition *of,* cannot be a subject.]
>
> The *cost* of replacing the asbestos shingles with cedar shakes *was* [not *were*] considerable.
>
> *Tact,* as well as patience, *is* [not *are*] required.

> *Mr. Sheldon,* together with several other division heads, *has* [not *have*] left.
>
> *Each* of the plans *has* [not *have*] its good points.
> *Is* [not *Are*] *either* of the contestants ready?

Determine the *real* subject of the verb; watch out for intervening words that might mislead you. The number of the verb is not altered when other nouns are attached to the subject by means of prepositions such as *in addition to, together with, as well as, with,* and *along with.* Remember that indefinite pronoun subjects like *either, neither, each, one, everyone, no one,* and *somebody* take singular verbs. *None* may take either a singular or a plural verb, depending on whether the writer wishes to emphasize "not one" or "no members" of the group.

> *None* of us *is* [or *are*] perfect.

2. A verb agrees with its subject even when the subject follows the verb.

> On the wall *hangs* a *portrait* of his father. [*portrait hangs*]
> On the wall *hang portraits* of his parents. [*portraits hang*]
> He handed us a piece of paper on which *was scribbled* a *warning.* [*warning was scribbled*]
> There *was* barely enough *time* remaining.
> There *were* only ten *minutes* remaining.
> There *seems* to be one *problem* remaining.
> There *seem* to be a few *problems* remaining.
> Here *is* a free *ticket* to the game.
> Here *are* some free *tickets* to the game.

Be especially careful to find the real subject in sentences starting with there or here.

3. Compound subjects joined by *and* take a plural verb.

> A little *boy* and his *dog were* playing in the yard.
> On the platform *were* a *table* and four *chairs.*

But the verb should be singular if the subjects joined by *and* are thought of as a single thing, or if the subjects are considered separately, as when they are modified by *every* or *each:*

> Plain *vinegar* and *oil is* all the dressing my salad needs. [one thing]
> Every *man* and every *woman is* asked to help. [considered separately]

4. Singular subjects joined by *or* or *nor* take singular verbs.

> Either a *check* or a money *order is* required.
> Neither the *manager* nor his *assistant has* arrived yet.
> *Was* Mr. Phelps or his *son* put on the committee?

In some sentences of this pattern, especially in questions like the last example, a plural verb is sometimes used, both in casual conversation and in writing. In serious and formal writing, the singular verb is considered appropriate. If the subjects joined by *or* or *nor* differ in number, the verb agrees with the subject nearer to it:

> Neither the *mother* nor the two *boys were* able to identify him.
> Either the *players* or the *coach is* responsible for the defeat.

5. Plural nouns of amount, distance, and so on, when they are used as singular units of measurement, take singular verbs.

> A hundred *dollars was* once paid for a single tulip bulb.
>
> Thirty *miles seems* like a long walk to me.
>
> Seven *years* in prison *was* the penalty that he had to pay.

6. A collective noun is considered singular when the group is regarded as a unit; it is plural when the individuals of the group are referred to.

> The *audience is* very enthusiastic tonight.
>
> The *audience are* returning to their seats. [Notice pronoun *their.*]
>
> The *band is* playing a rousing march.
>
> Now the *band are* putting away their instruments. [Again note *their.*]
>
> *Most* of the book *is* blatant propaganda.
>
> *Most* of her novels *are* now out of print.
>
> The *rest* of the fortune *was* soon gone.
>
> The *rest* of his debts *were* left unpaid.
>
> The *number* of bank failures *is* increasing.
>
> A *number* of these bank failures *are* being investigated.

Words like *number, all, rest, part, some, more, most, half* are singular or plural, depending on the meaning intended. A word of this type is often accompanied by a modifier or referred to by a pronoun, either of which gives a clue to the number intended. When the word *number* is a subject, it is considered singular if it is preceded by *the* and plural if it is preceded by *a.*

7. When the subject is a relative pronoun, the antecedent of the pronoun determines the number (and person) of the verb. (See Lesson 23, page 243.)

> He told a joke *that was* pointless. [*joke was*]
>
> He told several jokes *that were* pointless. [*jokes were*]
>
> I paid the expenses of the trip, *which were* minimal. [*expenses were*]
>
> Jack is one of those boys *who enjoy* fierce competition. [*boys enjoy*]

The last example, sometimes called the "one of those…who" sentence, is particularly troublesome. Often a singular verb is used. If we recast the sentence to read "Of those boys who enjoy fierce competition, Jack is one," however, it becomes clear that the logical antecedent of *who* is the plural noun *boys.* However, usage is divided. And notice that a singular verb must be used when the pattern is altered slightly:

> Jack is the only *one* of my friends *who enjoys* fierce competition.

Because a relative pronoun subject nearly always has an antecedent that is third-person singular or third-person plural, we are accustomed to pronoun-verb combinations like these:

> A boy *who is...*
>
> Boys *who are...*

A woman *who knows...*
Women *who know...*

But in those occasional sentences in which a relative pronoun subject has an antecedent that is in the first or second person, meticulously correct usage calls for subject-verb combinations like the following:

I, *who am* in charge here, should pay the bill. [*I...am*]
They should ask me, *who know* all the answers. [*I...know*]
You, *who are* in charge here, should pay the bill. [*You...are*]
They should ask you, *who know* all the answers. [*you...know*]

SUPPLEMENT

One particular error of subject-verb agreement warrants special attention. The third-person singular present tense form of the verb *do* is *does*. The plural form is *do*. The misuse of the negative contraction *don't* (instead of *doesn't*) with a third-person singular subject is quite often encountered in spoken English. Many people, justly or unjustly, look on the it-don't misuse as an important marker of grossly substandard English. Such forms as the following should be avoided in all spoken and written English:

Faulty: My father *don't* like broccoli.

Faulty: It really *don't* matter.

Faulty: Jack Johnson *don't* live here now.

Faulty: One of her teachers *don't* like her.

Faulty: This fudge tastes good, *don't* it?

Faulty: The fact that the bill is overdue *don't* bother him.

SUMMARY OF CORRECT VERB USE

1. The principal parts of a verb are the present, the past, and the past participle. Avoid confusing the principal parts of irregular verbs (*run, ran, run; eat, ate, eaten; fly, flew, flown*) with those of regular verbs (*study, studied, studied*). Be especially careful with the often confused principal parts of *lie* and *lay, sit* and *set*.

2. Singular verbs are used with singular subjects; plural verbs are used with plural subects.
    a. Nouns intervening between the subject and the verb do not determine the number of the verb. (Resistance to the actions of these government agencies *is* [not *are*] growing.)
    b. Singular subjects joined by *and* normally take plural verbs. Singular subjects joined by *or* or *nor* normally take singular verbs.
    c. Some nouns and pronouns (collective nouns, and words like *number, all, half,* etc.) are singular in some meanings, plural in others.

Using Verbs Correctly: Subject-Verb Agreement

NAME _____ SCORE _____

Directions: These sentences are examples of structures that often lead to errors in subject-verb agreement. In the space at the left, copy the correct verb in parentheses. In each sentence, the subject of the verb is printed in bold type.

_____ 1. The narrow **range** of temperatures during the past twenty-four hours (is, are) somewhat misleading.

_____ 2. Included in the schedule of events at the picnic (was, were) a three-legged **race**, a sack **race**, and a pie-eating **contest**.

_____ 3. The **quality** of the recorded message and of the recorded music that followed it (was, were) terrible.

_____ 4. Remember that neither **time** nor **tide** (waits, wait) for any man, or for any woman, for that matter.

_____ 5. By the time we arrived at the theater there (was, were) several dozen **people** already standing in line.

_____ 6. A **number** of rumors about the mayor (has, have) been circulating around City Hall lately.

_____ 7. The **number** of bank robberies in our county (has, have) increased alarmingly.

_____ 8. The **need** for skilled counselors to assist concerned students on this campus (has, have) never been greater.

_____ 9. It is generally admitted that the **use** of insecticides (has, have) saved millions of lives.

_____ 10. The police **sergeant**, as well as three outside experts, (has, have) testified concerning the signatures on the bill of sale.

_____ 11. In British Columbia, the recreational **use** of handguns (is, are) regulated by the province.

_____ 12. One passenger, in addition to the driver, was injured, but the **extent** of his injuries (is, are) unknown at this time.

_____ 13. Here (comes, come) **Jim Hawthorne** and his two noisy **sons**.

_____ 14. Political and economic **instability** in drug-producing areas around the world (has, have) resulted in seemingly insoluble problems.

_____ 15. Hanging on the office wall (was, were) a faded three-year old **calendar** and several dust-covered **pictures of** some children.

239

Directions: If you find an error in subject-verb agreement, underline the incorrect verb and write the correct form in the space at the left. Circle the subject of every verb you change. Some of the sentences may be correct.

_____ 1. The financial aspects of the three-million-dollar-plus annual budget of the golf club sometimes becomes overwhelming.

_____ 2. The nature of the experiments conducted on the last two space flights remain a secret.

_____ 3. In the back seat of the small car, in addition to Herb, Ernie, and me, were a record player and five ski poles.

_____ 4. Haven't you sometimes wondered why a knowledge of past wars and catastrophes have had so little effect on man's thinking?

_____ 5. One fashion commentator observed that neither comfort nor aesthetic consideration justify such a silly fad.

_____ 6. Also included in the package is a travel guide, some special trip tips, and two exceptional bonus gifts.

_____ 7. The lecturer convinced me that long hours of sitting before a TV screen were affecting my children's mental development.

_____ 8. You should visit the advisory office because information about scholarships and teaching fellowships are available there.

_____ 9. Mrs. Fellowes remarked that there's few ceremonies as interesting to women as weddings.

_____ 10. Does any one of those rims look like the one that is missing from your car?

_____ 11. One item that the agenda should include are the revised procedures for appointing new staff.

_____ 12. Neither my roommate nor I was sure that the spelling of every word in my report was correct.

_____ 13. There was at most, I dare say, only five or six people who asked sensible questions of our guest speaker.

_____ 14. Many people do not realize that continued exposure to loud noises are likely to damage the nerve cells of the inner ear.

_____ 15. Eight weeks do seem to me to be a long enough period for the completion of your term paper.

NAME _____   SCORE _____

Directions: If you find an error in subject-verb agreement, underline the incorrect verb and write the correct form in the space at the left. Circle the subject of every verb you change. Some of the sentences may be correct.

_____   1. Everyone connected with the community theater, right down to the school children, have helped in the fund raising.

_____   2. For me, at least, after that disastrous trip, the appeal of snow-covered slopes, slalom races, and after-ski gatherings have been dimmed.

_____   3. Basic to the success of our annual conference is careful planning, hard work, and quite a bit of good luck.

_____   4. "My experience in business, government, and community services surely qualify me for this office," the candidate concluded.

_____   5. After all, don't it seem possible that ignorance of the past can result in even more trouble than we now have?

_____   6. The prospect of solving local problems of water supply, garbage disposal, and transportation depend heavily on good relations among officials.

_____   7. The wide expanse of clean beach, plus the attractions of the nearby resort, makes Lake Crystal an ideal picnic spot.

_____   8. The safety of people, as well as of fish and animals, seem to be endangered by the continued use of certain fertilizers.

_____   9. The lecturer warned that the lure of hooking a few thirty-pound salmon sometimes cause fishermen to take needless risks.

_____   10. Francie liked the green scarf and bought it, although she realized that either tan or brown go better with her new coat.

_____   11. One of the first things Marilyn bought for her new apartment were a pair of table lamps.

_____   12. "Hurry, men," said the captain. "There's still ten or a dozen people on the roof waiting to be rescued."

_____   13. His wife, together with his mother-in-law and three cousins, are scheduled to arrive tomorrow from Prague.

_____   14. The schedule showing plane arrivals and departures needs to be brought up to date.

_____ 15. In general, the record of a student's past ability, effort, and accomplishments are an indication of his or her future progress.

_____ 16. The greatly increased number of students who are signing up this year for the pre-law program puzzles the advisory staff.

_____ 17. In every political campaign, it seems that there is always ill-mannered name-calling and wild, impossible promises.

_____ 18. Our first sight of the sage-covered hills, the whirling dust, and the clusters of half-starved cattle were depressing.

_____ 19. Another unpleasant aspect of the town are the garish neon signs that seem to be everywhere.

_____ 20. The prediction of the number of highway fatalities over the three-day holiday makes gloomy reading.

_____ 21. There's almost sure to be five or six stragglers who forgot to order their tickets before the deadline.

_____ 22. The only thing I forgot to put in my backpack were my extra pair of sunglasses.

_____ 23. Strategically arranged on the platform were a lectern, a standing lamp, and four overstuffed chairs.

_____ 24. Not one of the more than two thousand quiz answers submitted in the recent *Clarion* contest was 100 percent correct.

_____ 25. I admit that on the whole trip I was able to relax only when either one of the two older boys were driving the bus.

_____ 26. The documentary film showed us how the drabness of the surroundings and the ceaseless struggle for a bare existence affects the natives.

_____ 27. Neither of these raincoats is exactly what I had in mind.

_____ 28. The fact that the bill is only three months overdue don't justify a lawsuit, does it?

_____ 29. In addition to the tennis courts, there is a nearby golf course, and in the evenings there is dancing, bingo, and movies.

_____ 30. Over 24,000 board feet of prime cedar siding was destroyed in the fire.

As you learned in Lesson 1, a pronoun is a word that substitutes for a noun or another pronoun. The word for which a pronoun stands is called the pronoun's **antecedent**:

> I called *Harry*, but *he* didn't answer. [*He* substitutes for *Harry*. *Harry* is the antecedent of *he*.]
>
> My *cap and scarf* were where I had left *them*. [The antecedent of *them* is the plural unit *cap and scarf*.]
>
> *I* will wash *my* car tomorrow.
>
> *One* of my friends is painting *his* house.
>
> *Three* of my friends are painting *their* houses.

To use pronouns effectively and without confusing your reader, you must follow two basic principles:

1. Establish a clear, easily identified relationship between a pronoun and its antecedent.
2. Make the pronoun and its antecedent agree in person, number, and gender.

Let us examine these requirements more fully.

ROLE OF ANTECEDENTS

Personal pronouns should have definite antecedents and should be placed as near their antecedents as possible. Your readers should know exactly what a pronoun stands for. They should not be made to look through several sentences for a pronoun's antecedent, nor should they be asked to manufacture an antecedent for a pronoun. When you discover in your writing a pronoun with no clear and unmistakable antecedent, your revision, as many of the following examples demonstrate, will often require rewriting to remove the faulty pronoun from your sentence.

Faulty:	A strange car followed us closely, and *he* kept blinking his lights at us.
Improved:	A strange car followed us closely, and the driver kept blinking his lights at us.
Faulty:	Although Jenny was a real sports fan, her brother never became interested in *them*.
Improved:	Although Jenny really liked sports, her brother never became interested in them.
Faulty:	Mike is an excellent typist, although he never took a course in *it*.
Improved:	Mike is an excellent typist, although he never took a course in typing.

The indefinite *you* or *they* is quite common in speech and in chatty, informal writing, but one should avoid using either in serious writing:

Faulty:	In Alaska *they* catch huge king crabs.
Improved:	In Alaska huge king crabs are caught. [Often the best way to correct an indefinite *they* or *you* sentence is to use a passive verb.]

Faulty:	Before the reform measures were passed, *you* had few rights.
Improved:	Before the reform measures were passed, people had few rights.
	Before the reform measures were passed, one had few rights.

Faulty:	At the employment office *they* gave me an application form.
Improved:	A clerk at the employment office gave me an application form.
	At the employment office I was given an application form.

A pronoun should not appear to refer equally well to either of two antecedents:

Faulty:	Frank told Bill that *he* needed a haircut. [Which one needed a haircut?]
Improved:	"You need a haircut," said Frank to Bill. [In sentences of this type, the direct quotation is sometimes the only possible correction.]

Avoid the Indefinite *It*

The "it says" or "it said" introduction to statements, although common in informal language, is objectionable in serious writing because the *it* has no antecedent. (See Supplement.)

Faulty:	*It* says in the directions that the powder will dissolve in hot water.
Improved:	The directions say that the powder will dissolve in hot water.

Faulty:	*It* said on the morning news program that a bad storm is coming.
Improved:	According to the morning news program, a bad storm is coming.

Avoid Unclear References

Avoid vague or ambiguous reference of relative and demonstrative pronouns.

Faulty:	Only 20 people attended the lecture, *which* was due to poor publicity.
Improved:	Because of poor publicity, only 20 people attended the lecture.

Faulty:	Good writers usually have large vocabularies, and *this* is why I get poor grades on my papers.
Improved:	I get poor grades on my papers because my vocabulary is inadequate; good writers usually have large vocabularies.

Special Cases: *Which, This, That*

Sometimes the antecedent of the pronouns *which, this,* and *that* is an idea rather than the expressed noun. In a sentence such as "The children giggled, *which* annoyed the teacher" or "The children giggled, and *this* annoyed the teacher," what annoyed the teacher is not the *children* but "the giggling of the children" or "the fact that the children giggled." This kind of reference to a preceding idea rather than to an expressed noun is unobjectionable provided that the meaning is instantly and unmistakably clear. But you should avoid sentences like those shown below. In the first example, readers would be hard pressed to discover exactly what the *which* means, and in the second, they must decide whether the antecedent is the preceding idea or the noun immediately preceding the *which:*

Faulty:	Hathaway's application was rejected because he spells poorly, *which* is very important in an application letter.
Improved:	Hathaway's application was rejected because he spells poorly; correct spelling is very important in an application letter.

Faulty: The defense attorney did not object to the judge's concluding remark, *which* surprised me.

Improved: I was surprised that the defense attorney did not object to the judge's concluding remark.

PRONOUN AGREEMENT

Pronouns should agree with their antecedents in person, number, and gender. The following chart classifies the three forms of each personal pronoun on the basis of person, number, and gender:

	Singular	*Plural*
1st person	*I, my, me*	*we, our, us*
2nd person	*you, your, you*	*you, your, you*
3rd person	*he, his, him*	
	she, her, her	*they, their, them*
	it, its, it	

A singular antecedent is referred to by a singular pronoun; a plural antecedent is referred to by a plural pronoun.

> Dad says that *he* is sure that *his* new friend will visit *him* soon.
>
> Dad and Mother say that *they* are sure that *their* new friend will visit *them* soon.

This principle of logical pronoun agreement is not as simple as these two examples might suggest. Recent language practices have given rise to two situations for which it is impossible to make rules that apply in every instance. Student writers must, first, be aware of certain changing ideas about pronoun usage; they must then prepare themselves to make decisions among the choices available.

Indefinite Pronouns

The first of these two troublesome situations relates to some of the indefinite pronouns: *one, everyone, someone, no one, anyone, anybody, everybody, somebody, nobody, each, either,* and *neither.* These words have generally been felt to be singular; hence, pronouns referring to them have customarily been singular and, unless the antecedent specifies otherwise, masculine. Singular pronouns have also been used in formal writing and speaking to refer to noun antecedents modified by singular qualifiers such as *each* and *every.* The four following examples illustrate the traditional, formal practice:

> Everybody has *his* faults and *his* virtues.
>
> Each of the sons is doing what *he* thinks is best.
>
> England expects every man to do *his* duty.
>
> No one succeeds in this firm if Dobbins doesn't like *him.*

The principal difficulty with this usage is that these indefinites, although regarded by strict grammarians as singular in form, carry with them a group or plural sense, with the result that people are often unsure whether pronouns referring to them should be singular or plural. Despite traditional pronouncements, every day we hear sentences of the "Every-one-will-do-*their*-best" type. Beginning writers, however, would do well to follow the established practice until they feel relatively secure about recognizing the occasional sentence in which a singular pronoun referring to an indefinite produces a strained or unnatural effect even though it agrees in form with its antecedent.

Gender Issues

Closely related to this troublesome matter of pronoun agreement is the second problem, gender. What reference words should be used to refer to such a word as *student*? Obviously there are both female students and male students. Plural nouns present no problem; *they, their,* and *them* refer to both masculine and feminine. Singular nouns take *she, hers, her* and *he, his, him,* but no pronoun refers to third-person singular words that contain either male or female members.

Here again, as with the reference to third-person singular indefinites, the traditional practice is to use masculine singular pronouns. Eighty or so years ago, Henry James wrote the following sentence: "We must grant the artist his subject, his idea, his *donné;* our criticism is applied only to what he makes of it." In James's day, that sentence was undoubtedly looked upon as unexceptionable; the pronouns followed what was then standard practice. But attitudes have changed. These days, if that sentence got past the eyes of an editor and appeared on the printed page, its implication that artists are exclusively male would make the sentence unacceptably discriminatory to many readers.

Reliance on the *he or she* pronoun forms is an increasingly popular solution to some of these worrisome problems of pronoun reference. The *he or she* forms agree in number with the third-person singular indefinites, and the use of these forms obviates any possible charge of gender preference. However, excessive use of *he or she, his or her,* and *him or her* is undesirable. (Notice the cumbersome result, for instance, if a *he or she* form is substituted for all four of the third-person singular masculine pronouns in the Henry James sentence.)

Here is an important point to remember: When you are worried about a third-person singular masculine pronoun you have written, either because its reference to an indefinite antecedent does not sound quite right to you or because it shows an undesirable gender preference, you can remove the awkwardness, in nearly every instance that arises, by changing the antecedent to a plural noun, to which you then refer by using *they, their,* and *them.*

By way of summary, study these four versions of a sentence as they relate to the two problems just discussed:

Every member of the graduating class, if *he* wishes, may have *his* diploma mailed to *him* after August 15. [This usage reflects traditional practice that is still quite widely followed. The objection to it is that the reference words are exclusively masculine.]

Every member of the graduating class, if *he or she* wishes, may have *his or her* diploma mailed to *him or her* after August 15. [The singular reference is satisfactory, but the avoidance of masculine reference has resulted in clumsy wordiness.]

Every member of the graduating class, if *they* wish, may have *their* diplomas mailed to *them* after August 15. [This version, particularly if used in spoken English, would probably not offend many people, but the lack of proper number agreement between the pronouns and the antecedent would rule out its appearance in edited material.]

Members of the graduating class, if they wish, may have their diplomas mailed to them after August 15. [In this version the pronouns are logical and correct in both number and gender.]

A few other matters of pronoun reference, mercifully quite uncomplicated, should be called to your attention. If a pronoun refers to a compound unit or to a noun that may be either singular or plural, the pronoun agrees in number with the antecedent. (See Lesson 22, Rule 6.)

Wilson and his wife arrived in *their* new car.

Neither Jill nor Martha has finished *her* term paper.

The rest of the lecture had somehow lost *its* point.

The rest of the workers will receive *their* money soon.

The 8-o'clock class has *its* test tomorrow.

The 10-o'clock class finished writing *their* themes.

Beware of *You*

An antecedent in the third person should not be referred to by the second person *you*. This misuse develops when writers, forgetting that they have established the third person in the sentence, shift the structure and begin to talk directly to the reader:

Faulty: In a large university a *freshman* can feel lost if *you* have grown up in a small town.

Improved: In a large university a freshman can feel lost if he or she has grown up in a small town.

Faulty: If a *person* really wants to become an expert golfer, *you* must practice every day.

Improved: If a person really wants to become an expert golfer, *she or he* must practice every day.

SUPPLEMENT

At this point, you should be reminded that *it* without an antecedent has some uses that are completely acceptable in both formal and informal English. One of these is in the delayed subject or object pattern. (See Lesson 10.) Another is its use as a kind of filler word in expressions having to do with weather, time, distance, and so forth.

It is fortunate that you had a spare tire.

I find *it* difficult to believe Ted's story.

It is cold today; *it* snowed last night.

It is 12 o'clock; *it* is almost time for lunch.

How far is *it* to Phoenix?

NAME _____ SCORE _____

Directions: One sentence in each of the following pairs is correct; the other contains at least one reference word that is poorly used. In the space at the left, write the letter that identifies the correct sentence. In the other sentence, circle the pronoun or pronouns that have vague or incorrect reference.

_____ 1. a. Professor Graf has resigned from the chairmanship, and the college trustees have accepted his resignation.
　　　　　 b. Professor Graf has resigned from the chairmanship, and the college trustees have accepted it.

_____ 2. a. Ginny arrived just as they announced that every passenger for Flight 72 should show their boarding pass.
　　　　　 b. Ginny arrived just as it was announced that all passengers for Flight 72 should show their boarding passes.

_____ 3. a. Mrs. Thomas told her niece that she should eat more fruit and fewer sweets.
　　　　　 b. Mrs. Thomas told her niece, "I should eat more fruit and fewer sweets."

_____ 4. a. According to the morning broadcast, there has been a bad earthquake in Honduras.
　　　　　 b. It said on the morning broadcast that they had a bad earthquake in Honduras.

_____ 5. a. In today's China, a woman has something to say about her marriage, and you can even get a divorce.
　　　　　 b. In today's China, a woman has something to say about her marriage, and she can even get a divorce.

_____ 6. a. When her stolen car was recovered, Terry discovered that the spare tire had been removed.
　　　　　 b. When her stolen car was recovered, Terry discovered that they had removed the spare tire.

_____ 7. a. A copy of the annual report of the Children's Hospital is mailed to every one of their donors.
　　　　　 b. A copy of the annual report of the Children's Hospital is mailed to every one of its donors.

_____ 8. a. In Dickens's London, they could put you in prison for even a ridiculously small debt.
　　　　　 b. In Dickens's London, one could be put in prison for even a ridiculously small debt.

_____ 9. a. Mrs. Dressler is a talented cook, but as yet neither of her two daughters has shown any interest in cooking.
　　　　　 b. Mrs. Dressler is a talented cook, but as yet neither of her two daughters has shown any interest in it.

249

_____ 10. a. The advertisement maintains that a woman will have clearer skin after she has used the soap for two weeks.
　　　　 b. The advertisement maintains that a woman will have clearer skin after they have used the soap for two weeks.

_____ 11. a. The Busy Bee Mart wants its customers to know that it still has the best bargains in town.
　　　　 b. The Busy Bee Mart wants their customers to know that they still have the best bargains in town.

_____ 12. a. *Laugh with Us*, a new program, will replace *Guess Again*, which surprised many viewers.
　　　　 b. Many viewers were surprised to learn that *Laugh with Us*, a new program, will replace *Guess Again*.

_____ 13. a. Anyone handling a bear cub will learn that it will fight back if a person gets rough with it.
　　　　 b. Anyone handling a bear cub will learn that they will fight back if you get rough with them.

_____ 14. a. The owner spoke no Spanish, and the prospective buyer spoke little English, and it complicated the transaction.
　　　　 b. The fact that the owner spoke no Spanish and the prospective buyer spoke little English complicated the transaction.

_____ 15. a. If tourists have their traveler's checks stolen, you should report it and they will reimburse you.
　　　　 b. A tourist having his or her traveler's checks stolen will be reimbursed after reporting the loss.

_____ 16. a. The label warns that people who have ulcers should not use this medicine.
　　　　 b. It says on the label that a person should not use this medicine if they have ulcers.

_____ 17. a. Stan told his younger brother, "You ought to try out for the tennis team."
　　　　 b. Stan told his younger brother that he ought to try out for the tennis team.

_____ 18. a. Anyone who is a poor speller should feel better when they remember that nearly everybody has trouble with it.
　　　　 b. A poor speller should feel better when he or she remembers that nearly everybody has trouble with spelling.

_____ 19. a. Tonight's lecture deals with compulsive overeating, which I think you might enjoy.
　　　　 b. Tonight's lecture deals with compulsive overeating, a subject that I think you might enjoy.

_____ 20. a. Beekeeping can be a profitable avocation if one can conquer his or her fear of bees.
　　　　 b. Beekeeping can be a profitable avocation if one can conquer your fear of them.

NAME _____   SCORE _____

Directions: In the space at the left, copy the correct pronoun, or pronoun-verb combination, given in parentheses. Circle the antecedent of the pronoun.

_____ 1. Every young woman in this room believes that (she, you, they) will find a special place in the world.

_____ 2. "In the good old days," said Grandmother, "if one expected a day's pay, (he, you, they) gave a day's work."

_____ 3. I can't understand how anyone in (his or her, their) right mind would drive a car without any insurance.

_____ 4. The Homestead Marching and Chowder Society will hold (it's, its, their) annual parade and clambake next Monday afternoon.

_____ 5. Very few upper-echelon executives can remember what life was like when (he was, they were) starting out and struggling to get ahead in business.

_____ 6. My father's insurance agency will be moving into (its, it's, their) new office about the first of next month.

_____ 7. When I remember that several important elections have been decided by only a few votes, I realize how vital it is that every voter cast (his or her, their) vote.

_____ 8. A homeowner who wants to maintain the value of (his or her, your, their) property must be sure to take good care of the home.

_____ 9. "Somehow," said Jim, "I never seem to get credit for my good ideas; my boss always claims (it, them) as his own and gets the credit."

_____ 10. Not a single person out of the hundred or so we surveyed said that (he or she, they) remembered our product's advertisements.

_____ 11. At Camp Woonsocket every girl learned how to paddle (her, their) own canoe and how to survive a boating accident.

_____ 12. Everyone likes to believe that (he or she has, you have, they have) succeeded through intelligence and skill rather than by luck.

_____ 13. The Letterman's Club sends out (its, it's, their) members regularly to help underprivileged children develop athletic skills.

_____ 14. "In the business world," said the cynical old professor, "it's every man, uh, every person for (himself, himself or herself, themselves)."

_____ 15. The members of the homeowners' association will meet next Tuesday to decide how (it wants, they want) to vote in the next election.

Directions: Each sentence contains at least one reference word that is poorly used. In the space at the left, copy the pronoun or pronouns that have vague or incorrect reference. In the space below each sentence, rewrite enough of the sentence to make the meaning clear.

_____ 1. Mary explained to her sister that she needed to work harder on her physical conditioning if she intends to play volleyball.

_____

_____ 2. It says on the money-back guarantee that anyone who is not satisfied with a piece of merchandise can return it and get their money back.

_____

_____ 3. Anyone interested in becoming a doctor should know that there is a long road ahead of them and you have to be tough and dedicated to reach your goal.

_____

_____ 4. On television last night they said that they were expecting a sellout at today's game and you couldn't get a ticket anymore.

_____

_____ 5. Bobbie always insisted that she wanted to go into horse racing even though you have a hard time finding steady work and they don't pay much money to beginners.

_____

_____ 6. Anyone driving through Locust Grove on the state highway should know that they enforce the speed limits quite strictly and you will surely get a ticket if they catch you speeding.

_____

_____ 7. The city has been in a sort of recession for two years, but they seem to be coming out of it now.

_____

_____ 8. In our tennis club every player, regardless of their skill level, can find an opponent who is just about at their level.

_____

_____ 9. People who hike the trails in the state park can be certain that they will rescue you if you get lost in the forest.

_____

_____ 10. My father used to tell his brother that he should use his time and money wisely so that he could be successful and wealthy in his old age.

_____

In Lesson 23, the chart on page 245 classifies the personal pronouns on the basis of person, number, and gender. The three forms that are listed there for each person—first, second, and third, singular and plural—illustrate the three cases nouns and pronouns fall into: nominative, possessive, and objective. *I* and *they* are nominative, *my* and *their* are possessive, and *me* and *them* are objective, for example.

The way you use these pronouns in everyday language, in sentences such as "Two of *my* books have disappeared; *they* cost *me* 20 dollars, and *I* must find *them*," demonstrates that the case form you choose depends on how the word is used within the sentence. In this lesson we examine instances where the wrong choice of pronoun form is possible.

The only words in modern English that retain distinctions between nominative and objective case forms are the first- and third-person personal pronouns and the relative pronouns *who* and *whoever*. In nouns, the nominative and objective forms are identical, and the correct use of the one distinctive form, the possessive, requires essentially only a knowledge of how the apostrophe is used. (See Lesson 19.)

Here are the pronouns arranged according to their case forms. The first eight are the personal pronouns; notice that the only distinctive form of *you* and *it* is the possessive. The last three pronouns, which we examine separately from the personal pronouns, are used only in questions and in subordinate clauses. (See Supplement for a discussion of *which* in the possessive case.)

Nominative	*Possessive*	*Objective*
I	my, mine	me
you	your, yours	you
he	his, his	him
she	her, hers	her
it	its, its	it
we	our, ours	us
you	your, yours	you
they	their, theirs	them
which	——	which
who	whose	whom
whoever	whosever	whomever

PERSONAL PRONOUNS IN THE POSSESSIVE CASE

The **possessive case** is used to show possession. Review carefully the following three possible trouble spots.

Modifiers and Nominals

The preceding chart shows two possessive forms for the personal pronouns. The first form for each pronoun is used as a *modifier* of a noun. The second form is used as a nominal; in other words, it fills a noun slot, such as the subject, the complement, or the object of a preposition:

> This is *your* seat; *mine* is in the next row.
> Jane preferred *my* cookies; some of *hers* were burned.
> *Their* product is good, but the public prefers *ours*.

Indefinite Pronouns

The indefinite pronouns use an apostrophe to form the possessive case: *everybody's* duty, *one's* lifetime, *everyone's* hopes, someone *else's* car. But the personal pronouns do not:

> These seats are *ours* [not *our's*]. *Yours* [not *Your's*] are in the next row.

Learn to distinguish carefully between the following possessives and contractions that are pronounced alike: *its* (possessive), *it's* (it is, it has); *theirs* (possessive), *there's* (there is, there has); *their* (possessive), *they're* (they are); *whose* (possessive), *who's* (who is, who has); *your* (possessive), *you're* (you are):

> *It's* obvious that the car has outworn *its* usefulness.
> *There's* new evidence that *they're* changing *their* tactics.

Possessive Pronouns with Gerunds

Formal usage prefers the possessive form of pronouns (occasionally of nouns also) preceding gerunds in constructions like the following:

> He was unhappy about *my* [not *me*] voting for the bill.
> Her report led to *our* [not *us*] buying additional stock.
> Chad boasted about his *son's* [not *son*] having won the scholarship.

PERSONAL PRONOUNS IN THE NOMINATIVE AND OBJECTIVE CASES

The rules governing the uses of the other two cases are simple. A pronoun is in the **nominative case** when it is used

1. As a subject: *They* suspected that *he* was lying.
2. As a subjective complement: This is *she* speaking.
3. As an appositive of a nominative noun: *We* editors help young writers.

A pronoun is in the **objective case** when it is used

1. As an object of a verb or verbal: Ted told *her* the news. We enjoyed meeting *them*.
2. As an object of a preposition: Everyone except *me* had left the room.
3. As the subject of an infinitive: The police officer ordered *me* to halt.
4. As an appositive of an objective noun: Three of *us* truck drivers stopped to help.

We need not examine in detail every one of these applications. As people become more adept at using the English language, they learn that such usages as "*Them* arrived late" and

"I spoke to *she*" do not conform to the system of the language. Instead, we should examine the trouble spots where confusion may arise.

When you use the nominative and objective personal pronouns, exercise care in the following situations.

A Pronoun as Part of a Compound Unit

When the pronoun follows *and* (sometimes *or*) as part of a compound unit, determine its use in the sentence and choose the appropriate case form. The temptation here is usually to use the nominative, although the last example in the following list shows a trouble spot where the objective case is sometimes misused. If you test these troublesome constructions by using the pronoun by itself, you will often discover which form is the correct one:

The man gave Sue and *me* some candy. [Not: Sue and *I*. Both words are indirect objects. Apply the test. Notice how strange "The man gave...*I* some candy" sounds.]

Send your check to either my lawyer or *me*. [Not: to...*I*.]

Have you seen Bob or *her* lately? [Direct objects require the objective case.]

Just between you and *me*, the lecture was a bore. [Never say "between you and I." Both pronouns are objects of the preposition *between*. If this set phrase is a problem for you, find the correct form by reversing the pronouns: You would never say "between I and you."]

Ms. Estes took *him* and *me* to school.
[Not *he* and *I* or *him* and *I*. Both pronouns are direct objects.]

Will my sister and *I* be invited? [Not *me*. The subject is *sister* and *I*.]

Comparisons After As and Than

In comparisons after *as* and *than,* when the pronoun is the subject of an understood verb, use the nominative form:

He is taller than *I* [*am*]. I am older than *he* [*is*].
Can you talk as fast as *she* [*can talk*]?
No one knew more about art than *he* [*did*].

Sentences like these nearly always call for nominative case subjects. Occasionally the meaning of a sentence may demand an objective pronoun. Both of the following sentences are correct; notice the difference in meaning:

You trust Mr. Alton more than *I*. [Meaning "... more than I (trust Mr. Alton")."]
You trust Mr. Alton more than *me*. [Meaning "... more than (you trust) me."]

"It is" Expressions

Ordinarily, use the nominative form for the subjective complement. The specific problem here concerns such expressions as *It's me, It is I, It was they,* or *It was them.* Many people say *It's me,* but they would hesitate to say *It was her, It was him,* or *It was them,* instead of *It was she, It was he,* or *It was they.* However, this problem does not arise often in the writing of students. The following are examples of correct formal usage:

> It is *I.*
> It could have been *he.*
> Was it *she*?
> Was it *they* who called?

"We" Versus "Us" and "I" Versus "Me"

An appositive should be in the same case as the word that it refers to. Notice particularly the first three examples that follow. This usage employing *we* and *us* as an appositive modifier preceding a noun is a real trouble spot:

> *We* boys were hired. [The unit *We boys* is the subject and requires the nominative.]
> Two of *us* boys were hired. [The object of a preposition requires the objective case.]
> Mr. Elder hired *us* boys. [Not *we boys* for a direct object.]
> Two boys—you and *I*—will be hired. [In apposition with the subject.]
> Mr. Elder will hire two boys—you and *me.* [In apposition with the object.]

PROBLEMS WITH WHO AND WHOM

The only other pronouns in standard modern English that have distinctive nominative, possessive, and objective forms are *who/whose/whom* and *whoever/whosever/whomever.* (See Supplement.) The rules that apply to the personal pronouns apply to these words as well: In the subject position *who/whoever* should be used; in the direct object position *whom/whomever* should be used; and so forth. (These pronouns, it should be noted, are never used as appositives.)

The special problem in the application of the case rules to these words comes from their use as interrogatives and as subordinating words. As you learned in Lessons 6, 9, and 10, these words, because they serve as signal words, always stand at the beginning of their clauses. To locate the grammatical function of the pronoun within its clause, you must examine the clause to determine the normal subject-verb-complement positioning.

Direct Object or Object of a Preposition

In formal usage, *whom* is required when it is a direct object or the object of a preposition, even though it stands ahead of its subject and verb:

> *Whom* did Mr. Long hire?
> [If you are troubled by this sort of construction, try substituting a personal pronoun and placing it after the verb, where it normally comes: "Did Mr. Long hire *him*?" You would never say "Did Mr. Long hire *he*?" The transitive verb *hire* requires a direct object pronoun in the objective case.]
> He is a boy *whom* everyone can like. [*Whom* is the object of *can like*.]
> Wilson was the man *whom* everybody trusted. [Everybody trusted *whom*.]
> She is the girl *whom* Mother wants me to marry. [object of the verbal *to marry*]
> *Whom* was she speaking to just then? [To *whom* was she speaking?]

Beginning a Subordinate Clause

When *who(m)* or *who(m)ever* begins a subordinate clause that follows a verb or a preposition, the use of the pronoun *within its own clause* determines its case form:

We do not know *who* broke the window.

[*Who* is the subject of *broke*, not the direct object of *do know*.]

No one knows *who* the intruder was.

[*Who* is the subjective complement in the noun clause.]

We do not know *whom* the police have arrested.

[The objective form *whom* is used because it is the direct object of *have arrested*. The direct object of *do know* is the whole noun clause.]

I will sell the car to *whoever* offers the best price.

[The whole clause, *whoever offers the best price*, is the object of the preposition *to*. *Whoever* is the subject of *offers*. The subject of a verb must be in the nominative case.]

After a Parenthetical Insertion

When the pronoun subject is followed by a parenthetical insertion like *do you think, I suspect, everyone believes,* or *we know,* the nominative case form must be used:

Who do you think *has* the best chance of winning?

[*Who* is the subject of *has*. The *do you think* is a parenthetical insertion.]

Jenkins is the one *who* I suspect *will make* the best impression.

[Determine the verb that goes with the pronoun. If you are puzzled by this type of sentence, try reading it this way: "Jenkins is the one *who will make* the best impression—I suspect."]

But if the pronoun is not the subject of the verb, the objective form should be used:

He is an achiever *whom* I suspect you will eventually envy.

[*Whom* is the direct object of *will envy*.]

SUPPLEMENT

The chart on page 258 shows that the pronoun *which* has no possessive case form, a situation that brings about a minor problem of word choice. As you learned when you studied the adjective clause, *who(m)* normally refers to persons and *which* to things. But *whose* may be used in an adjective clause as the possessive form of *which* to refer to a nonhuman antecedent:

It is a disease *whose* long-term effects are minor.

If *whose* is not used in such a sentence, the "of-which" form must be used, producing a perfectly correct but cumbersome sentence:

It is a disease the long-term effects *of which* are minor.

SUMMARY OF CORRECT PRONOUN USE

1. A pronoun should have a clearly identified antecedent with which it agrees in person, number, and gender.

2. Be aware of the special problem of pronoun reference to third-person singular antecedents that include both masculine and feminine members—pronouns like *everybody* and *someone* and nouns like *person, student, employee,* and so on. *Note:* Using a plural rather than a singular antecedent is one obvious way of avoiding this problem.

3. Use nominative forms of pronouns for subjects, subjective complements, and appositives that rename nominative nouns. Use objective forms of pronouns for objects of verbs or prepositions, subjects of infinitives, and appositives that rename objective nouns.

4. Be aware of a particular pronoun problem when a personal pronoun is tied to a noun or another pronoun by *and* or *or:*

   Mickey and I [not *Mickey and me*] were sent to the principal's office.

   Mr. Case sent *Mickey and me* [not *Mickey and I*] to the principal's office.

   And so, neighbors, please vote for *Ms. Stone and me* [not *Ms. Stone and I*].

5. Remember that the case of *who* is determined by its use in its own clause. It may be a direct object that precedes the subject [*Whom* has your wife invited?] or a subject immediately following a verb or a preposition [We wonder *who* will win. Our dog is friendly with *whoever* pets it.]

NAME _____ SCORE _____

Directions: Each italicized pronoun in the following sentences is correctly used. In the space at the left, write one of the following numbers to identify the pronoun's use in the sentence:

1. Subject
2. Subjective complement
3. Appositive modifier of a nominative noun
4. Direct or indirect object
5. Object of preposition
6. Appositive modifier of an objective noun

_____   1. *Whomever* you saw at the door should have given you a schedule.

_____   2. You shouldn't worry so much about John and *me* when we are out on the snow-mobile.

_____   3. Billy deserves to play; no one else on the team has a higher batting average than *he.*

_____   4. Sandra enjoys playing cards more than *I.*

_____   5. "Honestly, " exclaimed Martha, "I think Jim loves that dog more than *me.*"

_____   6. For a few of *us* debate team members, the cancellation of the tournament was a big disappointment.

_____   7. The reporter didn't tell us *who* had given her the information about the election results.

_____   8. *Who* do you think can best answer that question?

_____   9. *Whom* did you call for help with that last computer problem?

_____   10. Except for Alice and *me*, everyone arrived early for the meeting.

_____   11. The teacher in the film class asked us *who* our favorite actors are.

_____   12. Yesterday at the mall I met a woman *whom* I had worked with briefly last year.

_____   13. Everyone except *him* and me got caught in that heavy rain.

_____   14. Charlie showed Jim and *me* how to fix the brakes on Jim's car.

_____   15. "Do you think that *we* students should be given free tickets to that game?" asked Al.

_____   16. None of *us* students could afford a ticket to that game.

_____   17. I wonder why you and *I* were chosen to work on that project.

_____   18. That's our new coach walking across campus; it was *he* who began the new fitness program for the team.

_____   19. *We* six graduating seniors will be honorary captains for that last game.

_____   20. The coach appointed *us* six graduating seniors as honorary captains for that game.

259

Directions: In the space at the left, copy the correct pronoun from within the parentheses.

_____ 1. Taller people like you and (she, her) have an advantage in basketball.

_____ 2. It was (I, me) who first found that reference for our group project.

_____ 3. Everyone in the class except Alex and (I, me) had seen that movie.

_____ 4. We are trying desperately to find out (who, whom) the winners of the election are.

_____ 5. There comes my brother Tom, (who, whom) you met last month in Vail.

_____ 6. (Whoever, Whomever) did you think knew the answer to that question, if it was not Alicia?

_____ 7. The boss asked me (who, whom) I was thinking about when I mentioned I knew someone else who wanted a job.

_____ 8. The judges have given you and (her, she) ten more minutes for your warm-up.

_____ 9. The candidate, (whoever, whomever) we choose, must be able to speak well in public.

_____ 10. It was (he, him) who suggested that we go out for dinner at a local restaurant.

_____ 11. (Who, Whom) do you think will be the nominees for president will be?

_____ 12. (Who, Whom) will the party choose as its candidate for president?

_____ 13. In that specialty, no one has more experience than (her, she).

_____ 14. Just between you and (I, me), I think the desktop computer is the most cost-effective choice.

_____ 15. Besides you and (her, she), did anyone else know the answer to that question?

_____ 16. Please send Jack, Marcia, and (I, me) copies of that report from the Houston office.

_____ 17. Tomorrow we will find out (who, whom) the boss has chosen to run that committee.

_____ 18. Tomorrow we will find out (who, whom) has been selected to run that committee.

_____ 19. If you were (I, me), which of those two shirts would you buy?

_____ 20. My grandfather asked (us, we) little kids where we had seen the flock of turkeys.

NAME _____ SCORE _____

Directions: If you find an incorrectly used pronoun, underline it and write the correct form in the space at the left. If a sentence is correct, leave the space blank.

_____ 1. As usual, the kitchen cleanup work was left to my sister and me.

_____ 2. Leonard boasted that none of us other men had worked as hard as him.

_____ 3. The old hermit would get out his shotgun and threaten whomever dared to walk across his property.

_____ 4. The small umbrella kept the doorman dry but not my escort or me.

_____ 5. Who do you suppose asked if she could go to the concert with you and I?

_____ 6. My sister Helen, who is ten years older than me, usually babysat with us younger children.

_____ 7. Regardless of who actually gave out the misinformation, all of us salespeople must share the blame.

_____ 8. I hope you don't object to me turning off this lamp; it's shining in my eyes.

_____ 9. Here are the names of a few candidates whom I hope you will vote against next Tuesday.

_____ 10. This responsibility, Mr. Chairman, should be everybody's, not solely your's.

_____ 11. The news had been leaked to only three of us people in the office—Mr. Fisher, his secretary, and me.

_____ 12. Not one of us guests knew whom the masked man in the clown suit was.

_____ 13. Among those selected to serve were my office mate, a new man from the accounting department, and I.

_____ 14. The strained relations between Professor Watkins and I began at the very first meeting of the committee.

_____ 15. The bank president hired a bodyguard whom, we later learned, had once been awarded a medal for bravery.

_____ 16. While our car was in the repair shop, Mrs. Langley occasionally would let my wife or me use her's.

_____ 17. Senator Williams is one leader who's support in the campaign we desperately need.

_____ 18. Who do you think Jean will invite to her party?

_____ 19. Who do you think will be invited to Jean's party?

_____ 20. I told Lucas that I'd get a second opinion, if I were he.

_____ 21. All the girls at camp except Jeanie and I were good swimmers.

_____ 22. Someone should have told one of we ushers that the main door was still locked.

_____ 23. Will your parents object to you dropping out of school for one semester?

_____ 24. "Who do you suggest that I vote for?" Valerie asked her father.

_____ 25. "Vote for whomever you think is the best candidate," her father replied.

_____ 26. "The record shows that the message was received by the office receptionist, not me," said the witness.

_____ 27. The bill will pass handily in the Senate, but it's fate in the House is uncertain.

_____ 28. My father-in-law is vacationing in Mexico; it couldn't have been he whom you saw at the auction.

_____ 29. Seated at the head table will be the club officers, the honored guests, and us hospitality committee members.

_____ 30. Jim admitted that there had been a mix-up in the ball handling between he and the quarterback.

NAME _____ SCORE _____

Directions: Copy incorrectly used pronouns in the spaces at the left. Then, in the space below each sentence, rewrite enough of the sentence to show how you would make it clear and correct. No sentence contains more than two poorly used pronouns; some sentences may be correct.

_____ 1. The director told we students that they've decided not to use any students as extras in the movie.

_____

_____ 2. Ask Jenny if that book on the back seat of my car is hers; it's not mine or yours.

_____

_____ 3. The clerk told Ed that you have to have your registration form signed by someone in the dean's office.

_____

_____ 4. Give this note to whoever you can find downstairs and tell them to take it to the coach's office, please.

_____

_____ 5. Mary asked Sue if her sister had brought back her clean laundry when she came for the weekend.

_____

_____ 6. It says in the handbook that March first is the last day you can withdraw from a course.

_____

_____ 7. "You can select whoever you wish for a partner; its your choice," said the teacher.

_____

_____ 8. The boss called earlier; she wants to know who we've hired and how we located them.

_____

_____ 9. Uncle Walt, who is a scuba diver, says he can teach us to dive if we are interested in it.

_____

_____ 10. Each student should have their own computer, and they should give each one individual instructions.

_____ 11. Jane Roberts, whom most of us think should be the next manager, has better credentials for it than anyone else.

_____ 12. I lost yesterday's lecture notes, but John and Anne, who sit next to me, will lend me their's.

_____ 13. On the television last night, they announced that people who use well water should boil it before drinking it.

_____ 14. Every entering freshman must attend orientation before they can sign up for their courses.

_____ 15. My parents, who both attended a local college, allowed my sister and I to choose an out-of-state school.

_____ 16. The guides gave each hiker a picnic lunch, but they had eaten everything well before noon.

_____ 17. "The climax of that movie was so frightening it made you forget how funny you thought the opening was," said Tom.

_____ 18. I wonder if our leaving the party early angered anyone who was there.

_____ 19. Everyone who my father employed last summer has returned to college to pursue their degree.

_____ 20. Please send copies of the schedule to all we freshmen so we can pick out our classes early.

In Lesson 2, you learned that an adjective is a word that describes or limits a noun or a pronoun. You also learned that an adverb modifies a verb, an adjective, or another adverb. Many adverbs end in *ly,* such as *happily, beautifully,* and *extremely.* But some adjectives—*lovely, likely, deadly, neighborly,* and *homely,* for instance—also end in *ly.* Some adverbs do not end in *ly,* and these happen to be among the most frequently used words in speech and writing: *after, always, before, far, forever, here, not, now, often, quite, rather, soon, then, there, too, very.* Some words can be used either as adjectives or as adverbs, as the following examples show:

Adverbs	Adjectives
He came *close.*	That was a *close* call.
She talks too *fast.*	She's a *fast* thinker.
Hit it *hard.*	That was a *hard* blow.
She usually arrives *late.*	She arrived at a *late* hour.
He went *straight* to bed.	I can't draw a *straight* line.

Some adverbs have two forms, one without and one with the *ly: cheap, cheaply; close, closely; deep, deeply; hard, hardly; high, highly; late, lately; loud, loudly; quick, quickly; right, rightly; slow, slowly.* In some of these pairs the words are interchangeable; in most they are not. The idiomatic use of adverbs is a rather complex matter; no rules can be made that govern every situation. We can, however, make a few generalizations that reflect present-day practice.

1. The shorter form of a few of these—*late, hard,* and *near,* for example—fills most adverbial functions because the corresponding *ly* forms have acquired special meanings:

We must not stay *late.*	I have not seen him *lately* [recently].
I studied *hard* last night.	I *hardly* [scarcely] know him.
Winter is drawing *near.*	I *nearly* [almost] missed the last flight.

2. The *ly* form tends toward the formal, with the short form lending itself to more casual, informal speech and writing:

Informal	Formal
It fell *close* to the target.	You must watch him *closely.*
They ate *high* off the hog.	She was *highly* respected.
Drive *slow*!	Please drive more *slowly.*
Must you sing so *loud?*	He *loudly* denied the charges.
We searched far and *wide.*	She is *widely* known as an artist.

3. Because the short form seems more direct and forceful, it is often used in imperative sentences:

Hold *firm* to this railing.

"Come *quick,"* yelled the officer.

4. The short form is often the one used when combined with an adjective to make a compound modifier preceding a noun:

a *wide*-ranging species	The species ranges *widely.*
a *slow*-moving truck	The truck moved *slowly.*

TYPICAL ADVERB/ADJECTIVE TROUBLE SPOTS

For the sake of simplifying the problem of the right use of adverbs and adjectives, we may say that there are three main trouble spots.

Misusing an Adjective for an Adverb

A word is an adverb if it modifies a verb, an adjective, or another adverb. The words that usually cause trouble here are *good, bad, well; sure, surely; real, really; most, almost; awful, awfully;* and *some, somewhat:*

Chip played *well* [not *good*] in the last game. [Modifies the verb *played.*]

This paint adheres *well* [not *good*] to concrete. [Modifies the verb *adheres.*]

Almost [not *Most*] every student has a job. [Modifies the adjective *every.*]

Today my shoulder is *really* [or *very*—not *real*] sore. [Modifies the adjective *sore.*]

He was driving *really* [or *very*—not *real*] fast. [Modifies the adverb *fast.*]

This rain has been falling *steadily* [not *steady*] for a week.

The champion should win his first match *easily* [not *easy*].

You'll improve if you practice *regularly* [not *regular*].

She wants that prize very *badly* [not *bad*].

Misusing Adverbs for Adjectives as Subjective Complements

The most common verb to take the subjective complement is *be;* fortunately, mistakes with this verb are nearly impossible. A few other verbs—like *seem, become, appear, prove, grow, go, turn, stay,* and *remain,* when they are used in a sense close to that of *be*—take subjective complements. This complement must be an adjective, not an adverb.

The house *seems empty.* [House *is* empty.]

Their plans *became apparent.* [Plans *were* apparent.]

The work *proved* very *hard.* [Work *was* hard.]

The adjective subjective complement is also used with another group of verbs, the so-called verbs of the senses. These are *feel, look, smell, sound,* and *taste:*

You shouldn't feel *bad* about this. [Not *badly.*]

His cough sounds *bad* this morning. [Not *badly.*]

At first our prospects looked *bad.* [Not *badly.*]

Doesn't the air smell *sweet* today? [Not *sweetly.*]

The verb *feel* is involved in two special problems. In the first place, it is often used with both *good* and *well.* These two words have different meanings; one is not a substitute for the other. When used with the verb *feel, well* is an adjective meaning "in good health."

The adjective *good*, when used with *feel*, means "filled with a sense of vigor and excitement." Of course, both *well* and *good* have other meanings when used with other verbs. In the second place, the expression "I feel badly" is used so widely, especially in spoken English, that it can hardly be considered an error in usage. Many careful writers, however, prefer the adjective here, with the result that "feel bad" is usually found in written English.

Misusing a Comparative or a Superlative Form of a Modifier

Most adverbs are compared in the same way as adjectives. (For a discussion of the comparison of adjectives, see Lesson 2.) Some common adverbs cannot be compared, such as *here, now, then, when,* and *before.* As you learned in Lesson 16, we use the comparative degree *(taller, better, more intelligent, more rapidly)* in a comparison limited to two things. We use the superlative degree *(tallest, best, most intelligent, most rapidly)* for more than two things.

Two other problems, both of minor importance, are involved in comparisons. First, we do not combine the two forms *(more + er, most + est)* in forming the comparative and superlative degrees:

> Later the landlord became *friendlier* [not *more friendlier*].
>
> Please drive *slower* [not *more slower*].
>
> Please drive *more slowly* [not *more slower*].

Second, some purists object to the comparison of the so-called absolute qualities, such as *unique* ("being the only one"), *perfect, round, exact,* and so forth. They argue that, instead of such uses as *most perfect, straighter, more unique,* the intended meaning is *most nearly perfect, more nearly straight, more nearly unique.* General usage, however, has pretty well established both forms.

PROBLEMS WITH PREPOSITIONS

Three reminders should be made about the use of prepositions. One problem is the selection of the exact preposition for the meaning intended.

Idioms Using Prepositions

Many words, especially verbs and adjectives, give their full meaning only when modified by a prepositional phrase. In most cases, the meaning of the preposition dictates a logical idiom: to sit *on* a couch, to walk *with* a friend, to lean *against* a fence, and so on. For some more abstract concepts, however, the acceptable preposition may seem to have been selected arbitrarily. Here are a few examples of different meanings of different prepositions:

> agree *to* a proposal, *with* a person, *on* a price, *in* principle
>
> argue *about* a matter, *with* a person, *for* or *against* a proposition
>
> compare *to* to show likenesses, *with* to show differences [sometimes similarities]
>
> correspond *to* a thing, *with* a person
>
> differ *from* an unlike thing, *with* a person
>
> live *at* an address, *in* a house or city, *on* a street, *with* other people

Note: Good modern dictionaries provide information about and examples of the correct usage of prepositions.

Unnecessary Prepositions

Although at colloquial levels of language we sometimes find unnecessary prepositions used, examples like the following are improved in serious contexts if written without the words in brackets:

> I met [up with] your uncle yesterday.
> We keep our dog inside [of] the house.
> Our cat, however, sleeps outside [of] the house.
> The package fell off [of] the speeding truck.

Avoid especially the needless preposition at the end of a sentence or the repeated preposition in adjective clauses and in direct or indirect questions:

> Where is your older brother *at*?
> He is one of the few people *to* whom I usually feel superior *to*.
> To what do you attribute your luck at poker *to*?
> [Use one *to* or the other, but not both.]

Repeated Prepositions in Compound Units

When two words of a compound unit require the same preposition to be idiomatically correct, the preposition need not be stated with the first unit:

Correct: We were both *repelled* and *fascinated by* the snake charmer's act.

But when the two units require different prepositions, both must be expressed:

Incomplete: The child shows an *interest* and a *talent for* music. [interest...*for* (?)]

Correct: The child shows an *interest in* and a *talent for* music.

Incomplete: I am sure that Ms. Lewis would both *contribute* and *gain from* a summer workshop. [contribute...*from* (?)]

Correct: I am sure that Ms. Lewis would both *contribute to* and *gain from* a summer workshop.

Using Modifiers Correctly

Directions: In the first space at the left, write the word (or words) that the italicized word modifies. In the second space, write **Adj.** if the italicized word is an adjective or **Adv.** if it is an adverb.

_____   1. The old district manager was *highly* respected by all the workers.
_____

_____   2. I saw two falcons soaring *high* above the mountaintop.
_____

_____   3. Despite the recession, we opened our new business with *high* hopes.
_____

_____   4. We were pleasantly surprised by the *gentlemanly* behavior of the boys at the dance.
_____

_____   5. We try to sympathize with Joan, although some of her problems are *real* and some are imaginary.
_____

_____   6. The doctor's prognosis on Anderson's knee injury was not *really* optimistic.
_____

_____   7. Sand the wood *well* before you apply the first coat of lacquer.
_____

_____   8. Last week my father was ill, but this week he is *well* again.
_____

_____   9. The spring weather, warm and breezy, made me feel *good* again.
_____

_____   10. The floors of the kitchen must be *spotless* before the inspector arrives.
_____

_____   11. That car would look *better* if you gave it a new coat of paint.
_____

_____   12. The engine will run *better* after a tune-up.
_____

_____   13. *Most* football players are fairly good students.
_____

_____   14. Hurricane Alma was our *most* destructive storm in the last five years.
_____

_____   15. The suburbs are growing *rapidly.*
_____

Directions: In the space at the left, copy the correct form given in parentheses.

_____ 1. George did not sound at all (happy, happily) when he heard the news from the main office.

_____ 2. The amount of rainfall in the valley has increased (considerable, considerably) over last year's.

_____ 3. The track team performed (good, well) at the state meet.

_____ 4. If we leave by 10 o'clock, we should (easy, easily) make it to St. Louis by dinnertime.

_____ 5. You punctuated nearly a dozen sentences in your paper (incorrect, incorrectly).

_____ 6. This money should be divided (equal, equally) among the four partners.

_____ 7. Jose wants very (bad, badly) to learn to play football.

_____ 8. Although I have taken some lessons, I still dance (awkward, awkwardly).

_____ 9. In spite of my lessons, I still felt (awkward, awkwardly) on the dance floor.

_____ 10. It rained (steady, steadily) for two weeks this summer.

_____ 11. When Paul had been missing for three days, we became (real, really) worried about him.

_____ 12. The butter-cream icing on the chocolate cake tasted very (sweet, sweetly).

_____ 13. The storm came up so (sudden, suddenly) that we did not have time to get the people off the island.

_____ 14. Frozen orange juice tastes (different, differently) from fresh juice.

_____ 15. This special glue bonds (good, well) on almost any surface.

_____ 16. We (sure, surely) hope that your brother will recover soon from his injury.

_____ 17. The musicians played so (bad, badly) that we could not recognize the tune.

_____ 18. He is quite short, but he can become a good basketball player if he practices (regular, regularly).

_____ 19. The blouse will look (good, well) with your new mauve slacks.

_____ 20. After a cold shower, Maria felt (some, somewhat) more cheerful.

NAME _____ SCORE _____

Directions: Study these sentences for misused adjectives, adverbs, and prepositions. Underline misused modifiers and write the correct forms in the spaces at the left. Circle superfluous prepositions and write **omit** in the spaces at the left. Write required prepositions in the spaces at the left and use a caret (ˇ) to show where they should be inserted. Some sentences are correct as they stand; in these cases, leave the spaces blank.

_____ 1. "It was real kind of you to speak well of my daughter's piano playing," Mrs. Hartwell told the teacher.

_____ 2. After the stern warning from the vice principal, the conduct of the class improved noticeable.

_____ 3. "The people here seem much more friendlier than those in Oakdale," said the new renter.

_____ 4. "Our quarterback was injured seriously," said Coach Saunders, "and we had to cut down on our offense and play more conservative."

_____ 5. The accused man testified that he had neither knowledge nor access to any secret Swiss bank accounts.

_____ 6. When I saw how weary the two old men looked, I admit that I felt somewhat guilty.

_____ 7. Mr. Evans confidently assured us that he could control the boat easy in any kind of weather.

_____ 8. Our chances for a successful season were hurt badly when Locke, the fastest of our two fullbacks, was declared ineligible.

_____ 9. Where do you think I might be able to buy two hubcaps for my 1977 Mustang at?

_____ 10. Your front yard certainly looks differently now that you have removed those two scraggly junipers.

_____ 11. Cynthia surely talks differently now that the braces have been removed from her teeth.

_____ 12. At the state meet last year, McCrae failed to place in the high jump but did real good in the 100-yard dash.

_____ 13. August Denby is a total incompetent local politician for whom I will never in my life cast a vote for.

_____ 14. At the recital Cathy's violin solo sounded good, and her accompanist played real well.

_____ 15. Brandowski's devotion and fascination with modern art led to the writing of his first critical essays.

_____ 16. If you use thinner as needed and clean your brushes regularly, you'll find that the painting job will move ahead more faster.

_____ 17. Although the scoutmaster set a rather leisurely pace, some of the boys were awful tired at the end of the hike.

_____ 18. Wally reluctantly admitted that, although his black eye looked ugly, it didn't hurt him real bad.

_____ 19. Dad and Fran worked hard and fast in the kitchen, and the excellent meal was ready for us promptly at 6 o'clock.

_____ 20. My uncle has always been interested in, in fact fascinated by, steam locomotives.

_____ 21. I am really sorry, Mrs. Frame, to have to report that your son has been behaving quite bad in class.

_____ 22. Mrs. Martin, the chairperson, made me promise solemnly that I would tell none of the children where I had hidden the Easter eggs at.

_____ 23. I'm sorry that Larry felt really bad when he confessed that he had not done very well on the final examination.

_____ 24. The author shows both a deep understanding and sympathy for the men who risk their lives fighting fires.

_____ 25. We had worried needlessly, for the young people behaved unusually well at the wedding reception.

The forms suggested in many of the entries in this glossary are those usually preferred in standard formal English—the English appropriate to your term papers, theses, term reports, examination papers in all your courses, and most of the serious papers written for your English classes. Many of the words or expressions in brackets are appropriate enough in informal conversation and in some informal papers.

Some of the entries are labeled *colloquial*, a term you should not think of as referring to slang, to forms used only in certain localities, or to "bad" English. The term applies to usages that are appropriate to informal and casual *spoken* English rather than to formal written English. However, expressions marked *substandard* should be avoided at all times.

A, an. Use *a* when the word immediately following it is sounded as a consonant; use *an* when the next sound is a vowel sound: *a, e, i, o,* or *u* (*a* friend, *an* enemy). Remember that it is the consonantal or vowel *sound,* not the actual letter, that determines the choice of the correct form of the indefinite article: *a* sharp curve, *an* S-curve; *a* eulogy, *an* empty house; *a* hospital, *an* honest person; *a* united people, *an* uneven contest.

Ad. Clipped forms of many words are used informally, such as *ad (advertisement), doc (doctor), exam (examination), gent (gentleman), gym (gymnasium), lab (laboratory), math (mathematics),* and *prof (professor).* Formal usage prefers the long forms.

Aggravate. In standard formal English the word means "make more severe," "make worse." Colloquially it means "annoy," "irritate," "exasperate."

Walking on your sprained ankle will *aggravate* the hurt. [*Informal:* All criticism aggravates him.]

Ain't. Substandard for *am not, are not, is not, have not.*

Am I not [not *Ain't I*] a good citizen?

The command *hasn't* [not *hain't* or *ain't*] been given yet.

They *are not* [not *ain't*] going either.

All the farther, all the faster, and the like. Generally regarded as colloquial equivalents of *as far as, as fast as,* and the like.

This is *as far as* [not *all the farther*] I care to go.

That was *as fast as* [not *all the faster*] he could run.

A lot. Always use as two words. See also *Lots of.*

A lot of. See *Lots of.*

Alright. This spelling, like *allright* or *allright,* although often used in advertising, is generally regarded as very informal usage. The preferred form is *all right.* In strictly formal usage, *satisfactory* or *very well* is preferred to *all right.*

Very well [not *Alright*], you may ride in our car.

The members agreed that the allocation of funds was *satisfactory* [not *all right*].

Among, between. *Among* is used with three or more persons or things, as in "Galileo was *among* the most talented people of his age," and "The estate was divided among his three sons." *Between* usually refers to two things, as in "between you and me," "between two points," "between dawn and sunset."

Amount, number. Use *number,* not *amount,* in reference to units that can actually be counted:

the *amount* of indebtedness, the *number* of debts

And, etc. Because *etc. (et cetera)* means "and so forth," *and etc.* would mean "and and so forth." You should not use *etc.* to replace some exact, specific word, but if you do use it, be sure not to spell it *ect.* And remember that *etc.* requires a period after it.

Anywheres. Colloquial for *anywhere.* Similar colloquial forms are *anyways* for *anyway* or *anyhow, everywheres* for *everywhere, nowheres* for *nowhere, somewheres* for *somewhere.*

I looked for my books *everywhere.*

They must be hidden *somewhere.*

Apt to, liable to, likely to. *Apt to* implies a natural tendency. *Liable to* implies a negative outcome or result. *Likely to* suggests a strong possibility.

That car is *apt to* increase in value.

We are *liable to* have a bad leak unless we fix the roof.

The new vaccine is *likely to* cause a disappearance of chicken pox.

As, like. See *Like.*

As to whether. *Whether* is usually enough.

Awful, awfully. Like *aggravate,* these words have two distinct uses. In formal contexts, they mean "awe-inspiring" or "terrifying." Often in conversation and sometimes in writing of a serious nature, *awful* and *awfully* are mild intensifiers, meaning "very."

Because. See *Reason is because.*

Because of. See *Due to.*

Being that, being as how. Substandard for *because, as,* or *since.*

Beside, besides. These two prepositions are clearly distinguished by their meanings. *Beside* means "at the side of" and *besides* means "in addition to."

Lucy sits *beside* me in class.

Did anyone *besides* you see the accident?

Between. See *Among.*

Bring, take. *Bring* means to convey from a farther to a nearer place. *Take* means to convey from nearer to farther.

Bring home a loaf of bread from the store.

Take that book back to the library.

But what, but that. Colloquial for *that.*

Both sides had no doubt *that* [not *but what*] their cause was just.

Calculate, figure, reckon. These are colloquial for *imagine, consider, expect, think,* and similar words.

He must have *expected* [not *calculated*] that she might not be pleased to see him after he did not return her calls.

Can, may. *Can* suggests ability to do something. *May* is the preferred form when permission is involved.

Little Junior *can* already count to ten.

May [not *Can*] I borrow your pencil?

Can't hardly, couldn't hardly, can't scarcely, couldn't scarcely. Substandard for *can hardly, could hardly, can scarcely, could scarcely.* These are sometimes referred to as double negatives.

I *can hardly* [not *can't hardly*] believe that story.

We *could scarcely* [not *couldn't scarcely*] hear the foghorn.

Caused by. See *Due to.*

Consensus means an agreement of the majority; thus, *consensus of opinion* is redundant. Say simply, "The consensus was…," not, "The consensus of opinion was…."

Continual, continuous. A fine distinction in meaning can be made if you remember that *continual* means "repeated regularly and frequently" and that *continuous* means "occurring without interruption," "unbroken."

Could(n't) care less. This worn-out set phrase indicating total indifference is a colloquialism. A continuing marvel of language behavior is the large number of people who insist on saying "I could care less" when they obviously mean the opposite.

Could of, would of, might of, ought to of, and so on. Substandard for *could have, would have,* and so on.

Couple, couple of. These expressions are fine for informal conversation but not precise enough for more formal occasions. In writing, be specific. Say "three points," for example, "four issues," rather than "a couple of points/issues."

Criteria. The singular noun is *criterion;* the plural is *criteria* or *criterions.* Such combinations as "a criteria," "one criteria," and "these criterias" are incorrect.

Data. Originally the plural form of the rarely used Latin singular *datum, data* has taken on a collective meaning so that it is often treated as a singular noun. "This data has been published" and "These data have been published" are both correct, the latter being the use customarily found in scientific or technical writing.

Different from, different than. *Different from* is generally correct. Many people object to *different than,* but others use it, especially when a clause follows, as in "Life in the Marines was different than he had expected it to be."

Their customs are *different from* [not *different than*] ours.

Life in the Marines was *different from* what he had expected it to be.

Different to, a form sometimes used by British speakers and writers, is rarely used in the United States.

Disinterested, uninterested. Many users of precise English deplore the tendency to treat these words as loose synonyms, keeping a helpful distinction between *disinterested* ("impartial," "free from bias or self-interest") and *uninterested* ("lacking in interest," "unconcerned"). Thus we would hope that a referee would be disinterested but not uninterested.

Due to, caused by, because of, owing to. *Due to* and *caused by* are used correctly after the verb *to be:*

His illness was *caused by* a virus.

The flood was *due to* the heavy spring rains.

Many people object to the use of *due to* and *caused by* adverbially at the beginning of a sentence, as in "Due to the heavy rains, the streams flooded," and "Caused by the storm, the roads were damaged." It is better to use *because of* or *owing to* in similar situations. *Due to* and *owing to* are also used correctly as an adjective modifier immediately following a noun:

Accidents *due to* excessive speed are increasing in number.

Note in the examples what variations are possible:

The streams flooded *because of* the heavy rains.

The flooding of the streams was *due to* the heavy rains.

The floods were *caused by* the rapid melting of the snow.

Emigrate, immigrate. To *emigrate* is to *leave* one region to settle in another; to *immigrate* is to *enter* a region from another one.

Enthuse. Colloquial or substandard (depending on the degree of a person's aversion to this word) for *be enthusiastic, show enthusiasm.*

The director *was enthusiastic* [not *enthused*] about her new program.

Everyday, every day. *Everyday* is an adjective meaning "ordinary." *Every day* is an adjective and noun combination.

Just wear your *everyday* clothes; don't dress up.

I wore those shoes almost *every day* last week.

Everywheres. See *Anywheres.*

Explicit, implicit. *Explicit* means "stated directly." *Implicit* means "implied," "suggested directly."

She *explicitly* told us to bring two pencils and ten pages of notebook paper.

The idea *implicit* in her statement was that we should come prepared to take the test.

Farther, further. Careful writers observe a distinction between these two words, reserving *farther* for distances that can actually be measured.

Tony can hit a golf ball *farther* than I can.

We must pursue this matter *further.*

Fewer, less. *Fewer* refers to numbers, *less* to quantity, extent, or degree.

Fewer [not *Less*] students are taking courses in literature this year.

Food costs *less,* but we have less money to spend.

Figure. See *Calculate.*

Fine. Colloquial, very widely used, for *well, very well.*

The boys played *well* [not *just fine*].

Graffiti. The singular form is *graffito.* In serious writing, *graffiti* takes a plural verb. Avoid combinations such as "a graffiti," "this graffiti," etc.

Had(n't) ought. *Ought* does not take an auxiliary.

You *ought* [not *had ought*] to apply for a scholarship.

You *ought not* [not *hadn't ought*] to miss the lecture.

Hardly. See *Can't hardly.*

Healthy, healthful. *Healthy* means "having health," and *healthful* means "giving health." Thus a person or an animal is *healthy*; a climate, a food, or an activity is *healthful.*

Immigrate. See *Emigrate.*

Implicit. See *Explicit.*

Imply, infer. Despite the increasing tendency to use these words more or less interchangeably, it is good to preserve the distinction: *Imply* means "to say something indirectly," "to hint or suggest," and *infer* means "to draw a conclusion," "to deduce." Thus you *imply* something in what you say and *infer* something from what you hear.

Incredible, incredulous. An unbelievable *thing* is incredible; a disbelieving *person* is incredulous.

In regards to. The correct forms are *in regard to* or *as regards.*

Inside of. *Inside* or *within* is preferred in formal writing.

We stayed *inside* [not *inside of*] the barn during the storm.

The plane should arrive *within* [not *inside of*] an hour.

Irregardless. Substandard or humorous for *regardless.*

The planes bombed the area *regardless* [not *irregardless*] of consequences.

Is when, is where. The *"is-when," "is-where"* pattern in definitions is clumsy and should be avoided. Write, for example, "An embolism is an obstruction, such as a blood clot, in the bloodstream," instead of "An embolism is where an obstruction forms in the bloodstream."

Kind, sort. These words are singular and therefore should be modified by singular modifiers. Do not write *these kind, these sort, those kind, those sort.*

> *Those kinds* [not *those kind*] of videos sell very well.
>
> Who could believe *that sort* [not *those sort*] of arguments?

Kinda, sorta, kind of a, sort of a. Undesirable forms.

Kind of, sort of. Colloquial for *somewhat, in some degree, almost, rather.*

> They felt *somewhat* [not *sort of*] depressed.

Learn, teach. *Learn* means "to acquire knowledge"; *teach* means "to give or impart knowledge."

> Ms. Brown *taught* [not *learned*] me Spanish.

Leave. Not to be used for let.

> *Let* [not *Leave*] me carry your books for you.

Less. See *Fewer.*

Let. See *Leave.*

Let's us. The *us* is superfluous because *let's* means "let us."

Liable to, likely to. See *Apt to.*

Like, as, as if. The use of *like* as a conjunction (in other words, to introduce a clause) is colloquial. It should be avoided in serious writing.

> *As* [not *Like*] you were told earlier, there is a small entry fee.
>
> She acts *as if* [not *like*] she distrusts us.
>
> Do *as* [not *like*] I tell you.

Line. Often vague and redundant, as in "What do you read in the line of books?" "Don't you enjoy fishing and other sports along that line?" It is better to say, more directly,

> What kind of books do you read?
>
> Don't you enjoy fishing and sports like that?

Lots of, a lot of. Used informally to mean a large extent, amount, or number, a usage that is enjoying increased acceptance. This usage should be avoided in formal writing.

> *A great many* [not *Lots of*] families vacation here every summer.
>
> The storms caused *a great deal* [not *lots of*] damage.
>
> All of us owe you *a great deal* [not *a lot*].

As one word, **alot** is still unacceptable spelling.

Mad. Colloquially, *mad* is often used to mean "angry." In formal English, it means "insane."

> Marge was *angry* [not *mad*] because I was late.

May. See *Can.*

Media. A plural noun referring to all mass communicative agencies. The singular is *medium.* Careful writers and speakers avoid the use of *media* as a singular noun, as in "Television is an influential media." Even more objectionable is the use of *medias* as a plural.

Might of. See *Could of.*

Most. This word is the superlative form of *much* and *many* (much, more, most; many, more, most). Its use as a clipped form of *almost* is colloquial.

> *Almost* [not *Most*] all of my friends work during the summer.

Nauseated, nauseous. Despite the increasingly wide use of these words as synonyms, there are still speakers and writers of precise English who insist that *nauseated* should be used to mean "suffering from or experiencing nausea" and that *nauseous* should be used only to mean "causing nausea."

Nohow. This emphatic negative is substandard.

Not all that. A basically meaningless substitute for *not very* or *not really;* it can easily become a habit.

> The movie was *not very* [not *not all that*] amusing.

Nowheres. See *Anywheres*.
Number. See *Amount*.
Of. See *Could of*.
Off of. Dialectal or colloquial for *off*.

She asked me to get *off* [not *off of*] my high horse.

OK. This form calls attention to itself in serious writing. It is appropriate only to business communications and casual speech or writing. Modern dictionaries offer several permissible forms: *OK, O.K.,* and *okay* for the singular noun; *OKs, O.K.s,* and *okays* for the plural noun; and *OK'd, OK'ing, O.K.'d, O.K.'ing, okayed,* and *okaying* for verb forms.

Ought. See *Had(n't) ought*.

Ought to of. See *Could of*.

Owing to. See *Due to*.

Party. Colloquial for "individual" in the sense of *man, woman, person*.

A man [not *A party*] called while you were out.

Percent, percentage. Use *percent* when referring to a specific number.

Ten *percent* of the class made an A.

Use *percentage* when referring to no specific number.

A small *percentage* of the class made an A.

Phenomenon, phenomena. A *phenomenon* is a single observable fact or event. *Phenomena* is a plural noun. When using either, be sure to make adjectives such as *this* and *these* and all verbs agree in number.

Plenty is a noun meaning "an abundance" and is used with the preposition *of*.

There are *plenty of* jobs available.

Do not use the word as an adverb meaning "very" or "quite."

It was *very* [not *plenty*] scary in that movie.

Pretty is an informal modifier. In writing, use *quite* or *very*.

The floodwaters were *very* [not *pretty*] deep.

Quote, unquote. Although these words may be needed in the oral presentation of quoted material, they have no use in written material, in which quotation marks or indentation sets off the quoted material from the text proper.

Real, really. The use of *real*, which is an adjective, to modify another adjective or an adverb is colloquial. In formal contexts, *really* or *very* should be used.

We had a *really* [not *real*] enjoyable visit.

The motorcycle rounded the corner *very* [not *real*] fast.

Reason is because, reason is due to, reason is on account of. In serious writing, a "reason is" clause is usually completed with *that*, not with *because, due to,* or *on account of*.

The *reason* they surrendered *is that* [not *because*] they were starving.

The *reason* for my low grades *is that* I have poor eyesight [not *is on account of* my poor eyesight].

Reckon. See *Calculate*.

Same. The use of *same* as a pronoun, often found in legal or business writing, is inappropriate in most other types of writing.

I received your report and look forward to reading *it* [not *the same*].

So, such. These words, when used as exclamatory intensifiers, are not appropriate in a formal context. Sentences like the following belong in informal talk: "I am *so* tired," "She is *so* pretty," or "They are having *such* a good time."

Some. Colloquial for *somewhat, a little*.

The situation at the border is said to be *somewhat* [not *some*] improved today.

Somewheres. See *Anywheres*.

Sort. See *Kind*.

Such. See *So*.

Suppose to, use to. Although these incorrect forms are difficult to detect in spoken

English, remember that the correct written forms are *supposed to, used to.*

Sure. *Sure* is correctly used as an adjective:

> We are not *sure* about her plans.
>
> He made several *sure* investments.

Sure is colloquial when used as an adverbial substitute for *surely, extremely, certainly, indeed, very, very much.*

> The examination was *surely* [not *sure*] difficult.
>
> The lawyer's plea *certainly* [not *sure*] impressed the jury.

Sure and. See *Try and.*

Suspicion. *Suspicion* is a noun; it is not to be used as a verb in place of *suspect.*

> No one *suspected* [not *suspicioned*] the victim's widow.

Swell. Not to be used as a general term of approval meaning *good, excellent, attractive, desirable,* and so on.

Take. See *Bring.*

Teach. See *Learn.*

That there, this here, those there, these here. Substandard for *that, this, those, these.*

Them. Substandard when used as an adjective.

> How can you eat *those* [not *them*] parsnips?

Try and, sure and. *Try to, sure to* are the preferred forms in serious writing.

> We shall *try to* [not *try and*] make your visit a pleasant one.
>
> Be *sure to* [not *sure and*] arrive on time.

Type. Colloquial when used as a modifier of a noun. Use *type of* or *kind of.*

> I usually don't enjoy that *type of* [not *type*] movie.

Uninterested. See *Disinterested.*

Unique. In its original meaning, the word meant either "the only example" or "without a like or equal." In modern use, it has also acquired an additional meaning: "unusual." In the first sense, it cannot be modified by an adjective.

> As a politician, he is *unique.*
>
> She gave him a *unique* [*very special*] pen as a present.

Many object to the use of a modifier with unique; in formal writing, it is best to choose some other adjective to convey the meaning "special" or "unusual."

Use to. See *Suppose to.*

Want in, want off, want out. Colloquial and dialectical forms for *want to come in, want to get off, want to go out.* Inappropriate in serious writing.

Ways. Colloquial for *way,* in such expressions as

> It is just a short *distance* [not *ways*] up the canyon.
>
> We do not have a long *way* [not *ways*] to go.

What. Substandard when used for *who, which,* or *that* as a relative pronoun in an adjective clause.

> His raucous laugh is the thing *that* [not *what*] annoys me most.

When, where clauses. See *Is when.*

Where...at. The *at* is unnecessary and undesirable in both speech and writing.

> *Where* [not *Where at*] will you be at noon?
>
> *Where* is your car? [Not *Where is your car at?*]

-wise. The legitimate function of this suffix to form adverbs like *clockwise* does not carry with it the license to concoct such jargon as "Entertainmentwise, this town is a dud" or "This investment is very attractive long-term-capital-gainswise."

Without. Not to be used as a conjunction instead of *unless.*

> He won't lend me his car *unless* [not *without*] I fill the gas tank.

Would of. See *Could of.*

Practice
Sheet 26

Appropriate Use

NAME _____ SCORE _____

Directions: In the space at the left, write the expression given in parentheses that you consider the more appropriate form to use in serious writing.

_____ 1. (Almost, Most) all of the people in the group would like to move
_____   to a place that has a (healthful, healthy) environment.

_____ 2. Some chose (among, between) a place in the mountains, where it
_____   rains (alot, a lot), and a place at the shore, where the sun shines
                     all the time.

_____ 3. "That's (all the faster, as fast as) he could move," said Grampa as
_____   he watched the old hound, "but I guess that's (alright, all right)."

_____ 4. The reason for the rain is (because, that) a tropical wave moved
_____   out of the ocean and stopped (beside, besides) the city.

_____ 5. Yesterday, I (brought, took) my library books back to the library,
_____   and then I (brought, took) a pizza home for supper.

_____ 6. (Somewhere, Somewheres) there must be a quiet, peaceful place
_____   where I can study, but I can't find one (anywhere, anywheres) on
                     this campus.

_____ 7. A (couple, couple of) problems that we (should have, should of)
_____   taken care of earlier today have stopped our progress temporarily.

_____ 8. (Because of, Due to) the heavy rains, I can't get too (enthused,
_____   enthusiastic) about going on a picnic today.

_____ 9. (As, Like) I told you earlier today, it makes the boss (angry, mad)
_____   when people don't answer her e-mails promptly.

_____ 10. The professor was (not all that, not very) amused by the (incredible,
_____   incredulous) story that silly freshman told her.

_____ 11. The single newspaper in our town is the only news (medium,
_____   media) available to us, so many people here are (quite, real)
                     ignorant in the realm of foreign affairs.

_____ 12. "I'm (pretty, very) (aggravated, annoyed) by the constant ringing
_____   of that telephone," said Barbara.

_____ 13. "(Let us, Let's us) go down to the cafeteria for a cup of coffee,"

_____   suggested Mark; "I (could, couldn't) care less about finishing that

     project."

_____ 14. People (use to, used to) enjoy taking their lunch down to the lake

_____   before the (nauseated, nauseous) smells began to drift over from

     the paper mill.

_____ 15. I cannot eat (them, those) artichokes; my mother never (learned,

_____   taught) me to enjoy them.

_____ 16. "My grandfather (emigrated, immigrated) from Norway and

_____   became an (emigrant, immigrant) to this country in the late 19th

     century," said Mark.

_____ 17. The judge at the dog show was (disinterested, uninterested), but

_____   we knew she was not (disinterested, uninterested) because she

     paid close attention to each dog.

_____ 18. A large (percent, percentage) of the class made fine grades; in

_____   fact, 10 (percent, percentage) made an A for the term.

_____ 19. The man said he was (plenty, very) tired at the end of the day, but

_____   I (suspect, suspicion) that he was exaggerating.

_____ 20. The reason I went to the store was (because, that) I needed to

_____   buy printer paper so I could try (and, to) print my paper for

     tomorrow's class.

_____ 21. "That key lime pie tastes (as, like) a real key lime pie, which has a

_____   (unique, very unique) taste, a taste unlike the taste of any other

     lime or lemon pie," said Jean.

_____ 22. The cabin was a long (way, ways) up the canyon, and we were

_____   delayed because the trail was (extremely, so) rough.

_____ 23. Julio won't lend me his glove (unless, without) I promise to

_____   (bring, take) it back here to the dorm after I finish using it.

_____ 24. "Do you (reckon, think) we can get back to the house (anywhere,

_____   anywheres) close to sunset?" asked Marcella.

_____ 25. (Leave, Let) me help you with that project; I've (implied, inferred)

_____   from your comments that you are running a bit behind schedule.

Directions: Each sentence contains two italicized words or expressions. If you think that a word or expression is inappropriate in serious writing, write an acceptable form in the space at the left. If an expression is correct, write **C** in the space.

_____ 1. The *prof* told me that the subject I'd selected for my term paper
_____ was *alright.*

_____ 2. I am studying *awful* hard this term, but my grades seem to be no
_____ *different from* my usual grades.

_____ 3. I *suspicion* that the mortgage receipts will be found *somewheres*
_____ in the old man's cluttered desk.

_____ 4. The reason I did not send you an *invite* is *that* I had been told you
_____ would be out of town.

_____ 5. Your theme would *of* received a better grade if you had made
_____ *fewer* errors in spelling and punctuation.

_____ 6. I *can't hardly* believe that Calvin is the *party* who reported us to
_____ the police.

_____ 7. It now looks *like* the remodeling will take *lots of* money.

_____

_____ 8. A very large gentleman sat down *besides* me and nearly crowded
_____ me *off of* the bench.

_____ 9. The insurance companies have paid off *almost* all claims for
_____ losses *due to* last year's tidal wave.

_____ 10. *Can* I have another one of *them* delicious muffins, Mrs. Loomis?

_____

_____ 11. I was *plenty* embarrassed when Lydia told me that I was *suppose*
_____ to have worn a tie and jacket.

_____ 12. *"In regards to* your summer schedule, I'll try *and* arrange early
_____ morning classes for you," said my adviser.

_____ 13. "I *sure* hope you can *learn* me how to avoid slicing my drives,"
_____ Mr. Todd said to the golf professional.

_____ 14. I'm *kinda* surprised that we can't find fresh pineapples *anywhere*
_____ in this town.

_____ 15. *That there* new postage meter in the business office will simplify
_____ our monthly billing *somewhat.*

_____ 16. I have never been particularly *enthusiastic* about *those kind of*

_____   *people*.

_____ 17. After the detective had looked into the case *farther*, he had no

_____   doubt *but what* the butler was guilty.

_____ 18. Admit it, Eric; you *ain't* as spry as you *use* to be.

_____

_____ 19. I'm *real* sure that the group will attempt the mountain climb

_____   *regardless* of the worsening weather.

_____ 20. I'm *so* glad to learn that Joan is no longer *mad* at me for copying

_____   her new dress.

NAME _____ SCORE _____

Directions: In the space at the left, write the expression given in parentheses that you consider the more appropriate form to use in serious writing.

_____   1. Bill was (plenty, very) upset when he learned that he was quartered

_____   in a hotel that was a long (way, ways) from the convention center.

_____   2. (Almost, Most) all of the students who attended the lecture were

_____   (enthused, enthusiastic) about it.

_____   3. We were served some (real, really) good snacks: doughnuts, pizzas,

_____   cake, soft drinks, (and etc., etc.).

_____   4. At first some of the young people acted (as if, like) they would

_____   prefer to be almost (anywhere, anywheres) except at this lecture.

_____   5. I now (believe, figure) that I (ought to of, ought to have) called

_____   ahead for an appointment.

_____   6. (Where, Where at) did you find all of them (them, those) statistics

_____   you used in your report?

_____   7. (Because of, Due to) the glare of the sun on the snow, you should

_____   wear (these, these here) sunglasses when you ski.

_____   8. I have (calculated, reckoned) that our profits are up by 12% but

_____   are (apt, likely) to decline next year.

_____   9. I was (rather, sort of) surprised that I had (fewer, less) misspelled

_____   words on this theme than I did on the last one.

_____   10. (Because, Being that) most of her friends are working, Dorothy

_____   has been (awful, very) bored this summer.

_____   11. The reason Clarence resigned from the committee is (because, that)

_____   he will be out of the city for the next (couple, couple of) months.

_____   12. (Lots of, Many) times Cresswell (aggravates, annoys) his coworkers

_____   with his silly practical jokes.

_____   13. I have no doubt (but what, that) the athletic department will

_____   receive complaints (in regard, in regards) to the increase in the
ticket price.

285

_____ 14. I (can hardly, can't hardly) believe that I am unable to find fresh

_____ strawberries available (anywhere, anywheres) in this town.

_____ 15. "(Let's, Let's us) go to a movie; it's been (a very, such a) long

_____ time since I've seen a good film," said Jenny.

_____ 16. I recently encountered an old friend who (use to, used to) work

_____ (beside, besides) me on the assembly line at the factory.

_____ 17. "I (sure, surely) hope that someone can (learn, teach) me how to

_____ play the guitar," said Billy Joe.

_____ 18. "You must (try and, try to) find some (disinterested, uninterested)

_____ third person to settle your dispute," the judge told the two of us.

_____ 19. "Mr. Chairman," said Senator Gibson, "(can, may) I be allowed

_____ ten more minutes so that I can discuss this matter (farther, further)?"

_____ 20. In her reply the secretary (implied, inferred) that she was not

_____ (suppose to, supposed to) work overtime.

_____ 21. In only a (couple, couple of) small details was Carsten's formula

_____ (different from, different than) yours.

_____ 22. (Where, Where at) can I buy one of (them, those) altimeters like

_____ the one you have in your car?

_____ 23. (Can, May) I make an appointment to meet with your lawyer (in

_____ regard to, in regards to) the renewed contract?

_____ 24. I (believe, figure) that Ethan is (not nearly, nowheres near) as

_____ young as he would like us to think he is.

_____ 25. Their new condominium is (real, very) comfortable, although it is

_____ a long (way, ways) from the campus.

_____ 26. The reason Junior has his arm in a sling is (because, that) yesterday

_____ in the park he fell (off, off of) one of the swings.

_____ 27. "I think we were (suppose, supposed to) connect the blue wire to

_____ (that, that there) black one," said Tim.

_____ 28. "I now think we (should have, should of) sent an (invitation,

_____ invite) to your uncle," said Fred to his wife.

_____ 29. A (party, person) completely unknown to me smiled cordially and

_____ then sat down (beside, besides) me.

_____ 30. (Because of, Due to) the heavy fog, there have been (lots of,

_____ many) delayed departures and canceled flights.

Directions: Each sentence contains two italicized words or expressions. If you think that a word or expression is inappropriate in serious writing, write an acceptable form in the space at the left. If an expression is correct, write **C** in the space.

_____ _____	1. We *should of* known that the meeting would not proceed exactly *like* we had planned it.
_____ _____	2. *Almost all* of the passengers had got *off of* the bus by the time we reached Rockford.
_____ _____	3. The student actors performed *really* well, and the audience was *enthusiastic* about the play.
_____ _____	4. The reason for the new regulation is *because* the number of accidents *due to* excessive speed has increased alarmingly.
_____ _____	5. Mr. Jameson will be *plenty* upset if he doesn't receive an *invite* to the inaugural ball.
_____ _____	6. I would *sure* like to have a set of *them* chrome dual pipes for my old Chevy.
_____ _____	7. *These data* should be shared with all scientists, *irregardless* of their political beliefs.
_____ _____	8. "I *suspicion* that next year *less* students will enroll in my Geology 223 class," said Professor Shanks.
_____ _____	9. The bill as passed by the house is *different from* the Senate version in a *couple of* minor details.
_____ _____	10. "*In regards to* your inquiry, I am happy to report that your friend's condition has improved *some*," said the nurse.
_____ _____	11. "After looking into your case *further,* I have no doubt *but what* you should sue your landlord," said the lawyer.
_____ _____	12. You *hadn't ought to* have eaten the entire pizza; you should have divided it *among* the four of us.
_____ _____	13. "*Can* I be so bold as to inquire *where at* you bought that painted velvet necktie you're wearing?" asked Terry.
_____ _____	14. "*Let's us* not tell anyone about our *awfully* extravagant shopping spree," said Meg.
_____ _____	15. The passenger sitting *besides* me said that we were *suppose to* fasten our seat belts.

_____ 16. *Being as how* I live a long *ways* from the campus, I must rely on

_____ the inadequate bus service.

_____ 17. *Lots of* voters *infer* from the governor's statement that he will not

_____ seek reelection.

_____ 18. Brent should realize that *those kind* of remarks can *aggravate*

_____ some people.

_____ 19. "I admit that I *use* to think that *these criteria* for promotion are

_____ too rigid," said Professor Hall.

_____ 20. Our rehearsal will have to be held *somewheres* else, *caused by*

_____ yesterday's fire in the auditorium.

_____ 21. "Mother says that we are *supposed to* eat these vegetables because

_____ they're *awful* good for us," said Edith.

_____ 22. In his note to me he said, "I have received your pamphlet in

_____ *regards to* value-added taxes and will read *the same* when time
permits."

_____ 23. The reason I turned down the *invite* to go skiing is *because* right

_____ now I am short of cash.

_____ 24. *Due to* your excellent tutoring, I made *fewer* mistakes on this test

_____ than I did on the one I took last week.

_____ 25. "*Leave* me help you with *them* heavy packages, Mrs. Taplinger,"

_____ said Leroy politely.

_____ 26. Linda's great-grandfather had *emigrated* from Finland in the

_____ 1850s and had settled *somewheres* in northern Minnesota.

_____ 27. "I *sure* hope that you'll be able to do something *beside* just criticize

_____ our efforts," said the chairperson bitterly.

_____ 28. If you get *off of* the bus at 24th and Elm, you will be only a short

_____ *ways* from our house.

_____ 29. "I *can hardly* imagine," said Jerry's mother, "why anyone would

_____ pay money to see this *type* movie."

_____ 30. I'm unsure *as to whether* or not *these data* should be used in my

_____ term paper.

Check Sheet

USAGE

☐ **Using Verbs Correctly**

☐ Using verb tenses correctly requires close attention to the principal parts of the verb:

run (the base or infinitive)
ran (the simple past tense)
run (the past participle)

☐ Tense formation is almost automatic in the present and the future tense:

I *run* that machine every day.   I *will run* that machine again next week.

☐ Shifting to the past tense and to the perfect tense requires careful attention to the principal parts of the verb. The past tense is always a single word: the second principal part.

Yesterday I *ran* that machine for two hours.

The three perfect tenses require the use of the third principal part and an auxiliary verb:

I *have run* that machine every day for the past three weeks. By last Friday, I *had run* that machine for a total of 72 hours. By next Monday, I *will have run* that machine for a total of 100 hours this month.

☐ *Troublesome Forms*

☐ Three pairs of verbs present especially troublesome problems because their spelling is similar and their principal parts seem to overlap. Three words are intransitive verbs and three are transitive:
  • I *lie* down for a nap, but I *lay* the book on the table.
  • I *sit* down in a chair, but I *set* the book on the shelf.
  • I *rise* from a sitting position, but I *raise* the flag.

The past tense of *lie* is *lay*; the past tense of *lay* is *laid*.

I *lay* down for a nap an hour ago, but I *laid* the book on the table this morning.

The perfect tense of *lie* uses *lain* as its principal part; the perfect tense of *lay* uses *laid*.

I *have lain* here peacefully for almost an hour, but I *have laid* that question to rest.

☐ *Subject-Verb Agreement*

☐ The basic rule for subject-verb agreement is that verbs agree with—that is, use the same number, singular or plural, as—the subject. This rule presents a problem only in the third-person singular present tense and in the third-person singular of certain auxiliary verbs:

> she *runs*
> she *has run*
> she *is running*
> she *does run*

☐ The problem is created by the fact that the third-person singular of these verbs ends in *s* but the other forms end without the *s*. Although *s* is the sign of the third-person singular in verbs, *s* is the sign of the plural for most nouns. Keep this concept straight, and most problems with verb forms in subject-verb agreement will solve themselves.

☐ The other problem in establishing subject-verb agreement is usually solved by determining the real subject of the verb:

- Prepositional phrases and other words that come between the subject and the verb do not dictate the number of the verb.
- The subject and verb agree in number even when the subject follows the verb.
- Compound subjects joined by *and* take a plural verb whether the nouns are singular or plural.
- When compound subjects have one noun singular and the other plural, the noun closer to the verb governs the number of the verb.
- Singular subjects joined by *or* or *nor* take a singular verb.
- When the subject of a verb is a relative pronoun, the verb takes its number from the antecedent.

☐ Reference and Agreement in Pronouns

☐ Two basic rules govern the connection between a pronoun and its antecedent.

1. Establish a clear, easily identified relationship between the pronoun and its antecedent.
   - This rule means, in its simplest form, that a noun must precede the pronoun when the pronoun replaces it.
   - Use a noun, not a clause or a phrase or an idea, as the antecedent of a pronoun.

   > I was tired from the hike, *which made Jan laugh at me.* [It is the fact that I was tired from the hike that made Jan laugh. The pronoun *which* has no antecedent in the sentence.]

2. Make the pronoun agree with its antecedent in gender and number.
   - Singular nouns are antecedents for singular pronouns; plurals are antecedents for plurals.
   - With personal pronouns and pronominal adjectives, use the gender that matches the antecedent.

   > Paul submitted *his* paper; Pauline submitted *her* paper. The car has lost *its* bumper.

☐ *Two Problem Areas*

☐ Indefinite pronouns such as *everyone, someone,* and *each* have always been considered, at least in formal language, singular, in spite of the fact that the pronouns seem to convey a sense of group or plural number. It is probably best

in academic writing to stick with the traditional usage and avoid structures that use a plural pronoun.
  • Avoid structures such as *Everyone* will certainly do *their* best.

☐ This use of indefinites leads to another problem related to the gender of pronouns.
  • Traditionally, sentences such as *Each student will do his best* were considered both correct and acceptable. The problem is that the use of *his* seems to suggest that all students are male—clearly an untrue idea.
  • One possible solution, a sentence that reads *Each student will do his or her best*, is both correct and acceptable, but it creates a kind of stumbling awkwardness in the rhythm of the sentence. The solution to this awkwardness is to make the noun plural and provide a plural pronoun.

> *All students* will do *their* best.

☐ *Case in Pronoun Usage*

☐ Certain pronouns change form to show their use in a clause or sentence.

Nominative	Possessive	Objective
I	my, mine	me
he	his	him
she	her, hers	her
we	our, ours	us
they	their, theirs	them
who	whose	whom
whoever	whosever	whomever

☐ Possessive case shows ownership. The first form is an adjective, sometimes called a *pronominal adjective* because it both shows possession and modifies a noun.

> That is *my* dog.

☐ The second form is a nominal; it fills a noun slot and thus is a true pronoun.

> That dog is *mine*.

☐ While indefinite pronouns use an apostrophe to show possession, personal pronouns do not even if they end in *s*. Make a sharp distinction between possessive forms *its* and *whose* and contracted forms such as *it's* (short for *it is*) and *who's* (short for *who is*).

☐ Use a possessive pronoun with a gerund.

> They had not planned on *my* [not *me*] coming with you.

☐ Nominative and Objective Cases
  • A pronoun is in the nominative case when it is used as
    > a subject (*He* arrived early yesterday.),
    > subjective complement (This is *he* speaking.),
    > an appositive with a nominative noun (*We* students appreciate your help.).

  • A pronoun is in the objective case when it serves as
    > the object of a verb or verbal (They told *me* the story. We saw *them* yesterday.),
    > the object of a preposition (Everyone but *him* left early.),
    > the subject of an infinitive (They asked *him* to come early.),
    > an appositive of an objective noun (Two of *us* players came back.).

☐ Pronoun case is sometimes a problem when the pronoun is part of a compound.

> Have you spoken to Juan or *her* [not *she*] today.
> Give your report to Jim or *me* [not *I*].

- Testing for correctness in these cases is simple. Omit the first noun in the compound and read the sentence. You are unlikely to say

> Give your report to *I*.

☐ In comparisons after *as* and *than,* when the pronoun is the subject of an omitted verb, use the nominative case.

> She is smarter than *I* (am).

- Most of the time, the sense of the sentence will demand a pronoun in the nominative case, but occasionally, the sentence can be taken in two ways:

> Sue loves that dog more than *I* (love that dog).
> Sue loves that dog more than *me* (more than she loves me).

Both sentences are correct, but the meanings are different. Be sure to specify your meaning by choosing the proper case for the pronoun.

☐ Who and Whom, Whoever and Whomever

☐ As an easily followed rule of thumb, remember that *who* and *whoever* can usually be replaced by *he* and *him,* or by *they* and *them* if the construction is plural. Test your choices by turning the clause into a single statement and replacing the relative or interrogative pronoun with one of the personal pronouns. The correct form will be easy to recognize.

> Yesterday I saw someone with *who/whom* I went to high school.
> Yesterday I saw someone. I went to high school with *he/him.*

It's obvious in the second pair of sentences that the form needed is *him,* so in the relative clause in the first sentence the form needed is *whom.* If the sentence changes to read

> Yesterday I saw someone *who/whom* went to high school with me.
> Yesterday I saw someone. *He/Him* went to high school with me.

It's unlikely that you would choose

> *Him* went to school with me.

If you select *He* went to school, then select *Who* went to school.

☐ When *who/whom, whoever/whomever* begins a noun clause, the case of the pronoun is determined by its role within the clause.

> Give the package to *whoever* comes to the door.
> I'll work with *whomever* you designate.

Make the *who*-to-*him* change again.

He comes to the door, [therefore the proper choice is *whoever* comes to the door]. You designate *him*, [not *he;* therefore, the proper choice is *whomever*].

☐ When a pronoun subject is followed immediately by a parenthetical expression such as *do you think* and then a verb, choose the nominative case (*who/whoever*) for the pronoun. When the pronoun is an object of a verb or preposition, choose *whom/whomever.*

Who/Whom do you think is the best choice?

Test your choice here by making the same change as above. Disregard the parenthetical expression and ask is the choice *he* or *him*? *He* is clearly the choice; therefore, the question should read *Who* do you think is the best choice?

☐ Modifiers and Prepositions

☐ Use the short forms of such adverbs as *late, hard,* and *near* because the *ly* forms of these adverbs have acquired special meanings. Among other adverbs, the short form serves well for informal writing, and the *ly* forms are better for more formal writing.

☐ Remember that adverbs modify verbs, adjectives, and other adverbs. Be careful to distinguish the adverb *well* from the adjective *good, almost* from *most, really* from *real, easily* from *easy,* an so on.

☐ Remember that *feels, sounds, smells,* and *looks* usually take adjectives, not adverbs.

☐ In English, we do not double intensifiers to make a point. We do not say *more friendlier* or *most friendliest.* If you uncertain about the correct way to form comparatives and superlatives in adjectives and adverbs, consult your dictionary.

Spelling and Capitalization

Lessons, Practice Sheets, and Exercises

Lesson 27   *Spelling Rules; Words Similar in Sound*

This lesson presents spelling rules that will help you improve your written work.

Rule 1: A word ending in a silent *e* generally drops the *e* before a suffix beginning with a vowel and retains the *e* before a suffix beginning with a consonant.

After *c* or *g*, if the suffix begins with *a* or *o*, the *e* is retained to preserve the soft sound of the *c* or *g*.

Drop E *Before a Vowel*					
become	+ ing	= becoming	hope	+ ing	= hoping
bride	+ al	= bridal	imagine	+ ary	= imaginary
conceive	+ able	= conceivable	noise	+ y	= noisy
desire	+ able	= desirable	remove	+ able	= removable
fame	+ ous	= famous	white	+ ish	= whitish
force	+ ible	= forcible	write	+ ing	= writing

Retain E *Before a Consonant*					
excite	+ ment	= excitement	life	+ like	= lifelike
force	+ ful	= forceful	pale	+ ness	= paleness
hope	+ less	= hopeless	sincere	+ ly	= sincerely

Retain E *After* C *or* G *if the Suffix Begins with* A *or* O					
advantage	+ ous	= advantageous	notice	+ able	= noticeable
change	+ able	= changeable	outrage	+ ous	= outrageous
manage	+ able	= manageable	service	+ able	= serviceable

(See Supplement.)

Rule 2: **In words with *ie* or *ei* when the sound is long *ee*, use *i* before *e* except after *c*.**

Use I Before E		
apiece	frontier	priest
belief	grieve	reprieve
fiend	niece	shriek
fierce	pierce	thievery
Except After C		
ceiling	conceive	perceive
conceited	deceit	receipt

The common exceptions to this rule may be easily remembered if you memorize the following sentence: Neither financier seized either species of weird leisure.

Rule 3: **In words of one syllable and words accented on the last syllable and, ending in a single consonant preceded by a single vowel, double the final consonant before a suffix beginning with a vowel.**

Words of One Syllable—Suffix Begins with a Vowel					
ban	banned	hit	hitting	rid	riddance
bid	biddable	hop	hopping	Scot	Scottish
dig	digger	quit	quitter	stop	stoppage
drag	dragged	["qu"-consonant]	wet	wettest	

Accented on Last Syllable—Suffix Begins with a Vowel			
abhor	abhorrence	equip	equipping
acquit	acquitted	occur	occurrence
allot	allotted	omit	omitted
begin	beginner	prefer	preferring
commit	committing	regret	regrettable
control	controlled	repel	repellent

Not Accented on Last Syllable—Suffix Begins with a Vowel			
differ	different	open	opener
happen	happening	prefer	preference
hasten	hastened	sharpen	sharpened

Suffix Begins with a Consonant			
allot	allotment	mother	motherhood
color	colorless	sad	sadness
equip	equipment	sin	sinful

(See Supplement.)

An apparent exception to this rule affects a few words formed by the addition of *ing, ed,* or *y* to a word ending in *c*. To preserve the hard sound of the *c*, a *k* is added before the vowel of the suffix, resulting in such spellings as *frolicking, mimicked, panicked, panicky, picnicked,* and *trafficking.*

Another irregularity applies to such spellings as *quitting* and *equipped.* One might think that the consonant should not be doubled, reasoning that the final consonant is preceded by two vowels, not by a single vowel. But because *qu* is phonetically the equivalent of *kw,* the *u* is a consonant when it follows *q.* Therefore, because the final consonant is actually preceded by a single vowel, the consonant is doubled before the suffix.

Rule 4: **Words ending in *y* preceded by a vowel retain the *y* before a suffix; most words ending in *y* preceded by a consonant change the *y* to *i* before a suffix.**

Ending in Y *Preceded by a Vowel*					
boy	boyish	coy	coyness	enjoy	enjoying
buy	buys	donkey	donkeys	stay	staying

Ending in Y *Preceded by a Consonant*					
ally	allies	easy	easiest	pity	pitiable
busy	busily	icy	icier	study	studies
cloudy	cloudiness	mercy	merciless	try	tried

The Y *Is Unchanged in Words Like the Following:*			
baby	babyish	lady	ladylike
carry	carrying	study	studying

WORDS SIMILAR IN SOUND

Accept. I should like to *accept* your first offer.

Except. He took everything *except* the rugs.

Advice. Free *advice* [noun] is usually not worth much.

Advise. Ms. Hull said she would *advise* [verb] me this term. (Similarly, *device* [noun] and *devise* [verb].

Affect. His forced jokes *affect* [verb] me unfavorably.

Effect. His humor has a bad *effect* [noun]. Let us try to *effect* [verb] a lasting peace.

All ready. They were *all ready* to go home.

Already. They had *already* left when we telephoned the house.

All together. Now that we are *all together,* let us talk it over.

Altogether. They were not *altogether* pleased with the results.

Altar. In this temple was an *altar* to the Unknown God.

Alter. One should not try to *alter* or escape history.

Ascent. The *ascent* to the top of the mountain was quite steep.

Assent. The judge did not *assent* to our request.

Bare. The *bare* and leafless limbs of the trees were a dark gray.

Bear. He could not *bear* to look at the accident.

Breath. His *breath* came in short gasps at the end of the race.

Breathe. The problem is solved; you can *breathe* easily now.

Canvas. We used a piece of *canvas* to shelter us from the wind.

Canvass. The candidate wanted to *canvass* every person in her precinct.

Capital. A *capital* letter; *capital* gains; *capital* punishment; state *capital*.

Capitol. Workers are painting the dome of the *Capitol*.

Cite. He *cited* three good examples.

Site. The *site* of the new school has not been decided on.

Sight. They were awed by the *sight* of so much splendor.

Climactic. The *climactic* moment in that movie was extremely exciting.

Climatic. According to NOAA, *climatic* conditions in North America have not changed much over the past 100 years.

Coarse. The *coarse* sand blew in my face.

Course. We discussed the *course* to take. Of course he may come with us.

Complement. Your intelligence is a *complement* to your beauty.

Compliment. It is easier to pay a *compliment* than a bill.

Consul. Be sure to look up the American *consul* in Rome.

Council. He was appointed to the executive *council*.

Counsel. I sought *counsel* from my friends. They *counseled* moderation. He employed *counsel* to defend him.

Decent. The workers demanded a *decent* wage scale.

Descent. The *descent* from the mountain was uneventful.

Dissent. The voices of *dissent* were louder than those of approval.

Desert. Out in the lonely *desert* [noun—desert], he tried to desert [verb—desert] from his regiment.

Dessert. We had apple pie for *dessert*.

Device. The *device* that controls the alarm system has malfunctioned.

Devise. We should *devise* a new system to cope with that problem.

Die. Old habits certainly *die* hard.

Dye. That *dye* produced a strange color in that new fabric.

Dining. We eat dinner in our *dining* room. *Dining* at home is pleasant.

Dinning. Stop *dinning* that song into my ears!

Fair. The decision of the umpire seemed very *fair*.

Fare. By plane, the *fare* from here to Toledo is $115.67.

Formerly. He was *formerly* a student at Beloit College.

Formally. You must address the presiding judge *formally* and respectfully.

Forth. Several witnesses came *forth* to testify.

Fourth. We planned a picnic for the *Fourth* of July.

Gorilla. The zoo has built a new habitat for the *gorillas*.

Guerrilla. The *guerrilla* forces are operating in the mountains beyond the city.

Heard. I had not *heard* that news.

Herd. The *herd* of cows moved slowly toward the barn.

Hole. The *hole* in my sock is growing bigger every minute.

Whole. The *whole* office is filled with a strange odor.

Incidence. Better sanitation lowered the *incidence* of communicable diseases.
Incidents. Smugglers were involved in several *incidents* along the border.

Instance. For *instance*, she was always late to class.
Instants. As the car turned, those brief *instants* seemed like hours.

Its. Your plan has much in *its* favor. [possessive of *it*.]
It's. *It's* too late now for excuses. [contraction of *it is, it has*.]

Later. It is *later* than you think.
Latter. Of the two novels, I prefer the *latter*.

Lead. Can you *lead* [lēd—verb] us out of this jungle? *Lead* [lĕd—noun] is a heavy, soft, malleable metallic element.
Led. A local guide *led* us to the salmon fishing hole.

Loose. He has a *loose* tongue. The dog is *loose* again.
Lose. Don't *lose* your temper.

Meat. We did not have any *meat* at lunch.
Meet. We intend to *meet* you after lunch.
Mete. The judge will *mete* out the punishment tomorrow.

Passed. She smiled as she *passed* me. She passed the test.
Past. It is futile to try to relive the *past*.

Patience. The teacher has little *patience* for lame excuses.
Patients. Twelve *patients* will be discharged from the hospital today.

Personal. Write him a *personal* letter.
Personnel. The morale of our company's *personnel* is high.

Pore. For hours they *pored* over the mysterious note.
Pour. Ms. Cook *poured* hot water into the teapot.

Precede. The Secret Service agents always *precede* the President when he enters a building.
Proceed. They all left the building and *proceeded* immediately to the parking lot.

Precedence. Tax reform takes *precedence* over all other legislative matters.
Precedents. The judge quoted three *precedents* to justify his ruling.

Presence. We are honored by your *presence*.
Presents. The child received dozens of Christmas *presents*.

Principal. The *principal* of a school; the *principal* [chief] industry; the *principal* and the interest.
Principle. He is a man of high *principles*.

Quiet. You must keep *quiet*.
Quite. The weather was *quite* good all week.

Rain. A soaking *rain* would help our crops greatly.
Reign. Samuel Pepys was briefly imprisoned during the *reign* of William III.
Rein. Keep a tight *rein* when you ride this spirited horse.

Right. Take a *right* turn on Oak Street.
Rite. Taking that course is a *rite* of passage for many students.
Write. Please *write* me a letter when you arrive.

Scene. The last *scene* in that movie was exceptionally touching.
Seen. I had not *seen* Frank for two weeks.

Sense. That statement makes a great deal of *sense* to me.
Since. Ten more people have arrived *since* we got here this morning.
Scents. The *scents* of those flowers are not easy to distinguish.

Sent. We *sent* a copy of the report to you yesterday.
Cent. We won't pay another *cent*.

Shone. The cat's eyes *shone* in the dark.
Shown. He hasn't *shown* us his best work.

Stationary. The benches were *stationary* and could not be moved.
Stationery. She wrote a letter on hotel *stationery*.

Statue. It was a *statue* of a pioneer.
Stature. Athos was a man of gigantic *stature*.
Statute. The law may be found in the 1917 book of *statutes*.

Than. She sings better *than* I.
Then. He screamed; *then* he fainted.

Their. It wasn't *their* fault. [possessive pronoun]
There. You won't find any gold *there*. [adverb of place]
They're. *They're* sure to be disappointed. [contraction of *they are*]

Thorough. We must first give the old cabin a *thorough* [adjective] cleaning.

Threw. The catcher *threw* the ball back to the pitcher.
Through. The thief had entered *through* [preposition] a hole in the roof.

To. Be sure to speak *to* her. [preposition]
Too. He is far *too* old for you. [adverb]
Two. The membership fee is only *two* dollars. [adjective]

Waist. She wore a beautiful silver belt around her *waist*.
Waste. Save every scrap; don't let anything go to *waste*.

Weather. The *weather* last week was very cold.
Whether. Do you know *whether* Jim has arrived?

Whose. *Whose* book is this? [possessive pronoun]
Who's. I wonder *who's* with her now. [contraction of *who is*]

Your. I like *your* new car. [possessive pronoun]
You're. *You're* not nervous, are you? [contraction of *you are*]

SUPPLEMENT

Rule 1: A few common adjectives with the suffix *able* have two correct spellings:

likable/likeable, lovable/loveable, movable/moveable, sizable/sizeable, usable/useable

Rule 2: Dictionaries show two spellings for the *ed* and *ing* forms (and a few other derived forms) of dozens of verbs ending in single consonants preceded by single vowels. In general, the single-consonant spelling is usually found in American printing; some of the dictionaries label the double-consonant spelling a British preference.

biased/biassed, canceling/cancelling, counselor/counsellor, diagraming/diagramming, equaled/equalled, marvelous/marvellous, modeled/modelled, totaling/totalling, traveler/traveller

NAME _____ SCORE _____

Directions: Each of the following sentences contains three italicized words, one of which is misspelled. Write the word, correctly spelled, in the space at the left.

_____ 1. The *inference* that our *capital* has been depleted caused a *noticable* drop in the sale of our stock.

_____ 2. *Achieving* a good score on that *controled* experiment was *quite* an accomplishment for Jimmy.

_____ 3. We had a *brief* opportunity to speak with him about some *desireable* changes in certain *policies.*

_____ 4. *Trafficking* in stolen goods brought a *heavier* sentence than our legal *council* had expected.

_____ 5. *Submitting* our proposal *earlier* than we had planned *altared* the strategies of our competitors.

_____ 6. The three *donkeys enjoyed* standing in the shade behind *they're* barn.

_____ 7. Her *loose* grasp of scientific *principals* caused several *deplorable* accidents in the laboratory.

_____ 8. Morton hasn't *shone* any *excitement* over the *outrageous* claims made by his opponent.

_____ 9. The *financeirs preferred* to *accept* the more positive predictions of their research department.

_____ 10. The gift of two *statues* to be put in the park forced the city *council* to change *it's* policy.

_____ 11. It is my *belief* that Marvin has *already* painted the hall and the *dinning* room.

_____ 12. To earn this degree, you must make a *commitment* to a long and *extremely* rigorous *coarse* of study.

_____ 13. Some of the men looked *to* young to be leaders of *two* of the largest *companies* in the state.

_____ 14. The *allied* force tried to find the *easiest* route across the vast, hostile *dessert.*

_____ 15. For your *journeys*, be sure that you are *equipped* with plenty of sturdy *canvass* to repair your tents.

301

_____ 16. The two leaders were *referred* to the head of our *personnel* department, who resolved *there* argument.

_____ 17. Our *differring* opinions about their *allotting* of the funds *led* to a long argument.

_____ 18. *Unfortunately,* the young man did not take the *priest's* good *advise.*

_____ 19. The *principal* of the school *complimented* us, saying that our class play was better *then* last year's.

_____ 20. *Whose* willing to set *forth* with me on the difficult *descent* down the icy glacier?

_____ 21. The partners *siezed* all of the *opportunities* and have paid off the debt *entirely.*

_____ 22. The *presence* of several *fameous* authors makes this *conference* an outstanding one.

_____ 23. My *niece* was *offered* several jobs, but the *salarys* were lower than she had expected.

_____ 24. During the *rein* of King Oswald, his *armies* often laid *siege* to neighboring castles.

_____ 25. "Because we're slowly *becomming* profitable," Jackson *admitted,* "the venture is still *exciting.*"

_____ 26. Word from the *Capitol* in Washington is that in all *liklihood* the dispute will be settled *peaceably.*

_____ 27. Our lawyers now *believe* that we can *retreive* those documents if the proposed law is *passed.*

_____ 28. Aunt Letty *poured* tea and then served us *raspberrys* and an *immensely* rich chocolate cake.

_____ 29. After the *fourth* one of these *regrettable incidence,* the police were notified.

_____ 30. Private Jesperson was teased by his *buddies* when he *received* a letter on pink, perfumed *stationary.*

NAME _____ SCORE _____

Directions: Each of the following sentences contains three italicized words, one of which
is misspelled. Write the misspelled word correctly spelled in the space at the left.

_____ 1. It seemed *advantageous* for us to leave the *dining* hall before
anyone noticed the theft of the *deserts*.

_____ 2. A loud *shreik* from the *dining* room frightened the three young
ladies.

_____ 3. The *sight* of that *glorious* chocolate cake destroyed my *all ready*
weakened willpower.

_____ 4. The oldest member of the city *council* is in her late *sixtys* and will
be *retiring* soon.

_____ 5. *They're* names were *omitted* from the list of those allowed to go
on the *field* trip.

_____ 6. All month I've been *pouring* over my books; getting *decent*
grades takes *precedence* over everything else.

_____ 7. Before her *descent* to the reef, the *cheif* diver put *heavier* weights
in her diving belt.

_____ 8. Horace's *fierce* dedication to his work left him little time for
leisure-time *activitys*.

_____ 9. "I *advice* you to put your *capital* into tax-free bonds rather *than*
lottery tickets," he answered.

_____ 10. Hotels *lose* money because of the *pilfering* of ashtrays and
stationary by guests.

_____ 11. The first speaker at the *conferrenc*e said that taxes now are
altogether too high.

_____ 12. *You're* show's ratings will be *adversely affected* by the departure
of the star comedian.

_____ 13. In that particular *instants*, Marlene rejected the *advice* Johnny
offered her.

_____ 14. The Brazilian *consul sited* several *statutes* to back up his argument.

_____ 15. Installing *serviceable batteries* in the toy had the desired *affect*.

_____ 16. The accountant had many *opportunitie*s to *altar* the figures on the firm's daily cash *receipts*.

_____ 17. Do you know the person *who's* car was recently *seized* by the local *authorities*?

_____ 18. *It's* been *shown* that this product is *quiet* effective in killing household pests.

_____ 19. The firm's *principal* lawyer *admitted* that the three unfortunate *occurences* could have been avoided.

_____ 20. Lindy has few *difficulties* with English *except* for the correct *useage* of personal pronouns.

_____ 21. I want to *complement* you on the *noticeable improvement* in your writing.

_____ 22. Of *coarse,* every investment carries *its* own risk, but this one, I'm sure, will be *profitable* for us.

_____ 23. Three weeks later, a second poll showed an *unmistakable preference* for the *incumbent*.

_____ 24. The *courageous cashier* entered the bank and then *lead* the hostages to safety.

_____ 25. The *financier,* a *personnel* friend of the governor, was *acquitted* of the charge.

_____ 26. In the *passed* four years, our *preferred* stock in the company has produced only a small *yield.*

_____ 27. After his *fourth* arrest, the man confessed that he had often resorted to *thievery* to provide himself with *luxurys.*

_____ 28. Jack's *attorneys* told him that his *presents* in the courtroom was not only *desirable* but necessary.

_____ 29. Seeing the *ninety* Olympic team members *enterring* the stadium was an *unforgettable* experience.

_____ 30. After *canvassing* the neighborhood, we learned that everyone *believes* that garbage service is *deploreably* bad.

Lesson 28 *Plurals and Capitals*

This lesson covers the formation of plurals and the conventions for using capitals.

PLURALS

Plurals of most nouns are regularly formed by the addition of *s*. But if the singular noun ends in an *s* sound *(s, sh, ch, x, z)*, *es* is added to form a new syllable in pronunciation:

crab, crabs	foe, foes	kiss, kisses	tax, taxes
lamp, lamps	box, boxes	church, churches	lass, lasses

Nouns ending in *y* form plurals according to Rule 4. (See Lesson 27.)

toy, toys	army, armies	fly, flies	attorney, attorneys
key, keys	lady, ladies	sky, skies	monkey, monkeys

Some words ending in *o* (including all musical terms and all words having a vowel preceding the *o*) form their plurals with *s*. But many others take *es:*

alto, altos	folio, folios	tomato, tomatoes
piano, pianos	hero, heroes	potato, potatoes

For several nouns ending in *o*, most modern dictionaries give both forms. Here are some examples, printed in the order they are found in most dictionaries. The first spelling is the more common one:

banjos, banjoes	frescoes, frescos	lassos, lassoes	volcanoes, volcanos
buffaloes, buffalos	grottoes, grottos	mottoes, mottos	zeros, zeroes
cargoes, cargos	halos, haloes	tornadoes, tornados	

Some nouns ending in *f* or *fe* merely add *s;* some change *f* or *fe* to *ves* in the plural; and a few *(hoofs/hooves, scarfs/scarves, wharves/wharfs)* use either form. Use your dictionary to make sure:

leaf, leaves	life, lives	half, halves	wolf, wolves
roof, roofs	safe, safes	gulf, gulfs	elf, elves

A few nouns have the same form for singular and plural. A few have irregular plurals:

deer, deer	ox, oxen	child, children	goose, geese
sheep, sheep	man, men	foot, feet	mouse, mice

Many words of foreign origin use two plurals; some do not. Always check in your dictionary:

alumna, alumnae	bon mot, bons mots
alumnus, alumni	crisis, crises
analysis, analyses	criterion, criteria
appendix, appendixes, appendices	datum, data
basis, bases	thesis, theses
beau, beaus, beaux	focus, focuses, foci
curriculum, curriculums, curricula	fungus, funguses, fungi
memorandum, memorandums, memoranda	index, indexes, indices
tableau, tableaus, tableaux	

Note: Do *not* use an apostrophe to form the plural of either a common or a proper noun.

Wrong: Our neighbor's, the Allen's and the Murray's, recently bought new Honda's.

Right: Our neighbors, the Allens and the Murrays, recently bought new Hondas.

CAPITALS

A capital letter is used for the first letter of the first word of any sentence, for the first letter of a proper noun, and, often, for the first letter of an adjective derived from a proper noun. Following are some reminders about situations that cause confusion for some writers.

1. Capitalize the first word of every sentence, every quoted sentence or fragment, and every transitional fragment. (See Lesson 14.)

   The building needs repairs. How much will it cost? Please answer me.
   Mr. James said, "We'll expect your answer soon." She replied, "Of course."
   And now to conclude.

2. Capitalize proper nouns and most adjectives derived from them. A proper noun designates by name an individual person, place, or thing that is a member of a group or class. Do not capitalize common nouns, which are words naming a group or class:

   Doris Powers, woman; France, country; Tuesday, day; January, month; Christmas Eve, holiday; Shorewood High School, high school; Carleton College, college; *Mauritania*, ship; Fifth Avenue, boulevard; White House, residence

   Elizabethan drama, Restoration poetry, Chinese peasants, Indian reservation, Red Cross assistance

3. Do not capitalize nouns and derived forms that, although originally proper nouns, have acquired special meanings. When in doubt, consult your dictionary:

   a set of china; a bohemian existence; plaster of paris; pasteurized milk; a mecca for golfers; set in roman type, not italics

4. Capitalize names of religions, references to deities, and most words having religious significance:

   Bible,* Baptist, Old Testament, Holy Writ, Jewish, Catholic, Sermon on the Mount, Koran, Talmud

---

*Note that "Bible" is lowercased when not used as a religious reference, as in "Chapman's *Piloting and Seamanship* is a bible for sailors everywhere."

5. Capitalize titles of persons when used with the person's name. When the title is used alone, capitalize it only when it stands for a specific person of high rank:*

> I spoke briefly to Professor Jones. He is a professor of history.
> We visited the late President Johnson's ranch in Texas.
> Jerry is president of our art club.
> Tonight the President will appear on national television.

6. Capitalize names denoting family relationship but not when they are preceded by a possessive. This rule is equivalent to saying that you capitalize when the word serves as a proper noun:

> At that moment Mother, Father, and Aunt Lucy entered the room.
> My mother, father, and aunt are very strict about some things.

7. Capitalize points of the compass when they refer to actual regions but not when they refer to directions:

> Before we moved to the West, we lived in the South for a time.
> You drive three miles west and then turn north on the Pacific Highway.

Do not capitalize adjectives of direction modifying countries or states:

> From central Finland, the group had immigrated to northern Michigan.

8. Capitalize names of academic subjects as they would appear in college catalog listings, but in ordinary writing capitalize only names of languages:

> I intend to register for History 322 and Sociology 188.
> Last year I took courses in history, sociology, German, and Latin.

9. In titles of books, short stories, plays, essays, and poems, capitalize the first word and all other words except the articles (*a, an, the*) and short prepositions and conjunctions. (See Lesson 19 for the use of italics and quotation marks with titles.)

> Last semester I wrote reports on the following: Shaw's *The Intelligent Woman's Guide to Socialism and Capitalism*, Joyce's *A Portrait of the Artist as a Young Man*, Pirandello's *Six Characters in Search of an Author*, Poe's "The Fall of the House of Usher," Yeats's "An Irish Airman Foresees His Death," Frost's "Stopping by Woods on a Snowy Evening," and Muriel Rukeyser's "The Soul and Body of John Brown."

Note: Traditionally, a capital letter begins every line of poetry. This convention, however, is not always followed by modern poets; when you quote poetry, be sure to copy exactly the capitalization used by the author.

*Captialize titles of people when used in direct address, as in "How do you respond, Senator?"

NAME _____   SCORE _____

Directions: Write the plural form or forms for each of the following words. When in doubt, consult your dictionary. If two forms are given, write both. Consult a standard college dictionary such as *Merriam Webster's Collegiate Dictionary, Tenth Edition* or *Random House Webster's Collegiate Dictionary.*

1. analysis _____   _____

2. aquarium _____   _____

3. archipelago _____   _____

4. assembly _____   _____

5. Charles _____   _____

6. commando _____   _____

7. Dutchman _____   _____

8. father-in-law _____   _____

9. flamingo _____   _____

10. folio _____   _____

11. fungus _____   _____

12. handful _____   _____

13. inferno _____   _____

14. lily _____   _____

15. mouse _____   _____

16. octopus _____   _____

17. plateau _____   _____

18. podium _____   _____

19. scarf _____   _____

20. sheriff _____   _____

21. spy _____   _____

22. thesis _____   _____

23. turkey _____   _____

24. vortex _____   _____

25. wife _____   _____

Directions: The following sentences contain 50 numbered words. If you think the word is correctly capitalized, write **C** in the space at the left with the corresponding number. If you think the word should not be capitalized, write **W** in the space.

____ ____ ____   (1) The guide told Mother and Aunt Mabel to walk two blocks farther
1   2   3   1   2

____ ____ ____   West to reach the Museum of Modern Art.
4   5   6   3   4   5   6

____ ____ ____   (2) Jerry's Uncle, who retired recently from the State Department and
7   8   9   7   8   9

____ ____ ____   who had served in many Countries in the Far East, often vacations
10   11   12   10   11   12

____ ____ ____   in the South Seas.
13   14   15   13   14

____ ____ ____   (3) Last Spring our Geology Professor scaled Mt. Rainier, the highest
16   17   18   15   16   17   18

____ ____ ____   Mountain in the Cascades.
19   20   21   19   20

____ ____ ____   (4) Wilma, who transferred from a Junior College in the South,
22   23   24   21   22   23

____ ____ ____   is majoring in Drama and Speech.
25   26   27   24   25

____ ____ ____   (5) Did you know that Professor Fry, our French teacher, has a Ph.D.
28   29   30   26   27   28 29

____ ____ ____   degree from Princeton University?
                              30

____ ____ ____   (6) A Librarian told me that material on African Pygmies could be found
31   32   33   31   32

____ ____ ____   in the *Americana*, the *Britannica*, or any other good Encyclopedia.
34   35   36   33   34   35

____ ____ ____   (7) When I was a Senior in High School, our class read Holmes's *The*
37   38   39   36   37   38   39

____ ____ ____   *Autocrat Of The Breakfast Table.*
40   41   42   40   41 42   43   44

____ ____ ____   (8) Besides courses in Psychology and Mathematics, Jane is taking
43   44   45   45   46

____ ____ ____   Literature 326, which deals with American novels written since
46   47   48   47   48

____ ____   World War I.
49   50   49   50

NAME _____   SCORE _____

Directions: Write the plural form or forms of each of the following words. When in doubt, consult your dictionary. If two forms are given, write both.

1. alto _____   _____

2. automaton _____   _____

3. belief _____   _____

4. cello _____   _____

5. census _____   _____

6. crisis _____   _____

7. curio _____   _____

8. difficulty _____   _____

9. fresco _____   _____

10. Frenchman _____   _____

11. journey _____   _____

12. latch _____   _____

13. man-of-war _____   _____

14. moose _____   _____

15. motto _____   _____

16. process _____   _____

17. roomful _____   _____

18. soprano _____   _____

19. stimulus _____   _____

20. stratum _____   _____

21. symposiums _____   _____

22. tableau _____   _____

23. waltz _____   _____

24. wharf _____   _____

25. zero _____   _____

Directions: The following sentences contain 50 numbered words. If you think the word is correctly capitalized, write **C** in the space at the left with the corresponding number. If you think the word should not be capitalized, write **W** in the Space.

_____ _____ _____ (1) In the Black Forest of Germany, I took several pictures of a partially
1   2   3   1   2

_____ _____ _____ ruined Benedictine Monastery.
4   5   6   3   4

(2) Miss Lambert, a Librarian at our local Junior College, told me that
5   6   7

_____ _____ _____ I could get the information I needed from *Britannica,* the *Americana,*
7   8   9   8   9

_____ _____ _____ or any other good Encyclopedia.
10 11 12   10

_____ _____ _____ (3) On her trip through the West last Fall, Mother bought some
13 14 15   11   12   13

beautiful baskets at an Indian reservation in Western Arizona.
14   15

_____ _____ _____ (4) My favorite teacher here is Professor Hill, who teaches Social
16 17 18   16   17

_____ _____ _____ Studies 223, but I like all of the Professors that I have met.
19 20 21   18   19

_____ _____ _____ (5) When you and I were in the Navy, I told you that I would probably
22 23 24   20

_____ _____ _____ major in Nuclear Physics or Electronics, but my Uncle persuaded me
25 26 27   21   22   23   24

_____ _____ _____ to get a a General Education first.
28 29 30   25   26

_____ _____ _____ (6) Over the Veteran's Day Holiday Weekend I read Holbrook's *The*
31 32 33   27   28   29   30   31

_____ _____ *Age Of The Moguls.*
34 35   32 33 34   35

_____ _____ _____ (7) Our doctor wrote to the Atlanta-based Centers For Disease Control
36 37 38   36   37   38   39

_____ _____ _____ for information about the effects of Agent Orange.
39 40 41   40   41

‾‾ ‾‾ ‾‾ (8) One of my Nephews, a retired Air Force Colonel, has returned
42 43 44   42   43   44   45

‾‾ ‾‾ ‾‾ to the Campus to work toward an M. A. in French Literature.
45 46 47   46   47 48   49   50

‾‾ ‾‾ ‾‾
48 49 50

This list includes words frequently misspelled by high-school and college students. Each word is repeated to show its syllabic division. Whether this list is used for individual study and review or in some kind of organized class activity, your method of studying should be the following: (1) Learn to pronounce the word syllable by syllable. Some of your trouble in spelling may come from incorrect pronunciation. (2) Copy the word carefully, forming each letter as plainly as you can. Some of your trouble may come from bad handwriting. (3) Pronounce the word carefully again. (4) On a separate sheet of paper, write the word from memory, check your spelling with the correct spelling before you, and, if you have misspelled the word, repeat the learning process.

abbreviate	ab-bre-vi-ate	audience	au-di-ence
absence	ab-sence	auxiliary	aux-il-ia-ry
accidentally	ac-ci-den-tal-ly	awkward	awk-ward
accommodate	ac-com-mo-date	barbarous	bar-ba-rous
accompanying	ac-com-pa-ny-ing	basically	ba-si-cal-ly
accomplish	ac-com-plish	beneficial	ben-e-fi-cial
accumulate	ac-cu-mu-late	boundaries	bound-a-ries
acknowledge	ac-knowl-edge	Britain	Brit-ain
acquaintance	ac-quaint-ance	bureaucracy	bu-reauc-ra-cy
acquire	ac-quire	business	busi-ness
across	a-cross	calendar	cal-en-dar
additive	ad-di-tive	candidate	can-di-date
admissible	ad-mis-si-ble	cassette	cas-sette
aggravate	ag-gra-vate	category	cat-e-go-ry
always	al-ways	cemetery	cem-e-ter-y
amateur	am-a-teur	certain	cer-tain
among	a-mong	chosen	cho-sen
analysis	a-nal-y-sis	commission	com-mis-sion
analytical	an-a-lyt-i-cal	committee	com-mit-tee
apartheid	a-part-heid	communicate	com-mu-ni-cate
apparatus	ap-pa-ra-tus	communism	com-mu-nism
apparently	ap-par-ent-ly	comparative	com-par-a-tive
appearance	ap-pear-ance	competent	com-pe-tent
appreciate	ap-pre-ci-ate	competition	com-pe-ti-tion
appropriate	ap-pro-pri-ate	completely	com-plete-ly
approximately	ap-prox-i-mate-ly	compulsory	com-pul-so-ry
arctic	arc-tic	computer	com-put-er
argument	ar-gu-ment	concede	con-cede
arithmetic	a-rith-me-tic	condominium	con-do-min-i-um
association	as-so-ci-a-tion	conference	con-fer-ence
astronaut	as-tro-naut	confidentially	con-fi-den-tial-ly
athletics	ath-let-ics	conscience	con-science
attendance	at-tend-ance	conscientious	con-sci-en-tious

conscious	con-scious	foreign	for-eign
consistent	con-sist-ent	forty	for-ty
continuous	con-tin-u-ous	frantically	fran-ti-cal-ly
controversial	con-tro-ver-sial	fundamentally	fun-da-men-tal-ly
convenient	con-ven-ient	generally	gen-er-al-ly
counterfeit	coun-ter-feit	ghetto	ghet-to
criticism	crit-i-cism	government	gov-ern-ment
criticize	crit-i-cize	graffiti	graf-fi-ti
curiosity	cu-ri-os-i-ty	grammar	gram-mar
curriculum	cur-ric-u-lum	grievous	griev-ous
decision	de-ci-sion	guarantee	guar-an-tee
definitely	def-i-nite-ly	guerrilla	guer-ril-la
describe	de-scribe	harass	ha-rass
description	de-scrip-tion	height	height
desperate	des-per-ate	hindrance	hin-drance
dictionary	dic-tion-ar-y	humorous	hu-mor-ous
difference	dif-fer-ence	hurriedly	hur-ried-ly
dilapidated	di-lap-i-dat-ed	hypocrisy	hy-poc-ri-sy
dinosaur	di-no-saur	imagination	im-ag-i-na-tion
disappear	dis-ap-pear	immediately	im-me-di-ate-ly
disappoint	dis-ap-point	impromptu	im-promp-tu
disastrous	dis-as-trous	incidentally	in-ci-den-tal-ly
discipline	dis-ci-pline	incredible	in-cred-i-ble
dissatisfied	dis-sat-is-fied	independence	in-de-pend-ence
dissident	dis-si-dent	indispensable	in-dis-pen-sa-ble
dissipate	dis-si-pate	inevitable	in-ev-i-ta-ble
doesn't	does-n't	influential	in-flu-en-tial
dormitory	dor-mi-to-ry	initiative	in-i-ti-a-tive
during	dur-ing	intelligence	in-tel-li-gence
efficient	ef-fi-cient	intentionally	in-ten-tion-al-ly
eligible	el-i-gi-ble	intercede	in-ter-cede
eliminate	e-lim-i-nate	interesting	in-ter-est-ing
embarrass	em-bar-rass	interpretation	in-ter-pre-ta-tion
eminent	em-i-nent	interrupt	in-ter-rupt
emphasize	em-pha-size	irrelevant	ir-rel-e-vant
enthusiastic	en-thu-si-as-tic	irresistible	ir-re-sist-i-ble
entrepreneur	en-tre-pre-neur	irritation	ir-ri-ta-tion
environment	en-vi-ron-ment	knowledge	knowl-edge
equipment	e-quip-ment	laboratory	lab-o-ra-to-ry
equivalent	e-quiv-a-lent	laser	la-ser
especially	es-pe-cial-ly	legitimate	le-git-i-mate
exaggerated	ex-ag-ger-at-ed	library	li-brar-y
exceed	ex-ceed	lightning	light-ning
excellent	ex-cel-lent	literature	lit-er-a-ture
exceptionally	ex-cep-tion-al-ly	livelihood	live-li-hood
exhaust	ex-haust	loneliness	lone-li-ness
existence	ex-ist-ence	maintenance	main-te-nance
exorbitant	ex-or-bi-tant	marriage	mar-riage
experience	ex-pe-ri-ence	mathematics	math-e-mat-ics
explanation	ex-pla-na-tion	memento	me-men-to
extraordinary	ex-traor-di-nar-y	miniature	min-i-a-ture
extremely	ex-treme-ly	miscellaneous	mis-cel-la-ne-ous
familiar	fa-mil-i-ar	mischievous	mis-chie-vous
fascinate	fas-ci-nate	misspelled	mis-spelled
February	Feb-ru-ar-y	mortgage	mort-gage

mysterious	mys-te-ri-ous	remembrance	re-mem-brance
naturally	nat-u-ral-ly	repetition	rep-e-ti-tion
necessary	nec-es-sar-y	representative	rep-re-sent-a-tive
ninety	nine-ty	respectfully	re-spect-ful-ly
ninth	ninth	respectively	re-spec-tive-ly
nowadays	now-a-days	restaurant	res-tau-rant
nuclear	nu-cle-ar	rhetoric	rhet-o-ric
obedience	o-be-di-ence	rhythm	rhythm
oblige	o-blige	ridiculous	ri-dic-u-lous
obstacle	ob-sta-cle	robot	ro-bot
occasionally	oc-ca-sion-al-ly	sacrilegious	sac-ri-le-gious
occurrence	oc-cur-rence	sandwich	sand-wich
omission	o-mis-sion	satellite	sat-el-lite
opportunity	op-por-tu-ni-ty	satisfactorily	sat-is-fac-to-ri-ly
optimistic	op-ti-mis-tic	schedule	sched-ule
original	o-rig-i-nal	scientific	sci-en-tif-ic
pamphlet	pam-phlet	secretary	sec-re-tar-y
parallel	par-al-lel	separately	sep-a-rate-ly
parliament	par-lia-ment	sergeant	ser-geant
particularly	par-tic-u-lar-ly	significant	sig-nif-i-cant
partner	part-ner	similar	sim-i-lar
pastime	pas-time	sophomore	soph-o-more
performance	per-form-ance	spaghetti	spa-ghet-ti
permissible	per-mis-si-ble	specifically	spe-cif-i-cal-ly
perseverance	per-se-ver-ance	specimen	spec-i-men
perspiration	per-spi-ra-tion	speech	speech
persuade	per-suade	strictly	strict-ly
politics	pol-i-tics	successful	suc-cess-ful
possession	pos-ses-sion	superintendent	su-per-in-ten-dent
practically	prac-ti-cal-ly	supersede	su-per-sede
preceding	pre-ced-ing	surprise	sur-prise
prejudice	prej-u-dice	suspicious	sus-pi-cious
preparation	prep-a-ra-tion	syllable	syl-la-ble
prevalent	prev-a-lent	synonymous	syn-on-y-mous
privilege	priv-i-lege	synthetic	syn-thet-ic
probably	prob-a-bly	technology	tech-nol-o-gy
procedure	pro-ce-dure	temperament	tem-per-a-ment
proceed	pro-ceed	temperature	tem-per-a-ture
processor	pro-ces-sor	together	to-geth-er
professional	pro-fes-sion-al	tragedy	trag-e-dy
professor	pro-fes-sor	truly	tru-ly
pronunciation	pro-nun-ci-a-tion	twelfth	twelfth
propaganda	prop-a-gan-da	unanimous	u-nan-i-mous
psychiatrist	psy-chi-a-trist	undoubtedly	un-doubt-ed-ly
psychological	psy-cho-log-i-cal	unnecessarily	un-nec-es-sar-i-ly
pursue	pur-sue	until	un-til
quantity	quan-ti-ty	usually	usu-al-ly
questionnaire	ques-tion-naire	various	var-i-ous
quizzes	quiz-zes	vegetable	veg-e-ta-ble
realize	re-al-ize	video	vid-e-o
really	re-al-ly	village	vil-lage
recognize	rec-og-nize	villain	vil-lain
recommend	rec-om-mend	Wednesday	Wednes-day
regard	re-gard	whether	wheth-er
religious	re-li-gious	wholly	whol-ly

NAME _____ SCORE _____

Directions: Each sentence contains two words from the first half of the spelling list. At least one letter is missing from each of these words. Write the words, correctly spelled, in the spaces at the left.

_____
_____ 1. At the conclusion of the first lecture, the members of the aud__nce were asked to send their criti__sms to the chairperson.

_____
_____ 2. Many residents of Great Brit__n see little reason for venturing beyond the bound__s of their own country.

_____
_____ 3. The secretaries are enthus__tic about the new equip__nt in the main office.

_____
_____ 4. Dur__ng the past decade our department has been housed in a d__apidated old building on the lower campus.

_____
_____ 5. Everyone in our tour group was dis__tisfied with the meager ac__modations at the hotel.

_____
_____ 6. The problem of overnight parking on city streets is a famil__r one, and one that is extre__ly difficult to solve.

_____
_____ 7. "It was," said Ms. Taylor, "one of the most embar__sing exp__ences of my entire life."

_____
_____ 8. It takes little im__gination to see how much the team has been helped by the new coach's strict dis__pline.

_____
_____ 9. The feeble old man was trying desp__tely to push his wheelbarrow a__ross the busy intersection.

_____
_____ 10. The results of our school's ath__ic contests this year have been, in general, dis__pointing.

_____
_____ 11. Staying in the new dorm__tory on the campus, Mary discovered, was a very conv__ent arrangement for her.

_____
_____ 12. "I wonder why my diction__ry seems to dis__pear from my desk every time I need it," complained Ellen.

_____   13. The man confessed to having imported from Libya an ex__rbitant
_____   number of counterf__t 20-dollar bills.

_____   14. Such practices could have disast__us effects on the fragile
_____   envi__nment of the marshlands.

_____   15. The child's health improved imme__ately under Dr. Swift's
_____   excel__nt care.

_____   16. It is not considered good practice to ab__iate ordinary words in a
_____   bu__iness letter.

_____   17. "Your theme was good, Tom," said Ms. Simms. "I espec__ly liked
_____   the hum__us examples you used."

_____   18. The a__ward, clumsy boy has fallen from nearly every exercise
_____   ap__ratus in the gymnasium.

_____   19. I'm sure Ben exag__rated when he told us that he jogged fo__ty
_____   miles yesterday.

_____   20. The participants are all amat__rs, but the comp__tition is fierce.
_____

_____   21. The child's skills in arith__etic have improved since her parents
_____   gave her a personal comput__r.

_____   22. Several spirited argu__ents developed shortly after the
_____   confer__nce opened.

_____   23. "I am proud to say that I number you am__ng my a__ainances,"
_____   she replied.

_____   24. Accompan__ng the letter was a brochure containing a detailed
_____   d__cription of the items offered for sale.

_____   25. "We have ch__sen a can__date who will surely win for us in
_____   November," said the chairperson.

NAME _____   SCORE _____

Directions: Each sentence contains three italicized words from the first half of the spelling list. One of the three words is misspelled. Underline the misspelled word and write it, correctly spelled, in the space at the left.

_____ 1. While I was out of town, pamphlets *describing* the qualifications of the *candidates accummulated* on my front porch.

_____ 2. A barrage of polysyllabic words *doesn't always accompolish* what the speaker had hoped for.

_____ 3. "We have an *efficient* staff, and we give *excelent* service," said the boastful *entrepreneur.*

_____ 4. "In my opinion," said Bert, "*compulsory attendance* at every class meeting is a *barbarious* regulation."

_____ 5. The personnel manager *apparently* considers Mike *exceptionly* well qualified for the insurance *business.*

_____ 6. It seems almost *incredible* that any *goverment* would inflict such *grievous* wrongs on its senior citizens.

_____ 7. *Fourty foreign* visitors were *frantically* arguing with one of the immigration officers.

_____ 8. *Finally*, late in *Febuary*, an *eminent* defense lawyer agreed to take our case.

_____ 9. I have checked my *calendar* and can report that I most *definately* will attend your next *committee* meeting.

_____ 10. The *astronaut hurriedly* retrieved the microphone that he had *accidently* dropped.

_____ 11. He tried *conscientiously* to *eliminate* all errors in spelling and *grammer* from his term paper.

_____ 12. The coach's *arguement* was that on the basis of *comparative* scores, our team *certainly* deserved a higher rating.

321

_____ 13. My friend lives in a *condominium* directly *accross* the street from the main entrance to the *cemetery.*

_____ 14. *Confidentially,* I am *desperately* in need of *approximatly* 400 dollars.

_____ 15. "I suppose, Harold," said the teacher, "that we can expect another of your *fascinating explainations* for your *absence* from class yesterday."

_____ 16. I *concede* that there has been nothing *extraordinary* in my rather drab *existance.*

_____ 17. You will *acknowledge*, won't you, that a *dictionary* is an *extreamly* valuable reference book for a student to own?

_____ 18. It was the family's *decision* to restore the *delapidated* farmhouse and give it to the State Historical *Association.*

_____ 19. A newly appointed *commission* will revise the *controvertial curriculum.*

_____ 20. *Incidentally,* if the *heighth* of your truck *exceeds* 11 feet, you cannot use the temporary underpass.

_____ 21. I predict that *during* the next week or ten days, the last remnants of dirty snow will have *dissappered completely* from my yard.

_____ 22. The recommendation read as follows: "This applicant is *competent,* she is neat in *appearance,* and she has done *consistantly* good work for our firm."

_____ 23. "My parents do not *appreciate* the fact that lately I have *aquired* passing grades in my *arithmetic* class," said Junior.

_____ 24. In these meetings we have our *differences,* of course, but we can *generally* settle them after short *conferrences.*

_____ 25. Experts agree that the cumbersome *bureaucracy* of the emerging country is a *continuous hinderance* to economic development.

NAME _____ SCORE _____

Directions: Each sentence contains two words from the second half of the spelling list. At least one letter is missing from each of these words. Write the words, correctly spelled, in the spaces at the left.

_____   1. Last semester I took one course in American lit__ture and one
_____   in spe__ch.

_____   2. For lunch Bob ordered a bowl of veg__ble soup and a tuna fish
_____   san__ich.

_____   3. I'm not a junior; because I have not yet earned ni__ty quarter
_____   hours of credit, I'm still a so__more.

_____   4. Dean Lange complained to her sec__tary about the excessive
_____   quan__ty of supplies used in the office.

_____   5. The very casual proc__ures followed in this office may at first
_____   su__prise you.

_____   6. Working under the blazing sun was par__cularly unpleasant,
_____   and soon all of us were covered with p__spiration.

_____   7. A knowl__ge of human nature is indispen__ble in the business
_____   of selling used cars.

_____   8. A team of experts trained in psych__ogical prop__ganda followed
_____   the army into the conquered province.

_____   9. My three business par__ners and I are opt__mistic about next
_____   year's prospects.

_____   10. "This is not an easy test," said the teacher, "and we shall prob__ly
_____   have simil__r assignments in future class meetings."

_____   11. The orig__nal report gave the police chief's interp__ation of the
_____   events leading to the riot.

_____   12. The counselor offered some int__sting ideas about what constitutes
_____   a happy, successful mar__age.

323

_____ 13. For 30 miles the highway runs pract__ly par__lel to the railroad
_____ tracks.

_____ 14. We do not yet know w__ther or not the police s__geant was
_____ seriously injured.

_____ 15. Matthew's favorite pas__ime is examining old and rare books
_____ at the city lib__ry.

_____ 16. The cook then proc__ded to show the children how to sep__rate
_____ the artichoke leaves.

_____ 17. Mr. Hawkins still has in his pos__sion several m__mentos of a
_____ trip he took to Mexico City in 1963.

_____ 18. After the thunder and light__ng storm, the temp__ture dropped
_____ nearly 20 degrees.

_____ 19. Mrs. Travis found it nec__sary to interc__de in the argument the
_____ two children were having.

_____ 20. On Tuesday evening a power shortage inter__pted the first
_____ p__rformance of the senior class play.

_____ 21. It is always permis__ble for a student to change his or her
_____ sched__le before the fourth class meeting.

_____ 22. Several of the spec__mens in our science museum are so out of date
_____ that they will undoubt__ly be replaced when funds are available.

_____ 23. "The prep__ation of this lengthy question__re required long hours
_____ of work on our part," said one of the committee members.

_____ 24. In these old mystery films, the vill__n was never apprehended and
_____ punished unt__l the final reel.

_____ 25. "The maint__nce of our independ__nce depends on our strong,
_____ well-equipped Army," declared General Martinson.

NAME _____ SCORE _____

Directions: A sentence may have no misspelled words, one misspelled word, or two misspelled words. Write the misspelled words correctly in the spaces at the left.

_____ 1. Your proposal seems fundamentally sound, but we are obliged to
_____   show it to the committee before we procede.

_____ 2. The county has purchased some kind of new firefighting apparatus
_____   designed to rescue people from skyscrapers.

_____ 3. My sister's allottment of Girl Scout cookies filled up our utility
_____   room and several shelfs in the garage.

_____ 4. Janie pleaded, "All I want is a good, servicable car, one that all
_____   ready has a few dents and scratches on it."

_____ 5. If you wish to start a business succesfully, you need capital, talant,
_____   and perspiration.

_____ 6. Athletics recieves entirely to much emphasis in some schools, but
_____   certainly not in ours.

_____ 7. Sometimes we have dificulty recognizing propaganda because it is
_____   cleverly perpared and extremely subtle.

_____ 8. "Pronunciation" and "pronouncement" are derived from the same
_____   root words in ancient languages.

_____ 9. The parrot mimiced my grandfather's words, saying each word
_____   presicely as my grandfather said it.

_____ 10. The donkeys are staying in the barn this mourning because the
_____   weather is all together too icy for them to be outside.

_____ 11. The casheir's nimble fingers flew over the keys of the cash register,
_____   never missing a number or making a mistake.

_____ 12. The company needs new stationary; the old letterhead has several
_____   mispelled names.

325

_____ 13. "Your presents here in court is a great assistence to my case," said
_____   the indicted city commissioner.

_____ 14. The Coast Guard Auxilary assists in porviding help to stranded
_____   boaters.

_____ 15. Be conscientous about attendance; you never know when you will
_____   learn something important in class.

_____ 16. The dinning hall had vegatables, roast beef, and strawberry short
_____   cake on the menu last night.

_____ 17. It will be necessary for ninety people to sign up for the trip before
_____   we can set up the schedule and make reservations.

_____ 18. Morris appeered embarrassed to be scene in his new lime-green
_____   sportcoat and yellow slacks.

_____ 19. Interpertation of that coded massage was necessary before the
_____   general could commit any troops.

_____ 20. To become an entrepenure and gain great wealth is a dream held
_____   by many and acheived by few.

NAME _____   SCORE _____

Directions: Correct all the errors of grammar, mechanics, spelling and punctuation in the following passage.

The Xerox machine is an absolute marvel of simplicity, and complexity. The machine is reletively easy to operate. Life the cover, and place the materiel to be copied on the glass plate. Select the number of copies and any other special formating items. Push the start button, and wait for the machine to do its work. Internaly the machine is amazingly complex. Physical principals, that involves oppositly charged substinces, and an application of heat provides the capability from making clean copies of print and pictures either black, white or color.Earlier methods of office copying had been cumbersome and slow—assigning a monk to make a copy or messy and smelly—mimeograph and ditto machines, which use volatile chemicals to make copies. Now since the invention the Xerox machine by Chester Carlson even the smallest business and many of us at home can make copies wit enormous ease.Copying is so easy that we all make copies of everything anytime the mood strikes us even if the document is unbelievable trivial. Building supply stores maintains a "bridal registry" of gifts, requested by prospective grooms. Someone on the staff will make a copy of the list if it is requested. Thus is cousin Max is marrying his true love Marcia he can go to the building supply store, and either enter his request for a air compressor or a hammer drill, and you can check you copy of the registry to see what Max requested, and know imediately weather or not another friend or relative has purchased the requested gift. This ability is a wonderful thing because it will prevent needless duplication of presence. After all no bride wants a second air compressor cluttering up the floor of her guest bedroom. The Xerox machine is a truly beautiful and wonderful device.

Writing Paragraphs and Essays

Although it may come as a surprise to you, you will be called on to do a great deal of writing in college and in your career. Lecture notes, essays, research papers, and tests are the stuff of which college courses are made. Memorandums, letters, e-mail correspondence, reports, and proposals are basic tools in almost any career you can name. And all this writing, whether in or out of college, is in great measure a key to your progress and success. In fact, in many large organizations, people are known to those in other areas more through their written work than through personal contact. Often, progress and promotion ride as much on the quality of written work as on any other factor. Writing skills, then, will be a major factor in your success.

Writing is also an effective tool for learning. Writing about a subject leads to greater understanding and control of the material itself and to new connections to other facts and concepts. Writing out lecture notes and textbook materials in your own words, for example, will give you better control of those materials and will help you connect the new materials with facts and concepts you learned earlier.

In the previous sections of this book, you examined the operating principles of the language and applied those principles to writing correct, effective sentences. Now you need to learn to combine those sentences into paragraphs and the paragraphs into papers that will fulfill your college writing assignments.

The assignments you receive in college may range from a single paragraph narrating an event in your life to a complex research paper. Look briefly at a list of these possible assignments:

1. *Personal Essays*
   - Recount an event in your life, explaining its importance.
   - Discuss your position on an upcoming election.

2. *Essay Tests*
   - Answer two of the following three questions, using well-developed paragraphs and complete sentences in your answer.

3. *Essays and Discussions*
   - Explain the causes of structural unemployment in our country today.
   - Discuss the ramifications of using gene therapy to treat diseases.

4. *Critical Papers*
   - Evaluate the enclosed proposal for the construction of a new dam.
   - Assess the legacy of industry irresponsibility toward the environment in the United States.

5. *Persuasive or Argumentative Papers*
   - Argue for or against the use of government spending to retrain displaced workers.
   - Discuss the arguments against universal military training in the United States.

6. *Documented Papers*
   - After thorough research into the subject, write a paper discussing the use of nuclear power in this country. Be sure to discuss the history, the current situation, and the arguments for and against continued use and further development.

Although this list may seem extremely diverse and the types of writing quite varied, you can take comfort in the fact that underneath this diversity and complexity lies a fairly straightforward process that can be applied to all types of writing. You need only to learn one set of steps, the basic writing process, in order to deal effectively with any writing project you might face.

THE WRITING PROCESS

Writing is a process, a set of steps, not a project that is started and finished in a single session. Often, people believe that successful writers have happened onto a secret method of production that allows them, almost by magic, to sit down and write out a nearly perfect draft on the first try. This happens only rarely and always to writers with long experience; most people can assume that good writing rises out of slow, painstaking, step-by-step work.

The steps in the writing process group themselves naturally into two phases, and each phase requires an approach, a mindset, that is quite different from the other. In the first phase, composing, you should be free and creative. Think of this phase as a search, an adventure, an opportunity to try out many possibilities for ideas, content, and strategies. In the second phase, revising, you must be critical of the materials you have composed. This is the time when you must evaluate, rewrite, reject, and correct the materials you developed while composing.

You must be careful not to mix the modes of operation. Don't edit when you should be composing. Don't delete materials, or decide not to pursue an idea, or ponder the correctness of a mark of punctuation. Such distractions will almost certainly stop your flow of ideas. But don't allow yourself to be free and creative when you are working as an editor. Keeping a word that is not quite right or failing to cut out a section that does not fit will produce papers that lack focus and are full of distractions. Remember that each phase in the process is separate and distinct. Each requires separate and distinct attitudes toward the work at hand.

The following brief explanation provides a general introduction to the steps that make up the writing process. In later sections, you will see these steps applied to different types of writing; those applications will illustrate minor changes to suit specific types of writing.

Composing

Step 1. Select or identify the subject.

Basic Question: What should I write about? or (if the assignment is very specific), What does the assignment require me to write about?

Strategy: Select the subject on the basis of these questions:
- Are you and your reader interested in it?
- Do you have enough knowledge to write on it? If not, can you locate enough?
- Can you treat the subject completely within the number of pages allotted for the assignment?

Step 2. Gather information about the subject.

Basic Question: What do I know about the subject? More important, what do I need to know to write about this subject fully and effectively?

Strategy: Record what you know, whether the information comes from recollection or research. Seek more information where necessary. Continue research and writing until you arrive at Step 3.

Step 3. Establish a controlling statement, or thesis, for the paper.

Basic Question: Exactly what can I say about this subject on the basis of the information and ideas I developed in Step 2?

Strategy: Continue to gather information and write about the subject until a specific idea develops. Write that idea in a single sentence.

Step 4. Select specific items of support to include in the paper.

Basic Question: What ideas, facts, and illustrations can I use to make the thesis completely clear to the reader?

Strategy: Review the stockpile of materials gathered in Step 2. Select from these materials only those ideas, facts, and illustrations that will develop and support the thesis.

Step 5. Establish an order for presenting the materials you have selected.

Basic Question: What is the most effective order for presenting the materials I have selected?

Strategy: Choose an order of presentation that offers your reader a logical progression for the development of your idea. The orders used in paragraph development are sometimes useful in developing an order for an essay. (See page 343.) Write the draft in any order you choose, starting with the easiest section. Assemble the draft in the order you have selected.

Step 6. Select a technique.

Basic Question: What is the most effective technique for presenting the materials I have selected?

Strategy: Explore different writing techniques to determine which one best complements your thesis and supporting materials.

Step 7. Write the first draft.

Basic Question:	What will the materials look like when presented in the order I have chosen?
Strategy:	Write out a complete version of the paper, following the plan developed in the first six steps.

Revising

Before you begin to revise the first completed draft of the paper, be sure that you shift from the role of composer/writer to the role of critic or editor. You have before you a completed product, not a perfect product. You must examine that product with a critical eye, testing and weighing each part to be sure that it is as good as it can be.

Step 8. Assess the thesis of the draft.

Basic Question:	Is the thesis a proper expression of your knowledge on the subject?
Strategy:	Read each supporting paragraph or section of the essay individually and create a sentence outline by writing a topic statement for each one. From the topic statements, produce a thesis statement for the draft. Compare it to the original thesis. If the two differ, create a new, better thesis.

Step 9. Assess the content.

Basic Question:	Does each paragraph or section offer genuine support for the thesis?
Strategy:	Check the topic statement for each paragraph or section to be sure each supports the new thesis. Remove and replace any paragraph or section that does not support the thesis.

Step 10. Assess the order of presentation.

Basic Question:	Does the order of presentation provide the reader with a logical progression or pathway through the essay?
Strategy:	Try different orders of presentation, shifting sections around to see if you can find a better order than the one you used for the first finished draft.

Step 11. Assess the paragraphs.

Basic Question:	Is each paragraph unified and complete? Is each paragraph developed following the best possible method of development?
Strategy:	Using the sentence outline created above, check the content of each paragraph to be sure it develops one idea and only one idea. Check the content to be sure that the paragraph contains enough specific, concrete details to make the topic statement clear to the reader.

Step 12. Assess the technique.

Basic Question:	Does this technique present my thesis and supporting materials in the best way possible?
Strategy:	Consider whether other techniques might better complement your thesis.

Step 13. Correct the mistakes in the draft.

Basic Question: What errors in grammar and mechanics do I need to correct?

Strategy: Read each sentence as an independent unit, starting at the end of the paper and working to the beginning. Reading "backward" in this fashion assures that you will not make mental corrections or assumptions as you read.

Step 14. Write the final draft.

Basic Question: What form shall I use for the final copy of the paper?

Strategy: Follow the guidelines for manuscript preparation specified by your teacher, printing or typing the final copy on plain white paper. Be sure to read the final copy carefully for errors.

A paragraph is a group of sentences (or sometimes just one sentence) related to a single idea. The paragraph originated as a punctuation device to separate ideas on paper and to assist readers in keeping lines separate as they read. Thus, each paragraph begins on a new line, and its first word is indented a few spaces from the left margin.

THE EFFECTIVE PARAGRAPH

The function of a paragraph is to state and develop a single idea, usually called a **topic.** The topic is actually the subject of the paragraph, what the paragraph is about. Everything in the paragraph after the statement of the topic ought to **develop the topic,** to explain and define, to discuss, to illustrate and exemplify the topic. From the reader's point of view, the content of the paragraph should provide enough information and explanation to make clear the topic of the paragraph and the function of the paragraph in the essay or the chapter.

The Topic Sentence

The first rule of effective paragraph writing is as follows:

   Usually, declare the topic of the paragraph early in a single sentence (called the *topic sentence***).**

Read the folowing paragraph about sea turtles.

Of the seven species of sea turtles, the green turtle is the largest and the most widely distributed, but it is nearing endangered status because it has commercial value. It is a large turtle, measuring between nearly 3 and 6 feet in length over the top of the shell and weighing on the average 200–300 pounds. The largest specimens are over 5 feet in length and weigh 800–1,000 pounds. The upper shell (carapace) is light to dark brown, shaded or mottled with darker colors ranging to an almost black-green. The lower shell (plastron) is white to light yellow. The scales on the upper surface of the head are dark, and the spaces between them are yellow; on the sides of the head, the scales are brown but have a yellow margin, giving a yellow cast to the sides of the head. The shell is broad, low, and more or less heart-shaped. The green turtle inhabits most of the warm, shallow waters of the world's seas and oceans, preferring areas 10–20 feet deep where it can find good sea grass pastures for browsing. The turtles prefer areas that have many potholes, because they sleep in the holes for security. In numbers and population trends, the status of the green turtle is in doubt. It is under great pressure in highly populated areas such as the Caribbean Sea, where it is avidly hunted for food and for use in making jewelry and cosmetics. However, because it occurs in large numbers in remote areas, it is not technically an endangered species at this time. It needs better protection in populated areas so that its numbers will not decline any further.

Note how the first sentence provides direction for the paragraph. It is, in other words, a topic sentence. Every paragraph you write should contain a sentence that names what the paragraph is about and indicates how the paragraph will proceed. It may do so in considerable detail:

> Although the green turtle—a large, greenish-brown sea turtle inhabiting warm, shallow seas over most of the world—is not yet generally endangered, it is subject to extreme pressure in populated areas.

or rather broadly:

> The green turtle is one of the most important of the seven species of sea turtles.

Both of these statements name a specific topic, the green turtle, but neither sentence stops with the name. A sentence that reads "This paragraph will be about green turtles" is not a complete topic sentence because it does not suggest the direction that the rest of the paragraph will take. Unlike the incomplete topic sentence, both good examples are phrased so that a certain type of development must follow. The first example anticipates a discussion that will mention size, color, habitat, and distribution but will focus on the green turtle's chances for survival. The second example anticipates a discussion that will develop the assertion that the species is one of the most important of the sea turtles. Note that neither example tries to embrace the whole idea of the paragraph. The topic sentence should lay the foundation for the paragraph, not say everything there is to be said.

Sometimes a paragraph has no topic sentence; occasionally the topic sentence occurs at the end of the paragraph. These exceptions are permissible, but the early topic sentence is more popular with both writers and readers because it helps in three ways to produce an effective message:

1. It defines your job as a writer and states a manageable objective—a single topic.
2. It establishes a guide for your development of the basic idea. You must supply evidence of or support for any assertion in the topic sentence. The topic sentence is only a beginning, but it predicts a conclusion that the paragraph must reach.
3. It tells your reader what the paragraph is going to contain.

Notice how the italicized topic sentence in the following paragraph controls the paragraph and provides clear direction for the reader:

> Of all the inventions of the last one hundred years, *the automobile assembly line has had the most profound effect on American life.* The assembly line provided a method for building and selling automobiles at a price many could afford, thus changing the auto from a luxury item owned by the wealthy few to an everyday appliance used by almost every adult in America. Universal ownership and the use of the automobile opened new occupations, new dimensions of mobility, and new areas of recreation to everyone. In addition, the automobile assembly line provided a model for the mass production of television sets, washing machines, bottled drinks, and even sailboats. All these products would have been far too expensive for purchase by the average person without the introduction of assembly-line methods to lower manufacturing costs. With the advent of Henry Ford's system, all Americans could hope to possess goods once reserved for a select class, and the hope changed their lives forever.

The italicized sentence states the topic and the purpose of the paragraph: The paragraph is going to argue that the assembly line, more than any other invention, changed America's way of life. The writer is controlled by this sentence because everything in the paragraph should serve to support this argument. Readers are assisted by the sentence, for they know that they can expect examples supporting the position stated in the sentence.

Complete Development

Writing a good topic sentence is only the first step in writing an effective paragraph, for an effective paragraph provides complete development of the topic—that is, it tells the readers all they need to know about the topic for the purposes at hand. This is the second basic rule of effective paragraph writing: **Always provide complete development in each paragraph.**

Complete development tells readers all that they need to understand about the paragraph itself and the way the paragraph fits into the rest of the essay or chapter. Complete development does not necessarily provide all the information the reader *wants* to know; rather, the reader receives what is *needed* for understanding the topic and its development (the internal working of the paragraph) and the relationship between the paragraph and the paper as a whole (the external connection). As an illustration of that rather abstract statement, read the following paragraph, which gives a set of instructions for a familiar process:

> Another skill required of a self-sufficient car owner is the ability to jump-start a car with a dead battery, a process that entails some important do's and don't's. First, make certain that the charged battery to be used is a properly grounded battery of the same voltage as the dead one. Put out all smoking material. Connect the first jumper cable to the positive terminal of each battery. Connect one end of the second cable to the negative terminal of the live battery, and then clamp the other end to some part of the engine in the car with the dead battery. DO *NOT* LINK POSITIVE AND NEGATIVE TERMINALS. DO *NOT* ATTACH THE NEGATIVE CABLE DIRECTLY TO THE NEGATIVE TERMINAL OF THE DEAD BATTERY. A direct connection is dangerous. Choose a spot at least 18 inches from the dead battery. Put the car with the live battery in neutral, rev the engine, and hold it at moderate rpm while starting the other car. Once the engine is running, hold it at moderate rpm for a few seconds and disconnect the NEGATIVE cable. Then disconnect the positive cable. It is wise to take the car to a service station as soon as possible to have the battery checked and serviced if necessary.

While the instructions in this paragraph are clear and will enable anyone to start a car with a dead battery, the reader may have certain questions in mind after reading the paragraph:

1. What is a properly grounded battery?
2. Why is it necessary to extinguish smoking materials?
3. To what parts of the engine may one attach the negative cable? (After all, attaching it to the fan will have exciting results.)
4. What is the danger of making a direct connection?

Also, at least two important steps are left out of the process:

Before connecting the two batteries,

1. Remove the caps to the cells of both batteries.
2. Check the fluid levels in the cells of both batteries.

Without these steps in the process, the car with the dead battery will start, but there is a chance of explosion. A paragraph that lacks material, that is not fully developed, probably won't explode. But it probably won't succeed, either. Questions raised in the mind of the reader will almost always weaken the effect of the paragraph. Sometimes the omissions are so important that the reader will miss the point or give up altogether in frustration.

Most of the time, you can write a well-developed paragraph by following three simple steps:

1. Make the topic statement one clear, rather brief sentence.
2. Clarify and define the statement as needed.
3. Illustrate or exemplify the topic statement concretely where possible.

As an example of this three-step process, follow the development of a paragraph written to answer the question "What is the most important quality that you are seeking in an occupation?" The student's answer, found after much preliminary writing and a good bit of discussion, led to the following topic sentence and rough paragraph:

> Above all other qualities, *I want to have variety in the tasks I perform and in the locations where I work.*
>
> I know I must do the general line of work for which I'm trained, but I want to do different tasks in that work every day if possible. Repeating the same tasks day after day must be a mind-numbing experience. Our neighborhood mechanic does one tuneup after another, five days a week. A doctor friend tells me that 90 percent of her practice involves treating people ill with a virus, for which she sometimes prescribes an antibiotic against secondary infection. I want no part of that sort of humdrum work. Variety means doing a different part of a job every day, perhaps working on the beginning of one project today and the completion of another tomorrow, or working on broad concepts one day and details the next. I'd also like to work at a different job site as often as possible. The field of architecture is one area that might suit me. I could work in drafting, and then switch to field supervision, and move from that task to developing the overall concepts of a large project. By doing this, I could vary my assignments and the locations of my work.

Following the three simple steps given above, you might revise this paragraph to read as follows:

Topic Sentence	Some people want salary and others want big challenges, *but in my career I want variety, in both assignment and work location,* more than
Clarification and Definition	any other single quality. As much as possible, I want to do a different part of a job every day. Perhaps I could work on the beginning of one project and shift to the completion of another, or work on details for a while and then shift to broad concepts involved in planning. For this reason architecture looks like a promising field for me. I could work in
Concrete Example	drafting and detailing, move next to on-site supervision, and then shift to developing the design concepts of a major project. I know that doing the same task in the same place would be a mind-numbing experience for me. Our family doctor says that 90 percent of her practice consists of treating patients who have a routine virus infection, for which she sometimes prescribes an antibiotic against secondary infection. Our neighborhood mechanic spends all his time doing tuneups. I want none of that humdrum sort of work. Variety is the spice of life; it is also the ingredient that makes work palatable for me.

Unity

Effective paragraphs have two other characteristics: unity and coherence. Maintaining unity in a paragraph would seem to be easy. After all, by definition, a paragraph should deal with only one idea that is completely developed. Second and subsequent ideas should be handled in separate paragraphs. Sometimes, however, ideas can trick you if you don't pay close attention to your topic sentence. A student wrote this paragraph on strawberries some years ago:

> Strawberries are my favorite dessert. Over ice cream or dipped in powdered sugar, they are so good they bring tears to my eyes. My uncle used to grow strawberries on his farm in New Jersey. Once, I spent the whole summer there, and my cousins and I went to the carnival. . . .

Things went pretty far afield from strawberries as the paragraph continued, and you can see how one idea, "used to grow strawberries on his farm," led to a recollection of a delightful summer on that farm and opened the door to a whole new idea and a change in form from discussion to narration. "Strawberries" and "that summer on the farm" are both legitimate, interesting, and perfectly workable topics for a paragraph. But they are probably not proper for inclusion in the same paragraph. Unity demands that each topic be treated in a separate paragraph. One paragraph handling one idea equals unity.

Coherence

In paragraph writing, the term *coherence* is used to describe a smooth flow between sentences within the paragraph. In other words, the sentences follow one another without abrupt changes. An effective paragraph reads smoothly, flowing from start to finish without choppiness to distract the reader.

The first step in establishing coherence occurs when you decide how you are going to develop the paragraph. (We discuss the various ways in which a paragraph can be developed in the next section.) The way in which you decide to develop the paragraph will help establish coherence because it will produce a flow and a movement in the paragraph and because it will serve as a frame for providing details of development. There are, however, other writing strategies that contribute to coherence. Three of these strategies are discussed next.

Repetition of Nouns and Use of Reference Words.

> My father asked me to dig some postholes. After I finished that, he told me the truck needed washing. It is Father's pride and joy, but I'm the one who has to do such jobs.

These three short sentences show a fairly clear pattern of development that in itself establishes coherence. Events occur one after another, establishing a chronological order for the development of the entire paragraph. But note how strongly the repeated nouns and reference words knit the sentences together within the paragraph:

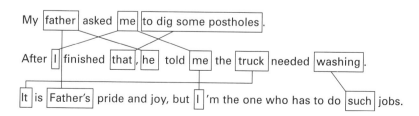

Use of Temporal Words: Conjunctions and Adverbs. Although a series of short, abrupt sentences may create chronological coherence, the paragraph may not read smoothly:

> I drove to the corner. I stopped for a light. A car smashed into the back of mine. I got out rubbing my neck. The driver of the other car sat behind the wheel and wept. I realized that the other driver was an elderly, gray-haired man.

A writer, sensing that something is lacking from the paragraph, might revise it this way:

> I drove to the corner. *While* I was stopped for a light, a car smashed into the back of mine. *As* I got out, rubbing my neck, the driver of the other car sat behind the wheel and wept. Only *then* did I realize that the other driver was an elderly, gray-haired man.

Two features of the revision have improved on the original draft. The first and most obvious is the addition of the words *while, as,* and *then* to connect the sentences by declaring the chronological sequence. Second, *while* and *as* convert short sentences into dependent clauses, thus replacing four choppy sentences with two longer ones and eliminating the jog-trot rhythm that gave the reader hiccups.

Transitional Words and Phrases At or Near the Beginning of Sentences. Coordinating conjunctions*; adverbs like *however, moreover, therefore, consequently, similarly,* and *thus;* and expressions like *on the other hand, in addition,* and *for example* can produce subtle transitional effects rather like that of reference words. They force the reader to recollect the preceding material, thus making a tie between the thoughts they introduce and what has already been stated. When you read *But* at the beginning of a sentence, the author is declaring to you in loud tones, "You are to interpret the forthcoming statement as being in opposition or in contrast to what you have just read." *Moreover,* in the same place, suggests that what is coming is an addition to the last remarks; *consequently* means "as a result of what I have just stated."

The ploy of cementing the parts of a paragraph together with these words and phrases is used by nearly every writer. It is a perfectly good device, but unfortunately it is also a seductively easy one. The unwary writer larding sentences with *however*'s and *therefore*'s in search of elegance and poise may get into trouble with logic. "Sam drank too much on our dinner date. Consequently he threw up," may leave one wondering whether the nausea stemmed from the liquor or the date.

---

*Disregard the myth that there is something wrong with starting a sentence with *and, but, for, or, nor, yet,* or *so.* Do realize, however, that these words at the opening of a sentence provide a special effect and call attention to themselves and to what follows them. Don't overuse them, and be sure of your purpose when you do launch a statement with one.

Once you have mastered the steps in the writing process by creating paragraphs, you will need to make only a few adjustments to follow that same process in writing a longer essay, the sort of essay you might be assigned in a college class in biology, business, or English. After all, whether you are writing essay test, special paragraph arrangements, or full-length essays, the writing process we described on pages 330–333 is the same.

COMPOSING

Let's assume you need to develop a paper for your English class. Because the paper is a class assignment, the first step requires a look at the nature of class assignments and the problems of defining the subject and limiting it to an appropriate, manageable length.

Step 1. Select the Subject

Usually, writing assignments fall into one of three categories.

1. **Very General:** Write a two-page paper on something we've covered in this course.

2. **Somewhat Specific:** Write a two-page paper on some aspect of the novel *Huckleberry Finn.*

3. **Very Directive:** Write a two-page paper explaining why Huck Finn's experiences led him to make his final statement: "Aunt Sally's going to adopt me and sivilize me and I can't stand it. I been there before."

The very general assignment grants considerable latitude in the selection of a subject for a paper. Often this latitude will prove more of a problem than a blessing because it is necessary to find something to write about that you *and* the teacher consider interesting and worthwhile. It is of little value to write a fine paper and find that the teacher (the grader) thinks the topic so insignificant that the whole effort can't be worth more than a C. The best approach here is to review the textbook, your lecture notes, and previous tests (if any); to select from these an important content area, concept, or personality; and to use that selection as a starting point for your work. Be sure to choose an area that interests you, an area about which you have some knowledge and some readily accessible sources of information. Once you have made this initial selection, you have converted the assignment from "general" to "somewhat specific." Next, you need to restrict the area you selected or were assigned so that you can develop it fully within the assigned length of the paper. Suppose, for example, the assignment said to write a two-page paper on *Huckleberry Finn.* Several areas are open to you:

1. Autobiographical aspects of the novel

2. Problems of plot and structure

3. Problems of characterization

4. Philosophical aspects of the novel

For the selection or restriction process, choose one of the areas and make a final selection of a topic within that area. The final selection should be fairly small in scope, something manageable within two pages. In the example of *Huckleberry Finn,* the process of restriction might look like this:

Philosophical aspects of the novel

1. The relationship between individuals and society

2. Huck Finn's attitude toward the world as he saw it

3. Why Huck's experiences led him to say that he couldn't stand to be "sivilized"

The final version of the topic (Number 3) is probably limited enough for it to be treated adequately within the assigned length. The topic asks a single question about one person. It should be possible to answer that question and offer examples supporting your answer in two pages.

Note that the way in which your teacher states the assignment dictates the starting point for your work. A general assignment requires that you go through three stages:

1. Selection of a general subject area

2. Selection of a portion or phase of this general area to form a limited subject area

3. Final selection of a specific limited topic within the limited subject area

A somewhat specific assignment completes the first two stages for you by limiting you to a general area. You need deal with only the third stage to complete the restriction process for this assignment. A very directive assignment accomplishes all three stages and leaves you free to begin work on the organization of the paper itself.

Step 2. Gather Information

Once you have established your topic, you need to establish what you know about the topic. Continuing with our *Huckleberry Finn* example, what were Huck's experiences? Why did they make him want to avoid Aunt Sally's attentions? List some of the experiences he had in the "sivilized" world. Here are some possibilities:

1. The confining life at the Widow Douglas's home and Miss Watson's efforts to teach Huck manners and religion

2. The brutal shooting of Boggs by Colonel Sherburn and the mob violence of the attempted lynching that was faced down by Sherburn's single-handed capacity for even greater violence

3. The Grangerford–Shepherdson feud

4. Huck's obvious pleasure at living outside civilization with Jim on Jackson's Island and on the raft

While other experiences may come to mind as you work on the paper, this list leads directly to Step 3.

Step 3. Establish a Controlling Statement

The controlling statement, or **thesis,** serves the longer essay much as the topic sentence serves the paragraph. The topic sentence states the subject of the paragraph and tells what will be said about it. The thesis statement controls the writer before the paper is written by defining the subject and what is to be said about it. The thesis keeps the writer from wandering away from the subject; sometimes it is so specific that it establishes the order in which the essay will be arranged. Reviewing your list of Huck's experiences, the thesis statement for your paper is obvious:

> Huck could not stand to be "sivilized" because his experiences in civilization were confining, frightening, or dangerous.

Step 4. Select Specific Items of Support

Keeping the thesis statement in mind, select from the book experiences and observations that will clearly illustrate the conditions in civilization. All the possible pieces of evidence listed above can be used to point out the conditions that Huck wanted to avoid. Even the pleasant experiences with Jim on Jackson's Island serve to make the bad experiences more vivid. As you select the content, you produce an outline, which is a simple list of the points you wish to make in support of your thesis. Each point in the outline then becomes a paragraph of support in your short paper. In a longer and therefore more complex paper, more than one paragraph may be required to develop a single point.

Step 5. Establish an Order of Presentation

Several orders are possible, but the easiest one to follow is to take the materials in the order in which they occur in the book.

Step 6. Write the First Draft

Begin by writing an introduction. The introduction might read this way:

> At the close of the novel *Huckleberry Finn,* Huck concludes his story by saying that he intends to "light out for the Territory" because Aunt Sally intends to "sivilize" him, and he feels that he can't stand any more efforts to make him an upstanding, moral, and religious citizen. His attitude is understandable, for his experiences in society as it existed along the Mississippi were confining, unpleasant, or downright terrifying.

We discuss introductions again in the next section.

Continue now to the **paragraphs of development.** Paragraphs of development are those you write to support your thesis. In this example, the paragraphs of development would discuss Huck's experiences with the "sivilized" world.

This completes the writing process through the writing of the rough draft.

The Introduction

The introduction should serve two important functions. *First,* and more important, the introduction must catch the interest of the reader. *Second,* it must give the reader an idea of the direction the paper will take. This sense of direction may come from a restating of the thesis statement you developed in Step 3 or from a paraphrase of your thesis statement. On the other hand, you may provide a sense of direction by offering a general identifying statement of the topic.

The Conclusion

Always provide a conclusion for your paper. As a rule, a short sentence of summary or a restatement of the topic will suffice. The function of a conclusion for a short paper is to let the reader know that the paper is complete. Don't leave readers with the impression that they ought to be looking for more material. Don't try to provide an extensive restatement or summary for a short paper. And be careful not to use the conclusion to introduce a new point or add additional information. A one-sentence conclusion is ample for most college essays.

REVISING

Keep in mind the completed version of the paper that comes out of Step 6 is *not*—repeat, *not*—the final version of the paper. Step 6 produces a rough draft, a version suitable for revision and not much else. Think of that draft as a good start, but remember that it is still a long way from completion. Use the remaining steps of the writing process in revising your draft. Wait a day or two (if possible) between completing the draft and undertaking the revision.

Step 7. Assess the Thesis of the Draft

Basic Question:	Is the thesis a proper expression of your knowledge on the subject?
Strategy:	Read each supporting paragraph or section of the essay individually and write a topic sentence for each one. From the topic statements, produce a thesis statement for the draft. Compare it to the original thesis. If the two differ, create a new, better thesis. Omit the introduction from the outline; it does not provide support for the thesis.

Step 8. Assess the Content

Basic Question:	Does each paragraph or section offer genuine support for the thesis?
Strategy:	Check the topic statement for each paragraph or section to be sure each one supports the new thesis. Remove and replace any paragraph or section that does not support the thesis.

Step 9. Assess the Order of Presentation

Basic Question: Does the order of presentation provide the reader with a logical progression or pathway through the essay?

Strategy: Try different orders of presentation, shifting sections around to see if you can find a better order than the one you used for the first finished draft.

Step 10. Assess the Paragraphs

Basic Questions: Is each paragraph unified and complete? Is each paragraph developed following the best possible method of development?

Strategy: Using the topic sentences from the sentence outline, check the content of each paragraph to be sure it develops one idea and only one idea. Check the content to be sure that the paragraph contains enough specific, concrete details to make the topic statement clear to the reader. Evaluate the introduction and conclusion separately as a single unit.

Step 11. Correct the Mistakes in the Draft

Basic Question: What errors in grammar and mechanics do I need to correct?

Strategy: Read each sentence as an independent unit, starting at the end of the paper and working to the beginning. Reading "backward" in this fashion assures that you will not make mental corrections or assumptions as you read.

- Check each sentence for errors in completeness (Lesson 13), subject-verb agreement (Lesson 22), pronoun-antecedent agreement (Lesson 23), pronoun case (Lesson 24), dangling or misplaced modifiers (Lesson 14), and the use of prepositions (Lesson 25). (Note: As you find errors in your papers and as marked errors appear on papers returned to you, keep a record of them—either by putting a check in the appropriate lessons of this book or by marking your reference handbook. You will soon discover whether you tend to repeat certain kinds of errors; simplify your proofreading by checking first for these errors. In a short time, you should be able to eliminate repeat faults from your writing.)
- Check each sentence for errors in punctuation; check for missing punctuation marks *and* for unneeded marks.
- Check for errors in mechanics, capitalization, and spelling.

Step 12. Write the Final Draft

Basic Question: What form shall I use for the final copy of the paper?

Strategy: Follow the guidelines for manuscript preparation specified by your teacher, printing or typing the final copy on plain white paper. Be sure to read the final copy carefully for errors.

Progress Tests

NAME _____ SCORE _____

Directions: Copy the subject of the sentence on the first line at the left and the verb on the second line.

_____ 1. Unfortunately, only a few of the choice seats remain.

_____

_____ 2. Next in line at the parade will be the bagpipe band from Lakeside
_____ High School.

_____ 3. All of this extra exertion has tired me out.

_____

_____ 4. Neither of these two plans seems workable.

_____

_____ 5. To the left of the main gate is a small guardhouse.

_____

_____ 6. Larry, together with three of his friends, spent the day at the
_____ beach.

_____ 7. Her constant expressions of dissatisfaction have not endeared her
_____ to the others in the office.

_____ 8. Here comes my next-door neighbor with her two mangy dogs.

_____

_____ 9. Not one of the three word processors is available at this time.

_____

_____ 10. There will very likely be another meeting of the committee soon.

_____

_____ 11. And there, in the peace and solitude of the mountain village, he
_____ spent the last few years of his life.

_____ 12. I have many times recalled our pleasant visit.

_____

_____ 13. One of our defensive backs intercepted the forward pass on the
_____ four-yard line.

_____ 14. Later in the meeting there will be time for questions for our guest
_____ speaker.

_____ 15. Suddenly from behind the shed appeared a snarling dog.

_____

Directions: Each sentence contains two italicized words. In the spaces at the left, write one of the following numbers to identify the part of speech of each italicized word:

1. Noun   3. Verb   5. Adverb
2. Pronoun   4. Adjective   6. Preposition

_____
_____   1. A *few* of the jewels *mysteriously* disappeared.

_____
_____   2. Only a *few* people were told about the *disappearance*.

_____
_____   3. The purpose of Stonehenge *still* remains a *mystery*.

_____
_____   4. George *sampled* several of the *desserts*.

_____
_____   5. *Several* girls were jogging *across* the meadow.

_____
_____   6. Today is *considerably colder* than yesterday.

_____
_____   7. *Later* he amassed a *considerable* fortune.

_____
_____   8. The *lateness* of the hour *disturbed* Aunt Mattie.

_____
_____   9. The mischievous boys *created* a *disturbance* at the picnic.

_____
_____   10. His most *creative* work was done *during* the last decade of his life.

_____
_____   11. Following my *advice*, the police searched the *nearby* area.

_____
_____   12. *Nearby*, there are three *fairly* good restaurants.

_____
_____   13. Although the test was a *fair* one, it *confused* me.

_____
_____   14. In his state of *confusion*, he walked *through* the wrong door.

_____
_____   15. The honored guest *arrived late* at the party.

_____
_____   16. She apologized for her *late arrival*.

_____
_____   17. The hostess *graciously* accepted the *apology*.

_____
_____   18. *Some* of the noisy clowns *frightened* the children.

_____
_____   19. *Some* changes will be made *before* the end of the semester.

_____
_____   20. *Sometimes* my brother's *changeable* moods upset me greatly.

_____

NAME _____ SCORE _____

Directions: Identify the italicized word in each sentence by writing one of the following abbreviations in the space at the left.

S.C. [subjective complement] I.O. [indirect object]
D.O. [direct object] O.C. [objective complement]

If the italicized word is *not* used as one of these complements, leave the space blank.

_____ 1. The next available time for an appointment will be next *Tuesd*ay.

_____ 2. How many outside readings did Ms. Grant assign the *class*?

_____ 3. How many outside *readings* did Ms. Grant assign the class?

_____ 4. In a short time, Jensen had become the most productive *salesman* in our division.

_____ 5. What *salary* did he offer you?

_____ 6. What salary did he offer *you*?

_____ 7. What *salary* were you offered?

_____ 8. A few passengers were tossing the *youngsters* coins from the ship.

_____ 9. "Feel the soft, silky *fur* on the collar of this jacket," said the saleswoman.

_____ 10. The fur on the collar of the jacket felt very *silky*.

_____ 11. *What* did they name their first child?

_____ 12. What did they name their first *child*?

_____ 13. The losing candidate had promised his *constituents* many favors.

_____ 14. You will find these people most *hospitable.*

_____ 15. Jeremy finally found the missing car *keys*.

_____ 16. The realtor found the *Petersons* a small but comfortable apartment.

_____ 17. *Whom* has the dictator appointed as his successor?

_____ 18. Whom has the dictator appointed as his *successor?*

_____ 19. Ms. Allerton has been named faculty *adviser* of the Drama Club.

_____ 20. You really should have made this path *wider*.

_____ 21. There might be *repercussions* from some of the delegates from African countries.

_____ 22. The usher handed *me* a souvenir program.

_____ 23. The usher handed me a souvenir *program*.

_____ 24. "Here is one of our souvenir *programs*," said the usher.

_____ 25. The two younger children are hopeless video game *addicts*.

_____ 26. Lately the days have been getting unpleasantly *humid*.

_____ 27. Mrs. Smith turned her *head* away from the blinding lights.

_____ 28. The leaves of my begonias have been turning *yellow*.

_____ 29. The heliotrope and related plants turn toward the *sun*.

_____ 30. The waiting period in the doctor's office seemed an *eternity*.

_____ 31. My broker considers *this* an attractive investment.

_____ 32. My broker considers this an attractive *investment*.

_____ 33. David showed *us* a picture of a moray eel.

_____ 34. For once, Professor Wilder was left *speechless*.

_____ 35. The guide pointed out *several* of the most beautiful orchids.

_____ 36. For 30 years, Bascom remained one of my closest *friends*.

_____ 37. When will you be *ready* for our tennis game?

_____ 38. You are surely being *stubborn* about this trivial matter.

_____ 39. Students in the top 10 percent are allowed a *choice* of elective courses.

_____ 40. How *tall* will the new headquarters building be?

NAME _____   SCORE _____

Directions: Each of the following sentences contains one subordinate clause. Use square brackets [ ] to mark the beginning and the end of each subordinate clause. Put parentheses ( ) around the subject, and underline the verb of each subordinate clause. Identify the clause by writing in the space at the left one of the following abbreviations:

Adv. [adverb clause]   Adj. [adjective clause]   N. [noun clause]

_____   1. The local bankers admitted that they could not handle the financing alone.

_____   2. How can you concentrate while that radio is blaring in your ear?

_____   3. The mechanic showed Estelle how the carburetor on that old car should be adjusted.

_____   4. I'd like to sit in the balcony if there are any seats available.

_____   5. Jill asked the usher if there were any seats available in the balcony.

_____   6. Della often writes glowing advertising copy for products for which she has little or no enthusiasm.

_____   7. We are all happy that you have joined our cycling club.

_____   8. Even though we argued for nearly an hour, the sergeant would not give entry passes to our whole group.

_____   9. On tests, the part my sister usually fails is the section on mathematics.

_____   10. The College Commons is a place where students from many countries meet each other.

_____   11. It soon became evident that neither of the two witnesses was reliable.

_____   12. Most of the young people with whom Treadwell worked on the project were high school juniors and seniors.

_____   13. Senator Ramsey always argues vehemently against whatever Senator Wilson proposes.

_____   14. Senator Ramsey always argues vehemently against anything Senator Wilson proposes.

_____   15. The council offered several plans, only two of which the mayor accepted.

_____   16. Experts consider it unlikely that the rebels can hold out much longer.

_____   17. I've heard from Glenn only twice since he moved to Iowa City.

_____   18. Since the auditorium seats only 300, many people were turned away.

_____   19. During the Civil War, Lincoln used powers that had not been authorized by law.

_____   20. A guinea pig, which is actually a type of rat, does not come from Guinea.

Directions: The italicized material in each of these sentences is a subordinate clause. In the first space at the left, write **Adv.**, **Adj.**, or **N.** to identify the clause. Within the italicized clause, the word in boldface type is a complement. Identify it by writing in the second space at the left one of the following:

S.C. [subjective complement]	I.O. [indirect object]
D.O. [direct object]	O.C. [objective complement]

If the word in boldface is not one of the above, leave the space blank.

_____ 1. The teacher told us *that every student must fill out a* **questionnaire**.
_____

_____ 2. The questionnaire asked for information *that the school requires.*
_____

_____ 3. We were not told *why the school requires this* **information**.
_____

_____ 4. Our geography period was cut short *because we filled out the* **questionnaires**.
_____

_____ 5. I'm sure *that the* **questionnaires** *will be put to good use.*
_____

_____ 6. According to Epictetus, you must write *if you would be a good* **writer**.
_____

_____ 7. I often wonder *if I'll ever become a good* **writer**.
_____

_____ 8. Did you seen the announcement *that was in the morning* **bulletin**?
_____

_____ 9. Did you see the announcement *that the afternoon* **assembly** *has been canceled?*
_____

_____ 10. The announcement was *that the afternoon* **assembly** *has been canceled.*
_____

_____ 11. *Were I* **you**, I'd look for a less expensive car.
_____

_____ 12. The earthquake was so severe *that all electric* **power** *in the area failed.*
_____

_____ 13. Do you know *how long Martha has been wearing a* **wig**?
_____

_____ 14. I remember the first time *I saw* **her** *without a wig.*
_____

_____ 15. She bought her first wig *when she lived in* **Dallas**.
_____

_____ 16. There was once a time *when all wealthy gentlemen wore* **wigs**.
_____

_____ 17. My roommate's monthly allowance is much larger *than* **mine** *is.*
_____

_____ 18. Is it possible *that someone else might have picked up your* **notebook**?
_____

_____ 19. One of our real worries now is *that Lake Elkins is becoming dangerously* **polluted**.
_____

_____ 20. At 10 o'clock, I usually have coffee with the man *whose office is* **next** *to mine.*
_____

Progress Test 4

Verbal Phrases (Lessons 11, 12)

NAME _____ SCORE _____

Directions: Each sentence contains one verbal phrase. Put brackets around the phrase, and, in the space at the left, write one of the following letters to identify the type of phrase:

G. [gerund phrase]   P. [participial phrase]

I. [infinitive phrase]   A. [absolute phrase]

_____ 1. Four days later, Enos returned the hacksaw without saying a word about the delay.

_____ 2. Right after lunch, I rushed home to pick up some needed class notes.

_____ 3. Successfully bunting down the third-base line, Caldwell put Lam in scoring position.

_____ 4. Elaine wanted Dean Alstock to approve her petition.

_____ 5. The storm having blown over, we resumed our ball game.

_____ 6. Darlene seemed almost insulted when her father suggested getting to the campus on a city bus.

_____ 7. The officers found the package of counterfeit bills hidden in the false bottom of a trunk.

_____ 8. Do you suppose they wanted us to leave early?

_____ 9. Here is a copy of the newspaper article describing your uncle's heroic act.

_____ 10. The engineers having repaired the bridge, our squad crossed over to the abandoned city.

_____ 11. A proposal calling for a new access road to the airport is being studied by city planners.

_____ 12. The children soon became bored with weeding their backyard vegetable garden.

_____ 13. Several witnesses reported overhearing the conversation between the two suspects.

_____ 14. Won't someone show me how to tie this knot?

_____ 15. He took as his model Cornelius Atterbury, called by some the Genghis Khan of Wall Street.

_____ 16. Beth's parents stayed overnight in a nearby motel, her apartment having only one bedroom.

_____ 17. Several members of the club heard Major Simms call Mr. Todd a liar.

_____ 18. Not having heard the chairman's remark, I was surprised by the laughter.

_____ 19. "I believe that increasing my allowance would improve my disposition," Jimmy told his parents.

_____ 20. It would not be convenient for me to attend a meeting tomorrow.

Directions: Each of the italicized words in the following sentences is used as a complement within a verbal phrase. In the first space at the left, identify the type of phrase by writing one of the following letters:

      G. [gerund phrase]   P. [participial phrase]

      I. [infinitive phrase]   A. [absolute phrase]

In the second space write one of the abbreviations to identify the complement:

      1. S.C. [subjective complement]   3. I.O. [indirect object]

      2. D.O. [direct object]   4. O.C. [objective complement]

_____   1. One of the clerks in the office recalled overhearing the telephone
_____   *conversation.*

_____   2. That being the *case*, we must find ways to get rid of the deficit.
_____

_____   3. Laying aside her *needlepoint*, Lydia turned on her favorite TV program.
_____

_____   4. It might be good strategy to make *them* a slightly higher offer for the property.
_____

_____   5. How many *cookies* did your Girl Scout troop manage to sell?
_____

_____   6. Thinking Carl's remark an idle *boast*, the teacher did not answer.
_____

_____   7. The lawyer could not locate the bill of sale, the original owner having left
_____   the *city.*

_____   8. Feeling *full* of self-pity, Sylvia sought comfort with some frozen yogurt.
_____

_____   9. Having given the *reporters* his version of the affair, Jim made a dash for his
_____   waiting taxicab.

_____   10. What *kind* of bribe did he offer to pay you?
_____

_____   11. I felt sorry for Jennifer when I saw her face turn *red* with embarrassment.
_____

_____   12. The lawyer's questions succeeded only in making the witness more
_____   *uncommunicative.*

_____   13. Having paid the part-time *workers* their wages, Marge walked slowly back
_____   to her truck.

_____   14. Did anyone actually hear the defendant threaten the *officer?*
_____

_____   15. Dan surprised us by remaining *silent* during the question period following
_____   the lecture.

NAME _____   SCORE _____

Directions: If a sentence is correct, write **C** in the space at the left. If you find a dangling modifier, underline it and write **W** in the space.

_____ 1. The water from those wells should not be drunk without boiling it.

_____ 2. The water from those wells should not be drunk without being boiled.

_____ 3. Having grown up in the Midwest, the lack of definite seasons here in the Southwest bothered me at first.

_____ 4. Looking out the window, I saw an unusual sight.

_____ 5. An unusual sight caught my eye while looking out the window.

_____ 6. The ceiling fan I assembled at home never worked properly in spite of following the directions explicitly.

_____ 7. While living in London shortly after the war, there was too much dampness and fog.

_____ 8. Meeting Bob after class, we arranged a tennis match.

_____ 9. Meeting Bob after class, I arranged a tennis match with him.

_____ 10. Meeting Bob after class, he suggested a tennis match.

_____ 11. Having recently returned from Hawaii, the Camera Club asked me to show my photographs.

_____ 12. Upon returning from Hawaii, I was asked by the Camera Club to show my photographs.

_____ 13. Frantically trying to start the outboard motor, the cord broke in two.

_____ 14. Today's agenda is already full enough without having to listen to the reading of the minutes of the last meeting.

_____ 15. We have a full enough agenda for today's meeting without having to listen to the reading of the minutes of the last meeting.

_____ 16. Walking back to the hotel at dawn, the air was soft and fresh.

_____ 17. As we walked back to the hotel at dawn, the air was soft and fresh.

_____ 18. While dressing for my son's commencement exercises, the phone rang.

_____ 19. While I was still a child, Father moved the family to Texas.

_____ 20. While still a child, Father moved the family to Texas.

Directions: Rewrite each of the following sentences twice:
    a. Change the dangler to a complete clause with subject and verb.
    b. Begin the main clause with a word that the dangler can logically modify.

1. By using a top-grade oil, the life of your car's engine can be extended.
    a. _____

    b. _____

2. Having been hastily proofread, there were several errors in my book report.
    a. _____

    b. _____

3. To ensure a trouble-free trip, maps of the region should be studied beforehand.
    a. _____

    b. _____

4. Graciously bowing in response to the applause, Julie's feet slipped on the polished platform and she fell down.
    a. _____

    b. _____

5. Upon totaling the receipts, a shortage of 42 dollars puzzled us.
    a. _____

    b. _____

NAME _____ SCORE _____

Directions: Study these paired sentences. One contains incompleteness, misplaced modifiers, faulty parallelism, and faulty comparisons; the other does not. In the space at the left, write the letter that identifies the sentence that is correct.

_____ 1. a. We learned that here in this desert community the sun shines 318 days a year from a Chamber of Commerce brochure.
 b. From a Chamber of Commerce brochure, we learned that here in this desert community the sun shines 318 days a year.

_____ 2. a. The fog being so thick at times that I could hardly see my hand in front of my face.
 b. The fog was so thick at times that I could hardly see my hand in front of my face.

_____ 3. a. You must remember that not all college students are interested in competitive sports.
 b. You must remember that all college students are not interested in competitive sports.

_____ 4. a. The accused man's nephew made statements about him that were not only malicious but also false.
 b. The accused man's nephew made statements about him that not only were malicious but also false.

_____ 5. a. The people living in Broadacre Estates are, I suspect, not much different from any middle-class suburb.
 b. The people living in Broadacre Estates are, I suspect, not much different from those in any other middle-class suburb.

_____ 6. a. "I don't know which is worst," said Ms. Lambert, "getting onto a crowded turnpike or or getting off one."
 b. "I don't know which is worse," said Ms. Lambert, "getting onto a crowded turnpike or getting off one."

_____ 7. a. On the first day of the term, we listed the activities that the students said they would be interested in doing on the blackboard.
 b. On the first day of the term, we listed on the blackboard the activities that the students said they would be interested in doing.

_____ 8 a. You should wear these sunglasses to protect yourself from the glare of the sun and also to look chic.
 b. You should wear these sunglasses for protection against the glare of the sun and also to look chic.

_____ 9. a. Jake thinks that the bear he saw yesterday is one of the largest, if not the largest bear, he's ever seen.
　　　　 b. Jake thinks that the bear he saw yesterday is one of the largest bears, if not the largest bear, he's ever seen.

_____ 10. a. You should be reminded again that opportunity only knocks once.
　　　　 b. You should be reminded again that opportunity knocks only once.

_____ 11. a. Marilyn is searching for the best way to properly and adequately repay her hosts.
　　　　 b. Marilyn is searching for the best way to repay her hosts properly and adequately.

_____ 12. a. I hope that my score on the test will be as high as, if not higher than, my older brother's.
　　　　 b. I hope that my score on the test will be as high, if not higher than, my older brother.

_____ 13. a. "Either you turn in your paper when it's due or have the grade lowered one letter," Dr. Pepper announced.
　　　　 b. "You either turn in your paper when it's due or have the grade lowered one letter," Dr. Pepper announced.

_____ 14. a. Lloyd maintains that his older sister talks more and says less than anyone else in the family.
　　　　 b. Lloyd maintains that his older sister talks more and says less than anyone in the family.

_____ 15. a. People who worked with asbestos are often subject to various kinds of lung afflictions.
　　　　 b. People who worked with asbestos often are subject to various kinds of lung afflictions.

_____ 16. a. A final examination so long and difficult that, from the comments I heard, no one in the class finished it.
　　　　 b. It was a final examination so long and difficult that, from the comments I heard, no one in the class finished it.

_____ 17. a. The broker predicts that the yield from these tax-free bonds will be as high as the yield from our stocks, if not higher.
　　　　 b. The broker predicts that the yield from these tax-free bonds will be as high, if not higher, than our stocks.

_____ 18. a. By bedtime I had read nearly 80 pages of the novel.
　　　　 b. By bedtime I had nearly read 80 pages of the novel.

_____ 19. a. Barbara took a part-time job to augment the family income and also because she was bored with housework.
　　　　 b. Barbara took a part-time job because she wanted to augment the family income and also because she was bored with housework.

_____ 20. a. Which has the largest population, Seoul or Mexico City?
　　　　 b. Which has the larger population, Seoul or Mexico City?

NAME _____ SCORE _____

Directions: Change the italicized sentence to the form indicated in the parentheses and write the two sentences as one sentence.

1. *The critics were unimpressed.* The play closed after four performances. (adverb clause of reason) _____
   _____

2. *The critics were unimpressed.* The play closed after four performances. (absolute phrase)
   _____
   _____

3. *The critics were unimpressed.* The play continued its run. (adverb clause of concession)
   _____
   _____

4. *Soak the codfish several times in cold water.* This will remove the excess salt. (gerund phrase)
   _____
   _____

5. *Soak the codfish several times in cold water.* This will remove the excess salt. (adverbial clause of condition)_____
   _____

6. *I finished the kitchen chores.* I turned on the TV to watch the ball game. (preposition plus gerund phrase) _____
   _____

7. *I turned on the TV to watch the ball game.* I had finished the kitchen chores. (participal phrase)
   _____
   _____

8. *The kitchen chores were finished.* I turned on the TV to watch the ball game. (absolute phrase)
   _____
   _____

9. The lawyer showed the letter to Dr. Ethel Lange. *She is a handwriting expert.* (adjective clause)
   _____
   _____

10. The lawyer showed the letter to Dr. Ethel Lange. *She is a handwriting expert.* (appositive)
    _____
    _____

Directions: Rewrite each of the following numbered sections as one complex sentence. In each case, use the italicized subject and verb for the main clause. Use a variety of the subordinating units listed on the first page of Lesson 15.

1. I painted the fence for nearly four hours. Then *I lay* in the hammock for a short time. I wanted to rest and cool off. _____

   _____

2. Our funds were limited. *We were forced* to make a choice. We could buy one small used car. Or we could buy two bicycles. _____

   _____

3. Carol had driven a car for nearly 60 years and never had an accident, but her eyesight is failing, and so *she has sold* her car. _____

   _____

4. He has two hobbies. One is hang-gliding. The other is guitar playing. *Freddie expends* most of his time and energies on these. _____

   _____

5. Jake's old *motorcycle* cost him only 200 dollars. He bought it five years ago. It still *serves* his needs well. _____

   _____

6. Greg's *parents were* once *interested* in horses. They raised them to show. That was several years ago. Greg was still in high school. _____

   _____

7. *Peg* borrowed my dictionary and she found several misspelled words in her theme and so she *made* a new and corrected copy. _____

   _____

8. I received an announcement today. *I was* happy to receive it. It informed me that Jim would soon get his MBA degree. Jim is my nephew. _____

   _____

9. There are many students like Ross. They resist learning in high school. Later they find the incentive to succeed. Every teacher *knows this*. _____

   _____

10. The *whippet* is a hunting dog. It hunts by sight rather than by smell. It *is* a combination of several breeds. Among these breeds are the terrier, the English greyhound, and the Italian greyhound. _____

    _____

NAME _____ SCORE _____

Directions: In each sentence, a **V** marks a point of coordination between (1) two verbs with a coordinating conjunction, (2) two independent clauses with a coordinating conjunction, or (3) two independent clauses without a coordinating conjunction. In the space at the left, write one of the following:

    0 (no punctuation is needed)

    C (a comma is needed)

    S (a semicolon is needed)

_____ 1. Ben toyed with the idea of applying for another credit card *V* but finally decided that three were enough.

_____ 2. The clerk listened patiently to my story *V* but he refused to summon the manager.

_____ 3. The clerk listened patiently to my story *V* he refused, however, to summon the manager.

_____ 4. The clerk listened patiently to my story *V* but refused to summon the manager.

_____ 5. A large air terminal is always an interesting place *V* during a time of minor crisis, it is a fascinating place.

_____ 6. As the professor had hinted, the textbook was indeed weighty *V* for it contained articles by more than 30 authors.

_____ 7. Mr. Stewart, please get Jean Barker on the phone *V* tell her that I'll be a few minutes late for our meeting.

_____ 8. Mr. Stewart, please get Joan Barker on the phone *V* and tell her that I'll be a few minutes late for our meeting.

_____ 9. As our group left the theater, a fire truck raced past us *V* and two police cars with sirens screaming followed it.

_____ 10. One of the assistant coaches usually conducts the interview *V* however, this time the head coach himself presided.

_____ 11. One of the assistant coaches usually conducts the interview *V* but this time the head coach himself presided.

_____ 12. One of the assistant coaches usually conducts the interview *V* but this time asked the head coach to preside.

_____ 13. Two of the firemen were overcome by smoke *V* and were taken to the Caldwell Street Hospital.

_____ 14. Some of the attempts to transplant foreign birds failed *V* but others succeeded beyond all hopes.

_____ 15. This small country has attracted the interest of foreign investors *V* for it has vast undeveloped mineral resources.

_____ 16. There followed a period of anxious concern *V* for nearly a week the expedition lost radio contact with the base camp.

_____ 17. The inspectors found structural flaws in three of the cranes *V* and rejected them.

_____ 18. Usually we require a 5 percent down payment *V* but we will change our rule in this special case.

_____ 19. Usually we require a 5 percent down payment *V* but will change our rule in this special case.

_____ 20. Usually we require a 5 percent down payment *V* in this special case, however, we will change our rule.

_____ 21. A headline on the front page of the paper caught my eye *V* it concerned a stray dog marooned on an ice floe in the river.

_____ 22. You must send us the delinquent payments before March 15 *V* otherwise you will hear from our lawyers.

_____ 23. Send us the delinquent payments before March 15 *V* or prepare to deal with our lawyers.

_____ 24. The popularity of basketball is unlimited *V* it is played summer or winter, indoors or outdoors.

_____ 25. "George, please drive slower," said Aunt Millie from the rear seat *V* "these wet roads make me nervous."

_____ 26. The floor manager would not exchange the merchandise *V* nor would he refund the original cost.

_____ 27. "I will not exchange the merchandise," said the floor manager *V* "moreover, I will not refund the original cost."

_____ 28. The floor manager would neither exchange the merchandise *V* nor refund the original cost.

_____ 29. The mayor and his party hesitated before mounting the hastily built platform *V* for the two-by-four supports looked unstable.

_____ 30. "It's lucky for you that you stopped by today," said the salesperson *V* "this sale ends tomorrow, you know."

NAME _____ SCORE _____

Directions: The following sentences contain 50 numbered spots that indicate punctuation problems. (The number is beneath the word when the problem involves the use of an apostrophe in that word, between words for all other problems.) In the correspondingly numbered spaces at the left, write **C** if the punctuation is correct, **W** if it is incorrect.

1. _____ (1) "I had a job three year's ago." said Brent, "that paid well, took little
                                             1

2. _____   of my time, and was interesting."
                               2

3. _____ (2) We were conducted around the island by a talkative, excitable guide,
                                                                      3   4

4. _____   he said we were the only customers he'd had all week.

5. _____ (3) The passenger pigeon whose extinction is known to most of us, serves
                                                     5

6. _____   as a warning that America must protect its birds.
                                                                 6

7. _____ (4) Coleridge's first volume was published in 1796, it preceded Keats' first
                                                                      7   8

8. _____   publication by twenty years.

9. _____ (5) "Miss. Abernathy knows more about this business than any of the
                        9

10. _____   high-salaried administrators," said the foreman.
                              10

11. _____ (6) Joanna, feeling slightly self-conscious in her new, party dress, had
                                                                          11

12. _____   absent-mindedly picked up someone elses purse.
                                                            12

13. _____ (7) Among the great English elegies are: Tennyson's *In Memoriam*,
                                                                     13

14. _____   Arnold's *Thyrsis,* and Milton's *Lycidas.*
                              14

15. _____ (8) Many adults now wonder if some of the values they were taught as

16. _____   youngsters should still be questioned?
                              15   16

17. _____ (9) Thousands of feet below the plane's shadow could be seen skimming
                                                          17

18. _____   over the brown, monotonous wasteland.
                                    18

19. _____ (10) My neighbor Mr. Allison, is now delivering the morning paper; his son
                                    19   20

20. _____   having broken his leg while skiing.

21. _____ (11) What's happening to this quiet friendly village of our's? asked
                                                          21   22

22. _____   Mr. Atwood.

365

23. _____ (12) The next test will cover the following materials: the class lectures
23

24. _____   to date and Chapters 4, 5, 6, and 7.
24

25. _____ (13) "Theres more to this case than meets the eye," said Stan; "we now
25   26

26. _____   realize that we should have called the police."

27. _____ (14) Trying to help the workmen, little Michael picked up some stones,
27   28

28. _____   and threw them in the cement mixer.

29. _____ (15) We first learned about the conflict on November 17, I remember that
29

30. _____   it was a dark, gloomy, day.
30

31. _____ (16) After Sue had finished mopping the children raced through the
31

32. _____   kitchen; their feet covered with wet grass clippings.
32

33. _____ (17) In Cooper's novels of Indians and woodsmen, his females, as he calls

34. _____   them, are unreal, two-dimensional characters.
33   34

35. _____ (18) "Let's not play with the rake, children," said the nurse, "you might
35

36. _____   trip over it, and hurt yourself."
36

37. _____ (19) "Have you noticed," asked Pat, "that some department store clerk's
37

38. _____   mispronounce 'accessories'?"
38

39. _____ (20) The judges, I'm convinced, showed favoritism toward Ms. Stark,
39

40. _____   whose entry showed less creativity than your's.
40

41. _____ (21) Instead of the anticipated twenty or thirty eight people remained after
41

42. _____   Dr. Jones' lecture to ask questions.
42

43. _____ (22) "Quite a bit of it is going around," said Dr. Allen, "take aspirin, and get
43   44

44. _____   plenty of rest."

45. _____ (23) "Here it is past noon, and no one's started to fix the childrens' lunches,"
45   46

46. _____   said Mother.

47. _____ (24) The judge, a fatherly, Irish, gentleman, assured Mother and me that we
47   48

48. _____   were free to leave.

49. _____ (25) "I wonder why I feel uneasy when I walk under a ladder or see a
49

50. _____   black cat cross my path?" said Jenny.
50

NAME _____ SCORE _____

Directions: The following sentences contain fifty numbered spots between words or beneath words. (The number is beneath the word when the punctuation problem involves the use of an apostrophe in that word.) In the correspondingly numbered spaces at the left, write **C** if the punctuation is correct or **W** if it is incorrect.

1. _____   (1)   "Lets have lunch at the Oak Tree," suggested Mark as we left Howell

                           1

2. _____   Hall where our last class had met.

               2

3. _____   (2)   Located ten miles offshore, its pipeline stretching across the ocean

                           3

4. _____   floor; this platform will house 50 technicians.

               4

5. _____   (3)   Many kinds of flowers grow well in this warm, humid climate,

                               5   6

6. _____   everywhere one sees hibiscus, oleander, and orchids.

7. _____   (4)   "I became uneasy," said Lew, "when the officer stopped us, and said,

                                                 7

8. _____   'Where there is smoke there is usually fire.'"

                                  8

9. _____   (5)   The calm, friendly garage attendant assured us, that we would have

                        9   10

10. _____   no problems on the detour.

11. _____   (6)   As we were leaving my uncle seemed strangely quiet, and I asked

12. _____   him if he was worried about something?

                                  12

13. _____   (7)   Yesterday we awoke to find the ground covered with wet heavy snow

                                       13   14

14. _____   and today's paper predicts more of the same.

15. _____   (8)   In the opinion of some elementary school teachers are the most

                                15

16. _____   influential in determining children's attitudes toward learning.

                                       16

17. _____   (9)   On a cold foggy night—it was January 9, 2001 if I remember

                                         17

18. _____   correctly—we left Regina for Arizona.

              18

19. _____ (10)   Don Kearns a senior in engineering, is finishing his course, he plans

                           19   20

20. _____   to do graduate work at Purdue next year.

21. _____ (11)   "Which one of the Roosevelt's was it," asked Andy, "who said,

                          21

22. _____   'Speak softly and carry a big stick'?"

                     22

23. _____ (12) Someone else's car is parked where our's should be.
       23   24

24. _____ (13) He concluded his speech as follows: "I won't make one more
                                25

25. _____   concession, and that ends the matter."
                   26

26. _____ (14) It was 4 o'clock of a warm, lazy afternoon, not one of us moved nor
                              27   28

27. _____   had any desire to move.

28. _____ (15) "I have never understood," said Dr. Tate, "why women so often weep
                              29

29. _____   at weddings?"
                   30

30. _____ (16) Long lines of tired, impatient freshmen stood in Perry Hall which
                              31   32

31. _____   houses the registrar's office.

32. _____ (17) "The attendance clerk wasn't impressed by my excuse and I doubt
                                             33

33. _____   that she'll find your's convincing," said Amy.
                   34

34. _____ (18) The muscular, young man gallantly picked up the child, and carried her
                              35   36

35. _____   across the muddy road.

36. _____ (19) Someone—probably one of the children—had left a wet, muddy towel
                          37   38

37. _____   on the dining room table.

38. _____ (20) After lunch Ted put a prime coat of paint on the new steps and his wife
                              39   40

39. _____   sandpapered the the railing.

40. _____ (21) Once again the ceremony was held in the outdoor theater but this time
                                                       41

41. _____   the weather was damp, cold, and disagreeable.
                   42

42. _____ (22) I wonder why Wyman, the regular center fielder, isn't in today's
                                                       43

43. _____   lineup?
                   44

44. _____ (23) Since I couldn't leave work early enough to get to the committee meeting

45. _____   on time; Miss. Steel took notes for me.
                   45   46

46. _____ (24) If it's after midnight when you return to the apartment the garage door
                      47   48

47. _____   will be locked.

48. _____ (25) "Your argument is absolutely invalid, it is nothing but name-calling,"
                              49

49. _____   answered the irate sergeant!
                   50

50. _____

NAME _____ SCORE _____

Directions: In the space at the left, write the number of the correct form given in parentheses.

_____ 1. Our political leaders should have (1. knew 2. known) that the damage done

_____ to land and water (1. is 2. are) almost irreparable.

_____ 2. As of this date, neither of the two candidates (1. has 2. have) (1. written 2.

_____ wrote) an acceptable speech.

_____ 3. The judge (1. raised 2. rose) from his bench and said, "The disposition of

_____ the charges (1. awaits 2. await) the recommendations of the committee."

_____ 4. Although discussions of the matter have (1. began 2. begun), the price of the

_____ new flights (1. has 2. have) not been determined.

_____ 5. (1. Here's 2. Here are) a few good secondhand parkas that have been

_____ (1. wore 2. worn) only a few times.

_____ 6. After finishing the floor polishing, Ned (1. lay 2. laid) down and said, "I intend

_____ to (1. lie 2. lay) here all afternoon."

_____ 7. "I (1. been 2. have been) fishing this lake for years and have never (1. caught

_____ 2. catched) my limit of bass," the old man said.

_____ 8. Not a single one of the valuable old coins that were (1. stole 2. stolen) from

_____ the museum (1. has 2. have) been recovered.

_____ 9. "The fact that you (1. lent 2. lended) us the start-up money (1. doesn't 2. don't)

_____ give you legal right to the patent," answered Mr. Thiel's lawyer.

_____ 10. Only one of the four Peterson children (1. has 2. have) (1. chose 2. chosen)

_____ to go to college.

_____ 11. It sometimes happens that my athletic neighbor, along with his four sons,

_____ (1. starts 2. start) a noisy game of touch football just as I (1. lie 2. lay) down

for a nap.

_____ 12. The sun has (1. shone 2. shined) every day for three weeks; not a drop of

_____ rain has (1. fell 2. fallen).

_____ 13. Yesterday I (1. paid 2. payed) Sissy for a tankful of gas because she

_____ (1. been 2. has been) giving me free rides to the campus.

_____ 14. As we were leaving the theater, a strange-looking man (1. came 2. come) up
_____ to us and said, "(1. Here's 2. Here are) some copies of my latest poems."

_____ 15. Placed about the lobby (1. is 2. are) soft lounge chairs and sofas so that
_____ guests may (1. set 2. sit) and relax.

_____ 16. Buford finished his coffee, left a large tip, and then (1. says 2. said) to the
_____ waiter, "That's the best meal I've (1. ate 2. eaten) since I left New Orleans."

_____ 17. The trust fund has (1. grew 2. grown) so that now an annual income of over
_____ $10,000 (1. is 2. are) available.

_____ 18. "Mr. Booth, the fact that not one of your algebra problems (1. was 2. were)
_____ solved correctly (1. doesn't 2. don't) seem to bother you unduly," said
Professor Elton.

_____ 19. Neither of the two elderly men (1. has 2. have) ever (1. flew 2. flown) in
_____ an airplane.

_____ 20. "I've (1. drove 2. driven) this old truck now for 16 hours," said Tom,
_____ "and several times I've nearly (1. fell 2. fallen) asleep at the wheel."

_____ 21. Every year the number of women who have (1. run 2. ran) in a major marathon
_____ race (1. has 2. have) increased.

_____ 22. After the guide (1. swam 2. swum) across the river, the water (1. rose 2. raised)
_____ and flooded the campsite.

_____ 23. Freddy removed his snow-covered boots and then (1. says 2. said) to no one
_____ in particular, "What a blizzard! I'm nearly (1. froze 2. frozen)."

_____ 24. As Martha was (1. lying 2. laying) on the sofa, the doorbell (1. rang 2. rung),
_____ announcing the arrival of guests.

_____ 25. After being (1. swore 2. sworn) in, the witness said that never in his life had
_____ he ever (1. saw 2. seen) the accused man.

_____ 26. Our old dog has been (1. lying 2. laying) all day in the driveway—not a very
_____ safe place for him to (1. lie 2. lay).

_____ 27. Sheriff Mason (1. began 2. begun) the activities by announcing, "Remaining
_____ to be sold in today's auction (1. is 2. are) a two-ton truck and two jeeps."

_____ 28. Mr. and Mrs. Samson have lived across the street from Verna for four months,
_____ but neither one of them (1. has 2. have) ever (1. spoke 2. spoken) a word
to her.

_____ 29. Carlson has (1. threw 2. thrown) two successful passes, but there (1. is 2. are
_____ still 12 yards to go for a first down.

_____ 30. The court hearing could have been set for next week if you had (1. written
2. wrote) or (1. spoke 2. spoken) to me earlier.

NAME _____ SCORE _____

Directions: Study the following sentences for poorly used pronouns. One sentence in each pair contains wrong case forms, misspelled possessives, or vague or inexact references. Circle each incorrect pronoun. In the space at the left, write the letter that identifies the correct sentence.

_____ 1. a. The colors of the autumn foliage were so glorious that the sight left my wife and me nearly speechless.
         b. The colors of the autumn foliage were so glorious that it left my wife and I nearly speechless.

_____ 2. a. If it wasn't him who borrowed your car, whom do you think it could have been?
         b. If it wasn't he who borrowed your car, who do you think it could have been?

_____ 3. a. A foreman told Fritz that he'd be lucky if he finished the job before quitting time.
         b. The foreman told Fritz, "I'll be lucky if I finish the job before quitting time."

_____ 4. a. Yesterday's *Journal* reported that the Peerless Bakery will move into its new quarters next month.
         b. It said in yesterday's *Journal* that the Peerless Bakery will move into their new quarters next month.

_____ 5. a. "When your dad and I were in high school," said Mother, "they never allowed you to question a teacher's authority."
         b. "When your dad and I were in high school," said Mother, "students were not allowed to question a teacher's authority."

_____ 6. a. My car has developed an alarming crack in it's windshield; we'll have to go to the game in your's.
         b. My car has developed an alarming crack in its windshield; we'll have to go to the game in yours.

_____ 7. a. A car bearing an Illinois license slowed down near the accident, but apparently the driver decided that he didn't want to get involved.
         b. A car bearing an Illinois license slowed down near the accident, but apparently he decided that he didn't want to get involved.

_____ 8. a. Every fellow in the dorm except Bert and I will spend the holiday at home with their family.
         b. Every fellow in the dorm except Bert and me will spend the holiday at home with his family.

_____ 9. a. All of we committee members will welcome whomever can volunteer a few hours of their time each week.
         b. All of us committee members will welcome whoever can volunteer a few hours of his or her time each week.

_____ 10. a. The reason I want to become an airline pilot is that the work gives one a chance to travel widely.
           b. The reason I want to become an airline pilot is that it gives you a chance to travel widely.

_____ 11. a. Some of us who know Cramdon well are amazed at his being invited to join the Junior Club.
           b. Some of us who know Cramdon well are amazed at him being invited to join the Junior Club.

_____ 12. a. If a visitor stays exclusively at a luxury beach hotel, this won't show you how the natives really live.
           b. Staying exclusively at a luxury beach hotel will not show a visitor how the natives really live.

_____ 13. a. Our plane was 50 minutes late leaving Milan, but by the time we reached Florence he had made up most of it.
           b. Our plane was 50 minutes late leaving Milan, but by the time we reached Florence the pilot had made up most of the lost time.

_____ 14. a. All freshmen must pass their physical examinations before attending their first class.
           b. Every freshman must pass his or her physical examination before attending his or her first class.

_____ 15. a. Ms. Willis, the landlady, told my roommate and me that she was unhappy about our moving out of town.
           b. Ms. Willis, the landlady, told my roommate and I that she was unhappy about us moving out of town.

_____ 16. a. Tell any friend of your's whom you think might apply for the job to be sure to type their application letter.
           b. Tell any friend of yours who you think might apply for the job to be sure to type his application letter.

_____ 17. a. Because Mother is a talented painter, she tried to get my sister and I interested in it.
           b. Because Mother is a talented painter, she tried to get my sister and me interested in painting.

_____ 18. a. I'm not surprised that whoever drew that outrageous caricature of Professor Lucas didn't sign his or her name to it.
           b. I'm not surprised that whomever drew that outrageous caricature of Professor Lucas didn't sign their name to it.

_____ 19. a. "Let's just assume that the responsibility for this mixup is someone elses, not our's," said Matt.
           b. "Let's just assume that the responsibility for this mixup is someone else's, not ours," said Matt.

_____ 20. a. We endured another long interview, and then Wally and I were told to come back in two weeks.
           b. We endured another long interview, and then they told Wally and I to come back in two weeks.

NAME _____ SCORE _____

Directions: In the space at the left, write the number of the correct form given in parentheses.

_____ 1. After we replaced the spark plugs, the motor ran (1. real 2. very) (1. smooth
_____   2. smoothly).

_____ 2. (1. Lots of 2. Many) of the high school boys seem to be having their hair cut
_____   (1. shorter 2. more shorter) this season.

_____ 3. "I maintain that the (1. older 2. oldest) of the two boys is always (1. suppose
_____   to 2. supposed to) protect his baby brother," said Father.

_____ 4. "You can't buy better vegetables than these (1. anywhere 2. anywheres) in
_____   town, not vegetables priced (1. reasonable 2. reasonably)," she announced
              vehemently.

_____ 5. The boys deserve a bonus, (1. being as how 2. because) they have worked
_____   (1. steady 2. steadily) for ten hours.

_____ 6. After this day full of wholesome outdoor activities, the children (1. ought
_____   2. had ought) to sleep (1. good 2. well) tonight.

_____ 7. The driving instructor boasts that (1. almost 2. most) all of his students do
_____   (1. good 2. well) on the written test.

_____ 8. Sedgewick, the (1. better 2. best) passer of our two quarterbacks, was injured
_____   quite (1. bad 2. badly) early in the second quarter.

_____ 9. Bert looks (1. healthy 2. healthful) because he follows a (1. healthy
_____   2. healthful) regimen of regular exercise and sensible eating.

_____ 10. In his reply to the reporter's question, the senator (1. implied 2. inferred)
_____   that he feels (1. bad 2. badly) about the results of the election.

_____ 11. Had I been driving, we (1. could have 2. could of) made the trip to Alabama
_____   (1. easy 2. easily) in four hours.

_____ 12. The reason Phil did not attend the celebration is (1. because 2. that) he was
_____   (1. awful 2. very) tired after the track meet.

373

_____ 13. "I have no doubt (1. but what 2. that) this year's team will be (1. considerable
_____   2. considerably) better than last year's team," said Coach Watkins.

_____ 14. Allan has been training hard; it now looks (1. as if 2. like) he has a
_____   (1. reasonable 2. reasonably) good chance of setting a new pole vault record.

_____ 15. "(1. Where 2. Where at) did you buy (1. them 2. those) spectacular earrings?"
_____   Josie asked her boyfriend.

_____ 16. "The VCR should sound (1. different 2. differently) now, because yesterday
_____   I cleaned the heads (1. good 2. well)," said Mrs. Easton.

_____ 17. The food at our dormitory is (1. not all that 2. not very) tempting, but some
_____   of us think that lately it has been improving (1. some 2. somewhat).

_____ 18. (1. Because of 2. Due to) the improved bus service, I can now get to the
_____   campus (1. earlier 2. more earlier) than I could last semester.

_____ 19. "I (1. can hardly 2. can't hardly) believe that I did (1. good 2. well) enough
_____   on that test to get a passing grade," moaned Jeff.

_____ 20. It was a long (1. way 2. ways) to the next rest stop, and the hikers were
_____   (1. sure 2. surely) exhausted when they arrived.

_____ 21. "When I was young I (1. use to 2. used to) (1. believe 2. figure) that I was
_____   put on this earth to become an international tennis star," Beth admitted.

_____ 22. "(1. Let's 2. Let's us) see if the two of us can move (1. that 2. that there)
_____   fallen tree limb from the sidewalk," said Jake's neighbor.

_____ 23. (1. In regard 2. In regards) to your late uncle's property, I can now report
_____   that the will divides it (1. between 2. among) you five nieces and nephews.

_____ 24. "We could finish this tiresome chore (1. faster 2. more faster) if we would
_____   all (1. try and 2. try to) help one another," said the troop leader.

_____ 25. Several others in the office (1. besides 2. beside) me (1. suspect 2. suspicion)
_____   that Edward wants to get the receptionist fired.

NAME _____ SCORE _____

Directions: Each sentence has two italicized words or expressions. If you think that a word or expression is inappropriate in serious writing, write a correct form in the space at the left. If a word or expression is correct, write **C** in the space.

_____ 1. If the coach or one of his assistants *don't* show up for the interview,
_____   the reporters will be *plenty* upset.

_____ 2. *There's* five or six good accountants in town *who* I can recommend
_____   to you wholeheartedly.

_____ 3. I'm proud to report that every one of *us* workers in the shipping
_____   department has already paid *their* share for the upcoming Christmas
                         party.

_____ 4. "*Somewheres* in this big city there must be someone *whose* as
_____   desperate for companionship as I am," said Charlie dramatically.

_____ 5. An elderly woman stopped near the park bench and said to Ellen,
_____   "Do you mind if I *set* here *besides* you?"

_____ 6. Florence told Jenny and *me* that for skiers, a wardrobe containing
_____   ski pants, boots, sweaters, scarves, gloves, and wraparound sun
                         glasses *is* indispensable.

_____ 7. On the trip some of us got *awful* cold because the car heater wasn't
_____   working *good.*

_____ 8. The number of students already waiting in the long line *was*
_____   enough to discourage *we* latecomers.

_____ 9. "If anyone ever gives me an *invite* to go rock climbing again,"
_____   said Pete, "I'll tell *them* I'm too busy."

_____ 10. *Irregardless* of your warning, I intend to go ahead with this
_____   investment just *like* I had planned.

_____ 11. Our parents had given each of *us* three children a musical instrument,
_____   but none of us could play very *good.*

_____ 12. In fact, no one else could be less musical than *I*; every note I
_____   played on the clarinet sounded *bad.*

_____ 13. Andy glanced at the empty pizza delivery box *lying* on my desk

_____ and said, "Surely you haven't *ate* the whole thing, have you?"

_____ 14. I realize now that I *had ought to have* bought a camcorder exactly

_____ like *your's*.

_____ 15. "These *criteria* should not be used to evaluate the work of really

_____ creative artists like you and *me*," exclaimed Theodora.

_____ 16. A shopper who refuses to attend *this here* grand opening sale will

_____ never know what bargains *they* missed.

_____ 17. "Don't fret, Mrs. Alwig," said Jude Tate; "one must expect *those*

_____ *kind* of responses from people *whom* we oldsters consider misfits."

_____ 18. Only a short *ways* from our condominium *are* a well-stocked

_____ supermarket, two filling stations, and a branch library.

_____ 19. There were hard feelings between the foreman and *me* because of

_____ a *couple* snide remarks he had made about my driving.

_____ 20. By the end of the first day of camp, one of my playmates had fallen

_____ into the creek, two had been *stung* by wasps, and most of *us*

younger ones wanted to go home.

_____ 21. Anyone *whom* the regents select for the acting presidency must

_____ reconcile *themself* to a short and thankless tenure.

_____ 22. *Due* to the bomb threat, every passenger had to agree to a thorough

_____ search of *their* luggage.

_____ 23. Because we were *setting* in the top row of the huge stadium, we

_____ *couldn't hardly* see the action on the playing field.

_____ 24. *Who* do you think will be assigned to room with you and *me* for

_____ next semester?

_____ 25. The reason for *me* accepting this rather unexciting job is *because* I

_____ need the money.

NAME _____ SCORE _____

Directions: In the spaces at the left, copy the correct form of each pair in parentheses.

_____   1. "I (beleive, believe) that (your, you're) next," the dentist's nurse
_____   said to the terrified youngster.

_____   2. The new work schedule will have a (noticable, noticeable) (affect,
_____   effect) on my study periods.

_____   3. "I have (all ready, already) (confered, conferred) with my business
_____   partners on the matter," she replied.

_____   4. "I fear that I might (loose, lose) my original investment," said the
_____   worried (financeir, financier).

_____   5. After a lengthy (conference, conferrence), the city engineers
_____   agreed on the (cite, sight, site) for the new garbage-collection
                       facility.

_____   6. Our (attornies, attorneys) have (adviced, advised) us against signing
_____   the contract.

_____   7. Franklin recently placed a bid on a very (desirable, desireable)
_____   (peice, piece) of waterfront property.

_____   8. "In this office," said the receptionist, "such (coarse, course) language
_____   is not (permited, permitted)."

_____   9. The rebel forces marched across the barren (desert, dessert) and
_____   (seized, siezed) the British outpost.

_____ 10. Yesterday Melba painted the (ceiling, cieling) of her (dining, dinning)
_____   room.

_____ 11. Mrs. Ludlow (complemented, complimented) her (neice, niece) on
_____   earning a a straight-A grade average.

_____ 12. "The price you offer is (deplorably, deploreably) low," he said,
_____   "but I must (accept, except) it to avoid bankruptcy."

377

_____ 13. I hope that (later, latter) in the year I'll have more (leisure,
_____ liesure) time.

_____ 14. "We cannot change the seating arrangement," said the teacher,
_____ "because, (unfortunately, unfortunatly), the desks are (stationary,
stationery)."

_____ 15. Martha's former college roommate has written three novels that
_____ have made her (quiet, quite) (fameous, famous).

_____ 16. "I have a new boyfriend (whose, who's) uncle is (outrageously,
_____ outragously) wealthy," boasted Sandra.

_____ 17. "These recent (incidence, incidents) are proof," said the judge,
_____ "that the old law is (unenforcable, unenforceable)."

_____ 18. The attempt to rob the bank was thwarted by the action of the
_____ (courageous, couragous) (casheir, cashier).

_____ 19. The hidden cameras in the bank took pictures of the robbers that
_____ ultimately (lead, led) to (their, there, they're) arrest.

_____ 20. In this particular (instance, instants), the advertisement is obviously
_____ trying to (deceive, decieve) the buyer.

_____ 21. "This toy does not come (equiped, equipped) with (batteries,
_____ batterys)," said the salesperson.

_____ 22. Our candidate will appear at (rallies, rallys) in all of the (principal,
_____ principle) cities of the state.

_____ 23. This ridiculous fad had (its, it's) greatest popularity in the late
_____ (sixties, sixtys).

_____ 24. The president of our city (consul, council, counsel) is surprisingly
_____ (knowledgable, knowledgeable) about federal tax regulations.

_____ 25. "The evidence has (shone, shown) that this witness is a (personal,
_____ personel) friend of the accused man," said the lawyer.

NAME _____   SCORE _____

Directions: Each sentence contains two words from the first half of the spelling list. In each of these words, at least one letter is missing. Write the words, correctly spelled, in the spaces at the left.

_____   1. You defin__tely will notice a differ__nce in the young man's
_____   behavior.

_____   2. Many of the graduate students were dis__pointed in the lecture
_____   given by the em__nent critic.

_____   3. The store owner is being crit__cized because many in the
_____   neighborhood think his prices are ex__bitant.

_____   4. Cert__n members objected to the appointment of Carstairs to the
_____   finance com__tee.

_____   5. Our can__date for mayor gave an excel__nt speech at the rally.
_____

_____   6. Specialists attending the confer__nce discussed new methods of
_____   detecting counterf__t money.

_____   7. Appar__ntly the ac__modations at the beach resort did not please
_____   your uncle and aunt.

_____   8. The technician's expl__nation of the cause of the disast__us
_____   explosion left many unanswered questions.

_____   9. A recently appointed com__sion of legal experts will explore
_____   ways to elim__nate needless and overlapping regulations.

_____   10. Your volunteer groups worked comp__tently and accomp__ished
_____   much good.

Directions: These sentences contain italicized words from the first half of the spelling list. A sentence may have no misspelled words, one misspelled word, or two misspelled words. Underline each misspelled word and write it, correctly spelled, in a space at the left.

_____
_____

1. *Accompaning* the letter was an *exceptionally* detailed *analysis* of the proposed reclamation project.

_____
_____

2. *Guerrilla* fighters continue to *harrass* loyal troops along our eastern and northern *boundries*.

_____
_____

3. At the *heighth* of the *arguement* between the two speakers, some in the *audience* began to applaud.

_____
_____

4. In his presentation the *entrepreneur* made a *grievious* error in *grammar*.

_____
_____

5. Those *familiar* with the new *curriculum* hope that the new materials will result in better *discipline* at the school.

_____
_____

6. The witness's *extremely* vivid *discription* of the encounter *emphasized* the humane behavior of the guards.

_____
_____

7. You must *concede* that the principal of the school *doesn't appreciate* our helpful suggestions.

_____
_____

8. Our *compitition* this year has been *especialy* weak, and our profit should *exceed* last year's.

_____
_____

9. "*Apartheid* is *barbarious,* and as a matter of *conscience* we must protest," shouted the speaker.

_____
_____

10. This *extraordinary* and *fascinating* poem is *finally* being translated into English.

NAME _____ SCORE _____

Directions: Each sentence contains two words from the second half of the spelling list. In each of these words, at least one letter is missing. Write the words, correctly spelled, in the spaces at the left.

_____
_____   1. Tonight I shall prob__ly eat dinner at some rest__nt near the campus.

_____
_____   2. The best bridge player at the Faculty Club is a venerable prof__r of American lit__ture.

_____
_____   3. A strange looking man approached us and said, "I have in my pos__sion a limited quan__ty of bargain watches to sell."

_____
_____   4. The sec__tary of the club explained the proc__ure that would be followed in the money__raising campaign.

_____
_____   5. Last We__sday I spent two hours pulling weeds from my veg__ble garden.

_____
_____   6. Oc__sionally the temp__ture here passes the one-hundred degree mark.

_____
_____   7. I was su__rised to learn that freshmen and sop__mores must have the instructor's permission to enroll in Sociology 342.

_____
_____   8. Local police have learned of simil__r occur__nces in neighboring towns.

_____
_____   9. Mrs. Thorne had the good sense to send the unusual specim__ns to the college lab__atory to be identified.

_____
_____   10. I strongly rec__mend that you seize the opp__tunity to hear this outstanding concert.

Directions: These sentences contain italicized words from the second half of the spelling list. A sentence may have no misspelled words, one misspelled word, or two misspelled words. Underline each misspelled word and write it, correctly spelled, in a space at the left.

_____   1. You must speak to your *sergeant respectfully wheather* you like
_____   him or not.

_____   2. His *pronounciation* was so distinct that we heard *practicly* every
_____   *syllable* of his oration.

_____   3. *Truly religious* persons are *particularily* interested in the welfare
_____   of their community.

_____   4. Your *interpretation* of the poem is both *interesting* and *origional.*
_____

_____   5. The *superintendent persuaded* Clark that he should take another
_____   course in *speech.*

_____   6. Our *schedules* are so full that my *pardner* and I rarely have time
_____   for more than a *sandwich* at noon.

_____   7. People of Andrew's *temperment* often become *unnecessarily* agitated
_____   about *politics.*

_____   8. Jane's *perseverance* kept her at the task *untill* it was completed
_____   *satisfactorily.*

_____   9. If his *rediculous preformance* last night is *representative,* he
_____   should be urged to give up his acting career.

_____   10. *Knowledge* of *mathematics* is *indispensable* in our line of work.
_____

NAME _____   SCORE _____

Directions: Write the plural form or forms for each of the following words. When in doubt, consult your dictionary. When two forms are give, write both of them.

1. assembly _____   _____

2. cargo _____   _____

3. commando _____   _____

4. complexity _____   _____

5. convoy _____   _____

6. cookie _____   _____

7. crash _____   _____

8. cupful _____   _____

9. fungus _____   _____

10. half _____   _____

11. hoof _____   _____

12. housewife _____   _____

13. inferno _____   _____

14. lunch _____   _____

15. mango _____   _____

16. mosquito _____   _____

17. ne'er-do-well _____   _____

18. reef _____   _____

19. referendum _____   _____

20. salmon _____   _____

21. sanatorium _____   _____

22. Scotsman _____   _____

23. stratum _____   _____

24. tempo _____   _____

25. thesis _____   _____

Directions: The following sentences contain fifty numbered words. If a word is correctly capitalized, write **C** in the space with the corresponding number. If a word should not be capitalized, write **W** in the space.

____ ____ ____ (1) Last Spring I talked over my College plans with Dan Howard,
1   2   3

____ ____ ____ a Professor who teaches French and Social Studies at Lakeview
4   5   6

____ ____ ____ Community College.
7   8   9

____ ____ ____ (2) The photograph, taken on the lawn of the White House, shows
10   11   12

____ ____ ____ the President, the Speaker Of The House, and the Secretary
13   14   15

____ ____ ____ Of Defense, along with the Ambassadors from two countries in
16   17   18

____ ____ ____ the Middle East.
19   20   21

____ ____ ____ (3) On my recent visit to South Florida, I spent two days with Uncle
22   23   24

____ ____ ____ Daniel, Mother's younger brother, who is a Captain in the Navy.
25   26   27

____ ____ ____ (4) In Professor Allen's course, the reading list includes several
28   29   30

____ ____ ____ Restoration comedies, one being Congreve's *The Way Of The World.*
31   32   33

____ ____ ____ (5) In 1830 in Fayette, New York, Joseph Smith founded the Church
34   35   36

____ ____ ____ Of Jesus Christ Of Latter-day Saints, now commonly referred to
37   38   39

____ ____ ____ as the Mormon Church.
40   41   42

____ ____ ____ (6) Last Thanksgiving Day I met Jack's Father, an Anthropologist who
43   44   45

____ ____ ____ had been making plaster of Paris casts of Dinosaur footprints
46   47   48

____ ____ near an Indian village in the southwest.
49   50

NAME _____ SCORE _____

Directions: If you find a misspelled word, underline it and write it correctly in the space at the left. (Consider an omitted or misused apostrophe a punctuation error, not a spelling error.) In the column of figures at the left, circle numbers that identify errors in the sentence. Each sentence contains at least one error.

1. Incomplete sentence
2. Dangling or misplaced modifier
3. Misused verb (wrong number, tense, or principal part)
4. Misused pronoun (wrong number or case form or weak reference)
5. Error in punctuation

_____
1 2 3 4 5

1. While hurriedly walking down the slippery steps of the library, a most embarrasing thing happened to Paula and I.

_____
1 2 3 4 5

2. The reason for her attitude being, I suppose, that she had always been told to remain in the background by her stern parents.

_____
1 2 3 4 5

3. "It is apparent, Mr. Toomey," he explained, "that the omission of two commas, one apostrophe, and one key word have produced a humorous affect in your opening sentence."

_____
1 2 3 4 5

4. To accomplish anything really meaningful in college, both discipline and perseverance is undoubtedly necessary.

_____
1 2 3 4 5

5. The dean of the law school explained the proposed law designed to control goverment spending, which he thinks is desperately needed.

_____
1 2 3 4 5

6. Located in a setting of unbeleivable beauty, I think that Dew Drop Inn is an unusually desirable vacation spot.

_____
1 2 3 4 5

7. The manager of the tour group will be frantic, there's only accommodations for 40 guests.

_____
1 2 3 4 5

8. The troop leader asked if either of the two girls had brought their camping equipment?

_____
1 2 3 4 5

9. On entering the Palace of Primitive Art, everyones camera has to be checked at at the door or they won't let you in.

_____
1 2 3 4 5

10. The truth of the matter being that by Wednesday I nearly had used up all of my allowance for February.

_____
1 2 3 4 5   11. Whom did you say found the missing mail pouch laying on the municipal beach.

_____
1 2 3 4 5   12. While performing a rather complicated experiment in the labratory, some acid was spilled and burned the instructors hand.

_____
1 2 3 4 5   13. The fire could have been disasterous, there only were two guards on duty in the entire factory.

_____
1 2 3 4 5   14. Having directed the sergeant to the place where the accident occurred; we went to a nearby restaurant for sandwitches and coffee.

_____
1 2 3 4 5   15. The instructor asked how many of we sophomores had taken a coarse in advanced mathematics.

_____
1 2 3 4 5   16. "I'm sure that everybody who attended the fair today got their moneys worth," said the announcer.

_____
1 2 3 4 5   17. We looked in amazement at the psychiatrist's secretary, neither of us girls were expecting such a question.

_____
1 2 3 4 5   18. Having become involved in a rediculous argument about capital gains; it is now too close to dinner time to begin any studying.

_____
1 2 3 4 5   19. Just between you and me, I suspect that not more then one out of ten of the dormitory residents approve of the new dining-room regulations.

_____
1 2 3 4 5   20. If a person only earns a minimum wage, they cant be expected to contribute much to charity.

_____
1 2 3 4 5   21. If you was me, would you ask to be assigned to someone elses class?

_____
1 2 3 4 5   22. The dampness of the early-morning fog drifting down on ones face and hair being one of the most peaceful expieriences that I know of.

_____
1 2 3 4 5   23. Marilyn received a silver cup on which was inscribed the names of all of the preceeding winners of the award.

_____
1 2 3 4 5   24. Three counselors—Marvin, Arnold, and me—removed the peices of broken glass that were laying in the middle of the path.

_____
1 2 3 4 5   25. It's hard to understand, isn't it, how anyone could have drove their car into that deep ditch without injuring themself seriously.

General Review: Proofreading

NAME _____ SCORE _____

Directions: If you find a misspelled word, underline it and write it correctly in the space at the left. (Consider an omitted or misused apostrophe a punctuation error, not a spelling error.) Circle at least one of the numbers at the left:

1. The sentence is correct.
2. The sentence contains a dangling or misplaced modifier.
3. The sentence contains a misused verb.
4. The sentence contains a misused pronoun.
5. There is an error in punctuation.

---
1 2 3 4 5
1. Ted was surely surprised to learn that no sophomore in the English literature class except Jerry and him was required to take the test.

---
1 2 3 4 5
2. "Just between you and I, the prospect of a vacation at that fishing lodge, with it's primitive accommodations, realy don't fascinate me," Fran told her husband.

---
1 2 3 4 5
3. I like Professor Woodward better then any of my other teachers, she always tries to without embarrassing me answer my stupid question satisfactorily.

---
1 2 3 4 5
4. Handing each of us teachers a sheet of paper, the superintendent of schools said, "Here are the criteria we must apply when we hire our next vice-principal."

---
1 2 3 4 5
5. High on the list of building prioritys are the construction of play grounds and swimming pools in the western part of town.

---
1 2 3 4 5
6. Mrs. Wilkins managed to keep the family intact while her husband was in the hospital doing odd jobs for the neighbors.

---
1 2 3 4 5
7. Shirley and I studied the questions with shock and disbeleif, neither one of us were prepared for a test like this.

---
1 2 3 4 5
8. The delivery boy entered the kitchen, smiled disarmingly, and announced, "Here's the three pizzas someone ordered."

---
1 2 3 4 5
9. "I'm quiet sure the person the boss was referring to is not you or I," said Julia Stowe who had just joined our group around the water cooler.

---
1 2 3 4 5
10. "Remember, you new students," said the adviser, "it's every-ones responsibility to consistantly and conscientiously follow these regulations."

1 2 3 4 5

11. Our committee not only was dissappointed but also angry to learn that not one of our six proposals were accepted.

1 2 3 4 5

12. The new athletic director is an extremely pleasant young man who, I have been told, spent three years playing professional soccer.

1 2 3 4 5

13. Laying in my parking place was a large piece of paint-stained canvass and several empty bottles that someone has thrown from their car.

1 2 3 4 5

14. "Don't it seem strange that your's was the only car on the block that was given a parking ticket?" asked Lillian.

1 2 3 4 5

15. Having selected a seat in the back row, emptied my briefcase, and hastily reviewed my class notes; the teacher announced that the test was postponed.

1 2 3 4 5

16. The police sargeant asked if any of we neighbors had ate in the new restaurant during the past two weeks?

1 2 3 4 5

17. Is either of your two tow trucks in good enough condition to at a moments notice get to a highway emergancy?

1 2 3 4 5

18. "Lately there have been rumors that two of us representatives will face stiff compitition in next year's primaries," said the eminent politician)

1 2 3 4 5

19. Crossing the boundary into Clay County, long delays ocurred because they were repairing the road for a stretch of approximately four miles.

1 2 3 4 5

20. I can recommend Ms. Jamison enthusiastically, every editing job she did for either my business partner or I was done promptly and efficiently.

1 2 3 4 5

21. "There's probably not more than a dozen people in this town who I'd trust any farther than I could throw them," said the sheriff.

1 2 3 4 5

22. Ben is one of those people who think of only their own convenience and who are sure that their ideas are better than anyone else's.

1 2 3 4 5

23. It nearly took me 90 minutes to fill out the questionnaire and then they told me to come back next Wednesday.

1 2 3 4 5

24. The teacher asked Colleen how the migration of early Germanic tribes affected the development of the English language?

1 2 3 4 5

25. "When only eight years old," Edith explained, "Father took my older brother and I to France and Great Britian."

Sentence combining is a simple process designed to help you write more sophisticated and effective sentences. You began to employ combining techniques in Lesson 7 and its accompanying exercises, so the following exercises ought to be familiar to you. The exercises in Appendix A begin with the simplest kinds of combining, embedding an adjective from one sentence into another sentence, thus enriching one sentence and eliminating the other. The exercises then move through the formation of compound sentences and into complex sentences, those constructed with verbal phrases and subordinate clauses.

Every set in these exercises can be done in several ways, each one correct. The first set offers a good example of the possibilities:

> The man was tall.
> He was thin.
> He walked down the street.

The simplest combined form puts the adjectives *tall* and *thin* in the sentence immediately before the noun:

> The tall, thin man walked down the street.

But it is possible to move the adjectives into more emphatic positions:

> Tall and thin, the man walked down the street.
> The man, tall and thin, walked down the street.

Each of these options is correct, and each creates a slightly different sentence—a sentence that draws the reader's attention to the facts in slightly different ways.

These additional combining exercises will help your writing in two ways. First, they will remind you of different ways of expressing the same idea, and thus they will expand the range of constructions you employ in your writing. Second, the exercises will focus your attention on punctuation as you make up the combinations.

Remember that every set in these exercises can be done in several ways, all of them correct. For each set, test the various ways of creating combinations, and you will make yourself a more flexible and more effective writer.

Combine the sentences in each numbered unit into a single longer sentence.

1. The man was tall.
   He was thin.
   He walked down the street.

   _____

   _____

2. The tall, thin man walked down the street.
   A woman walked with him.
   She was short.
   She was blonde.

   _____

   _____

3. The man and the woman walked down the street.
   The street was dusty.
   The street was crowded.

   _____

   _____

4. The tall, thin man and the short, blonde woman walked down the dusty, crowded street.
   They walked slowly.
   They walked into a cold north wind.

   _____

   _____

5. The man and the woman were very cold.
   They stopped in front of a store.
   Then they went inside.
   They went inside for a cup of coffee.

   _____

   _____

Combine the sentences in each unit into a single sentence by using compound verbs.

6. Jim walked down the hall.
   He entered the last classroom on the right.

   _____

   _____

7. Robert and the girls parked the car in the student parking lot.
   They made the long walk to the library.

   _____

   _____

8. The office building is seven stories high.
   It has a long circular drive in front of it.

   _____

   _____

9. We went to the soccer field.
   Then we walked into the picnic area.

   _____

   _____

10. Tom went to the basketball game.
    Sue went to the basketball game.
    They sat at midcourt behind the team's bench.

    _____

    _____

Combine the sentences in each unit into a single sentence by putting the items into a series.

11. Joan picked up her purse.
    She picked up her umbrella.
    She picked up a set of car keys.

    _____

    _____

12. She walked slowly down the stairs.
    She got into her car.
    She drove happily off to work.

    _____

    _____

13. Jim opened the windows.
    He turned on the fan.
    Then he began to work on the test.

    _____

    _____

14. I have lost my textbook.
    I have lost my lecture notes.
    I have lost my workbook.

    _____

    _____

15. I have called all my friends.
    I have searched the trunk of my car.
    I have even looked on my desk.

    _____

    _____

Combine the sentences in each unit into a single compound sentence.

16. The bus arrived late.
    George didn't mind waiting for it.

    _____

    _____

17. The tall boy looks like a basketball player.
    He would rather study nuclear physics.

    _____

    _____

18. I spend a great deal of time at the Student Union.
    It is a wonderful place.

    _____

    _____

19. The three little boys went to the soccer game.
    They stayed only a few minutes.

    _____

    _____

20. Thunder and lightning hit the area very suddenly.
    Both teams left the field in a great hurry.

    _____

    _____

Combine these same sentences in each unit by using **adverbial clauses**.

21. The bus arrived late.
    George didn't mind waiting for it.

    _____

    _____

22. The tall boy looks like a basketball player.
    He would rather study nuclear physics.

    _____

    _____

23. I spend a great deal of time at the Student Union.
    It is a wonderful place.

    _____

    _____

24. The three little boys went to the soccer game.
    They stayed only a few minutes.

    _____

    _____

25. Thunder and lightning hit the area very suddenly.
    Both teams left the field in a great hurry.

    _____

    _____

Combine the sentences in each unit into a single sentence by using **participial phrases**.

26. The tall, slender girl walked out of the garage.
    She moved close to a blue car.
    She inspected the outside of the car for dents and scratches.

    _____

    _____

27. The girl walked up to the car.
    She opened the door of the car.
    She checked the odometer reading.

    _____

    _____

28. The girl opened the hood of the car.
    She took a wrench out of her toolbox.
    She removed a spark plug so that she could check it.

    _____

    _____

29. The girl looked at the tip of the spark plug.
    She looked very carefully.
    She shook her head sadly.

    _____

    _____

30. She replaced the spark plug.
    She closed the hood.
    She walked slowly away from the car.

    _____

    _____

Combine the sentences in each unit into a single sentence by using adjective clauses and participial phrases.

31. The lifeguard sat in the tower.
    He scanned the water carefully.
    He was looking for people in distress.

    _____

    _____

32. Only a few people were at the beach that day.
    They sat on the sand.
    They listened to their CD players.

    _____

    _____

33. The lifeguard watched the ships.
    The ships sailed by on the horizon.
    He regularly checked two people.
    The people were swimming nearby.

    _____

    _____

34. About noon the lifeguard left the tower.
    He walked slowly across the sand.
    He was carrying his umbrella and sunscreen with him.

    _____

    _____

35. He sat quietly at the lunch counter.
    He ate a hot dog with onions and pickles.
    Then he took a short nap on a bench nearby.

    _____

    _____

Combine the sentences in each unit into a single sentence by using a variety of constructions.

36. Last night three guys came to visit Jim.
    The three guys had played on his high school soccer team.
    The four of them talked until 3:00 A.M.

    _____

    _____

37. One of them is studying accounting.
    He had been a weak student in high school.
    He now works very hard at his courses.

    _____

    _____

38. He had never enjoyed school very much.
    He finds several of his courses extremely interesting now.

    _____

    _____

39. The second guy is in the Air Force.
    He is a year older than the others.
    He is studying to be an electronics technician.

    _____

    _____

40. The third guy intends to enter the state university this fall.
   He has been working in construction since he graduated from high school.

   _____

   _____

Make the first sentence in each of the following units a participial phrase or a gerund combined with a preposition.

41. The two men were installing a satellite dish on the roof.
   They found a small suitcase on the roof of the building.

   _____

   _____

42. The girls were walking slowly down the hall.
   They stopped to talk to the other students.

   _____

   _____

43. The clouds built up slowly in the west.
   They brought lightning and thunder early in the evening.

   _____

   _____

44. The players saw that defeat was certain.
   They played even harder for the rest of the game.

   _____

   _____

45. The teacher walked into the room.
   She was rolling a cart.
   The cart had a computer and an LCD projector on it.
   She was carrying a laser pointer.

   _____

   _____

Combine the sentences in each unit into a single sentence by using a variety of constructions.

46. The woman was tall and slender.
    She was wearing a gray coat.
    She met a man.
    She met him in the lobby of the hotel.

_____

_____

47. The man was extremely young.
    He was poorly dressed.
    He had no important information to give her.

_____

_____

48. The man told the woman his sad story.
    She was disappointed.
    Her disappointment was extreme.
    She told him (two things).
    He was fired.
    He would never work in industrial espionage again.

_____

_____

49. In response, the man told her (something).
    He had just landed a job with IBM.
    The job was in their security office.

_____

_____

50. (Something) seems unlikely.
    The man was telling the truth.

_____

_____

Combine the sentences in each unit into a single sentence by using a variety of constructions.

51. The new office building down the street is finally finished.
    A few tenants are moving in.

_____

_____

52. Three lawyers moved into an office on the third floor yesterday.
    Today they installed a new phone system.

    _____

    _____

53. That building has 50 offices in it.
    Only six of them are occupied.

    _____

    _____

54. The rent for the offices is extremely high.
    Many of the offices are vacant.

    _____

    _____

55. The owners need to lower the rent.
    They might go into bankruptcy.

    _____

    _____

Appendix B *Diagnostic Tests*

NAME _____ SCORE _____

Directions: In the space at the left of each pair of sentences, write the letter that identifies the correctly punctuated sentence.

_____ 1. a. Although we prepared the ground carefully, watered regularly, and weeded thoroughly, we got very few decent vegetables from the garden.
b. Although we prepared the ground carefully, watered regularly, and weeded thoroughly; we got very few decent vegetables from the garden.

_____ 2. a. We began work on December 14, 1981, but complex evaluation procedures delayed the completion of the project beyond the four weeks, we had originally scheduled.
b. We began work on December 14, 1981, but complex evaluation procedures delayed the completion of the project beyond the four weeks we had originally scheduled.

_____ 3. a. I have studied economic theory, but I still do not understand what makes a weeks pay this year worth less than a weeks pay last year.
b. I have studied economic theory, but I still do not understand what makes a week's pay this year worth less than a week's pay last year.

_____ 4. a. The park is divided in half by a small stream; one half providing facilities for camping, and the other having open spaces for games.
b. The park is divided in half by a small stream, one half providing facilities for camping, and the other having open spaces for games.

_____ 5. a. To get the boat ready for summer, I scraped and painted the bottom, and my sister varnished all the exposed wood.
b. To get the boat ready for summer I scraped and painted the bottom and my sister varnished all the exposed wood.

_____ 6. a. The visual details of the building make it more interesting, unfortunately they also increase it's maintenance costs.
b. The visual details of the building make it more interesting; unfortunately they also increase its maintenance costs.

_____ 7. a. Trying to show off her literary knowledge, Julie used the word *illusion* when she meant to say *allusion*.
b. Trying to show off her literary knowledge Julie used the word, *illusion* when she meant to say *allusion*.

_____ 8. a. Before sunset on Friday, we need to have the car washed, the yard raked and the screen door repaired.
b. Before sunset on Friday we need to have the car washed, the yard raked, and the screen door repaired

_____ 9. a. "I intend to vote for Harold Sanchez, who is clearly the most able candidate running for the office," replied Jerry.

b. "I intend to vote for Harold Sanchez who is clearly the most able candidate running for the office," replied Jerry.

_____ 10. a. The mechanic smiled and said, "The reason your car is in such fine shape is that you have maintained it carefully all these years."

b. The mechanic smiled, and said, "The reason your car is in such fine shape, is that you have maintained it carefully all these years."

_____ 11. a. Fuel economy has become very important in this country, therefore manufacturers are building smaller lighter cars.

b. Fuel economy has become very important in this country; therefore manufacturers are building smaller, lighter cars.

_____ 12. a. Piping hot, scrambled eggs and country sausage are on todays breakfast menu, and almost every student is coming to the cafeteria.

b. Piping hot scrambled eggs and country sausage are on today's breakfast menu, and almost every student is coming to the cafeteria.

_____ 13. a. Jim walked to the microphone and said, "It's wonderful, isn't it, that we've been able to gather so many representatives from other schools."

b. Jim walked to the microphone, and said, "Its wonderful, isn't it, that we've been able to gather so many representatives from other schools?"

_____ 14. a. Tomorrow at 10 o'clock we'll be able to witness one of nature's most awesome sights: a total eclipse of the sun.

b. Tomorrow at 10 o'clock we'll be able to witness one of nature's most awesome sights; a total eclipse of the sun.

_____ 15. a. When we decided to leave, the attendant in the cloakroom handed Bert someone else's hat, which was so large it slipped down over his eyes.

b. When we decided to leave the attendant in the cloakroom handed Bert someone else's hat, which was so large it slipped down over his eyes.

_____ 16. a. Through the window of the cabin we could see a tall pine tree, some blueberry bushes, and an azalea in full bloom.

b. Through the window of the cabin we could see: a tall pine tree, some blueberry bushes, and an azalea in full bloom.

_____ 17. a. The *Herald* reported the incident in a story headed "Local Farmer Discovers Giant Mushroom," since it was buried on the last page few people noticed it.

b. The *Herald* reported the incident in a story headed "Local Farmer Discovers Giant Mushroom"; since it was buried on the last page, few people noticed it.

_____ 18. a. We walked for miles to the headwaters of the river, where we saw a very high, awesomely beautiful waterfall.

b. We walked for miles to the headwaters of the river where we saw a very high, awesomely beautiful waterfall.

_____ 19. a. Although Mr. Joneses car is almost new, its condition is deteriorating because he does not care for it properly.

b. Although Mr. Jones' car is almost new; it's condition is deteriorating because he does not care for it properly.

_____ 20. a. Some of us wonder if Mr. Brown should have hired his father-in-law, who is close to retirement age.

b. Some of us wonder if Mr. Brown should have hired his father-in-law who is close to retirement age.

_____ 21. a. The main speaker's oration was so long, so rambling, and so uninteresting that it's no wonder many in the audience left early.

b. The main speaker's oration was so long, so rambling and so uninteresting, that it's no wonder many in the audience left early.

_____ 22. a. "The outcome of the evaluation has been very positive," said Mr. Jordan, "we have made remarkable improvement in our management system this year."

b. "The outcome of the evaluation has been very positive," said Mr. Jordan; "we have made remarkable improvement in our management system this year."

_____ 23. a. "It was crafty old Sam Johnson, wasn't it," asked Dr. Allen; "who said, 'Let me smile with the wise and feed with the rich?'"

b. "It was crafty old Sam Johnson, wasn't it," asked Dr. Allen, "who said, 'Let me smile with the wise and feed with the rich'?"

_____ 24. a. Joe has tried sky diving and scuba diving; now he is looking around for more excitement to drive away life's boredom.

b. Joe has tried sky diving and scuba diving, now he is looking around for more excitement to drive away lifes' boredom.

_____ 25. a. "I don't understand why you want one of those imported cars," said Dad, "for over 20 years Ford's and Buick's have suited our family well."

b. "I don't understand why you want one of those imported cars," said Dad; "for over 20 years Fords and Buicks have suited our family well."

NAME _____ SCORE _____

Directions: Each of the following sentences contains one misspelled word. Underline the misspelled word and write it, correctly spelled, in the space at the left.

_____ 1. The secretary offered to drive the eminent visitors to the restaurant and then return the reference books to the village libary.

_____ 2. The authorities have received word that there have been several troublesome incidence at our embassies in two countries.

_____ 3. During these desperate emergencies it was not permissible for anyone to travel accross the boundaries into foreign lands.

_____ 4. All of the sophomores and some of the athletes will definately attend the meeting of dissatisfied students tonight in the dormitory.

_____ 5. I acknowledge that my enthusiastic craving for pecan pie often exeeds my limited capacity for sweet desserts.

_____ 6. My cousin Bill is, quite naturally, already making preparations for his seperation from military service next February.

_____ 7. I truly cannot describe my excitement at funding a servicable car among the dilapidated old junkers at the used car lot.

_____ 8. At the heighth of the storm a bolt of lightning struck a tree near the theater, and the audience hurriedly fled from the building.

_____ 9. Our amateur guide was embarrassed when he admitted that he had chosen the wrong route and had lead us to the wrong airport.

_____ 10. My partner reminded me that it's undoubtably more profitable for a businessman to win an argument.

_____ 11. "For this job," he answered, "a knowledge of Spanish grammar and literature is not absolutely necessary but would be desireable."

_____ 12. On a similar occassion a governmental commission had asked for and received a unanimous vote of approval from Parliament.

_____ 13. The candidate for the open position on the city council faced the committee and proceeded with his explaination.

_____ 14. Marcia admitted that Hank is competent and efficient in a mathematics classroom but is awkward and entirely lacking in rhythm on a dance floor.

_____ 15. Because the preceding speakers at the teachers' conference had been extremely boreing, the principal limited his remarks to 90 minutes.

_____ 16. The outrageous propoganda in the controversial pamphlet about nuclear energy was apparently the work of a fanatic.

_____ 17. The visiting superintendent gave an impromptu speech that dragged on for more then 40 minutes.

_____ 18. This lovely calendar with its description of several cathedrals in Great Britain is an appropriate momento of our trip.

_____ 19. Since meeting Bernard, Jenny no longer grieves about her lonliness, and there has been a noticeable improvement in her appearance.

_____ 20. My advise to you is this: A person of your intelligence and imagination really should acquire an excellent education.

_____ 21. "I'm probably prejudiced," said Jack, "but compulsery attendance of classes is a barbarous custom in a free world."

_____ 22. "I concede," said the famous financier, "that your amendment is basically beneficial, and I reccommend that it be passed."

_____ 23. A few more disastrous experiences like that one and I believe you'll loose what few friends you still have.

_____ 24. An acquaintance of mine played the part of the villain in a humerous play, the first performance of which occurred last Wednesday.

_____ 25. We are dissappointed that the exorbitant cost of the new equipment for the laboratory forces us to reduce the size of the order.

NAME _____ SCORE _____

Directions: In the space at the left, copy from within the parentheses the form appropriate in serious writing.

_____ 1. Your response to the questionnaire, along with almost 1,000 other responses, (has, have) been entered into the computer for collating.

_____ 2. It was (sure, surely) good to see Joe again after all these years.

_____ 3. "Charles, is there anyone in your office (who, whom) you think will be available to help us next week?" asked the president.

_____ 4. I have talked to (almost, most) everyone in the club, but I've found no one willing to run for president.

_____ 5. "Remember, fellows," said Peg, "that no one sold more raffle tickets for your silly club than (us, we) girls on the pep squad."

_____ 6. Each of the hikers felt that (his, their) effort on the trail that day had been extraordinary.

_____ 7. Cathy maintains that either she or Marge (deserves, deserve) this year's prize for outstanding service.

_____ 8. The telephone had (rang, rung) 12 times before I was able to answer it.

_____ 9. At 5 o'clock this afternoon I (laid, lay) down to take a short nap, drowsy from my work in the yard.

_____ 10. Have you (taken, took) all of your vacation days already?

_____ 11. I don't believe that we have a chance in Saturday's game, (being as how, because) our goalie is still injured.

_____ 12. You may choose (whoever, whomever) you wish as your assistant in this experiment.

_____ 13. I did not see a single one of my classmates studying over the weekend for (his, their) exams.

_____ 14. "Let's just keep this story a secret among (us, we) guys," suggested Jim.

_____ 15. Although the term has barely (began, begun), Shawn has already missed two classes.

_____ 16. Your ideas on developing efficient power sources seem quite different (from, than) mine.

_____ 17. No one but members of that club (was, were) invited to the conference with the president.

_____ 18. The old man picked up the ship model lovingly and (sat, set) it carefully on the top shelf of the bookcase.

_____ 19. The reason for postponing the game was (because, that) the field had been soaked that morning by a downpour.

_____ 20. My score on that test would have been (considerable, considerably) higher if I had been able to use my calculator.

_____ 21. Malcolm said that he couldn't agree with Knox and (I, me) that Coleman is the best state senator we've ever had.

_____ 22. George says that there (seem, seems) to be several good prospects for the treasure's job.

_____ 23. Each of the carpenters on that job has a helper assigned to (him, them).

_____ 24. My car runs so (bad, badly) that I hesitate to take it on a long trip.

_____ 25. We have found the person (who, whom) we are sure will do the best job as head of that committee.

Sentence Structure

NAME _____   SCORE _____

Directions: Study these sentences. One sentence in each pair suffers from incompleteness, dangling or misplaced modifiers, faulty parallelism, or faulty comparisons. In the space at the left, write the letter that identifies the grammatically correct sentence.

_____ 1. a. When I was barely five years old, my family visited New York City with my uncle.
   b. When barely five years old, my family visited New York City with my uncle.

_____ 2. a. The company's fear now is that the union delegates intend neither to ask the members vote on the offer nor to return soon to the bargaining table.
   b. The company's fear now is that the union delegates neither intend to ask the members vote on the offer nor to return soon to the bargaining table.

_____ 3. a. Having told him about my plan for producing methanol, Professor Hartline said he would investigate funding for the project.
   b. After I told him amount my plan for producing methanol, Professor Hartline said he would investigate funding for the project.

_____ 4. a. The yearly salary Bob Rockham receives in the NFL exceeds the average college president's.
   b. The yearly salary Bob Rockham receives in the NFL exceeds the average college presidents.

_____ 5. a. For several years, running has been an increasingly popular sport among older men and women.
   b. Running for several years has been an increasingly popular sport among older men and women.

_____ 6. a. Carefully checking the map and the landmarks in front of us, the obvious conclusion was that we were lost.
   b. Carefully checking the map and the landmarks in front of us, we came to the obvious conclusion that we were lost.

_____ 7. a. Jan told us that we ought to wind up our business in the hardware store as quickly as possible.
   b. Jan told us that we ought to as quickly as possible wind up our business in the hardware store.

_____ 8. a. My experience in the local newspaper taught me about thorough investigation, being careful of my sources, and to avoid using lengthy quotations.
   b. My experience in the local newspaper taught me to investigate thoroughly, to be careful about my sources, and to avoid using lengthy quotations.

411

_____ 9. a. My income tax refund this year should be higher than last year's because I overestimated my income.

b. My income tax refund this year should be higher than last year, having overestimated my income.

_____ 10. a. The agenda including a discussion of a plan to within six months reduce the club's indebtedness by 30 percent.

b. The agenda included a discussion of a plan to reduce the club's indebtedness by 30 percent within six months.

_____ 11. a. My sister was delighted by my willingness to help her with her algebra and by my skill as a tutor.

b. My sister was delighted by my willingness to help her with her algebra and by my being a skillful tutor.

_____ 12. a. Reaching the bottom of the canyon at long last, I looked up at a powerful waterfall cascading down near me.

b. Reaching the bottom of the canyon at long last and looking up, a powerful waterfall cascaded down near me.

_____ 13. a. My old Aunt Kate talked earnestly about the value of following a sound diet whenever we had a rich dessert.

b. Whenever we had a rich dessert, my old Aunt Kate talked earnestly about the value of following a sound diet.

_____ 14. a. By examining the spark plugs carefully, I determined that the car was burning oil rather heavily.

b. I determined that, by examining the spark plugs carefully, the car was burning oil rather heavily.

_____ 15. a. The property includes a section flat and level enough for a tennis court but which is, I'm afraid, not quite large enough.

b. The property includes a section that is flat and level enough for a tennis court but not, I am afraid, quite large enough.

_____ 16. a. Crawling carefully to the edge of the cliff, we saw the entire valley spread out magnificently before us.

b. Crawling carefully to the edge of the cliff, the entire valley spread out magnificently before us.

_____ 17. a. Joanne is one of the most intelligent, if not the most intelligent, person I know.

b. Joanne is one of the most intelligent persons, if not the most intelligent person, that I know.

_____ 18. a. In shocked disbelief, the loyal Striker fans have watched their team lose 8 of their last 11 games.

b. Loyal Striker fans have watched their team lose 8 of their last 11 games in shocked disbelief.

_____ 19. a. Rolling the large, flat stone over carefully, a small, brownish snake lay coiled underneath.
        b. Rolling the large flat stone over carefully, I found a small, brownish snake lying coiled underneath.

_____ 20. a. Although working students have less time for studying than nonworking students do, their education seems to be as good as that of nonworking students.
        b. Although working students have less time for studying than nonworking, their education seems to be as good as nonworking students.

_____ 21. a. Mr. Thomas's construction company has not only built condominiums but also commercial buildings.
        b. Mr. Thomas's construction company has built not only condominiums but also commercial buildings.

_____ 22. a. I'd prefer to invest the surplus funds rather than let them sit idle in the safe-deposit box.
        b. I'd prefer to invest the surplus funds rather than letting them sit idle in the safe-deposit box.

_____ 23. a. Either you must repeat the course spring term or come back to summer school to make up the four-credit course.
        b. You must repeat the course spring term or come back to summer school to make up the four-credit course.

_____ 24. a. Lydia's face turned flaming red upon hearing that her grade was higher than anyone's in her sociology class.
        b. Lydia's face turned flaming red when she heard that her grade was higher than anyone's in her sociology class.

_____ 25. a. The reason I resigned is that the school has one of the worst retirement plans in the state, if not the worst.
        b. The reason I resigned being that the school has one of the worst retirement plans in the state, if not the worst.

Appendix C
Answer Key to Practice Sheets

Practice Sheet 1, Page 5

1. drives
2. follows
3. stands
4. built
5. park
6. employs
7. were
8. came
9. increased
10. sells
11. line
12. provides
13. held
14. occurred
15. are
16. offers
17. attracts
18. are
19. led
20. decorated

Practice Sheet 1, Page 6

1. Some
2. men
3. They
4. Jim
5. gift
6. salesperson
7. I
8. Jamie
9. Tom
10. shortstop
11. batter
12. snake
13. line
14. craftsman
15. crawl
16. announcement
17. coaches
18. sister
19. cause
20. play

Practice Sheet 2, Pages 15–16

1. 6,1	6. 1,3	11. 3,4	16. 4,4	21. 1,5	26. 4,4	31. 2,5	36. 6,2
2. 3,4	7. 2,6	12. 6,4	17. 1,3	22. 1,1	27. 3,5	32. 1,5	37. 4,4
3. 2,4	8. 2,5	13. 2,1	18. 1,4	23. 3,1	28. 1,1	33. 4,1	38. 5,4
4. 2,1	9. 5,6	14. 5,5	19. 2,1	24. 6,1	29. 4,5	34. 5,2	39. 1,1
5. 1,3	10. 2,6	15. 4,1	20. 1,1	25. 5,3	30. 2,4	35. 5,6	40. 5,1

Practice Sheet 3, Page 27

1. player
2. fan
3. sport
4. source
5. part
6. president
7. employee
8. graduate
9. director
10. mentor
11. major
12. study
13. specialty
14. writers
15. contributors
16. scholar
17. inventor
18. machine
19. asset
20. man

Practice Sheet 3, Page 28

1. exhausted
2. confident
3. able
4. best
5. enthusiastic
6. good
7. brilliant
8. renowned
9. acceptable
10. high
11. skilled
12. famous
13. successful
14. weary
15. sour
16. happier
17. talented
18. customary
19. comfortable
20. successful

Practice Sheet 4, Page 35

1. All want holiday
2. we took tests
3. assistant announced assignment
4. paper will provide treatment
5. people have chosen topics
6. reporters issued warning
7. front will cover part
8. weather threatens game
9. game will decide championship
10. college might postpone game
11. One hiked trail
12. She carried pack
13. she saw bear
14. bear was stealing honey
15. bear frightened friend
16. I found copy
17. Some held meeting
18. people left meeting
19. person needs raise
20. None makes money

Practice Sheet 4, Page 36

1. I.O.
2. D.O.
3. O.C.
4. D.O.
5. D.O.
6. I.O.
7. D.O.
8. O.C.
9. D.O.
10. O.C.
11. D.O.
12. I.O.
13. I.O.
14. D.O.
15. O.C.
16. O.C.
17. D.O.
18. O.C.
19. I.O.
20. O.C.

Practice Sheet 5, Pages 43, 44

1. 3, could have	11. 2, has	21. 4, did	31. 2, might
2. 2, would have	12. 5, has	22. 5, has	32. 1, should
3. 1, will have been	13. 4, Can	23. 1, need to	33. 3, has
4. 1, have been	14. 2, Does(n't)	24. 1, have been	34. 5, might
5. 3, Will	15. 3, ought to	25. 3, have	35. 4, will
6. 3, Can	16. 2, should	26. 5, has	36. 4, did
7. 3, could	17. 3, might have	27. 5, should	37. 2, used to
8. 1, is supposed to	18. 3, Will	28. 3, did	38. 1, might
9. 1, should have been	19. 1, could have	29. 3, will need to	39. 1, will have been
10. 3, do	20. 3, should have	30. 1, have been	40. 4, should have

Practice Sheet 6, Page 53

1. 3, was included	6. 3, should have been reported
2. 3, was elected	7. 4, should have been told
3. 3, was found	8. 3, could not have been discovered
4. 4, was given	9. 3, were not recognized
5. 5, are kept	10. 5, can be recalled

Practice Sheet 6, Page 54

1. cookies	4. proposal	7. who errors	10. who	13. who
2. copies	5. car	8. whom	11. whom	14. what
3. what	6. car	9. who	12. color	15. whom

Practice Sheet 7, Pages 65–66

1. S	6. S	11. C	16. C	21. S
2. C	7. O	12. S	17. C	22. C
3. O	8. S	13. C	18. S	23. O
4. C	9. O	14. O	19. C	24. C
5. C	10. O	15. O	20. C	25. O

Practice Sheet 8, Pages 77–78

1. 10	9. 9	17. 7	25. 5	33. 2
2. 9	10. 3	18. 1	26. 1	34. 9
3. 1	11. 1	19. 2	27. 3	35. 10
4. 8	12. 1	20. 8	28. 10	36. 9
5. 2	13. 3	21. 7	29. 5	37. 8
6. 7	14. 2	22. 10	30. 4	38. 2
7. 4	15. 6	23. 9	31. 6	39. 3
8. 10	16. 10	24. 1	32. 1	40. 1

Practice Sheet 9, Page 87

1. 1903	6. glider	11. gliders
2. gliders	7. gliders	12. wind tunnel
3. gliders	8. engines	13. strip
4. flight	9. Nikolaus Otto	14. updrafts
5. balloons	10. Dayton	15. design

Practice Sheet 9, Page 88

1. material I failed to study
2. Chapter 1, which I failed to study,
3. instructors who wrote that test
4. Mr. Smith and Mrs. Babson, who wrote that test,
5. students that are enrolled in an American history course
6. classes that meet at 8:00 A.M.
7. class, which meets at 8:00 A.M.,
8. Joe, who attends a college in the northern part of the state.
9. students who attend that school
10. Joe, who doesn't have a lot of money,
11. laptop that is older and less expensive than a new one.
12. laptop that is older
13. option, which doesn't seem very wise,
14. aunt who has quite a bit of money.
15. money he needs

Practice Sheet 10, Page 99

1. Ap.	6. O.P.	11. S.C.	16. S.
2. D.O.	7. Ap.	12. D.O.	17. S.
3. S.	8. D.O.	13. Ap.	18. D.O.
4. D.O.	9. Ap.	14. S.	19. D.O.
5. O.P.	10. S.	15. D.O.	20. S.C.

Practice Sheet 10, Page 100

1. D.O.   where he put his history textbook
2. S.   How he manages to lose so much of his stuff
3. Ap.   that he loses his book constantly
4. S.   Whatever table is handy when he walks in the door
5. S.C.   where he leaves his books.
6. S.   that he is so absent-minded
7. D.O.   that absent-mindedness is caused by stress
8. D.O.   that Sam is always very relaxed.
9. D.O.   that Sam does not seem to care about his possessions
10. D.O.   that his friends will be understanding about his attitude.
11. D.O.   who will take care of Sam next year in graduate school.
12. O.P.   whoever is willing to do the job.
13. S.   Whoever takes on that job
14. S.   Whomever he finds for that job
15. D.O.   that he had left his brother in a restaurant
16. Ap.   that he had left his brother behind.
17. D.O.   where he had left his brother.
18. S.   that they had been having lunch together
19. Ap.   that he had eaten a pastrami sandwich for lunch
20. Ap.   that in the future his memory will improve.

Practice Sheet 11, Page 113

1. D.O.	5. S.	9. S.	13. S.	17. D.O.
2. D.O.	6. D.O.	10. S.C.	14. O.P.	18. S.C.
3. O.P.	7. O.P.	11. O.P.	15. S.C.	19. O.P.
4. S.	8. D.O.	12. D.O.	16. O.P.	20. D.O.

Practice Sheet 11, Page 114

1. N   to know more about your experience in your last job
2. Adj.   to change a tire on a car
3. Adv.   To find that program in your computer
4. Adj.   to talk to him
5. N.   you select your courses for next term
6. N   anything but walk home
7. Adv.   to find those books somewhere in the college library
8. Adj.   to pick the lock and enter the hotel room
9. Adv.   to pick the lock and enter the hotel room
10. Adj.   to be studied for the next test
11. N   to know which trail to the top of the mountain is easier
12. Adv.   to study for the big test in history
13. Adv.   to play tennis
14. N   to exercise early in the morning,
15. Adj.   to drive that car on the test track
16. Adv.   to make fun of my unsuccessful woodworking projects.
17. N   to let Al choose the menu for the staff banquet
18. Adv.   To be sure you get the courses you need,
19. N   to spend the day looking for a new dress for that dance
20. Adj.   to be read for that class

Practice Sheet 12, Pages 123–124

1. _____	7. _____	13. _____	19. _____	25. _____
2. path	8. students	14. _____	20. Al	26. men
3. I	9. _____	15. letters	21. men	27. Jimmy
4. _____	10. you	16. _____	22. puppy	28. Jimmy
5. _____	11. _____	17. us	23. men	29. _____
6. coach	12. people	18. _____	24. _____	30. project

Practice Sheet 13, Pages 141–142

1. F	7. S	13. F	19. S	25. S
2. F	8. S	14. F	20. S	26. F
3. S	9. F	15. S	21. S	27. F
4. F	10. S	16. S	22. F	28. S
5. S	11. F	17. S	23. S	29. F
6. S	12. S	18. F	24. S	30. S

Practice Sheet 14, Page 151

1. A	3. B	5. B	7. A	9. B
2. B	4. A	6. B	8. B	10. B

Practice Sheet 14, Page 152

1. B	4. B	7. B	10. A	13. A
2. B	5. A	8. B	11. B	14. A
3. B	6. B	9. B	12. B	15. A

Practice Sheet 14A, Page 155

1. B	5. B	9. A	13. A	17. B
2. B	6. B	10. A	14. A	18. B
3. A	7. A	11. A	15. B	19. B
4. A	8. B	12. B	16. B	20. B

Practice Sheet 15, Page 163

1. 1	6. 7	11. 1	16. 7	21. 1
2. 2	7. 1	12. 5	17. 1	22. 3
3. 5	8. 4	13. 5	18. 5	23. 1
4. 2	9. 3	14. 4	19. 2	24. 7
5. 6	10. 1	15. 1	20. 2	25. 2

Practice Sheet 16, Page 171

1. b	3. a	5. b	7. a	9. a
2. b	4. a	6. a	8. b	10. a

Practice Sheet 16, Page 172

1. a	3. b	5. a	7. a	9. b
2. b	4. b	6. b	8. b	10. b

Practice Sheet 17, Page 183–184

1. 5, 1, after, work,
2. 4, 3, work, long,
3. 4, 2, engine, boy,
4. 2, 3, door, short,
5. 4, 1, action, court,
6. 5, 1, eating, table,
7. 3, 2, short, nap,
8. 4,1, report, work,
9. 2,3, tents, tasteless,
10. 5,2, five, lot,
11. 4,1, town, work,
12. 2,2, exhausted, days,
13. 1, 3, storm, long,
14. 4,2, been, friends,
15. 4,1, along, restaurant,
16. 4,2, sail, sail
17. 5,1, before, Canada,
18. 4,3, city, old,
19. 4,2, career, writing,
20. 4,2, spot, time,
21. 3,2, intense, Barb,
22. 4,2, note, buns,
23. 5,1, efforts, task,
24. 5,1, before, handwriting,
25. 2,1, coaches, day,

Practice Sheet 18, Page 193

1. 6 ended,
2. 4 came, understand,
3. 2 Jim Atkins, the unofficial leader of our little group,
4. 3 Folks,"
5. idea, Jim,"
6. 1 Elm Street,
7. 4 elm trees, people say,
8. 1 oak trees, which were planted to replace the elm trees,
9. trees, having grown . . . height,
10. 5 beautiful,
11. 2 mayor, Angela Lopez,
12. 4 crew, however,
13. 1 oaks, called
14. 1 oaks, which often live 200 to 400 years,
15. 2 Connecticut, the Charter Oak
16. 2 Andros, the governor of the Dominion of New England,
17. 1 charter, which was quite a controversial request,
18. 4 and, with the room dark,
19. 1. charter, which was hidden in the oak tree by Joseph Wadsworth, a member of the legislature,
20. 2 The Charter Oak, an important part of American history,

Practice Sheet 19, Page 194

1. R that will require little outside reading
2. N , which requires much outside reading
3. N , where the winters are mild
4. R where the winters are mild
5. N , having hung up his hat and coat,
6. R holding a small baby
7. R who gives us the correct answer
8. N , who thought she knew the answer,
9. N , where many of us went ashore.
10. R I'd like to visit

11. R knowing this man's whereabouts
12. N , having witnessed the accident,
13. N , whose opinion she valued highly.
14. R whose parents live in Bermuda
15. N , of whom you have heard me speak
16. R from whom you could borrow the money?
17. N , badly scorched in the fire,
18. R kept in the reserve library
19. R who really needs no introduction
20. N , who really needs no introduction

Practice Sheet 19, Page 207

1. C
2. W, Morris's lots
3. W, impressive:
4. W, lawyer's
5. W, else's, it's

6. W, in women's, men's, children's
7. C
8. W, It's people's
9. C
10. W, everyone's

11. W, Let's
12. C
13. W, car's with leather
14. W, years, year's
15. W, o'clock, cake's

Practice Sheet 19, Page 208

1. My brother said, "I have lost my wallet."
2. The sales manager observed, "I will need to hire two new division managers."
3. My teachers often tell me, "You are too talkative in class."
4. The policeman asked, "Do you need directions to the next town?"
5. Did she tell you, "The elevator is being repaired"?
6. The teller said to me that it would take only a minute to compute my interest.
7. My father said that he certainly appreciated all my hard work.
8. His sister answered that she did not want to go sailing in this rainy weather.
9. The salesman asked why I had selected the convertible.
10. Didn't she say that you (we) should take the right-hand fork after the covered bridge?

Practice Sheet 20, Page 215

1. W Mr. Johnson, please
2. W NASA Cape Kennedy,
3. C
4. W address: 646 Seneca Avenue, Madison,
5. W question?
6. 6. "Not otherwise specified," "nos"
7. W etc.
8. C
9. C
10. C

11. W No. 12,
12. W Delete quotation mark at beginning of sentence
13. W Main, located?
14. C
15. C
16. W Uncle Dan, who owns that beautiful sailboat out in the harbor,
17. C
18. W Lillian.
19. W me why I had been absent from the two previous classes.
20. W auditorium,

Practice Sheet 20 Page 216

1. Looming over the campsite is a huge white pine that is 150 feet tall; its branches are reflected in the lake lying just nearby.
2. This year's budget doesn't include any funds for hiring the new staff members that we need if we're going to implement that newly proposed quality control plan.
3. Smiling broadly at the team, the coach said, "I've been coaching for almost twenty years, and I don't believe I have ever had a team that plays with as much heart and courage as you displayed in today's game."
4. Al Lopez, the new engineer, came to us from a construction company where he was the assistant superintendent in charge of engineering for a parking garage project.
5. "My computer is older and slower than yours," laughed Nancy, "but it does what I need and doesn't cause me any problems."
6. It's time for the 6 o'clock news, but I think I will watch the motocross race on Cannel 237 instead.
7. You need to drive back to the library where you left your books before it closes and you have to wait until tomorrow morning to get them back.

8. Laughing softly, the manager looked at Gonzales and said, "I want you to play right field today even though you haven't played there since Little League."
9. Stretching out below us was a beautiful valley, its floor a vast green meadow and its far border a beautiful river.
10. Titan Corporation, a national security company, is opening a branch office in town so that it can offer its services to the new companies opening in the new industrial park outside of town.

Practice Sheet 21, Pages 229 and 230

1. drunk, climbed	11. eaten, laid	21. brought, paid
2. broken, dug	12. did, lent	22. became, taken
3. drowned, sunk	13. spent, shone	23. done written
4. torn, stung	14. bought, driven	24. swum, lay
5. dragged, blown	15. stole, caught	25. swore, stolen
6. ridden, swung	16. sworn, known	26. come, chose
7. brought, ate	17. lain, laid	27. lain, began
8. ran, flown	18. hung, taken	28. threw, climbed
9. chosen, gone	19. burst, rose	29. lay, eaten
10. begun, frozen	20. gone, swum	30. flown, clung

Practice Sheet 21, Page 231

1. C, came	6. became, C	11. C, C,	16. worn, paid
2. have been, have seen	7. C, broken	12. laid, announced	17. C, C
3. C, C	8. began, is	13. taken, have been sitting	18. have been, stolen
4. C, chosen	9. blown, C	14. sworn, saw	19. C, C
5. to admit, C	10. lying, came	15. said, C	20. C, C

Practice Sheet 22, Page 239

1. is	4. waits	7. has	10. has	13. come
2. were	5. were	8. has	11. is	14. has
3. was	6. have	9. has	12. is	15. were

Practice Sheet 22, Page 240

1. aspects become	6. guide, tips, and gifts are	11. item is
2. nature remains	7. C	12. C
3. C	8. information is	13. people were
4. knowledge has	9. ceremonies are	14. exposure is
5. consideration justifies	10. C	15. Eight weeks does

Practice Sheet 23, Page 249–250

1. A, it	6. A, they	11. A, their, they	16. A, it, they
2. B, they, their	7. B, their	12. B, which	17. A, he
3. B, she	8. B, they, you	13. A, they, you	18. B, they, it
4. A, It, they	9. A, it	14. B, it	19. B, which
5. B, you	10. A, they	15. B, their, you, it, they, you	20. A, your

Practice Sheet 24, Page 259

1. 4	6. 6	11. 1	16. 6
2. 5	7. 1	12. 5	17. 1
3. 1	8. 1	13. 5	18. 2
4. 1	9. 4	14. 4	19. 3
5. 4	10. 5	15. 3	20. 6

Practice Sheet 24, Page 260

1. her	5. whom	9. whomever	13. she	17. whom
2. I	6. Whoever	10. he	14. me	18. who
3. me	7. whom	11. Who	15. her	19. I
4. who	8. her	12. Whom	16. me	20. us

Practice Sheet 25, Page 269

1. respected, Adv.	4. behavior, Adj.	7. Sand, Adv.	10. floors, Adj.	13. players, Adj.
2. soaring, Adv.	5. some, Adj.	8. he, Adj.	11. car, Adj.	14. destructive, Adv.
3. hopes, Adj.	6. optimistic, Adv.	9. me, Adj.	12. will run, Adv.	15. are growing, Adv.

Practice Sheet 25, Page 270

1. happy	6. equally	11. really	16. surely
2. considerably	7. badly	12. sweet	17. badly
3. well	8. awkwardly	13. suddenly	18. regularly
4. easily	9. awkward	14. different	19. good
5. incorrectly	10. steadily	15. well	20. somewhat

Practice Sheet 26, Page 281–282

1. Almost, healthful	8. Because of, enthusiastic	15. those, taught	22. way, extremely
2. between, a lot	9. As, angry	16. emigrated, immigrant	23. unless, bring
3. as fast as, all right	10. not very, incredible.	17. disinterested, uninterested	24. think, anywhere
4. that, beside	11. medium, quite	18. percentage, percent	25. Let, inferred
5. took, brought	12. very, annoyed	19. very, suspect	
6. Somewhere, anywhere	13. Let us, couldn't	20. that, to	
7. Couple of, should have	14. used to, nauseous	21. like, unique	

Practice Sheet 26, Pages 283–284

1. professor, all right *or* acceptable	8. beside, off	15. That, C
2. awfully, C	9. C, C	16. C, those kinds of
3. suspect, somewhere	10. May, those	17. further, that
4. invitation, C	11. quite *or* very, supposed	18. are not, used
5. have, C	12. In regard to, try to	19. very *or* really C
6. can hardly, person	13. surely, teach	20. very, angry
7. as if, a great deal of	14. rather, C	

Practice Sheet 27, Pages 301–302

1. noticeable	7. principles	13. too	19. than	25. becoming
2. controlled	8. shown	14. desert	20. Who's	26. likelihood
3. desirable	9. financiers	15. canvas	21. seized	27. retrieve
4. counsel	10. its	16. their	22. famous	28. raspberries
5. altered	11. dining	17. differing	23. salaries	29. incidents
6. their	12. course	18. advice	24. reign	30. stationery

Practice Sheet 28, Page 309

1. analyses	7. Dutchmen	14. lilies	21. spies
2. aquariums, aquaria	8. fathers-in-law	15. mice	22. theses
3. archipelagos, archipelagoes	9. flamingos, flamingoes	16. octopuses, octopi	23. turkeys
4. assemblies	10. folios	17. plateaus, plateaux	24. vortexes, vortices
5. Charleses	11. fungi, funguses	18. podia, podiums	25. wives
6. commandos, commandoes	12. handfuls, handsful	19. scarfs, scarves	
	13. infernos	20. sheriffs	

Practice Sheet 28, Page 310

1. W	10. W	19. W	28. C	37. W	46. W
2. C	11. C	20. C	29. C	38. W	47. C
3. W	12. C	21. W	30. C	39. C	48. C
4. C	13. C	22. W	31. W	40. C	49. C
5. C	14. C	23. W	32. W	41. W	50. C
6. C	15. W	24. W	33. C	42. W	
7. W	16. W	25. W	34. C	43. C	
8. C	17. W	26. C	35. W	44. C	
9. C	18. C	27. C	36. W	45. W	

Practice Sheet 29, Pages 319–320

1. audience, criticisms
2. Britain, boundaries
3. enthusiastic, equipment
4. During, dilapidated
5. dissatisfied, accommodations
6. familiar, extremely
7. embarrassing, experiences
8. imagination, discipline
9. desperately, across
10. athletic, disappointing
11. dormitory, convenient
12. dictionary, disappear
13. exorbitant, counterfeit
14. disastrous, environment
15. immediately, excellent
16. abbreviate, business
17. especially, humorous
18. awkward, apparatus
19. exaggerated, forty
20. amateurs, competition
21. arithmetic, computer
22. arithmetic, conference
23. among, acquaintances
24. Accompanying, description
25. chosen, candidate

Practice Sheet 29A, Pages 323–324

1. literature, speech
2. vegetable, sandwich
3. ninety, sophomore
4. secretary, quantity
5. procedures, surprise
6. particularly, perspiration
7. knowledge, indispensable
8. psychological, propaganda
9. partners, optimistic
10. probably, similar
11. original, interpretation
12. interesting, marriage
13. practically, parallel
14. whether, sergeant
15. pastime, library
16. proceeded, separate
17. possession, mementos
18. lightning, temperature
19. necessary, intercede
20. interrupted, performance
21. permissible, schedule
22. specimens, undoubtedly
23. preparation, questionnaire
24. villain, until
25. maintenance, independence

Index